CLAY LORD

MASTER of GOLEMS

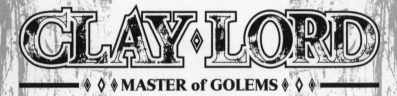

2

Jun Suzumoto

Characters

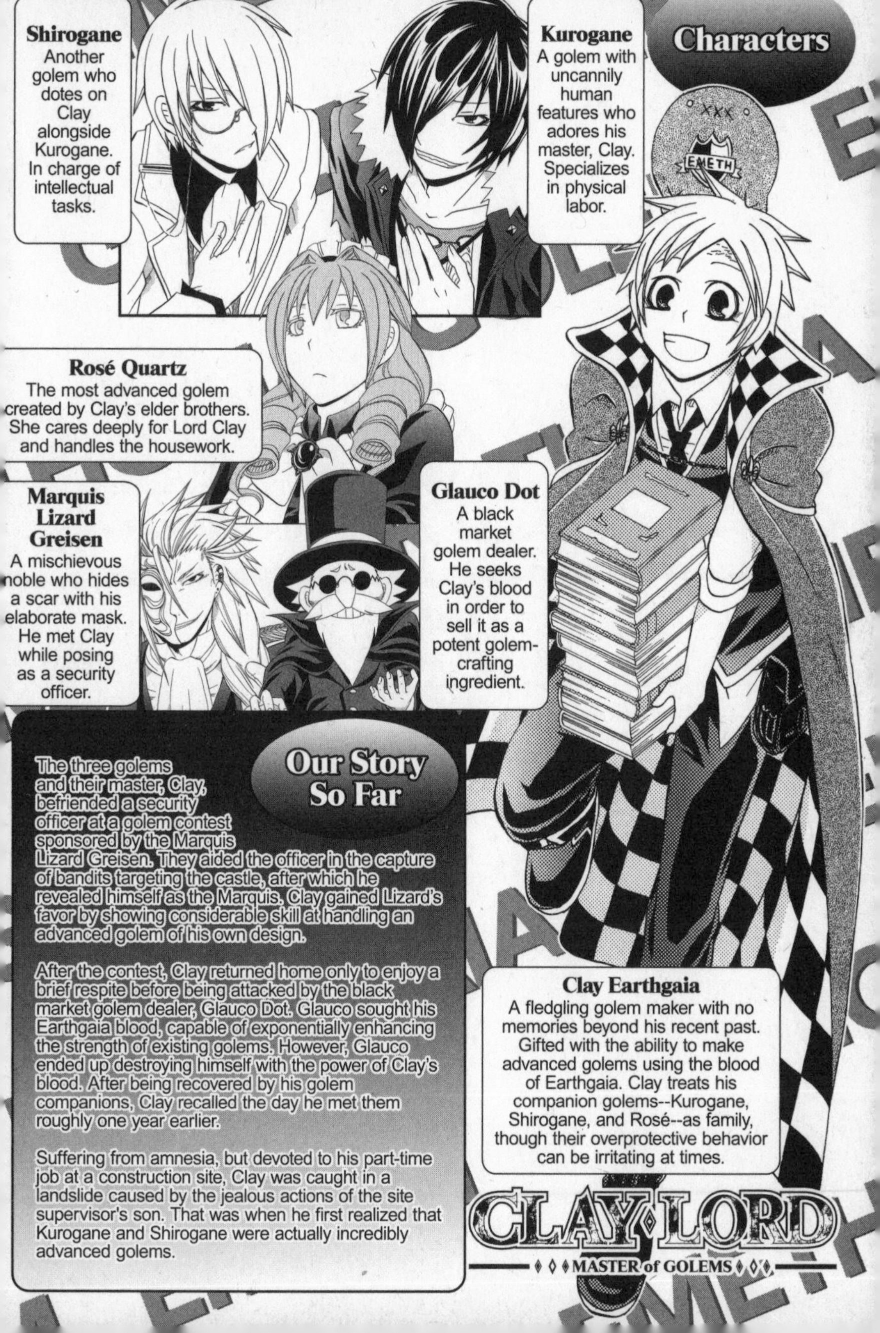

Kurogane
A golem with uncannily human features who adores his master, Clay. Specializes in physical labor.

Shirogane
Another golem who dotes on Clay alongside Kurogane. In charge of intellectual tasks.

Rosé Quartz
The most advanced golem created by Clay's elder brothers. She cares deeply for Lord Clay and handles the housework.

Glauco Dot
A black market golem dealer. He seeks Clay's blood in order to sell it as a potent golem-crafting ingredient.

Marquis Lizard Greisen
A mischievous noble who hides a scar with his elaborate mask. He met Clay while posing as a security officer.

Clay Earthgaia
A fledgling golem maker with no memories beyond his recent past. Gifted with the ability to make advanced golems using the blood of Earthgaia. Clay treats his companion golems--Kurogane, Shirogane, and Rosé--as family, though their overprotective behavior can be irritating at times.

Our Story So Far

The three golems and their master, Clay, befriended a security officer at a golem contest sponsored by the Marquis Lizard Greisen. They aided the officer in the capture of bandits targeting the castle, after which he revealed himself as the Marquis. Clay gained Lizard's favor by showing considerable skill at handling an advanced golem of his own design.

After the contest, Clay returned home only to enjoy a brief respite before being attacked by the black market golem dealer, Glauco Dot. Glauco sought his Earthgaia blood, capable of exponentially enhancing the strength of existing golems. However, Glauco ended up destroying himself with the power of Clay's blood. After being recovered by his golem companions, Clay recalled the day he met them roughly one year earlier.

Suffering from amnesia, but devoted to his part-time job at a construction site, Clay was caught in a landslide caused by the jealous actions of the site supervisor's son. That was when he first realized that Kurogane and Shirogane were actually incredibly advanced golems.

CLAY LORD

MASTER of GOLEMS

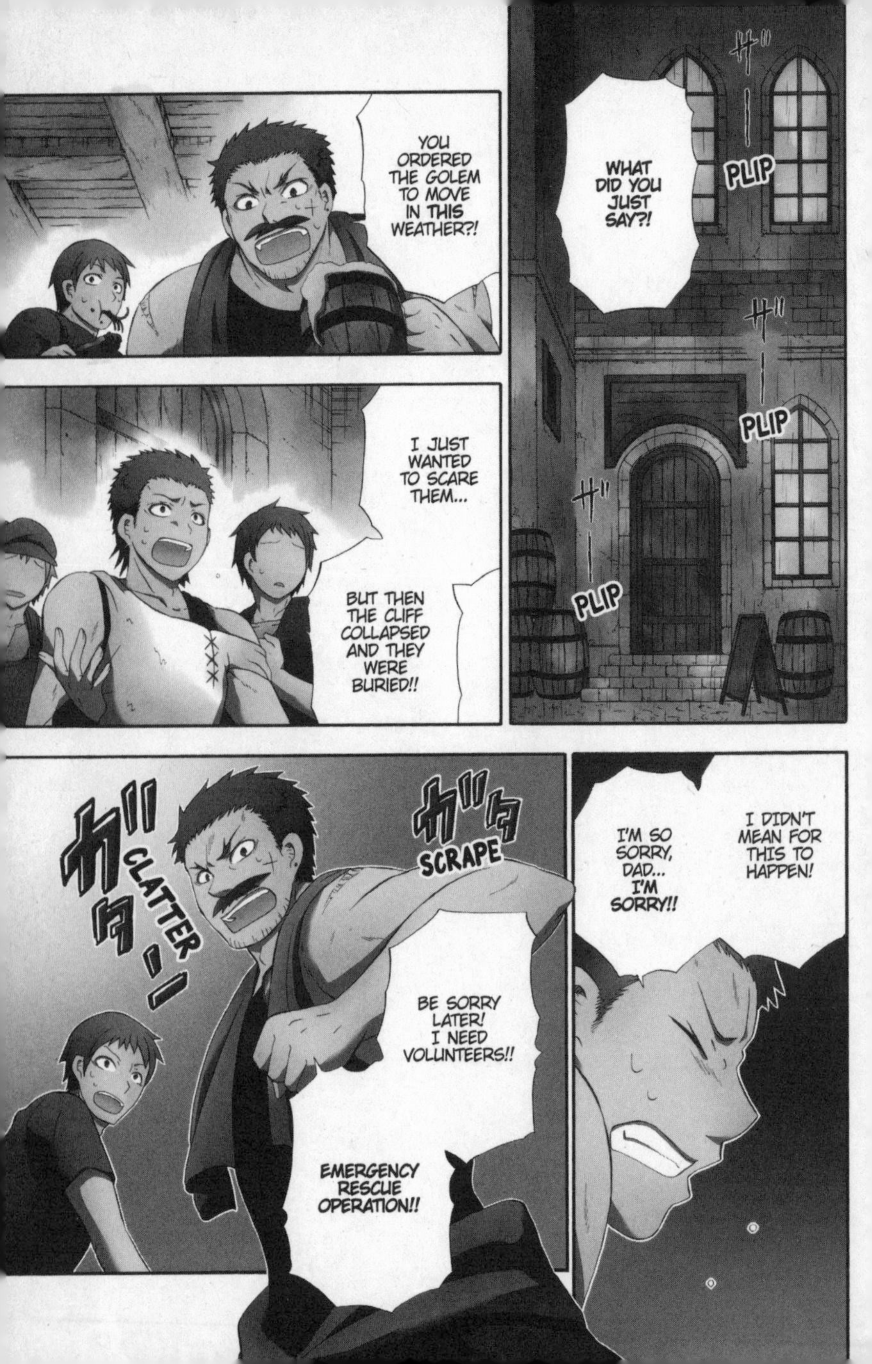
WHAT DID YOU JUST SAY?!
PLIP
PLIP
PLIP
YOU ORDERED THE GOLEM TO MOVE IN THIS WEATHER?!
I JUST WANTED TO SCARE THEM...
BUT THEN THE CLIFF COLLAPSED AND THEY WERE BURIED!!
I DIDN'T MEAN FOR THIS TO HAPPEN!
I'M SO SORRY, DAD... I'M SORRY!!
SCRAPE
CLATTER
BE SORRY LATER! I NEED VOLUNTEERS!!
EMERGENCY RESCUE OPERATION!!

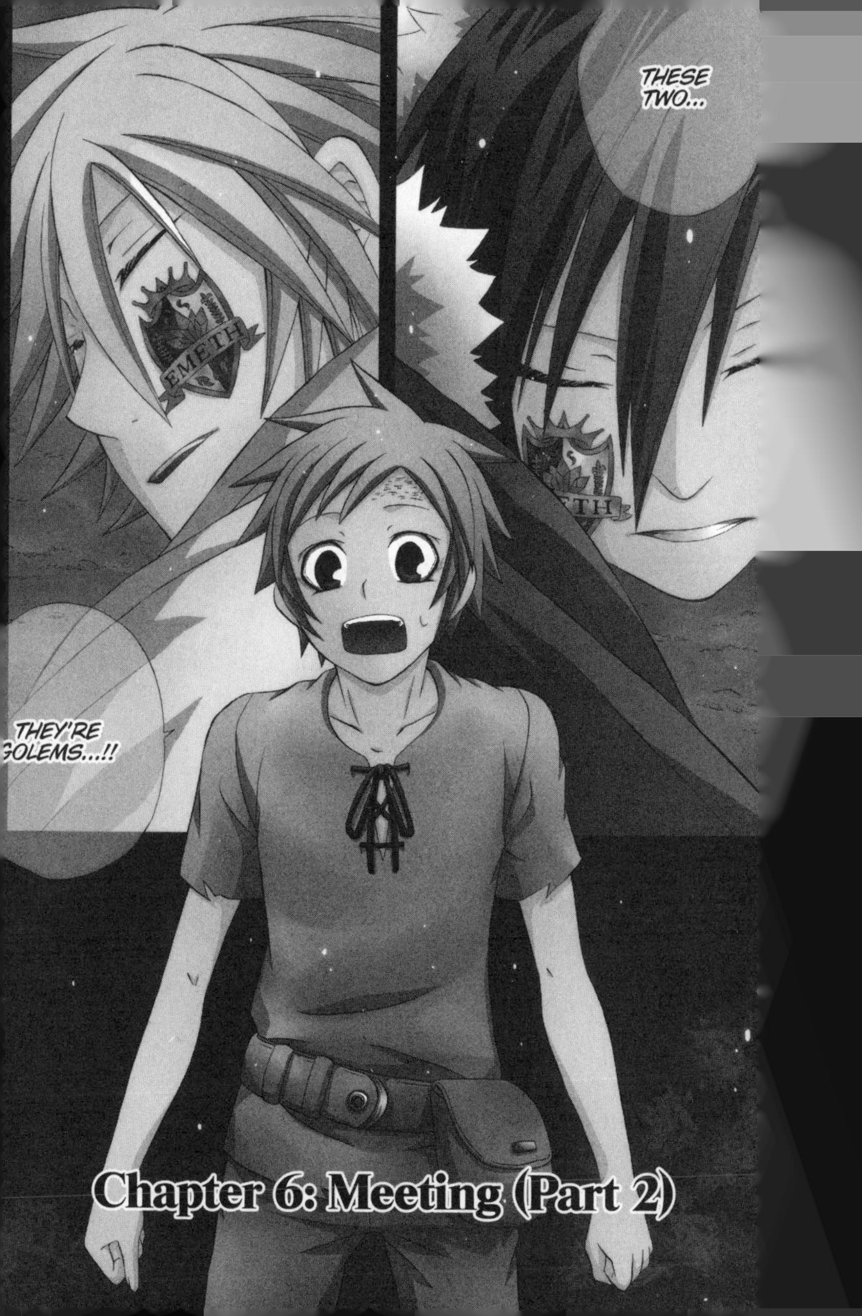
THESE TWO...
EMETH
THEY'RE GOLEMS...!!
Chapter 6: Meeting (Part 2)

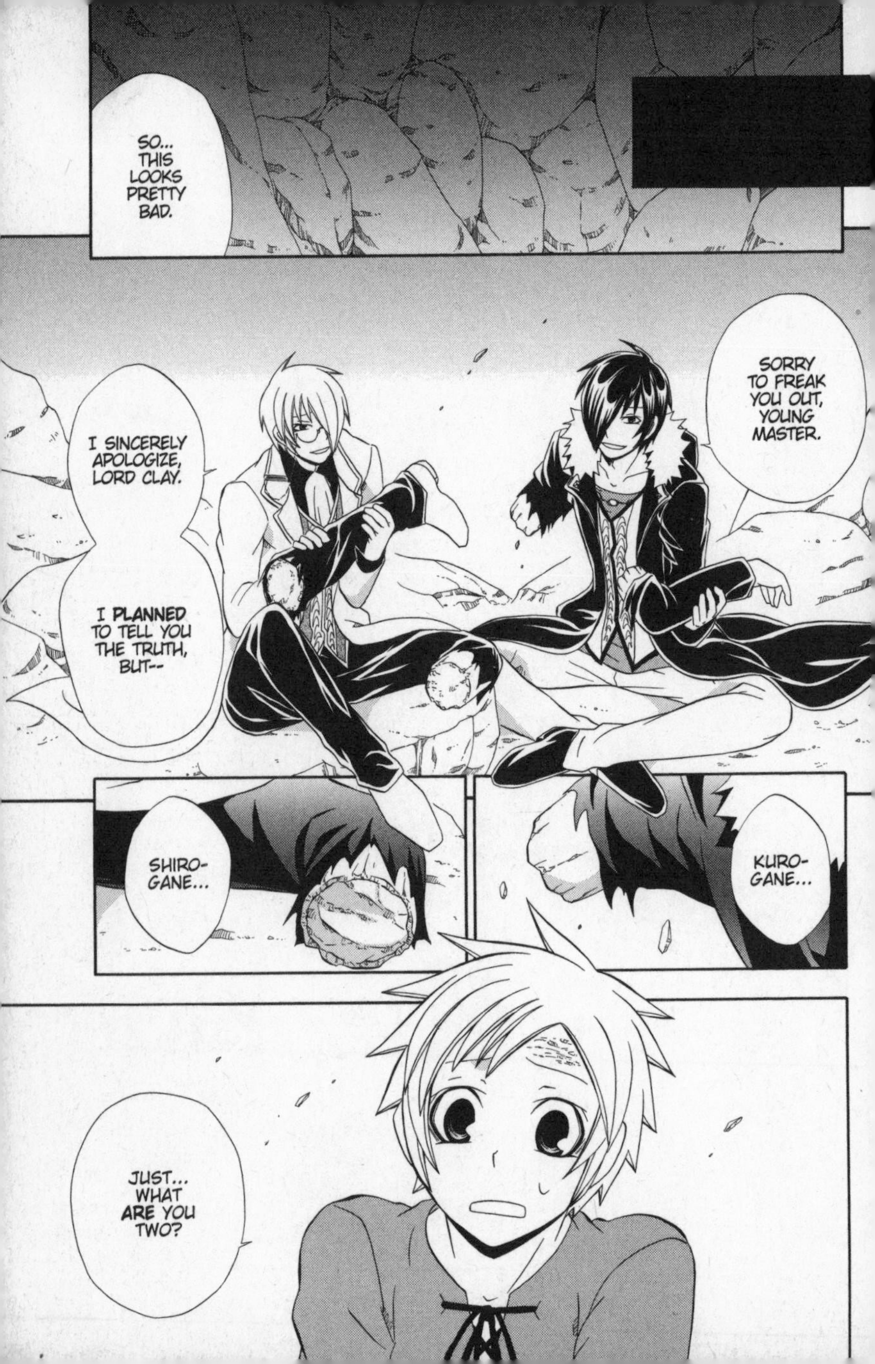
[redacted]
SO... THIS LOOKS PRETTY BAD.
SORRY TO FREAK YOU OUT, YOUNG MASTER.
I SINCERELY APOLOGIZE, LORD CLAY.
I PLANNED TO TELL YOU THE TRUTH, BUT--
KURO-GANE...
SHIRO-GANE...
JUST... WHAT ARE YOU TWO?

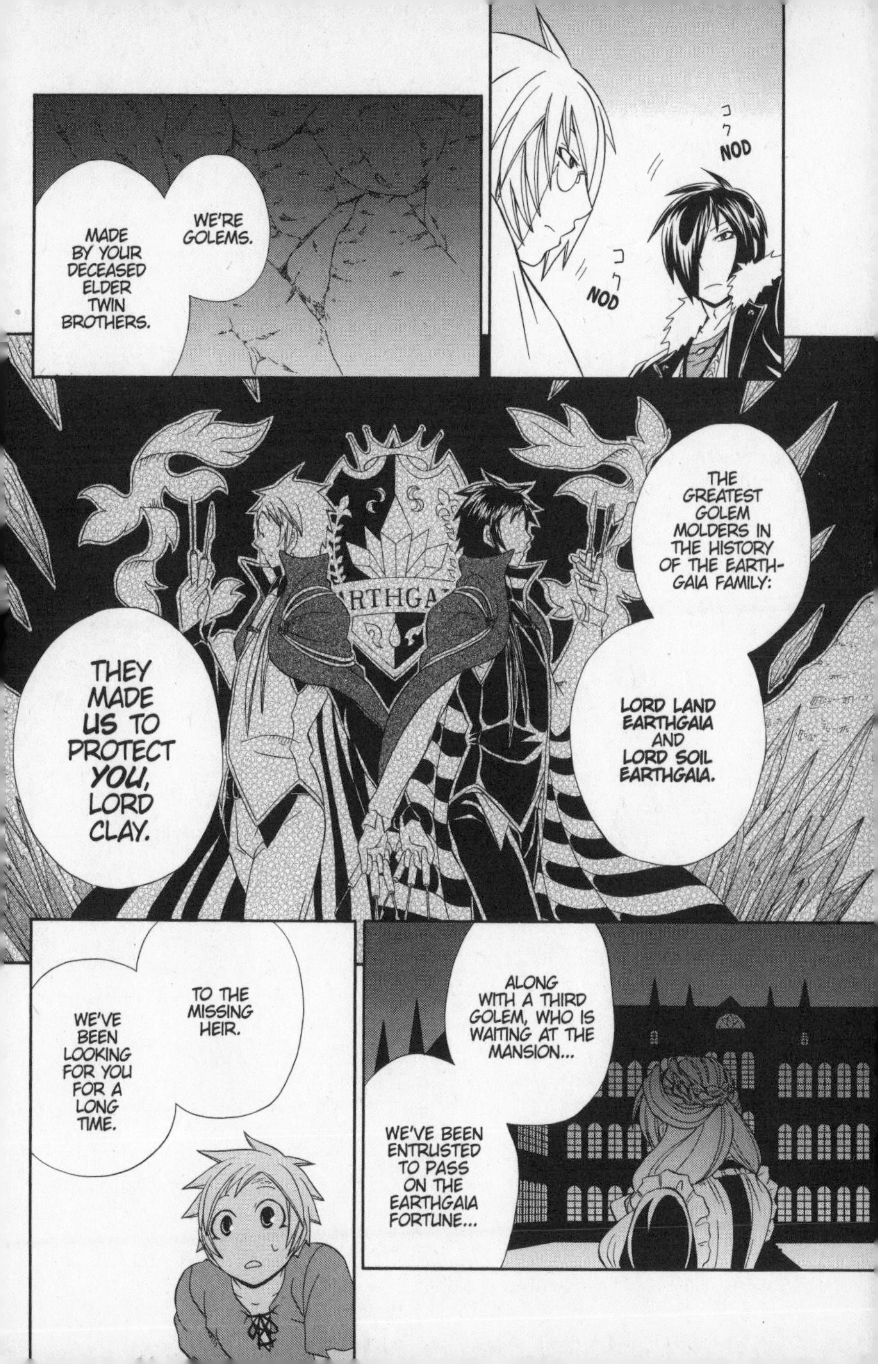
コク
NOD
コク
NOD
WE'RE GOLEMS.
MADE BY YOUR DECEASED ELDER TWIN BROTHERS.
THE GREATEST GOLEM MOLDERS IN THE HISTORY OF THE EARTH-GAIA FAMILY:
LORD LAND EARTHGAIA AND LORD SOIL EARTHGAIA.
THEY MADE US TO PROTECT YOU, LORD CLAY.
ARTHGA
ALONG WITH A THIRD GOLEM, WHO IS WAITING AT THE MANSION...
WE'VE BEEN ENTRUSTED TO PASS ON THE EARTHGAIA FORTUNE...
TO THE MISSING HEIR.
WE'VE BEEN LOOKING FOR YOU FOR A LONG TIME.

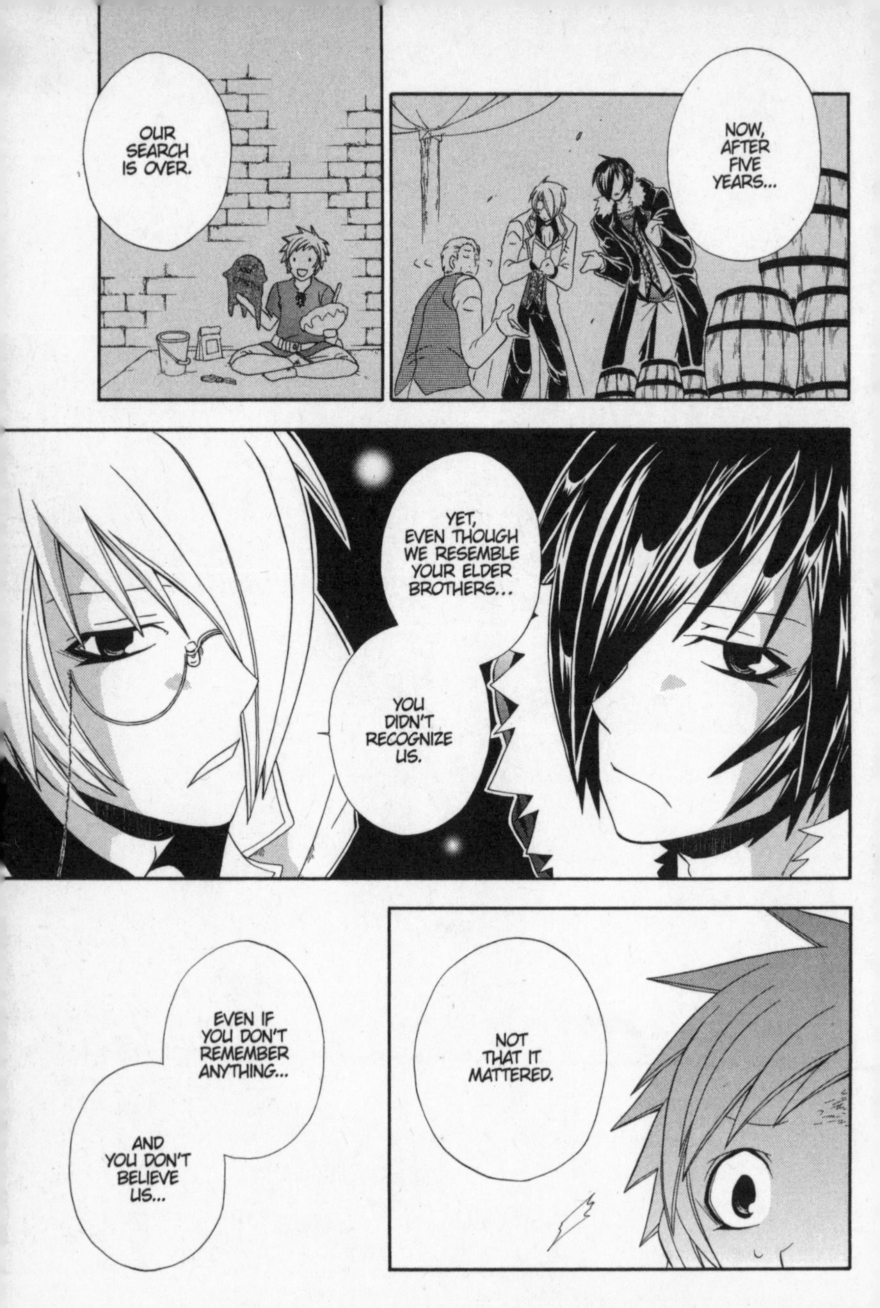
NOW, AFTER FIVE YEARS...
OUR SEARCH IS OVER.
YET, EVEN THOUGH WE RESEMBLE YOUR ELDER BROTHERS...
YOU DIDN'T RECOGNIZE US.
NOT THAT IT MATTERED.
EVEN IF YOU DON'T REMEMBER ANYTHING...
AND YOU DON'T BELIEVE US...

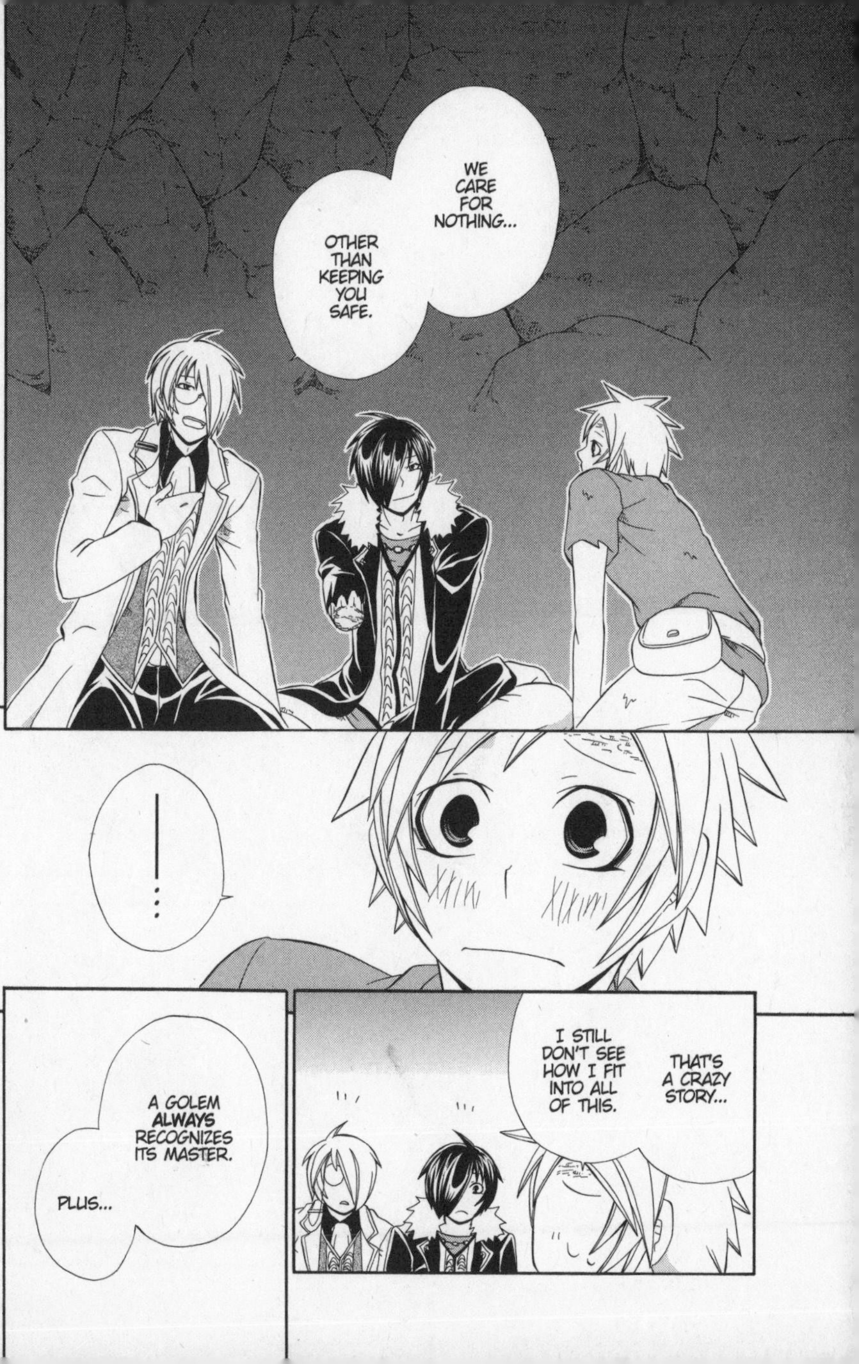
WE CARE FOR NOTHING...
OTHER THAN KEEPING YOU SAFE.
—...
THAT'S A CRAZY STORY...
I STILL DON'T SEE HOW I FIT INTO ALL OF THIS.
A GOLEM **ALWAYS** RECOGNIZES ITS MASTER.
PLUS...

THE EARTHGAIA BLOOD...

CALLS OUT TO US.

IF THAT'S TRUE... THEN...

．．．．．．

IS IT POSSIBLE THE FIGURES FROM MY DREAMS ARE ACTUALLY MY BROTHERS?

WAIT. THEY SAID I WAS THE HEIR.

AND... MY PARENTS?

WE CAN SENSE IT IN YOU.

I'M SORRY, YOUNG MASTER. THEY DIED WHEN YOU WERE VERY YOUNG.

YOUR ELDER BROTHERS RAISED YOU AFTER THAT, BUT THEY WERE CAUGHT IN A FIRE...

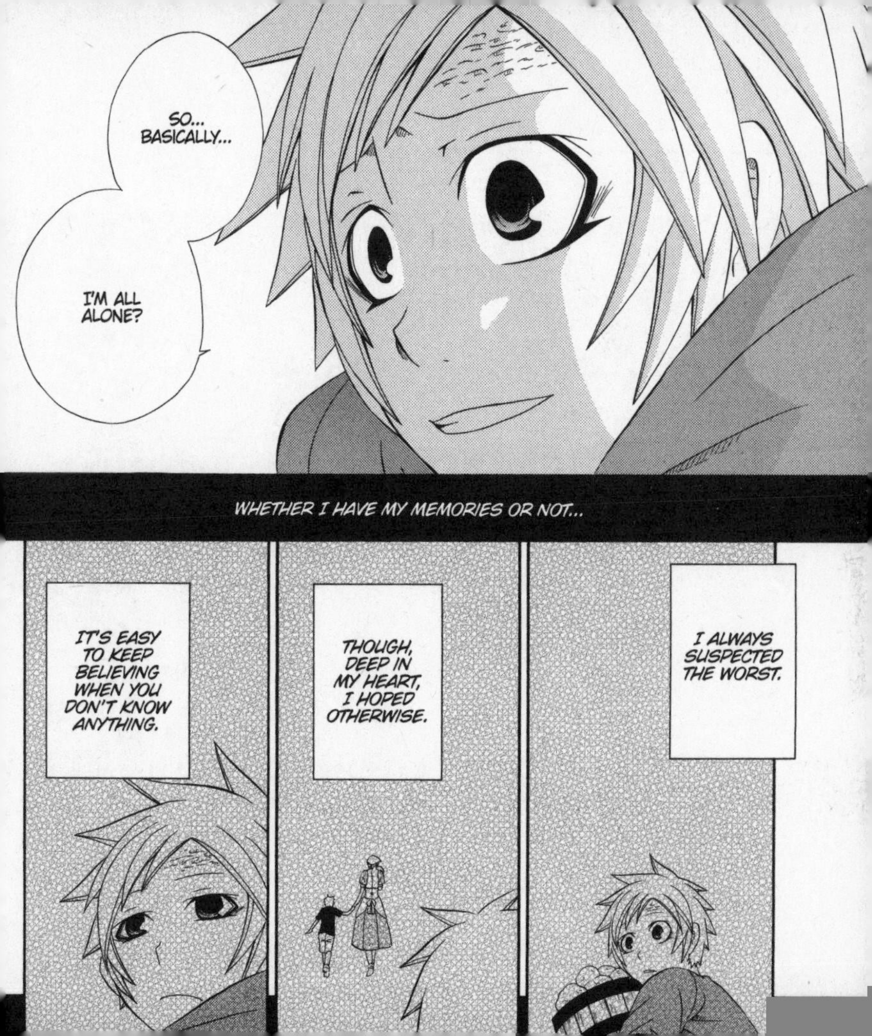
SO... BASICALLY...
I'M ALL ALONE?
WHETHER I HAVE MY MEMORIES OR NOT...
I ALWAYS SUSPECTED THE WORST.
THOUGH, DEEP IN MY HEART, I HOPED OTHERWISE.
IT'S EASY TO KEEP BELIEVING WHEN YOU DON'T KNOW ANYTHING.

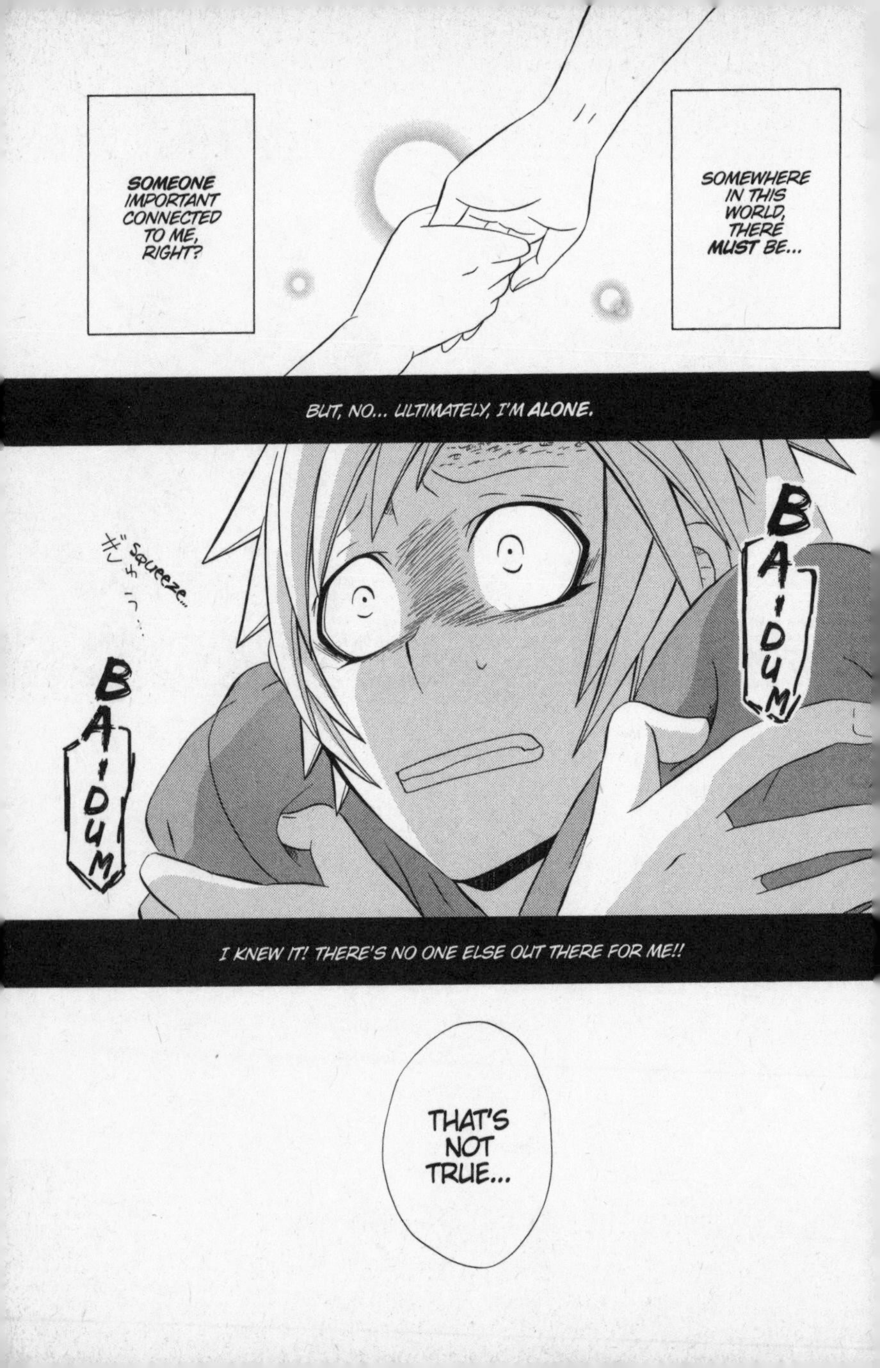
SOMEWHERE IN THIS WORLD, THERE MUST BE...
SOMEONE IMPORTANT CONNECTED TO ME, RIGHT?
BUT, NO... ULTIMATELY, I'M ALONE.
BA-DUM
Squeeze...
BA-DUM
I KNEW IT! THERE'S NO ONE ELSE OUT THERE FOR ME!!
THAT'S NOT TRUE...

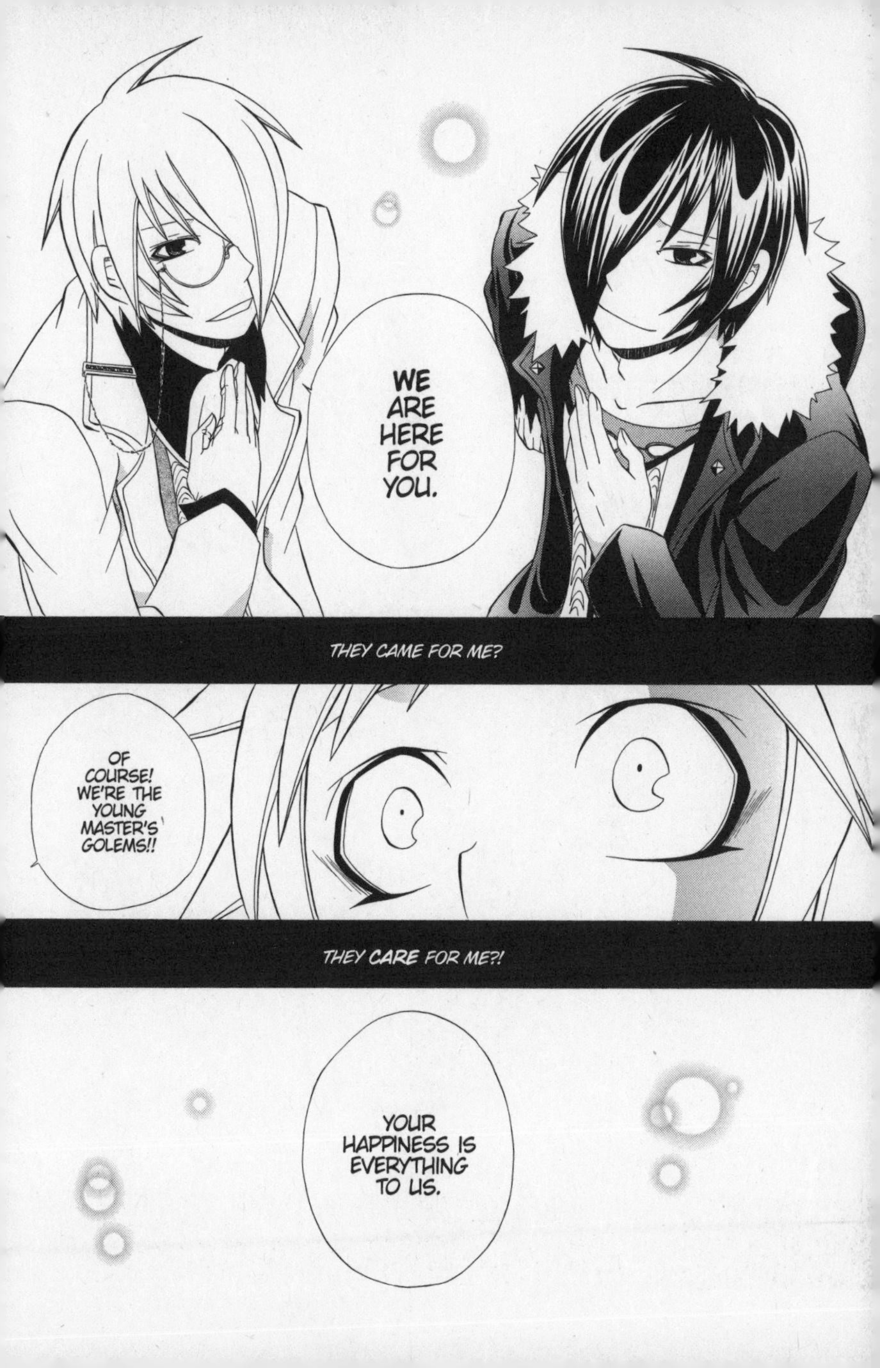
WE ARE HERE FOR YOU.
THEY CAME FOR ME?
OF COURSE! WE'RE THE YOUNG MASTER'S GOLEMS!!
THEY CARE FOR ME?!
YOUR HAPPINESS IS EVERYTHING TO US.

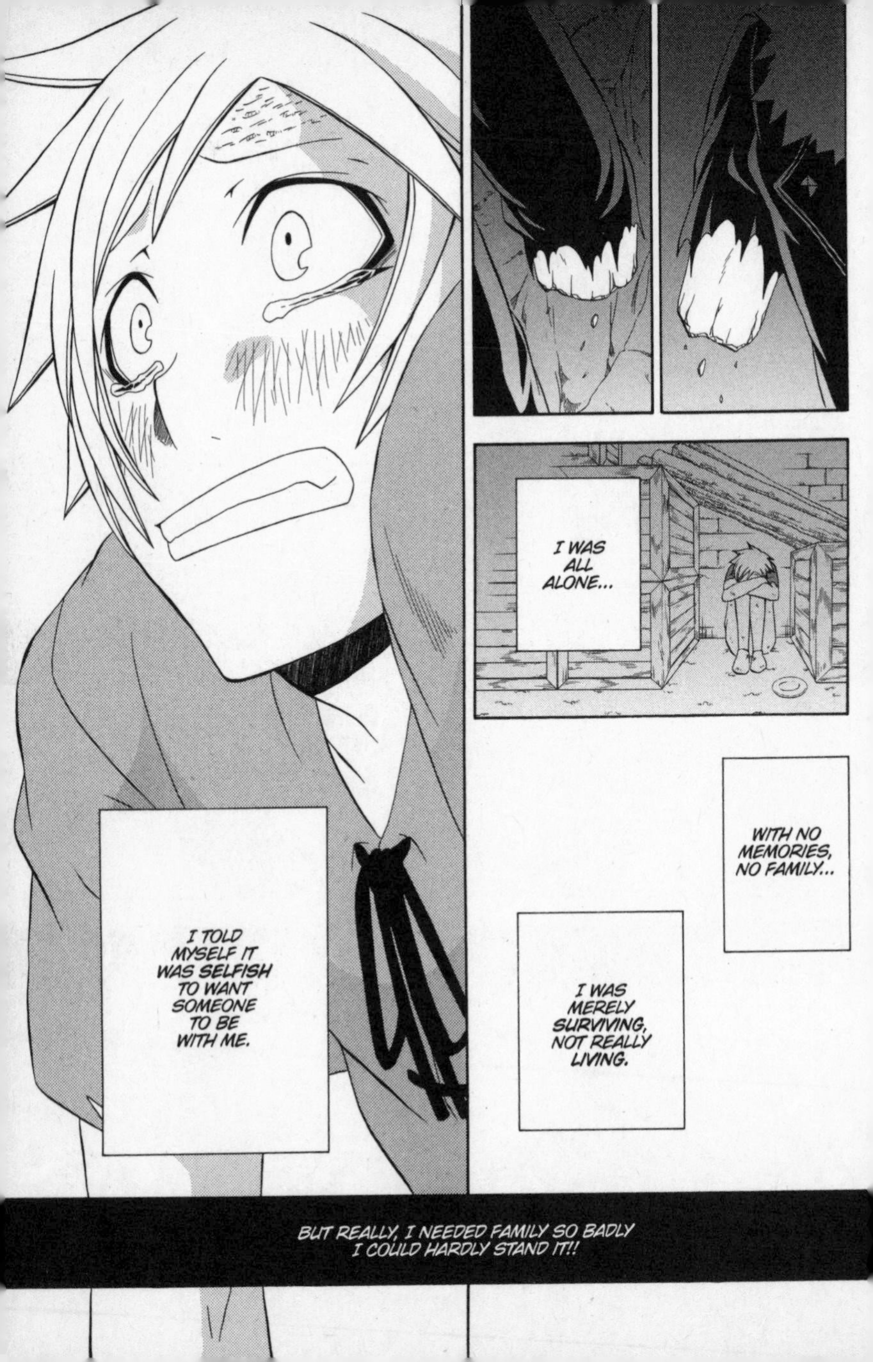
I WAS ALL ALONE...
WITH NO MEMORIES, NO FAMILY...
I WAS MERELY SURVIVING, NOT REALLY LIVING.
I TOLD MYSELF IT WAS SELFISH TO WANT SOMEONE TO BE WITH ME.
BUT REALLY, I NEEDED FAMILY SO BADLY I COULD HARDLY STAND IT!!

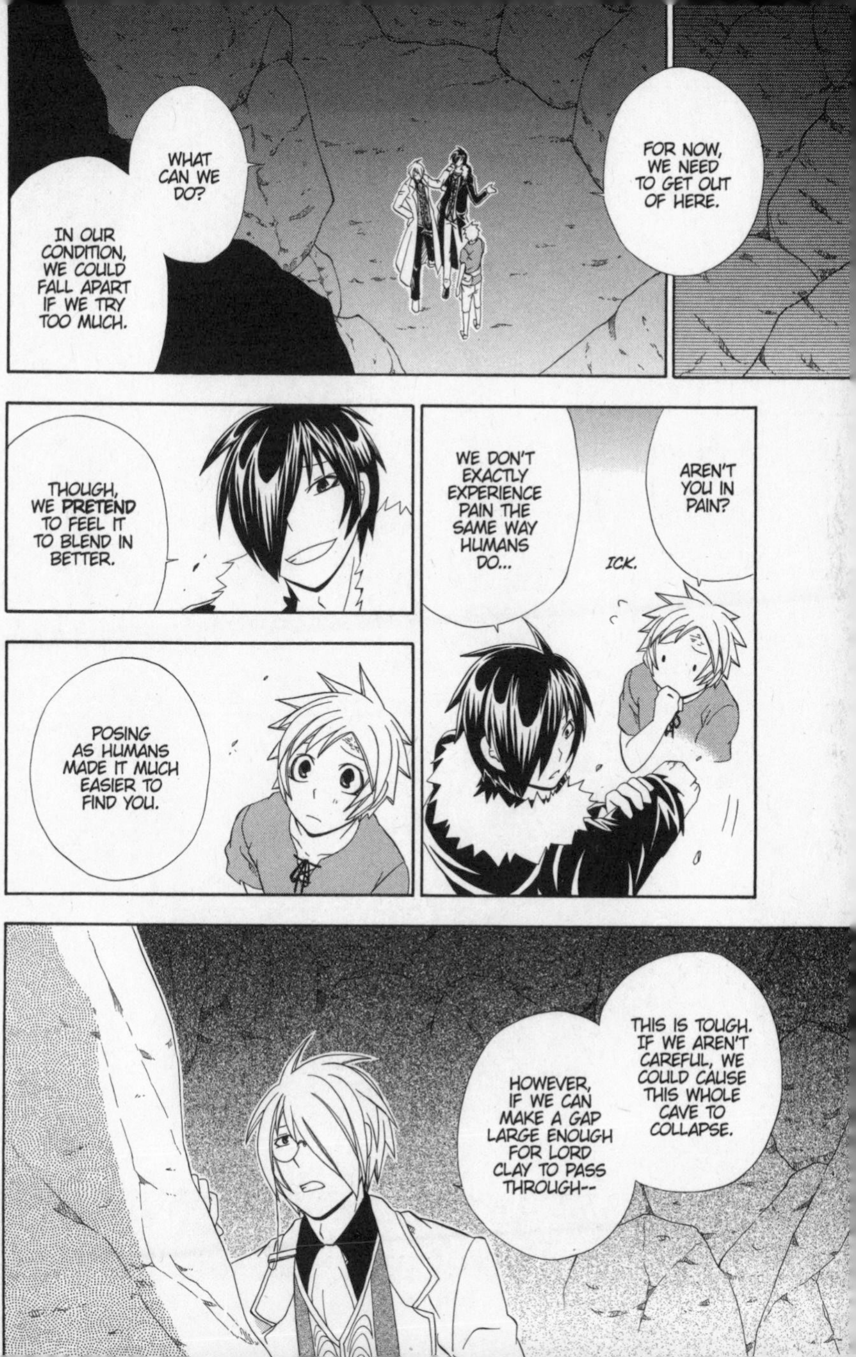
FOR NOW, WE NEED TO GET OUT OF HERE.
WHAT CAN WE DO?
IN OUR CONDITION, WE COULD FALL APART IF WE TRY TOO MUCH.
AREN'T YOU IN PAIN?
ICK.
WE DON'T EXACTLY EXPERIENCE PAIN THE SAME WAY HUMANS DO...
THOUGH, WE PRETEND TO FEEL IT TO BLEND IN BETTER.
POSING AS HUMANS MADE IT MUCH EASIER TO FIND YOU.
THIS IS TOUGH. IF WE AREN'T CAREFUL, WE COULD CAUSE THIS WHOLE CAVE TO COLLAPSE.
HOWEVER, IF WE CAN MAKE A GAP LARGE ENOUGH FOR LORD CLAY TO PASS THROUGH--

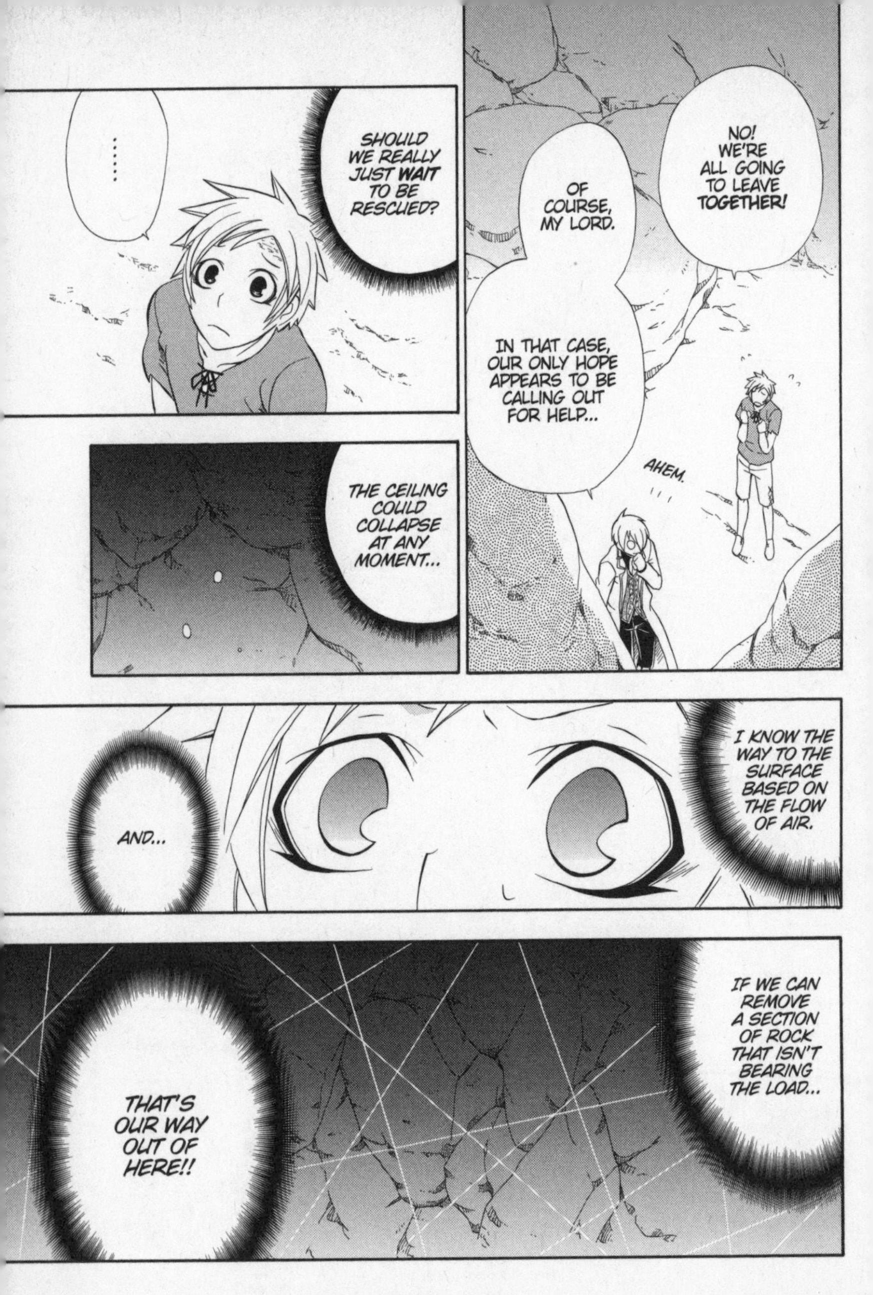
NO! WE'RE ALL GOING TO LEAVE TOGETHER!
OF COURSE, MY LORD.
IN THAT CASE, OUR ONLY HOPE APPEARS TO BE CALLING OUT FOR HELP...
AHEM.
SHOULD WE REALLY JUST WAIT TO BE RESCUED?
......
THE CEILING COULD COLLAPSE AT ANY MOMENT...
I KNOW THE WAY TO THE SURFACE BASED ON THE FLOW OF AIR.
AND...
IF WE CAN REMOVE A SECTION OF ROCK THAT ISN'T BEARING THE LOAD...
THAT'S OUR WAY OUT OF HERE!!

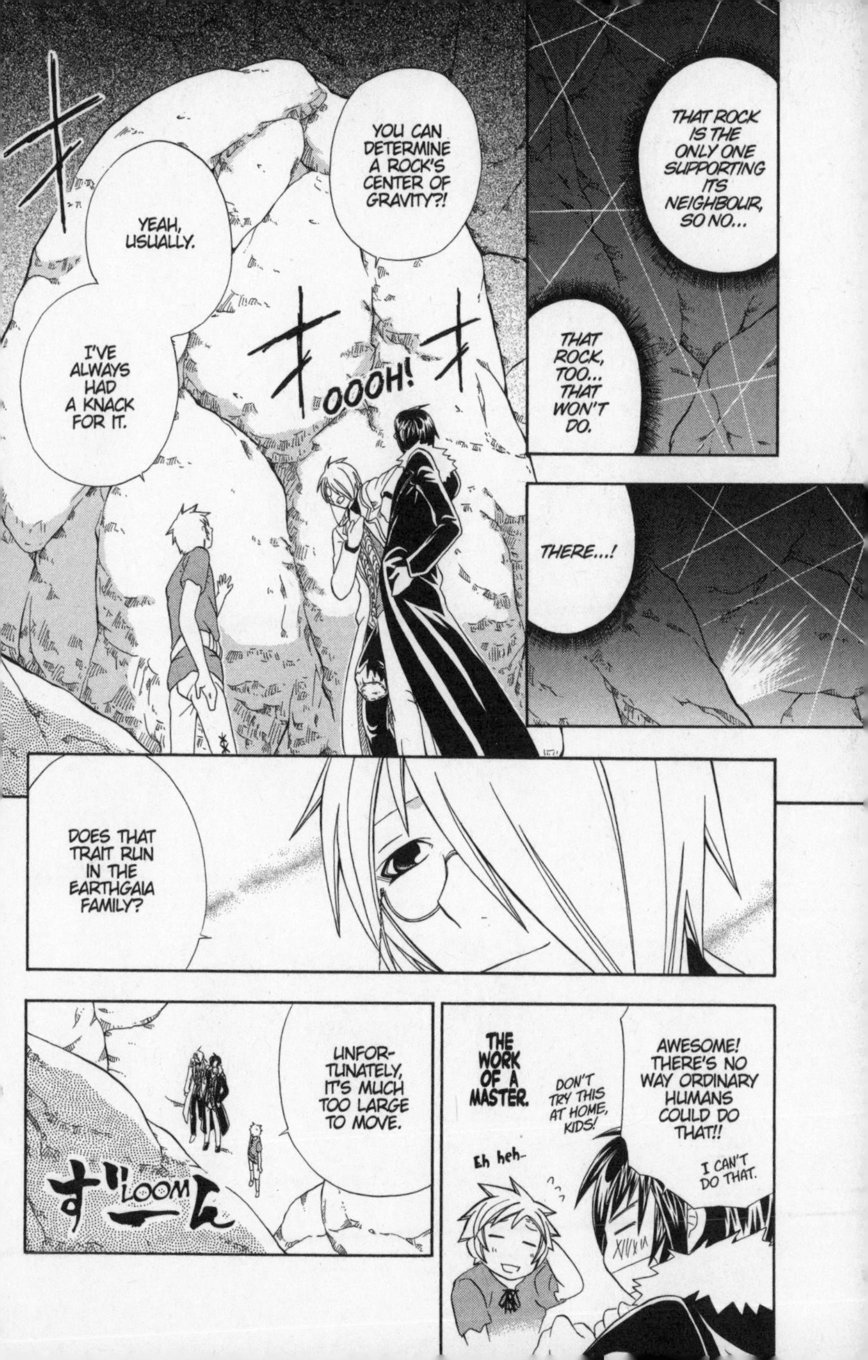
THAT ROCK IS THE ONLY ONE SUPPORTING ITS NEIGHBOUR, SO NO...
THAT ROCK, TOO... THAT WON'T DO.
THERE...!
YOU CAN DETERMINE A ROCK'S CENTER OF GRAVITY?!
YEAH, USUALLY.
I'VE ALWAYS HAD A KNACK FOR IT.
OOOH!
DOES THAT TRAIT RUN IN THE EARTHGAIA FAMILY?
AWESOME! THERE'S NO WAY ORDINARY HUMANS COULD DO THAT!!
I CAN'T DO THAT.
THE WORK OF A MASTER.
DON'T TRY THIS AT HOME, KIDS!
Eh heh-
UNFOR-TUNATELY, IT'S MUCH TOO LARGE TO MOVE.
LOOM

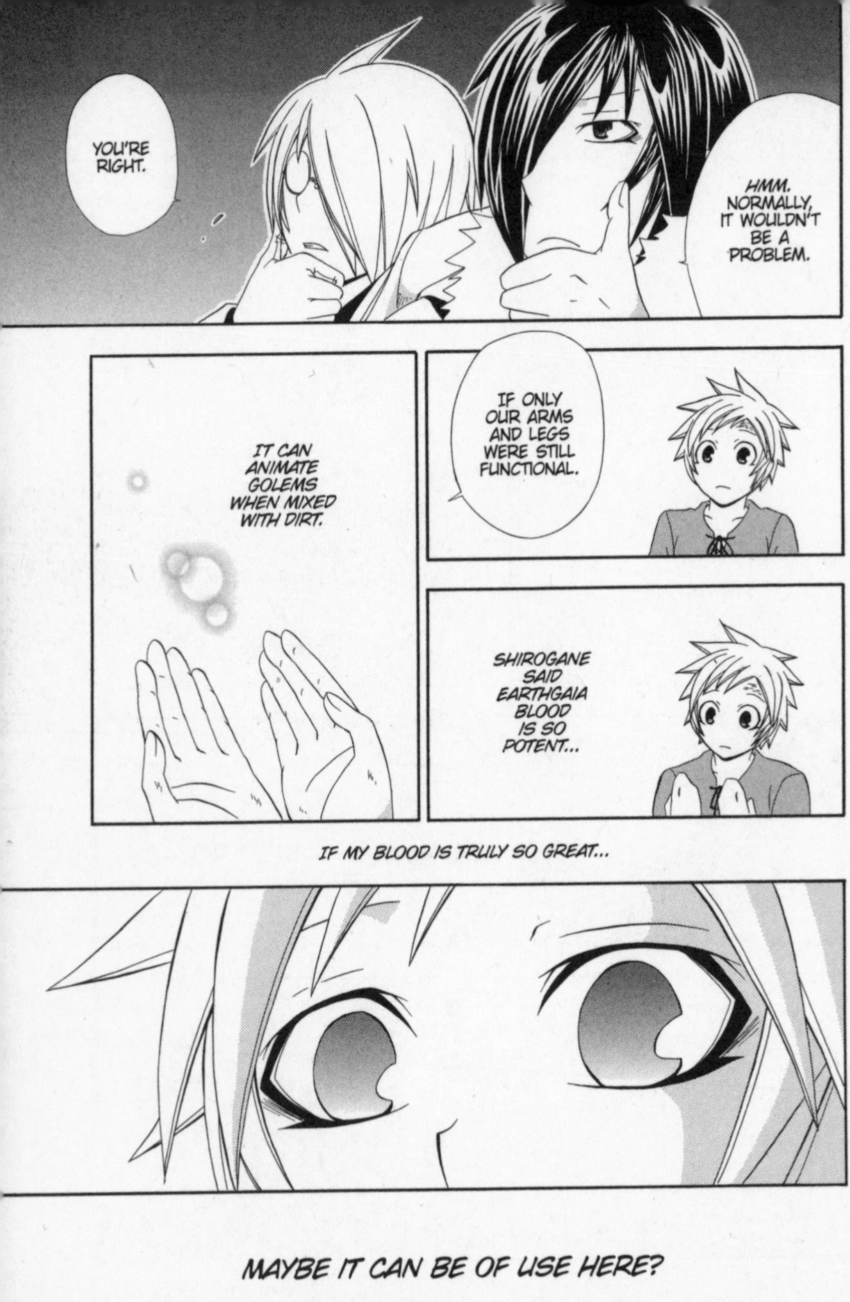
HMM. NORMALLY, IT WOULDN'T BE A PROBLEM.
YOU'RE RIGHT.
IF ONLY OUR ARMS AND LEGS WERE STILL FUNCTIONAL.
SHIROGANE SAID EARTHGAIA BLOOD IS SO POTENT...
IT CAN ANIMATE GOLEMS WHEN MIXED WITH DIRT.
IF MY BLOOD IS TRULY SO GREAT...
MAYBE IT CAN BE OF USE HERE?

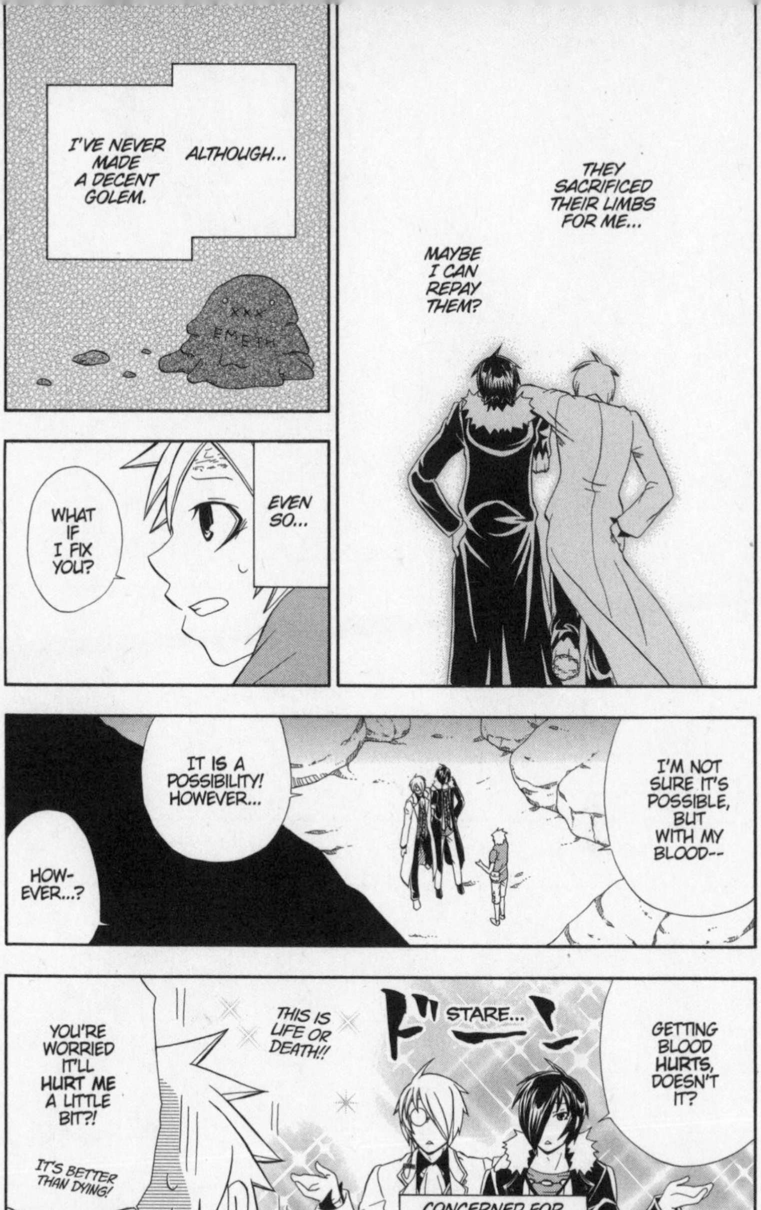
THEY SACRIFICED THEIR LIMBS FOR ME...
MAYBE I CAN REPAY THEM?
ALTHOUGH...
I'VE NEVER MADE A DECENT GOLEM.
EMETH
EVEN SO...
WHAT IF I FIX YOU?
I'M NOT SURE IT'S POSSIBLE, BUT WITH MY BLOOD--
IT IS A POSSIBILITY! HOWEVER...
HOW-EVER...?
GETTING BLOOD HURTS, DOESN'T IT?
STARE...
THIS IS LIFE OR DEATH!!
YOU'RE WORRIED IT'LL HURT ME A LITTLE BIT?!
IT'S BETTER THAN DYING!
CONCERNED FOR CLAY'S WELL-BEING.

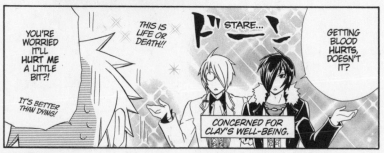

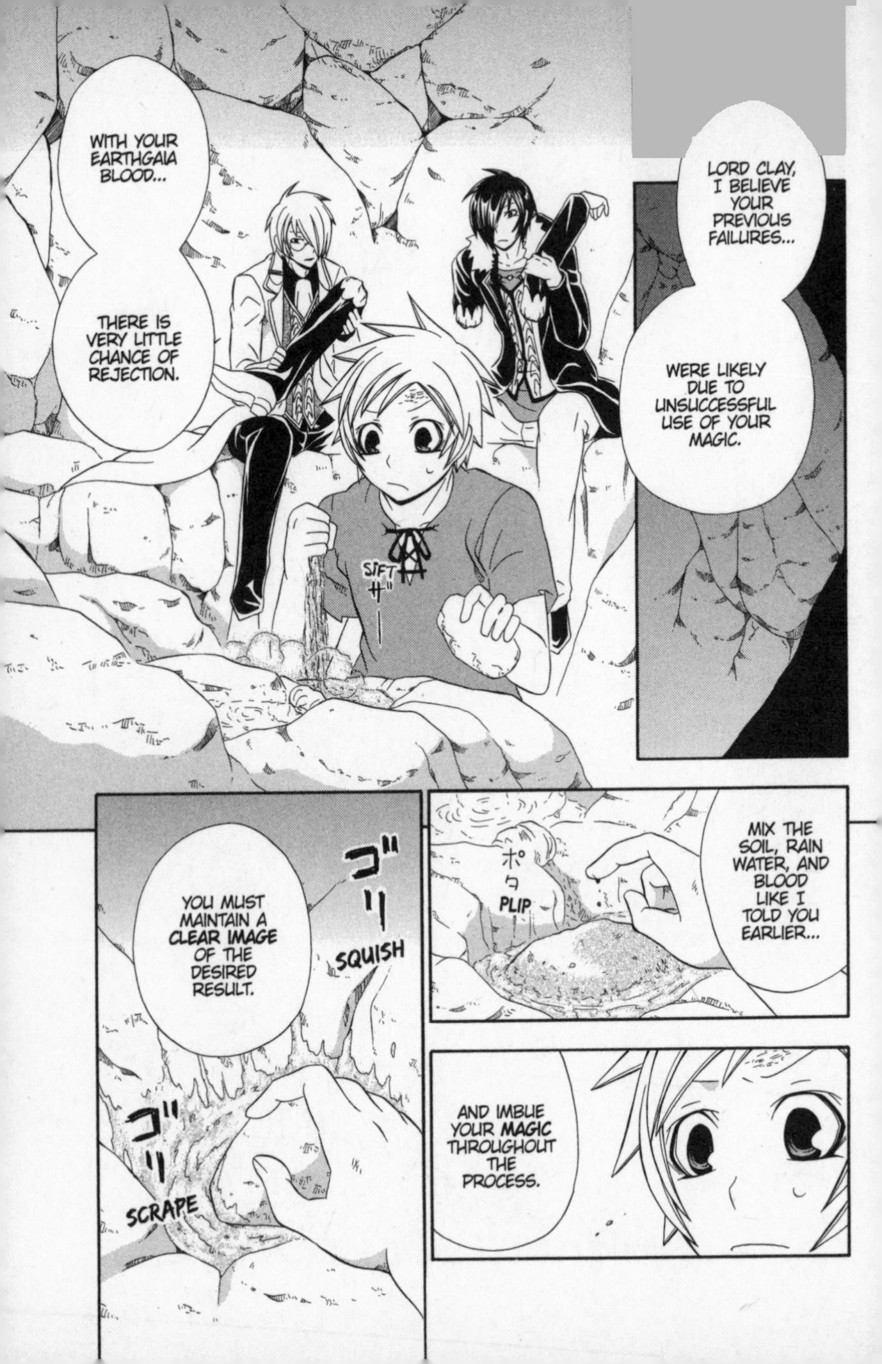
LORD CLAY, I BELIEVE YOUR PREVIOUS FAILURES...
WERE LIKELY DUE TO UNSUCCESSFUL USE OF YOUR MAGIC.
WITH YOUR EARTHGAIA BLOOD...
THERE IS VERY LITTLE CHANCE OF REJECTION.
SIFT ザー
MIX THE SOIL, RAIN WATER, AND BLOOD LIKE I TOLD YOU EARLIER...
ポタ PLIP
AND IMBUE YOUR MAGIC THROUGHOUT THE PROCESS.
YOU MUST MAINTAIN A CLEAR IMAGE OF THE DESIRED RESULT.
ゴリ SQUISH
ゴリ SCRAPE

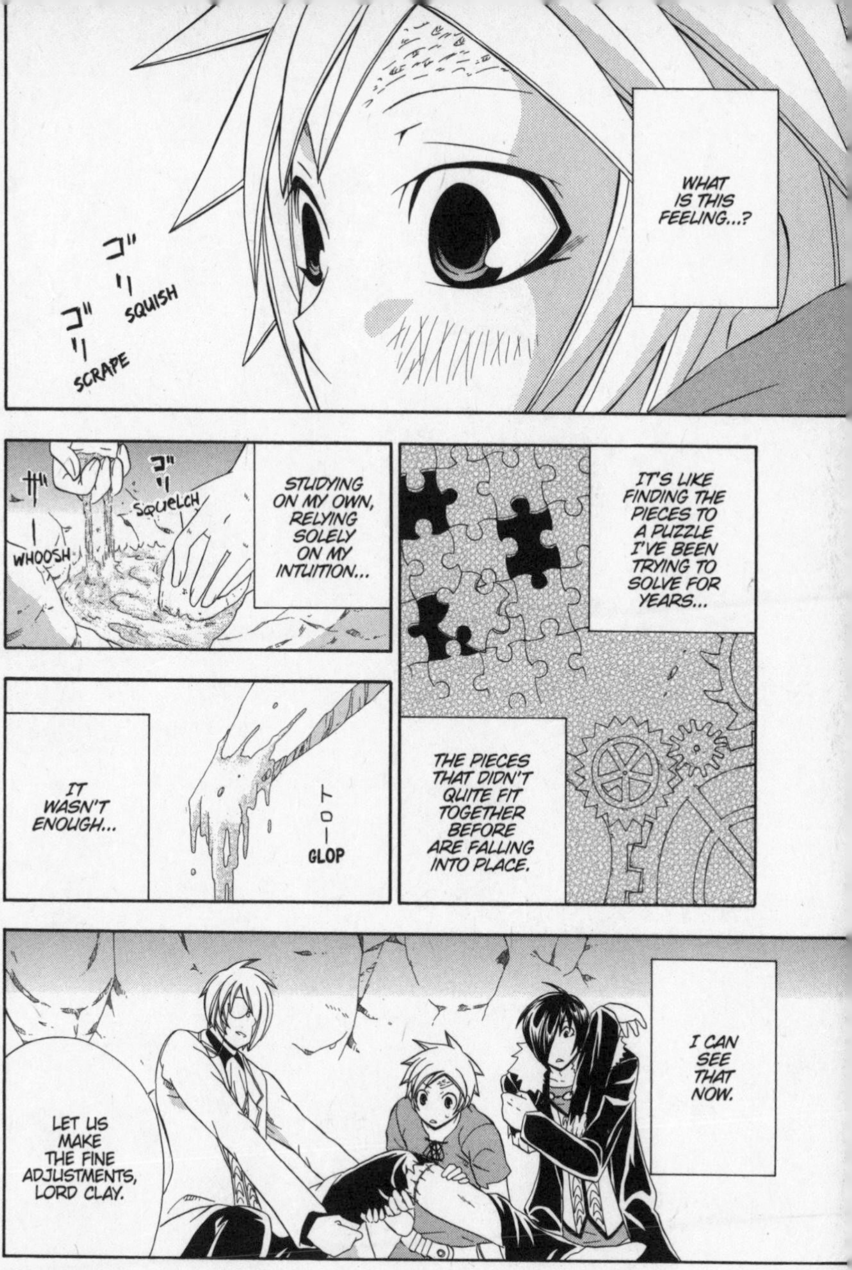
WHAT IS THIS FEELING...?
ゴリ
SQUISH
ゴリ
SCRAPE
IT'S LIKE FINDING THE PIECES TO A PUZZLE I'VE BEEN TRYING TO SOLVE FOR YEARS...
THE PIECES THAT DIDN'T QUITE FIT TOGETHER BEFORE ARE FALLING INTO PLACE.
STUDYING ON MY OWN, RELYING SOLELY ON MY INTUITION...
ゴリ
SQUELCH
ザー
WHOOSH
IT WASN'T ENOUGH...
GLOP
I CAN SEE THAT NOW.
LET US MAKE THE FINE ADJUSTMENTS, LORD CLAY.

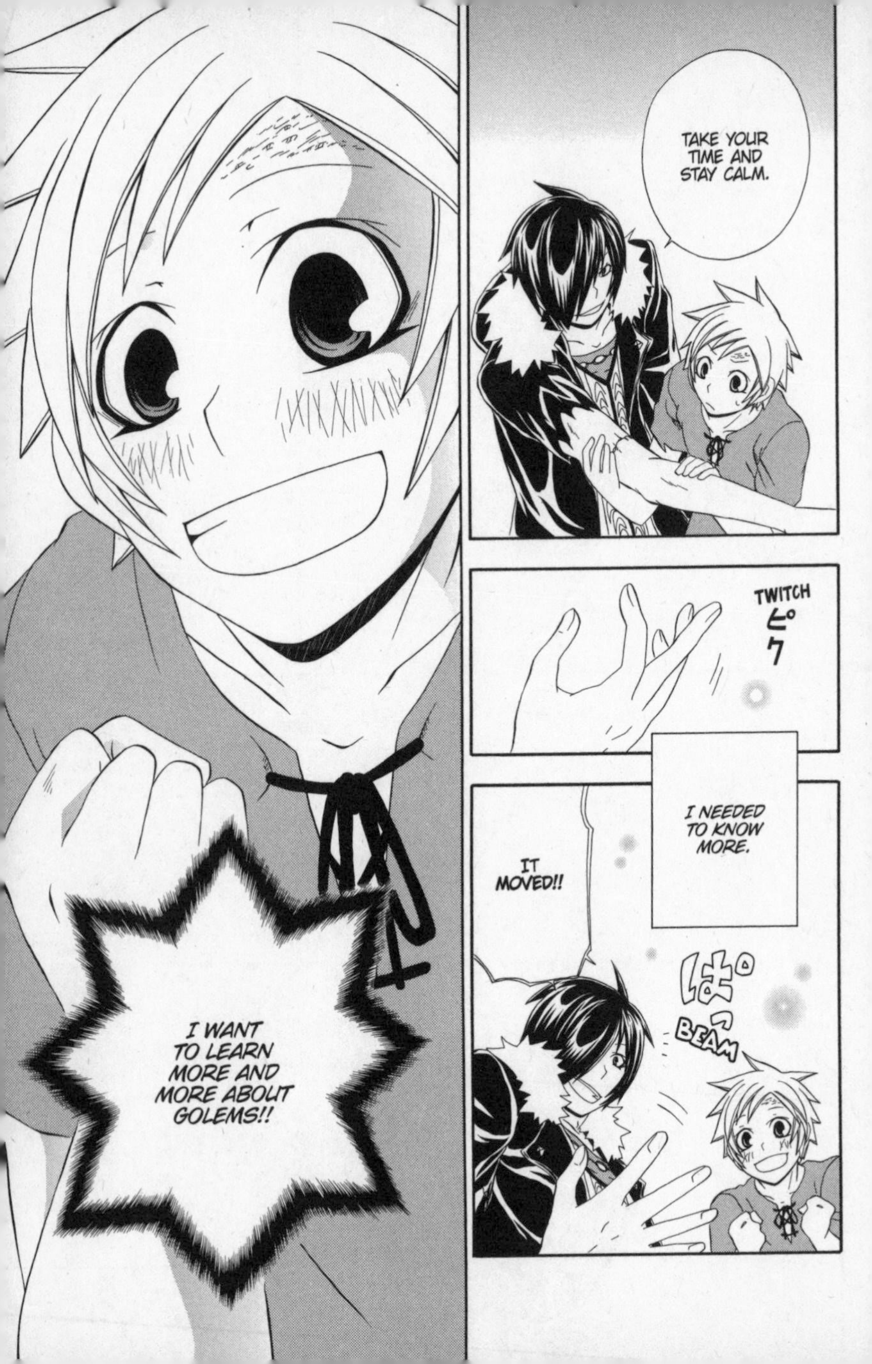
TAKE YOUR TIME AND STAY CALM.
TWITCH
ピク
I NEEDED TO KNOW MORE.
IT MOVED!!
はっ
BEAM
I WANT TO LEARN MORE AND MORE ABOUT GOLEMS!!

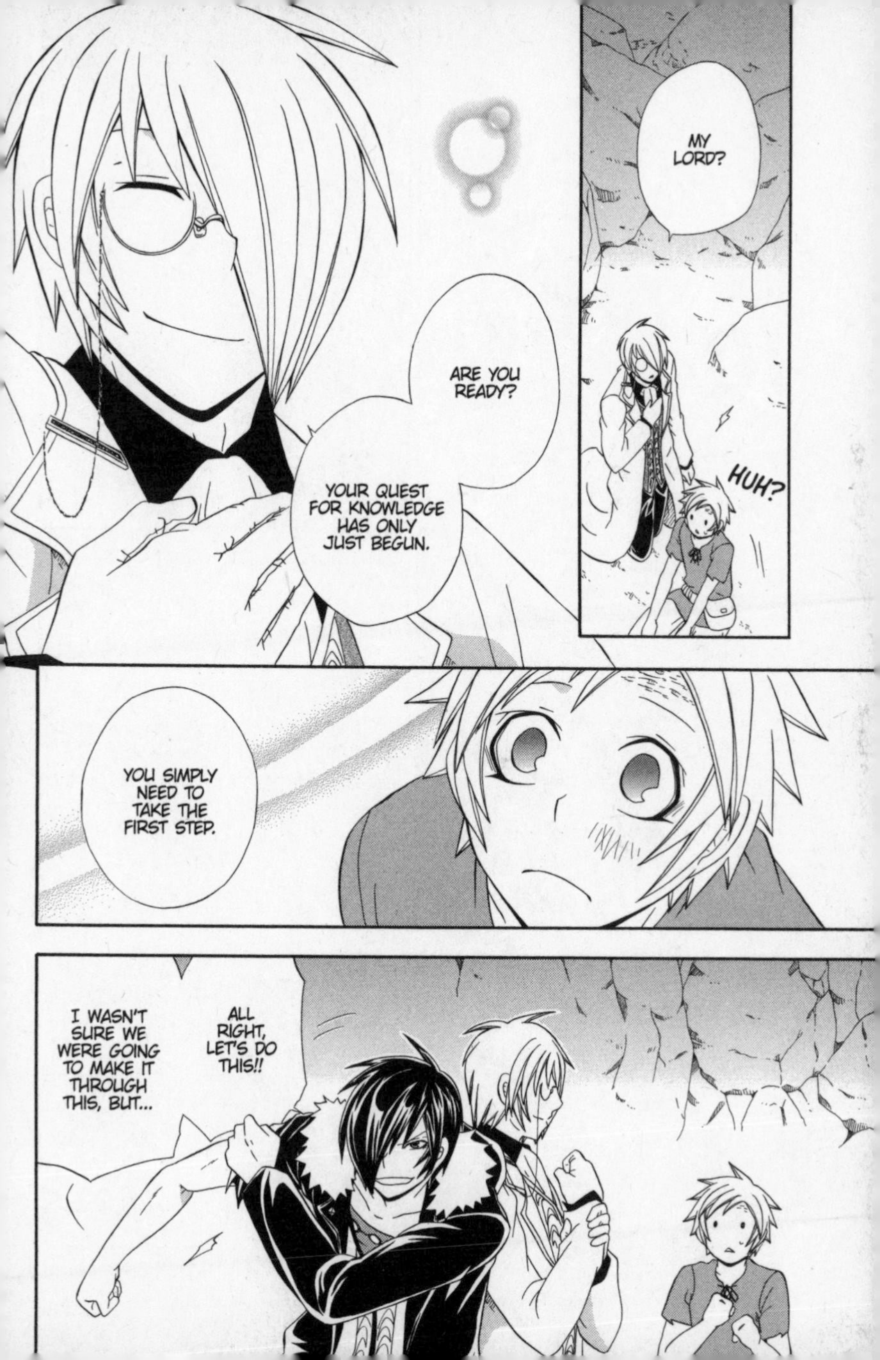
MY LORD?
HUH?
ARE YOU READY?
YOUR QUEST FOR KNOWLEDGE HAS ONLY JUST BEGUN.
YOU SIMPLY NEED TO TAKE THE FIRST STEP.
ALL RIGHT, LET'S DO THIS!!
I WASN'T SURE WE WERE GOING TO MAKE IT THROUGH THIS, BUT...

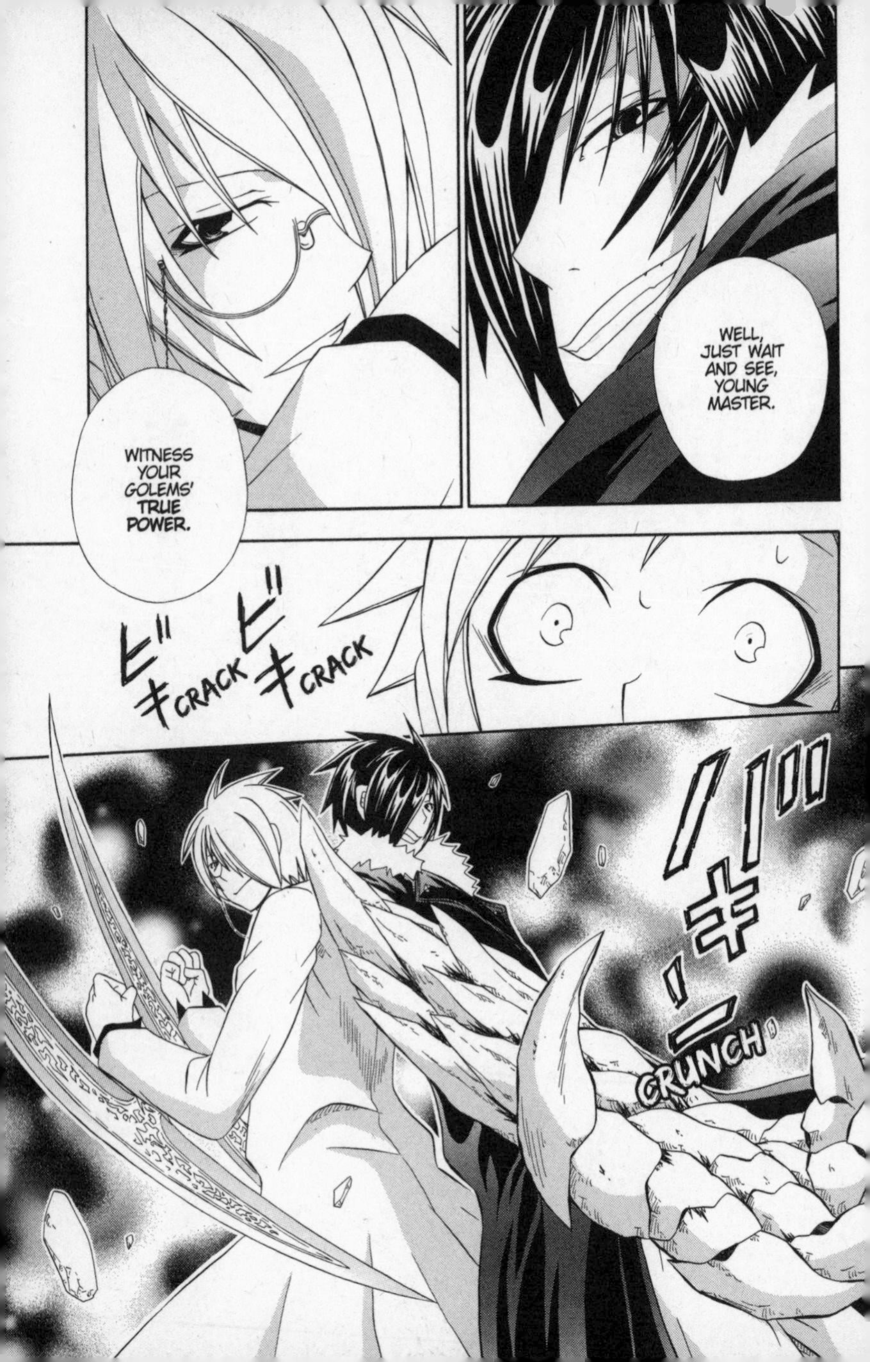

WELL, JUST WAIT AND SEE, YOUNG MASTER.
WITNESS YOUR GOLEMS' TRUE POWER.
ビキ CRACK
ビキ CRACK
CRUNCH

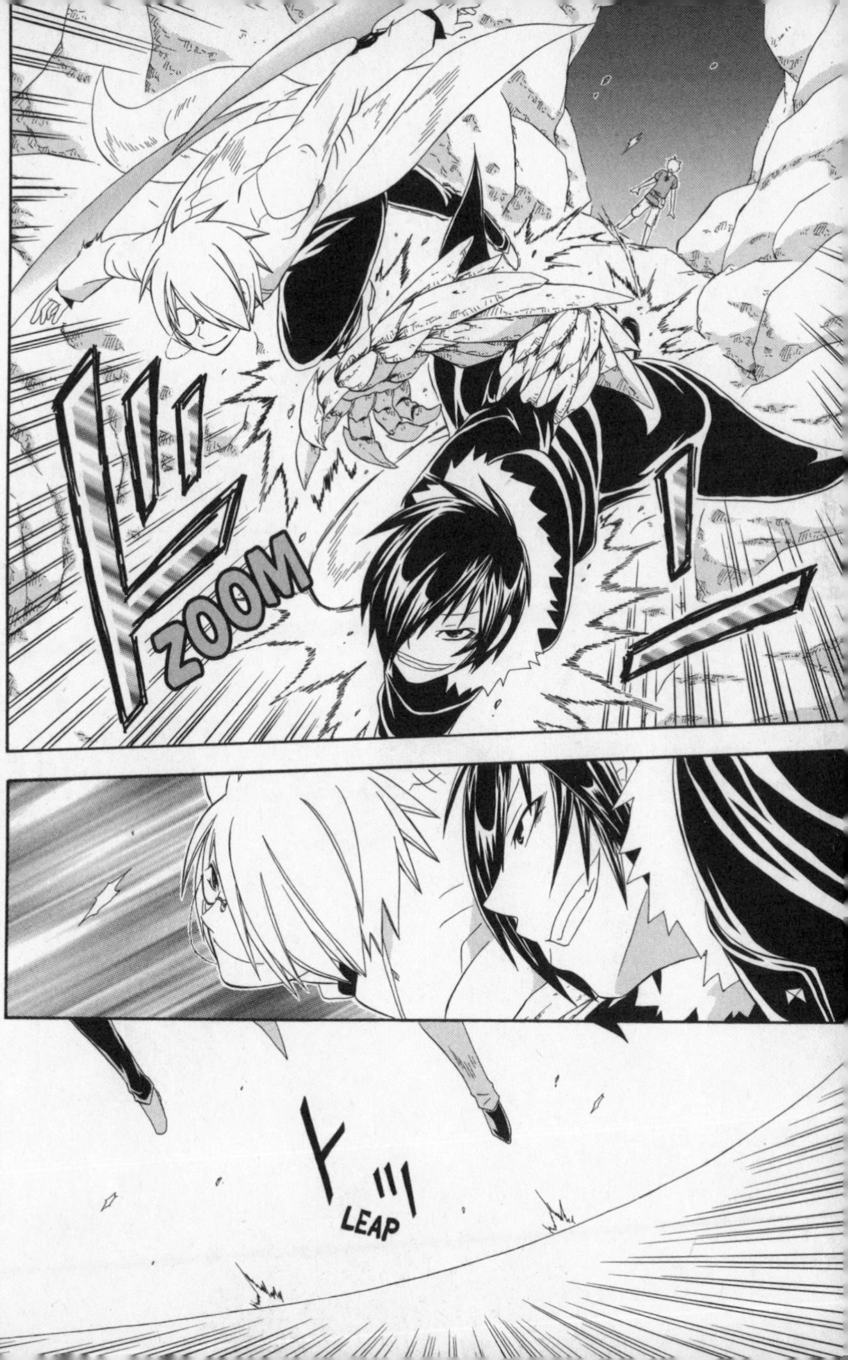
ZOOM
LEAP

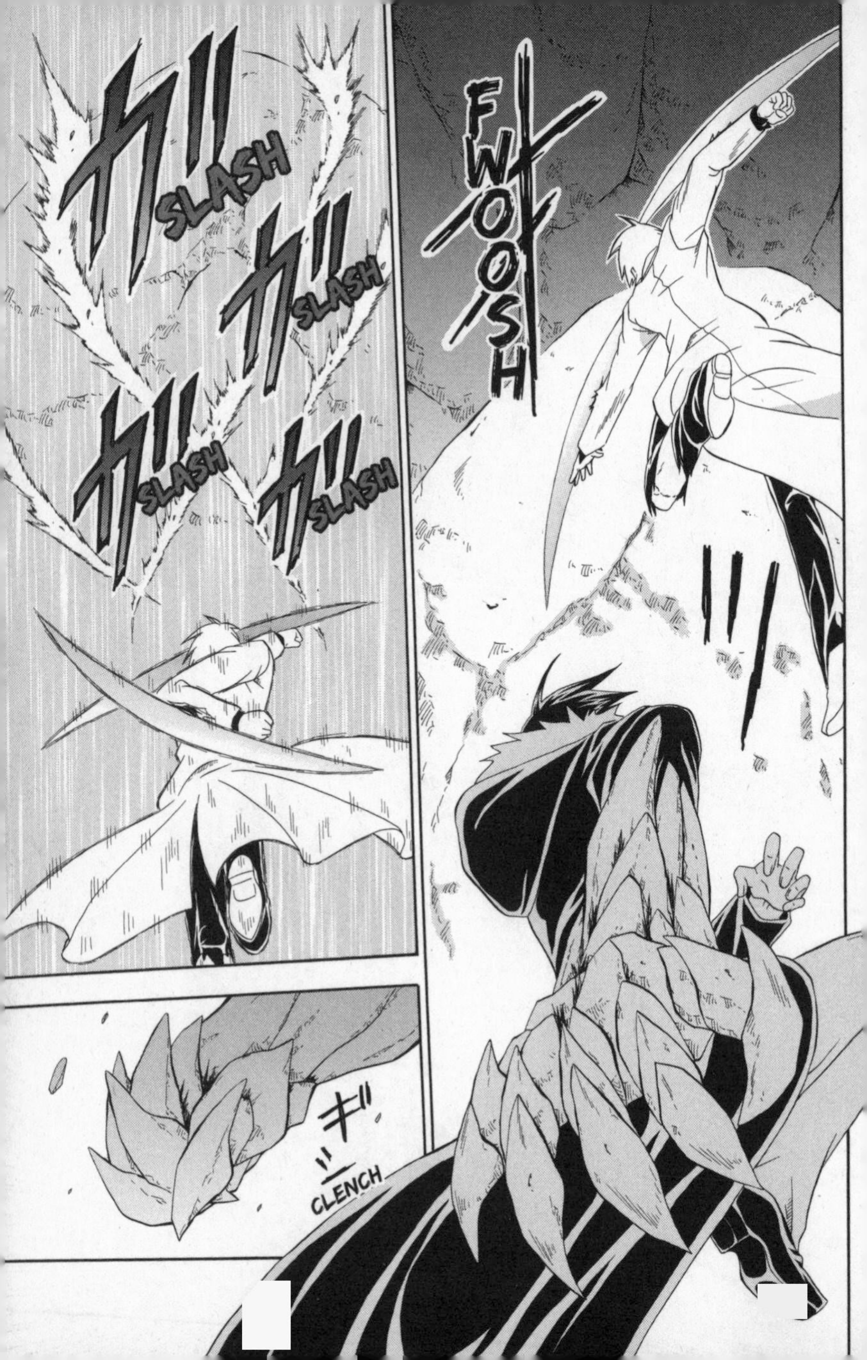
FWOOSH
SLASH
SLASH
SLASH
SLASH
CLENCH

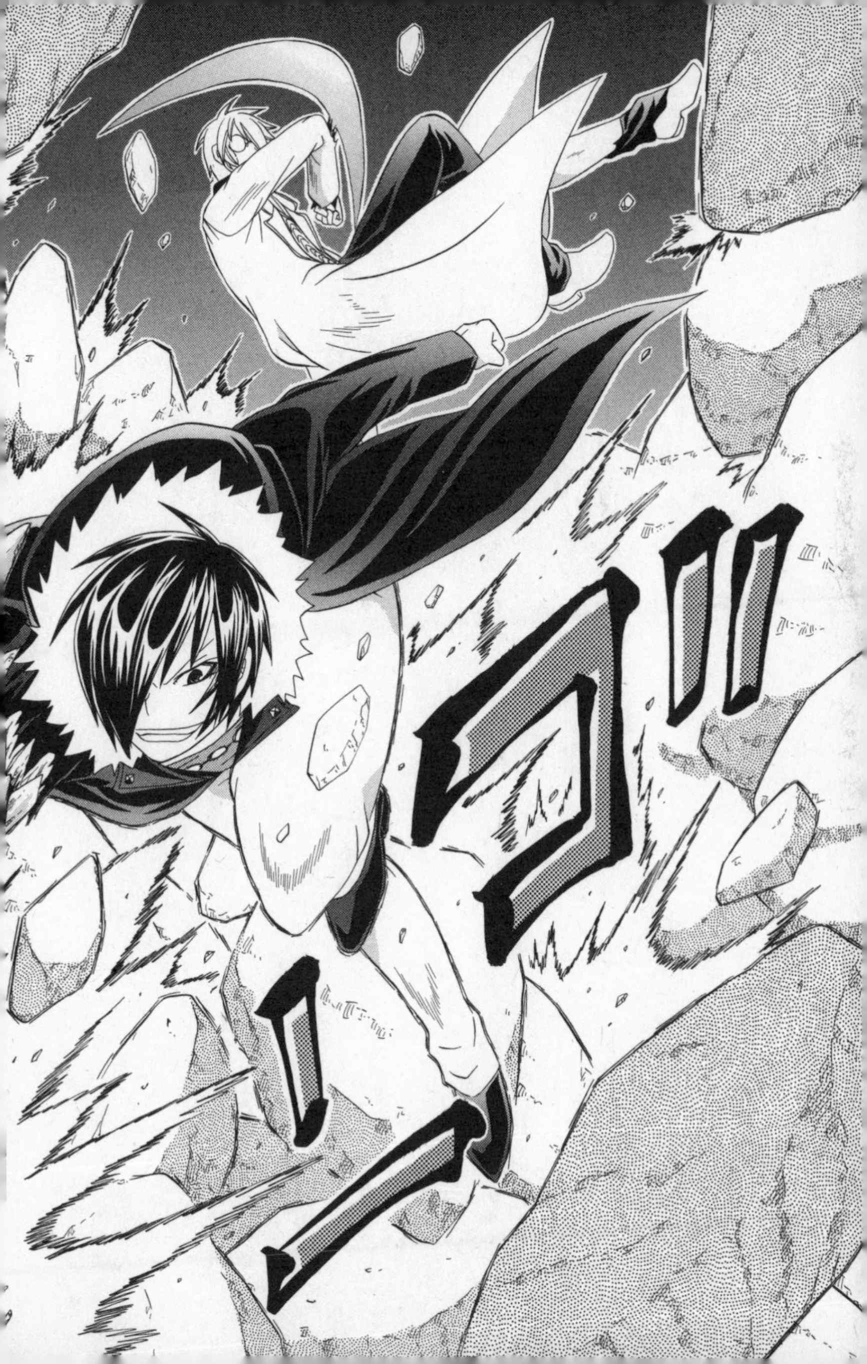

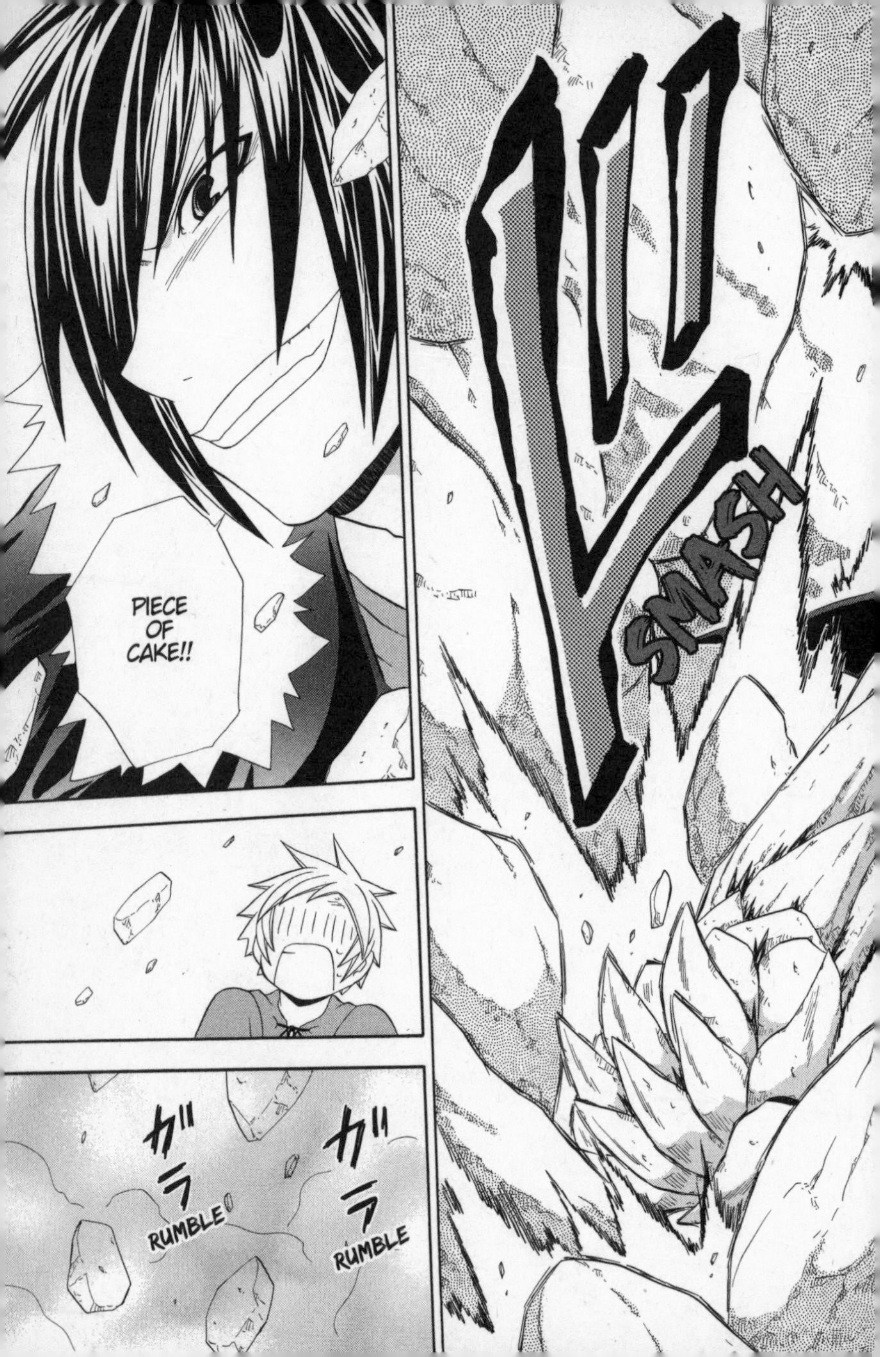
SMASH
PIECE OF CAKE!!
ガラ
RUMBLE
ガラ
RUMBLE

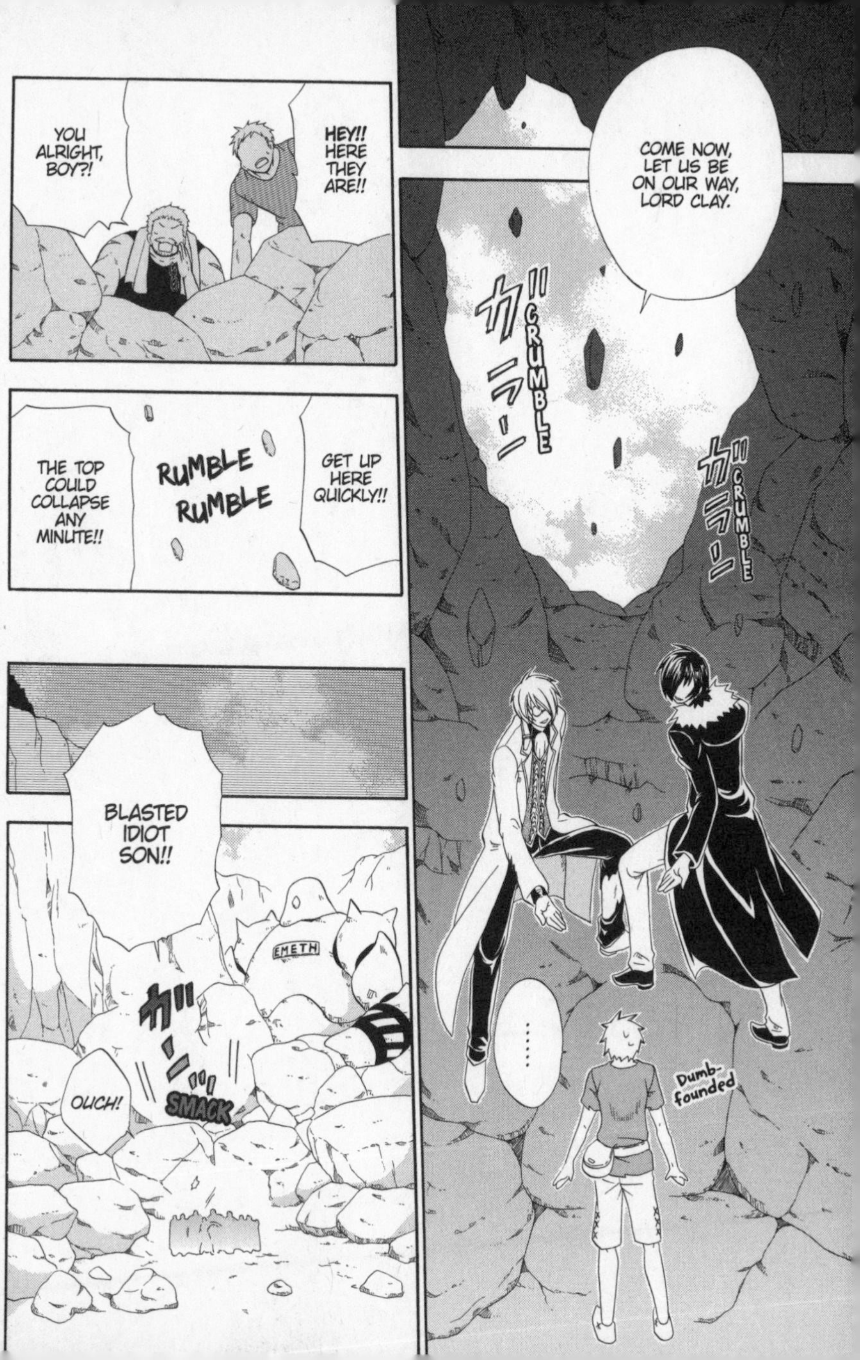

COME NOW, LET US BE ON OUR WAY, LORD CLAY.
CRUMBLE
CRUMBLE
......
Dumb-founded
HEY!! HERE THEY ARE!!
YOU ALRIGHT, BOY?!
GET UP HERE QUICKLY!!
RUMBLE RUMBLE
THE TOP COULD COLLAPSE ANY MINUTE!!
BLASTED IDIOT SON!!
EMETH
SMACK
OUCH!

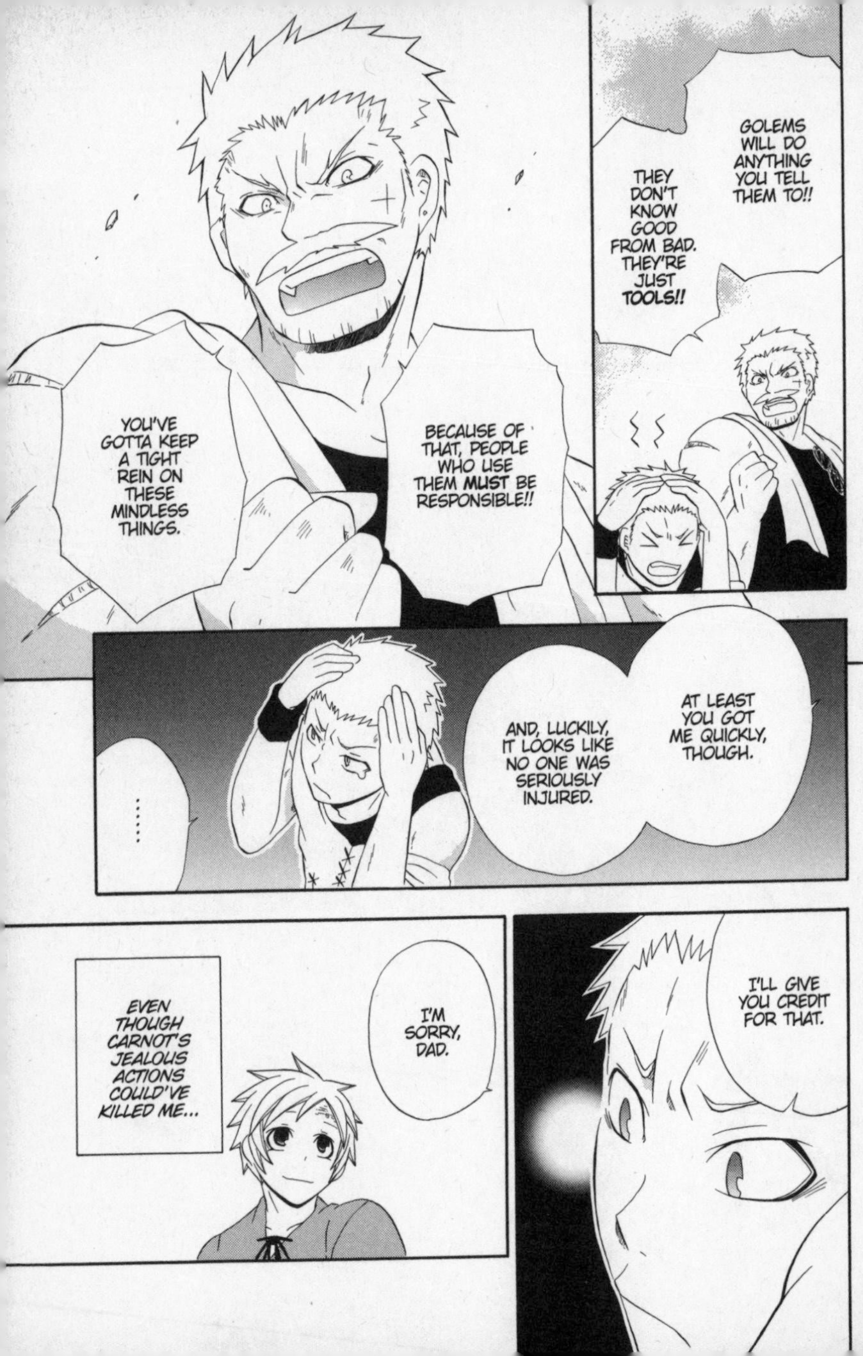
GOLEMS WILL DO ANYTHING YOU TELL THEM TO!!
THEY DON'T KNOW GOOD FROM BAD. THEY'RE JUST TOOLS!!
BECAUSE OF THAT, PEOPLE WHO USE THEM MUST BE RESPONSIBLE!!
YOU'VE GOTTA KEEP A TIGHT REIN ON THESE MINDLESS THINGS.
AT LEAST YOU GOT ME QUICKLY, THOUGH.
AND, LUCKILY, IT LOOKS LIKE NO ONE WAS SERIOUSLY INJURED.
......
I'LL GIVE YOU CREDIT FOR THAT.
I'M SORRY, DAD.
EVEN THOUGH CARNOT'S JEALOUS ACTIONS COULD'VE KILLED ME...

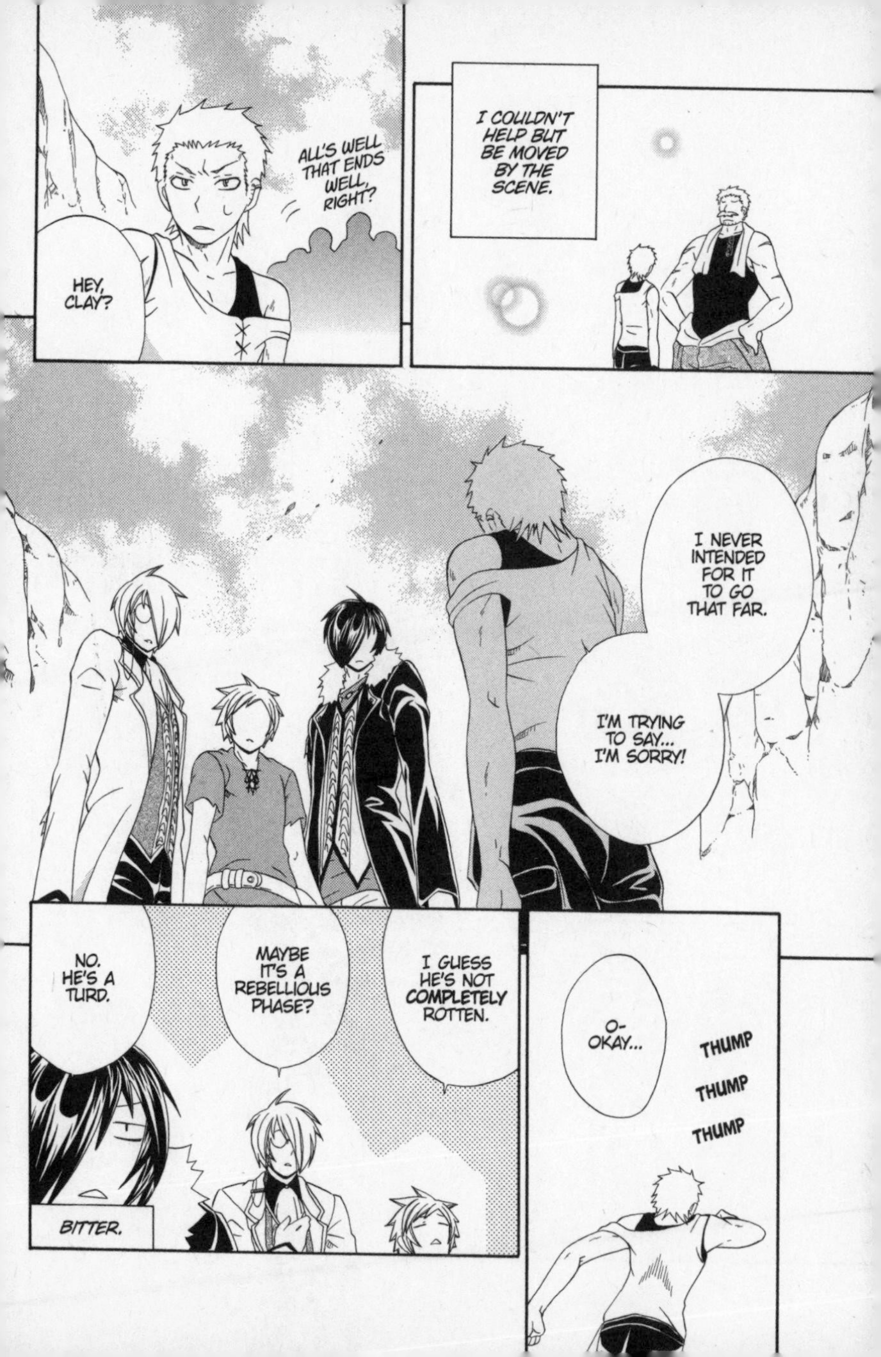
I COULDN'T HELP BUT BE MOVED BY THE SCENE.
ALL'S WELL THAT ENDS WELL, RIGHT?
HEY, CLAY?
I NEVER INTENDED FOR IT TO GO THAT FAR.
I'M TRYING TO SAY... I'M SORRY!
O-OKAY...
THUMP
THUMP
THUMP
I GUESS HE'S NOT COMPLETELY ROTTEN.
MAYBE IT'S A REBELLIOUS PHASE?
NO. HE'S A TURD.
BITTER.

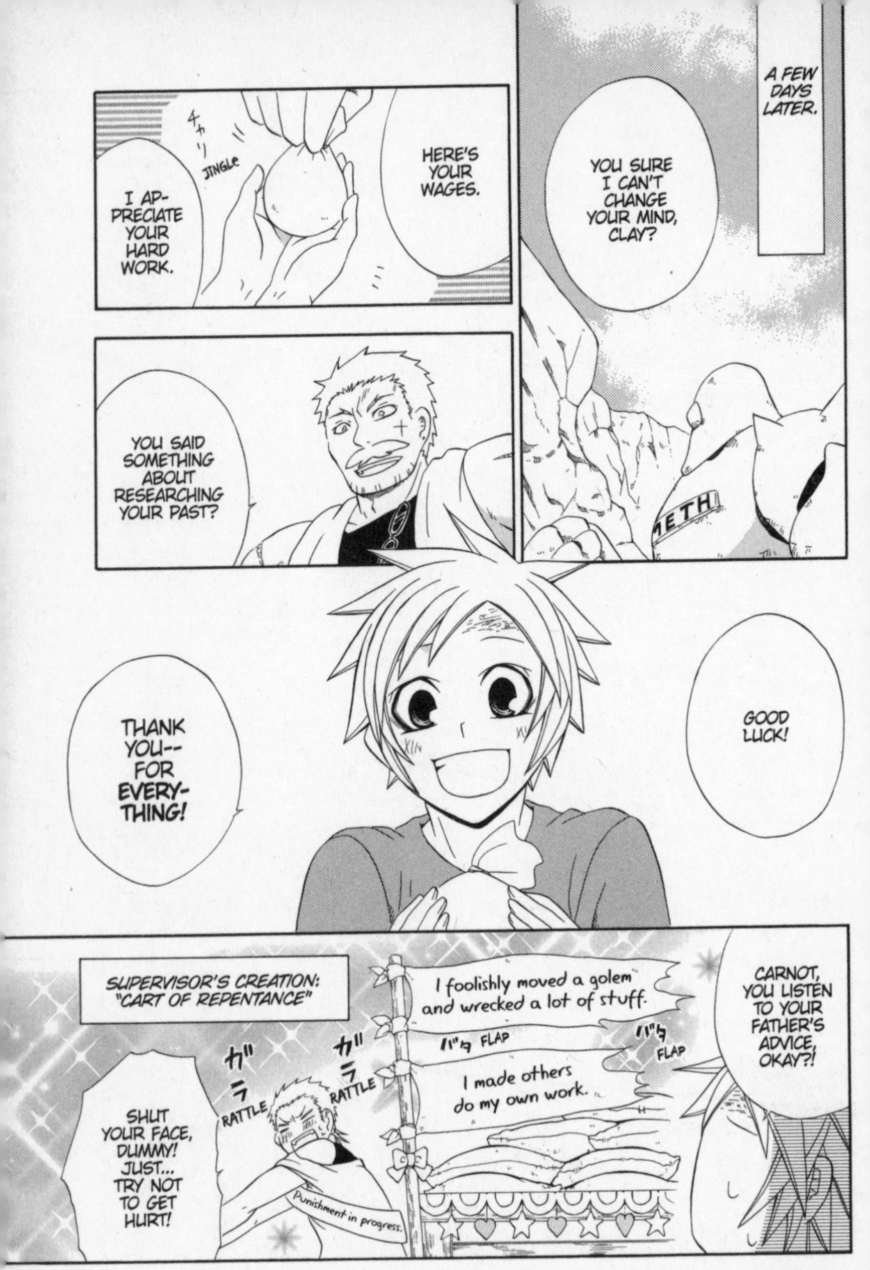
A FEW DAYS LATER.
YOU SURE I CAN'T CHANGE YOUR MIND, CLAY?
HERE'S YOUR WAGES.
チャリ JINGLE
I APPRECIATE YOUR HARD WORK.
YOU SAID SOMETHING ABOUT RESEARCHING YOUR PAST?
METH
GOOD LUCK!
THANK YOU-- FOR EVERYTHING!
CARNOT, YOU LISTEN TO YOUR FATHER'S ADVICE, OKAY?!
バタ FLAP
I foolishly moved a golem and wrecked a lot of stuff.
バタ FLAP
I made others do my own work.
ガラ RATTLE
ガラ RATTLE
SUPERVISOR'S CREATION: "CART OF REPENTANCE"
SHUT YOUR FACE, DUMMY! JUST... TRY NOT TO GET HURT!
Punishment in progress.

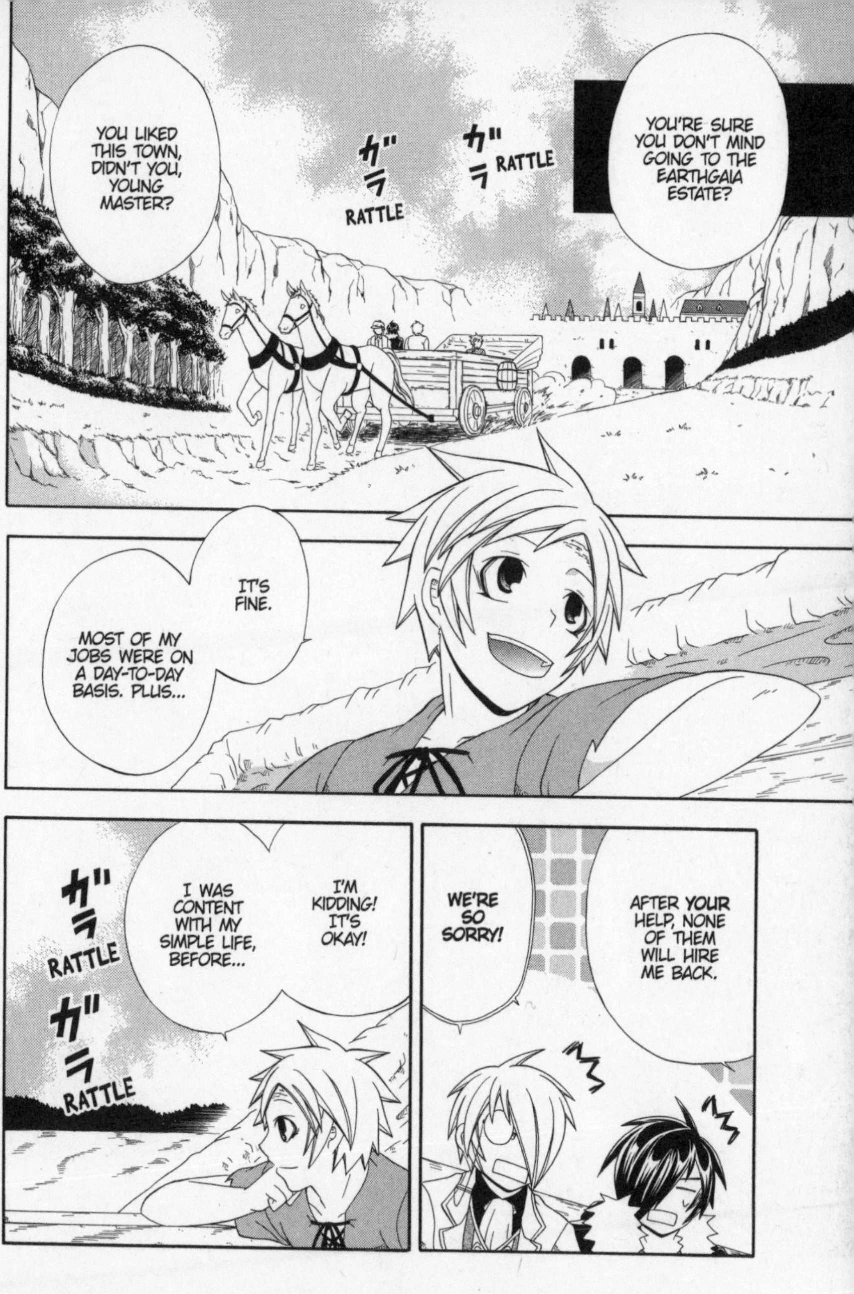
YOU'RE SURE YOU DON'T MIND GOING TO THE EARTHGAIA ESTATE?
ガラ RATTLE
ガラ RATTLE
YOU LIKED THIS TOWN, DIDN'T YOU, YOUNG MASTER?
IT'S FINE.
MOST OF MY JOBS WERE ON A DAY-TO-DAY BASIS. PLUS...
AFTER YOUR HELP, NONE OF THEM WILL HIRE ME BACK.
WE'RE SO SORRY!
I'M KIDDING! IT'S OKAY!
I WAS CONTENT WITH MY SIMPLE LIFE, BEFORE...
ガラ RATTLE
ガラ RATTLE

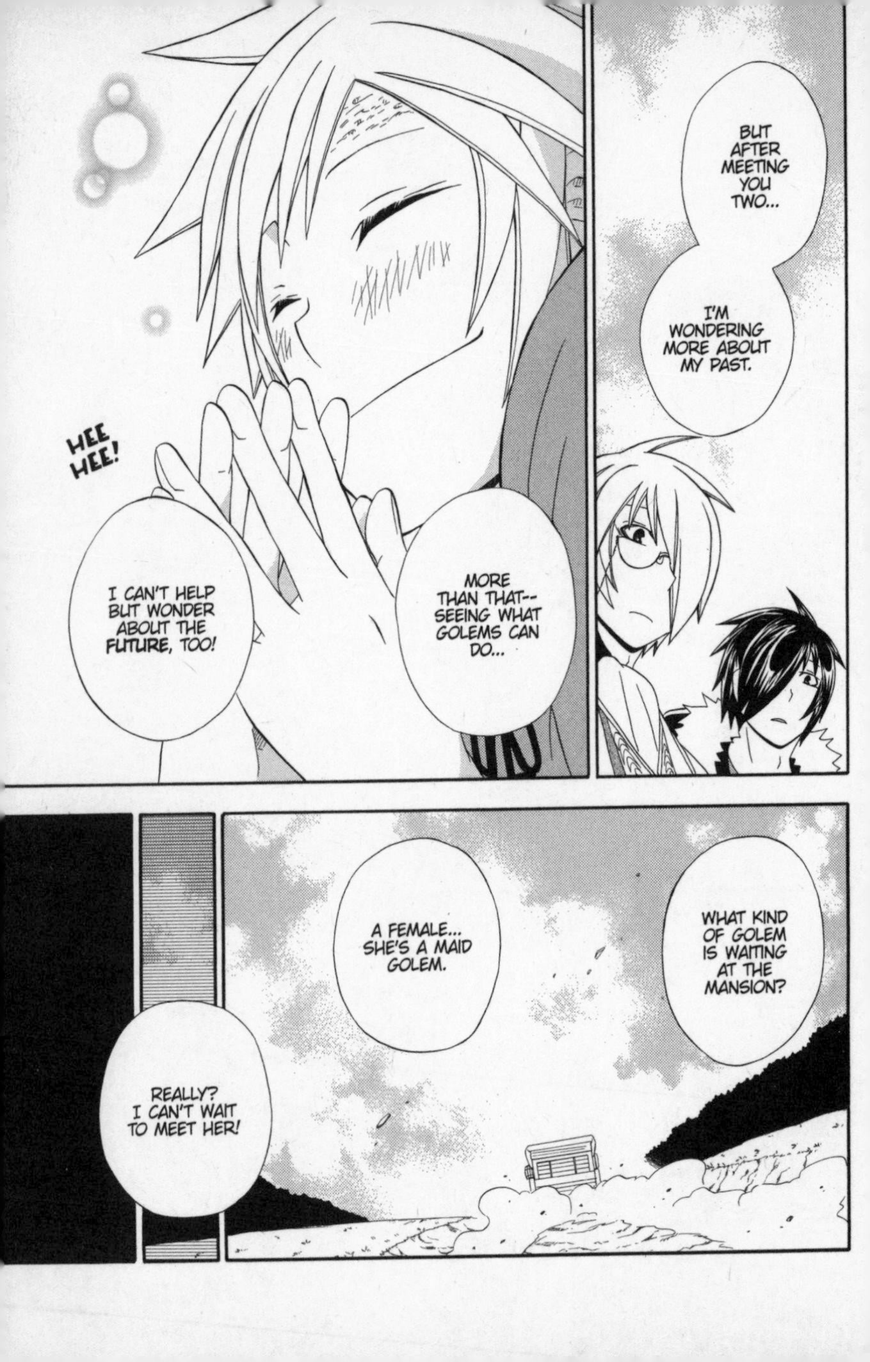
BUT AFTER MEETING YOU TWO...
I'M WONDERING MORE ABOUT MY PAST.
MORE THAN THAT-- SEEING WHAT GOLEMS CAN DO...
I CAN'T HELP BUT WONDER ABOUT THE FUTURE, TOO!
HEE HEE!
WHAT KIND OF GOLEM IS WAITING AT THE MANSION?
A FEMALE... SHE'S A MAID GOLEM.
REALLY? I CAN'T WAIT TO MEET HER!

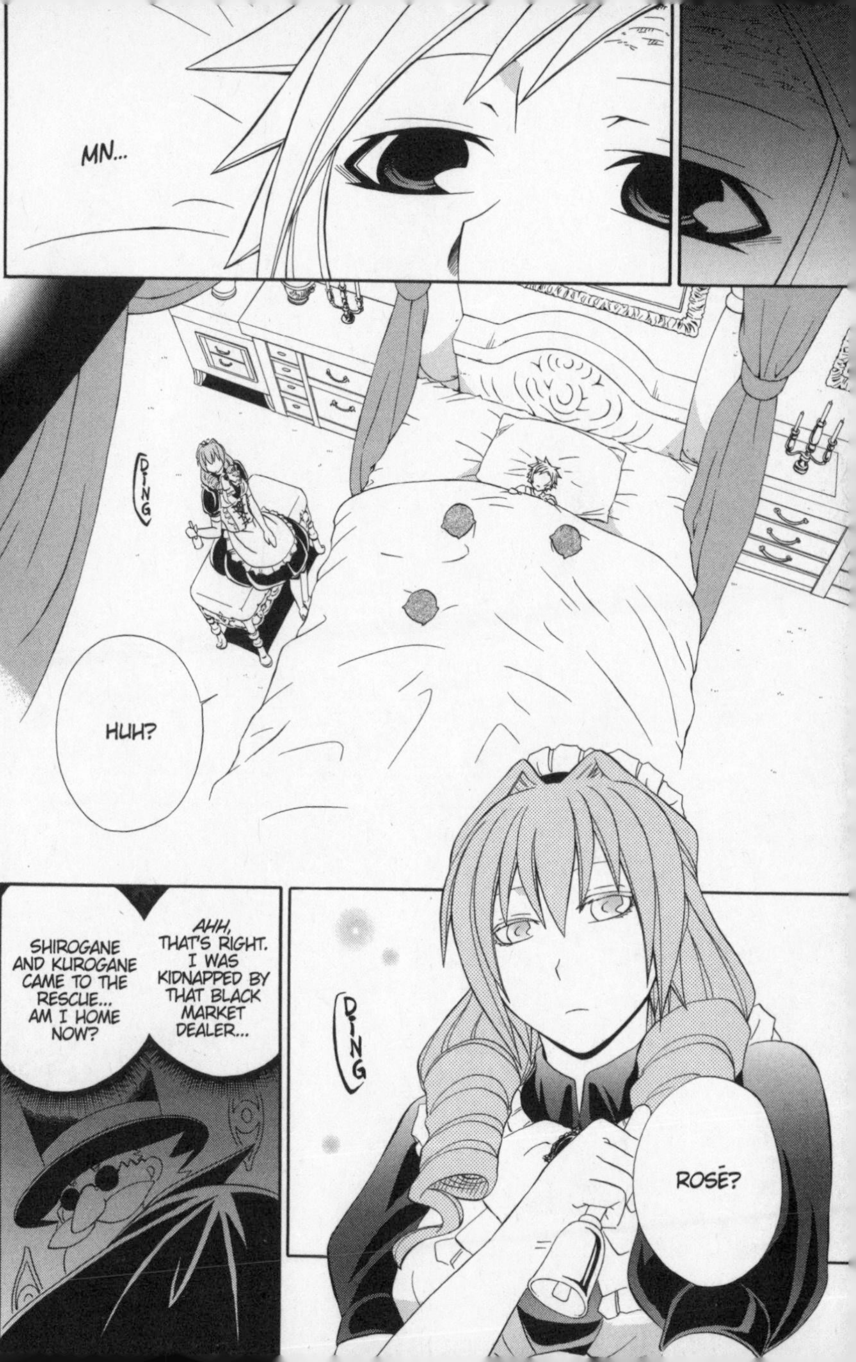
MN...
DING
HUH?
DING
ROSÉ?
AHH, THAT'S RIGHT. I WAS KIDNAPPED BY THAT BLACK MARKET DEALER...
SHIROGANE AND KUROGANE CAME TO THE RESCUE... AM I HOME NOW?

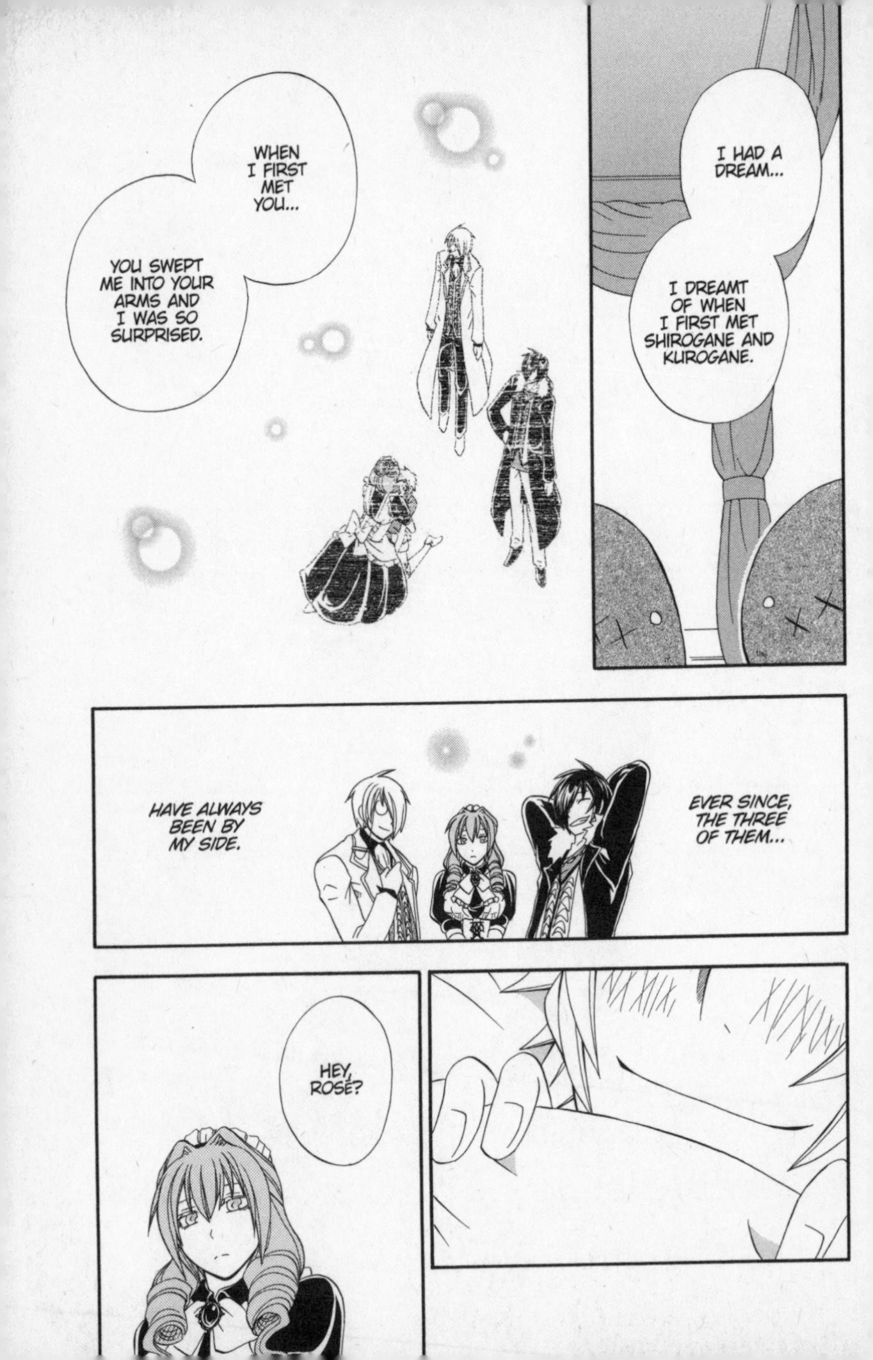
I HAD A DREAM...
I DREAMT OF WHEN I FIRST MET SHIROGANE AND KUROGANE.
WHEN I FIRST MET YOU...
YOU SWEPT ME INTO YOUR ARMS AND I WAS SO SURPRISED.
EVER SINCE, THE THREE OF THEM...
HAVE ALWAYS BEEN BY MY SIDE.
HEY, ROSÉ?

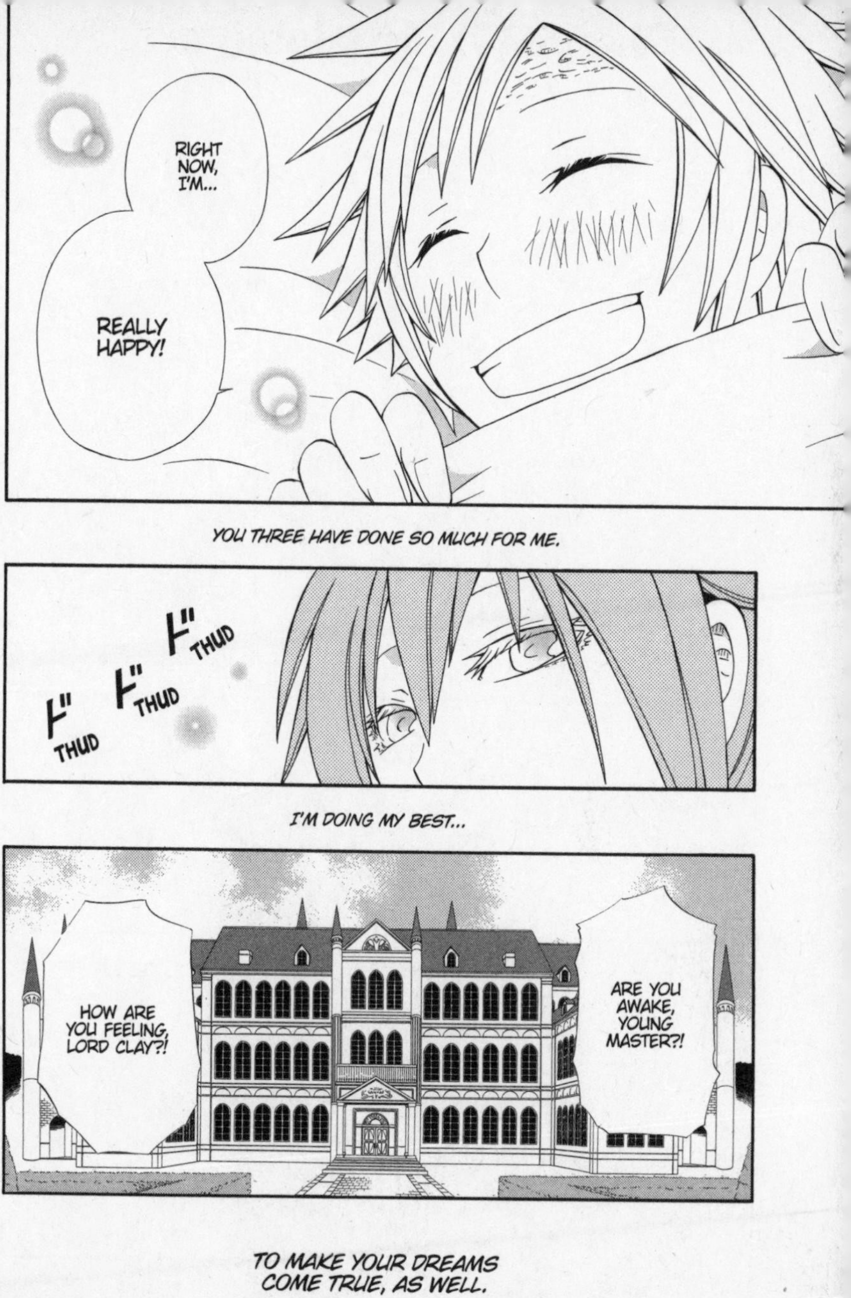
RIGHT NOW, I'M...
REALLY HAPPY!
YOU THREE HAVE DONE SO MUCH FOR ME.
ド THUD
ド THUD
ド THUD
I'M DOING MY BEST...
ARE YOU AWAKE, YOUNG MASTER?!
HOW ARE YOU FEELING, LORD CLAY?!
TO MAKE YOUR DREAMS COME TRUE, AS WELL.

Chapter 7: First Job (Part 1)

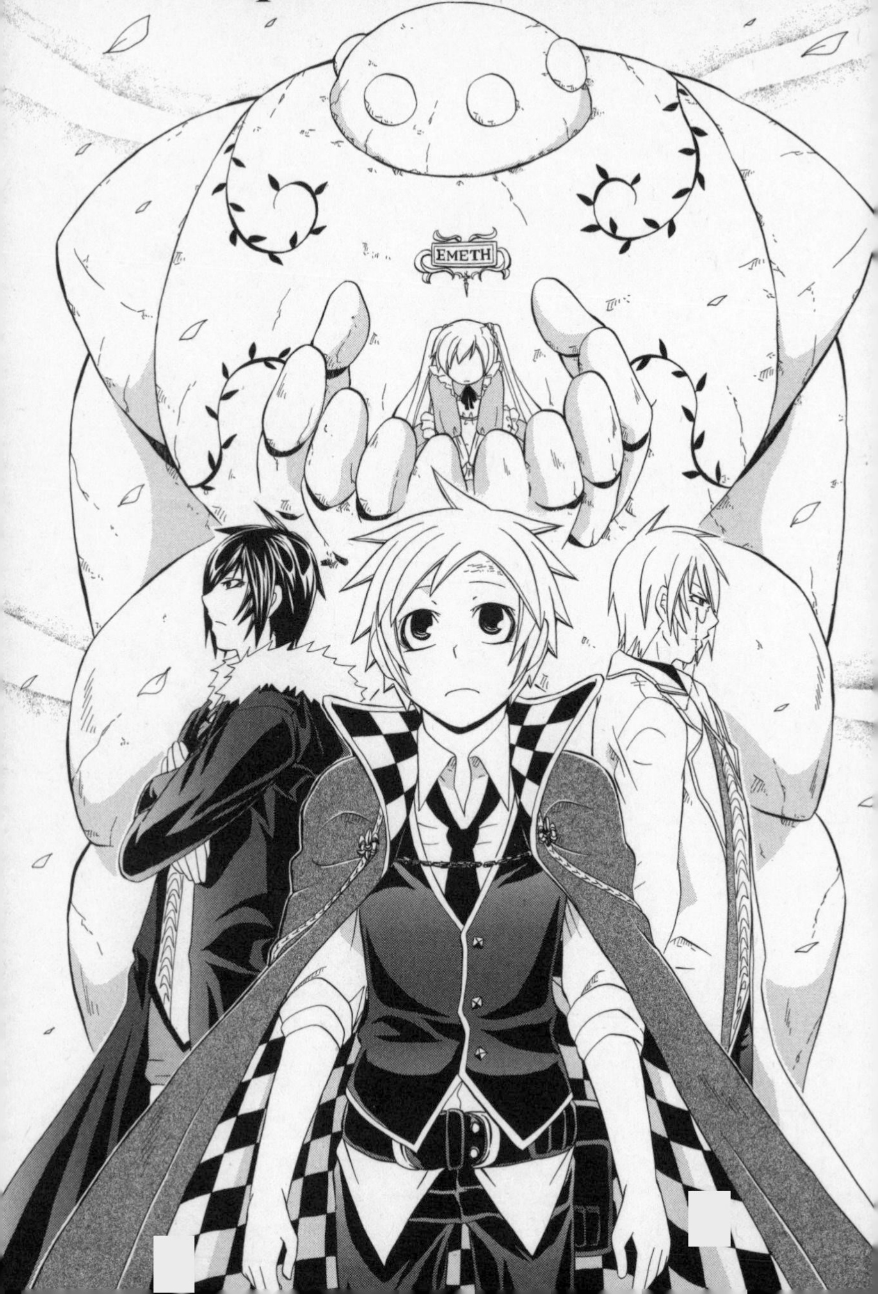
EMETH

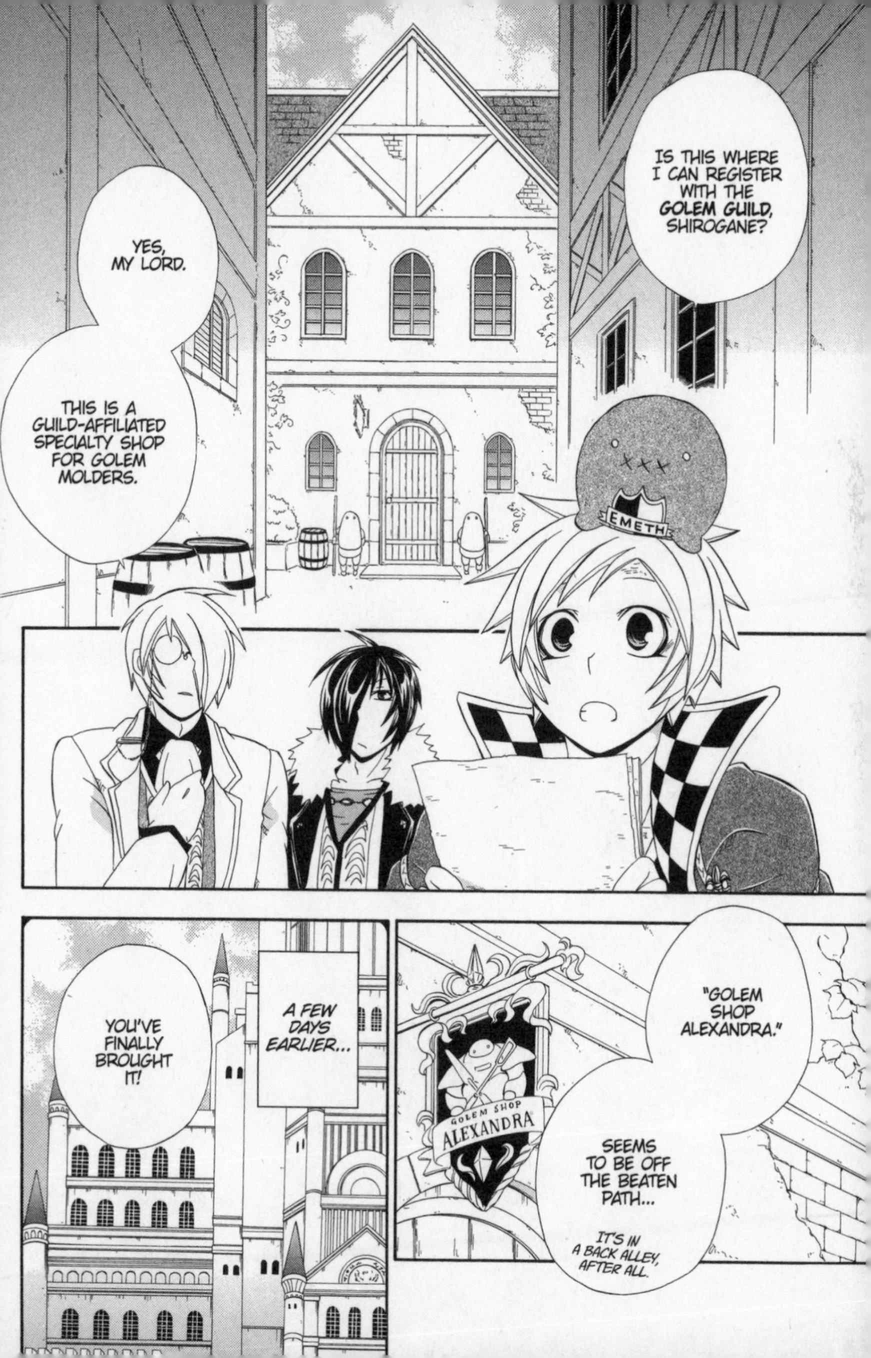
IS THIS WHERE I CAN REGISTER WITH THE GOLEM GUILD, SHIROGANE?
YES, MY LORD.
THIS IS A GUILD-AFFILIATED SPECIALTY SHOP FOR GOLEM MOLDERS.
EMETH
"GOLEM SHOP ALEXANDRA."
GOLEM SHOP ALEXANDRA
SEEMS TO BE OFF THE BEATEN PATH...
IT'S IN A BACK ALLEY, AFTER ALL.
A FEW DAYS EARLIER...
YOU'VE FINALLY BROUGHT IT!

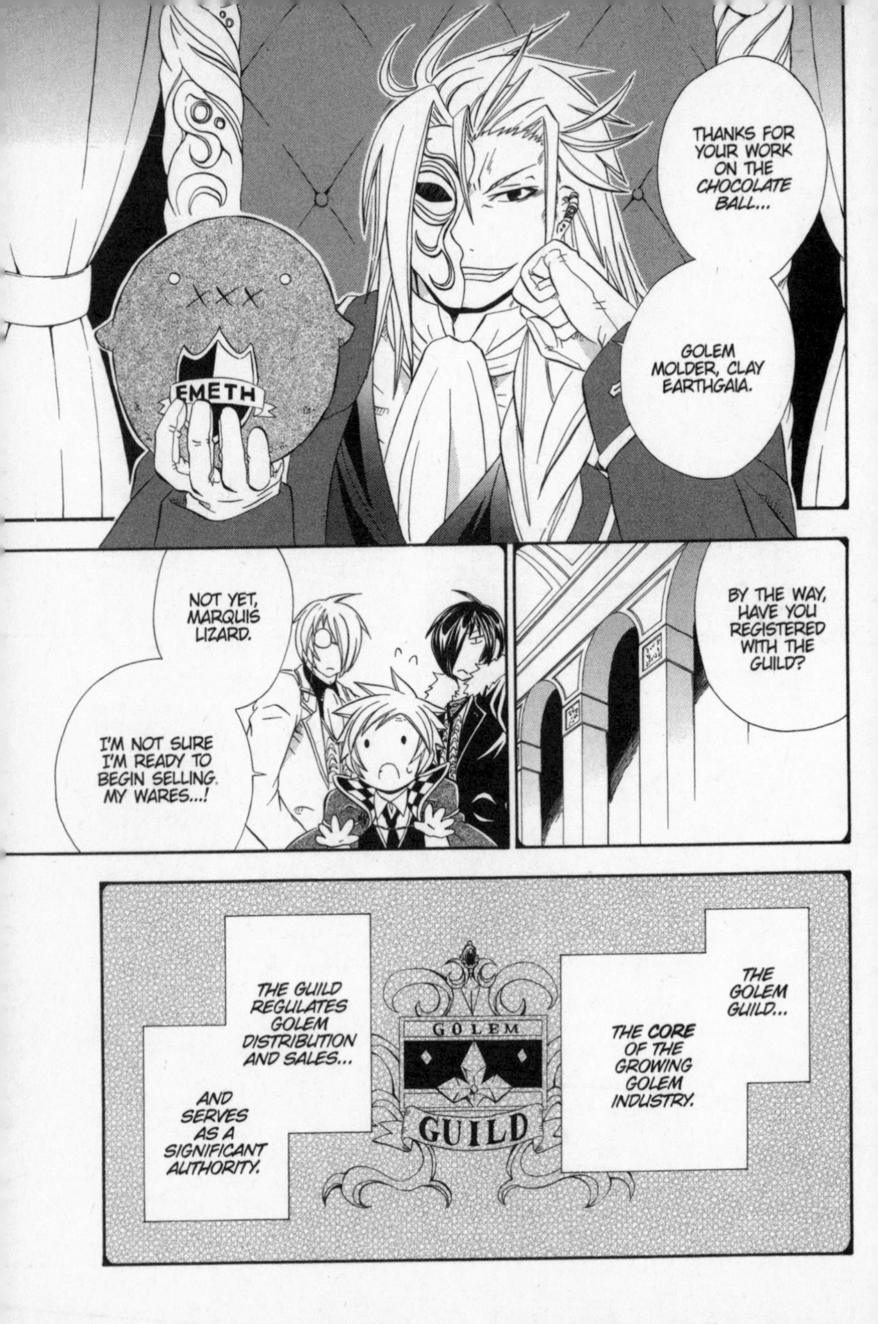
THANKS FOR YOUR WORK ON THE CHOCOLATE BALL...
GOLEM MOLDER, CLAY EARTHGAIA.
EMETH
BY THE WAY, HAVE YOU REGISTERED WITH THE GUILD?
NOT YET, MARQUIS LIZARD.
I'M NOT SURE I'M READY TO BEGIN SELLING MY WARES...!
THE GOLEM GUILD...
THE CORE OF THE GROWING GOLEM INDUSTRY.
GOLEM
GUILD
THE GUILD REGULATES GOLEM DISTRIBUTION AND SALES...
AND SERVES AS A SIGNIFICANT AUTHORITY.

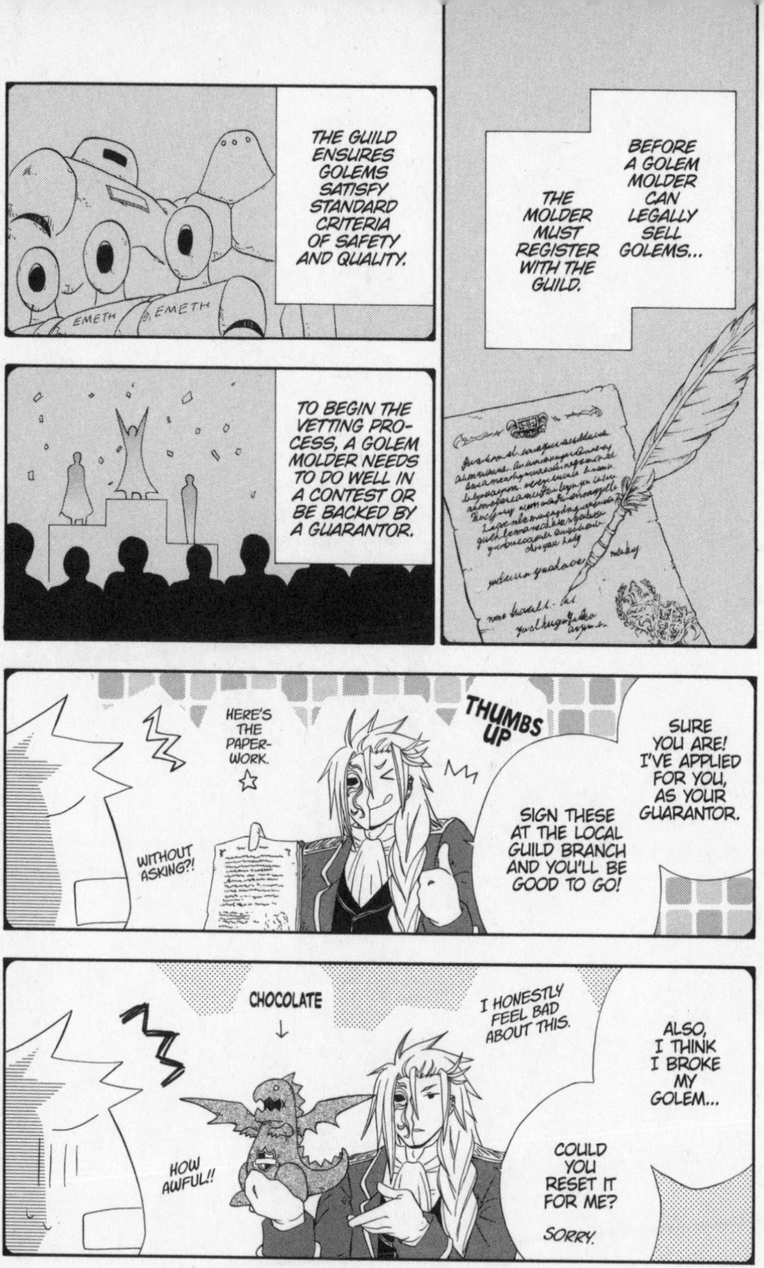
BEFORE A GOLEM MOLDER CAN LEGALLY SELL GOLEMS...
THE MOLDER MUST REGISTER WITH THE GUILD.
THE GUILD ENSURES GOLEMS SATISFY STANDARD CRITERIA OF SAFETY AND QUALITY.
EMETH
EMETH
TO BEGIN THE VETTING PRO-CESS, A GOLEM MOLDER NEEDS TO DO WELL IN A CONTEST OR BE BACKED BY A GUARANTOR.
SURE YOU ARE! I'VE APPLIED FOR YOU, AS YOUR GUARANTOR.
SIGN THESE AT THE LOCAL GUILD BRANCH AND YOU'LL BE GOOD TO GO!
THUMBS UP
HERE'S THE PAPER-WORK. ☆
WITHOUT ASKING?!
ALSO, I THINK I BROKE MY GOLEM...
I HONESTLY FEEL BAD ABOUT THIS.
COULD YOU RESET IT FOR ME?
SORRY.
CHOCOLATE ↓
HOW AWFUL!!

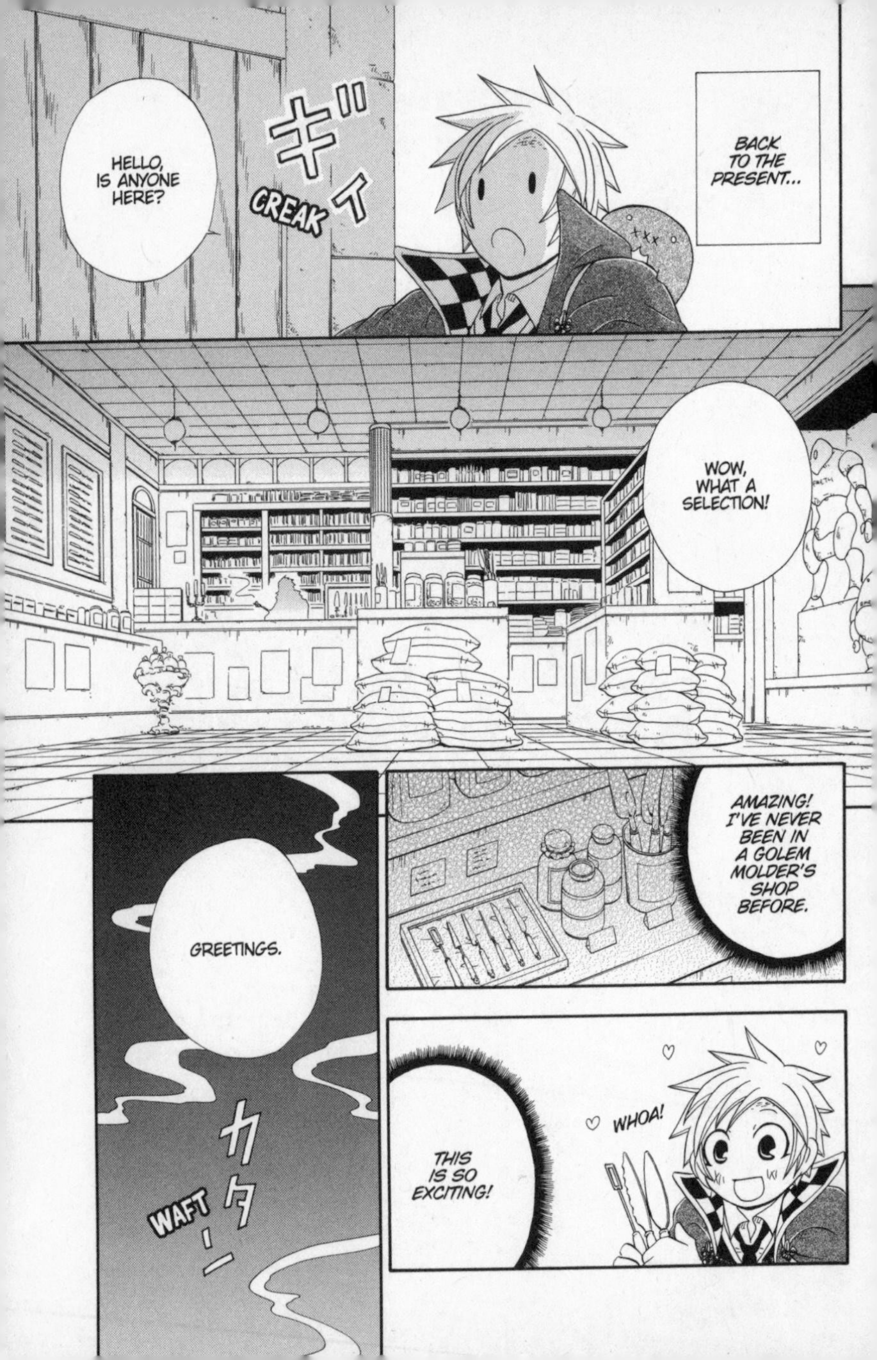
BACK TO THE PRESENT...
CREAK
HELLO, IS ANYONE HERE?
WOW, WHAT A SELECTION!
AMAZING! I'VE NEVER BEEN IN A GOLEM MOLDER'S SHOP BEFORE.
WHOA!
THIS IS SO EXCITING!
GREETINGS.
WAFT

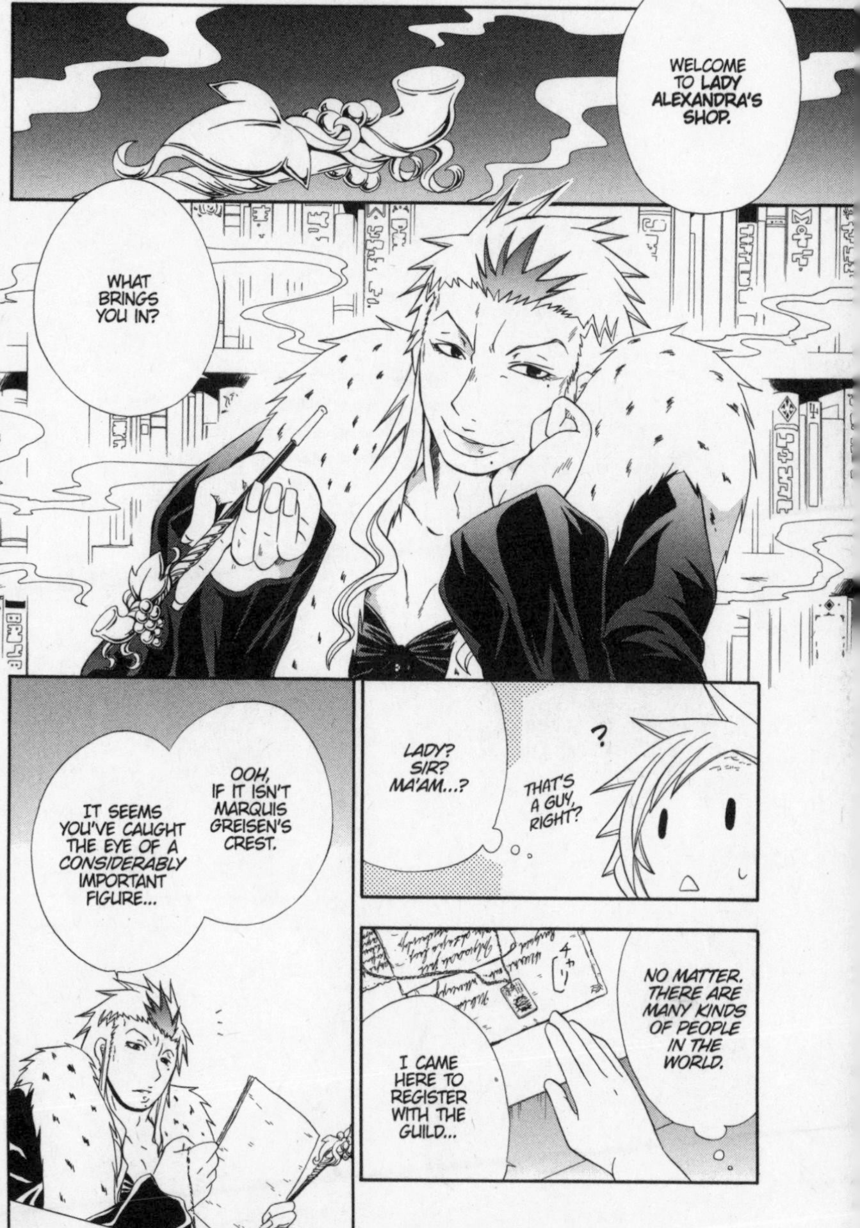
WELCOME TO LADY ALEXANDRA'S SHOP.
WHAT BRINGS YOU IN?
?
LADY? SIR? MA'AM...?
THAT'S A GUY, RIGHT?
NO MATTER. THERE ARE MANY KINDS OF PEOPLE IN THE WORLD.
I CAME HERE TO REGISTER WITH THE GUILD...
OOH, IF IT ISN'T MARQUIS GREISEN'S CREST.
IT SEEMS YOU'VE CAUGHT THE EYE OF A CONSIDERABLY IMPORTANT FIGURE...

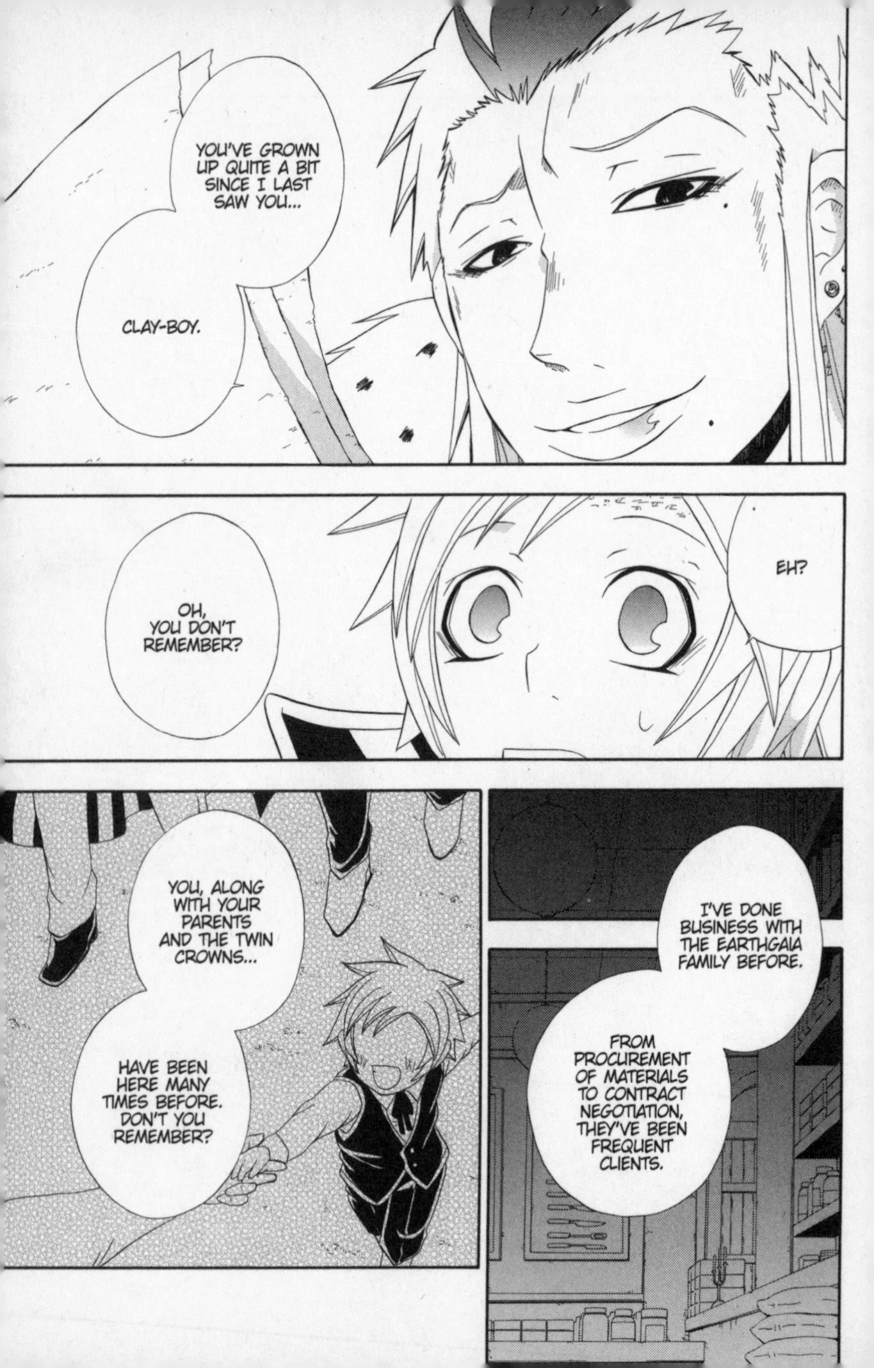
YOU'VE GROWN UP QUITE A BIT SINCE I LAST SAW YOU...
CLAY-BOY.
EH?
OH, YOU DON'T REMEMBER?
I'VE DONE BUSINESS WITH THE EARTHGAIA FAMILY BEFORE.
FROM PROCUREMENT OF MATERIALS TO CONTRACT NEGOTIATION, THEY'VE BEEN FREQUENT CLIENTS.
YOU, ALONG WITH YOUR PARENTS AND THE TWIN CROWNS...
HAVE BEEN HERE MANY TIMES BEFORE. DON'T YOU REMEMBER?

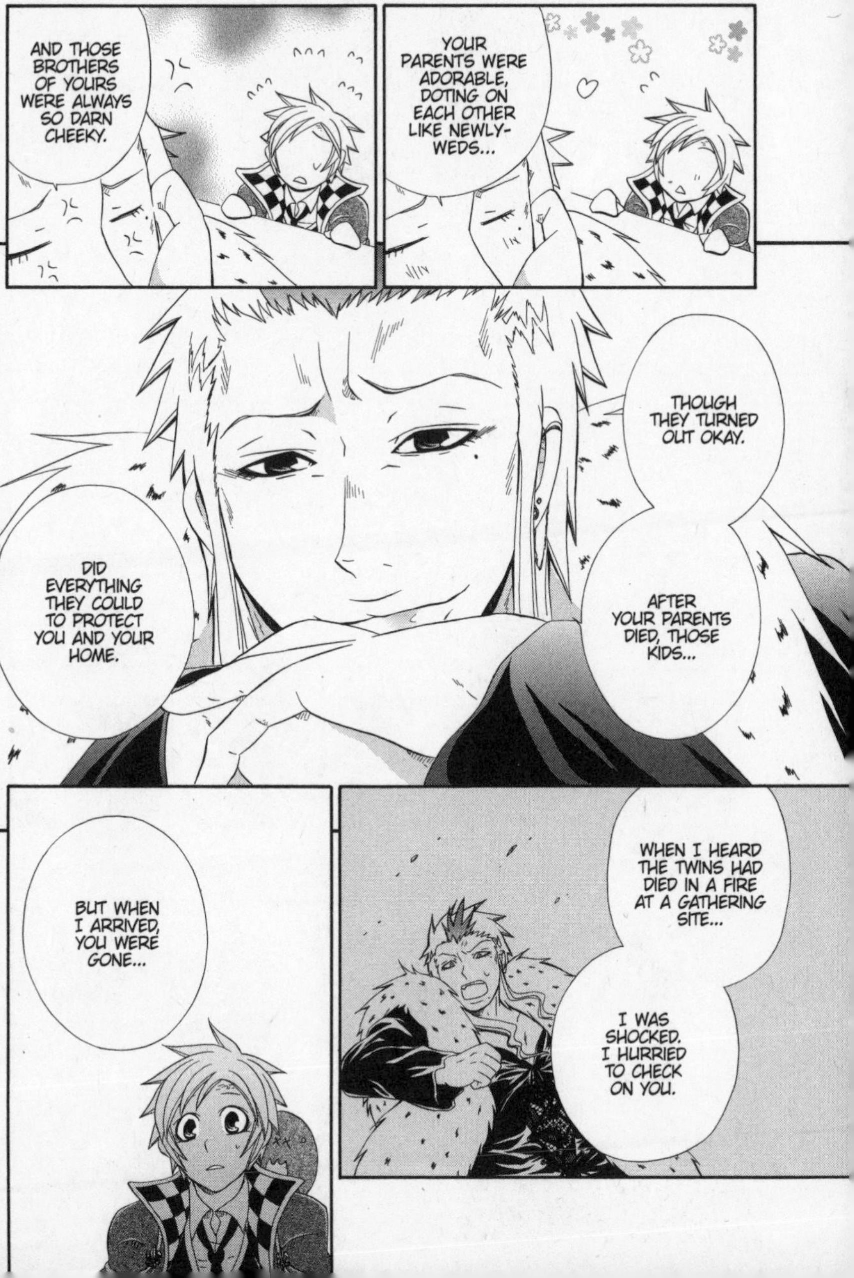
YOUR PARENTS WERE ADORABLE, DOTING ON EACH OTHER LIKE NEWLY-WEDS...
AND THOSE BROTHERS OF YOURS WERE ALWAYS SO DARN CHEEKY.
THOUGH THEY TURNED OUT OKAY.
AFTER YOUR PARENTS DIED, THOSE KIDS...
DID EVERYTHING THEY COULD TO PROTECT YOU AND YOUR HOME.
WHEN I HEARD THE TWINS HAD DIED IN A FIRE AT A GATHERING SITE...
I WAS SHOCKED. I HURRIED TO CHECK ON YOU.
BUT WHEN I ARRIVED, YOU WERE GONE...

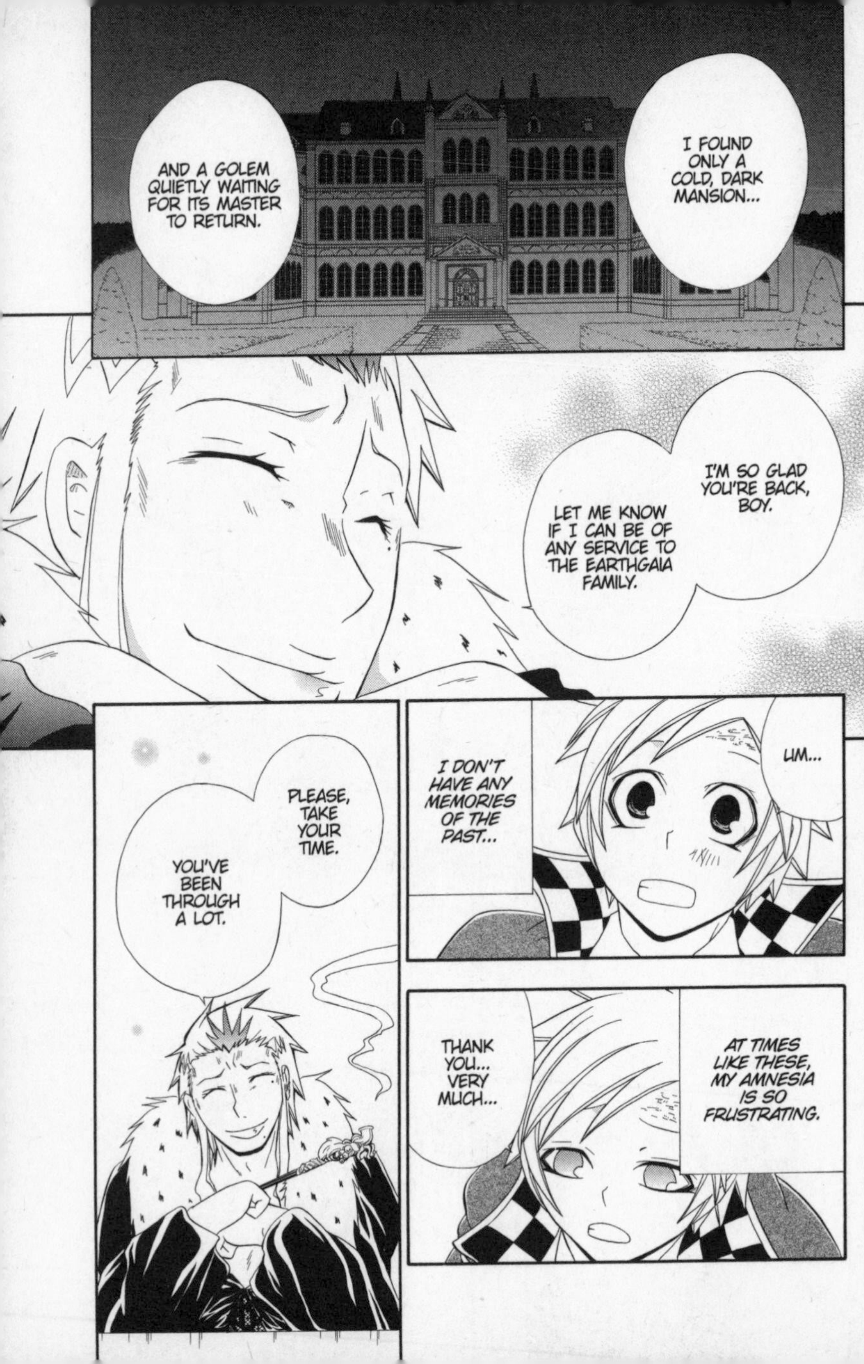
I FOUND ONLY A COLD, DARK MANSION...
AND A GOLEM QUIETLY WAITING FOR ITS MASTER TO RETURN.
I'M SO GLAD YOU'RE BACK, BOY.
LET ME KNOW IF I CAN BE OF ANY SERVICE TO THE EARTHGAIA FAMILY.
UM...
I DON'T HAVE ANY MEMORIES OF THE PAST...
AT TIMES LIKE THESE, MY AMNESIA IS SO FRUSTRATING.
THANK YOU... VERY MUCH...
PLEASE, TAKE YOUR TIME.
YOU'VE BEEN THROUGH A LOT.

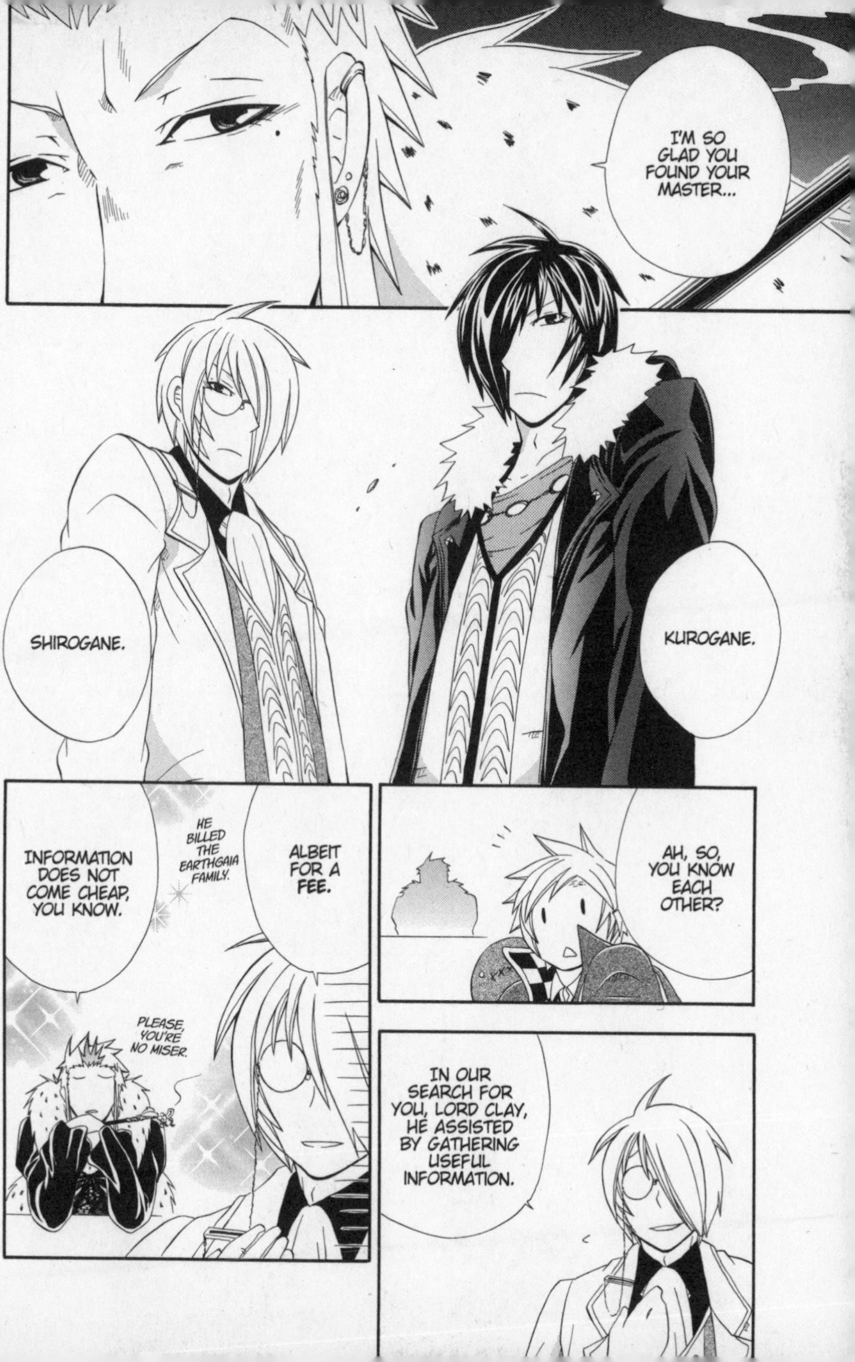
I'M SO GLAD YOU FOUND YOUR MASTER...
KUROGANE.
SHIROGANE.
AH, SO, YOU KNOW EACH OTHER?
IN OUR SEARCH FOR YOU, LORD CLAY, HE ASSISTED BY GATHERING USEFUL INFORMATION.
ALBEIT FOR A FEE.
HE BILLED THE EARTHGAIA FAMILY.
INFORMATION DOES NOT COME CHEAP, YOU KNOW.
PLEASE, YOU'RE NO MISER.

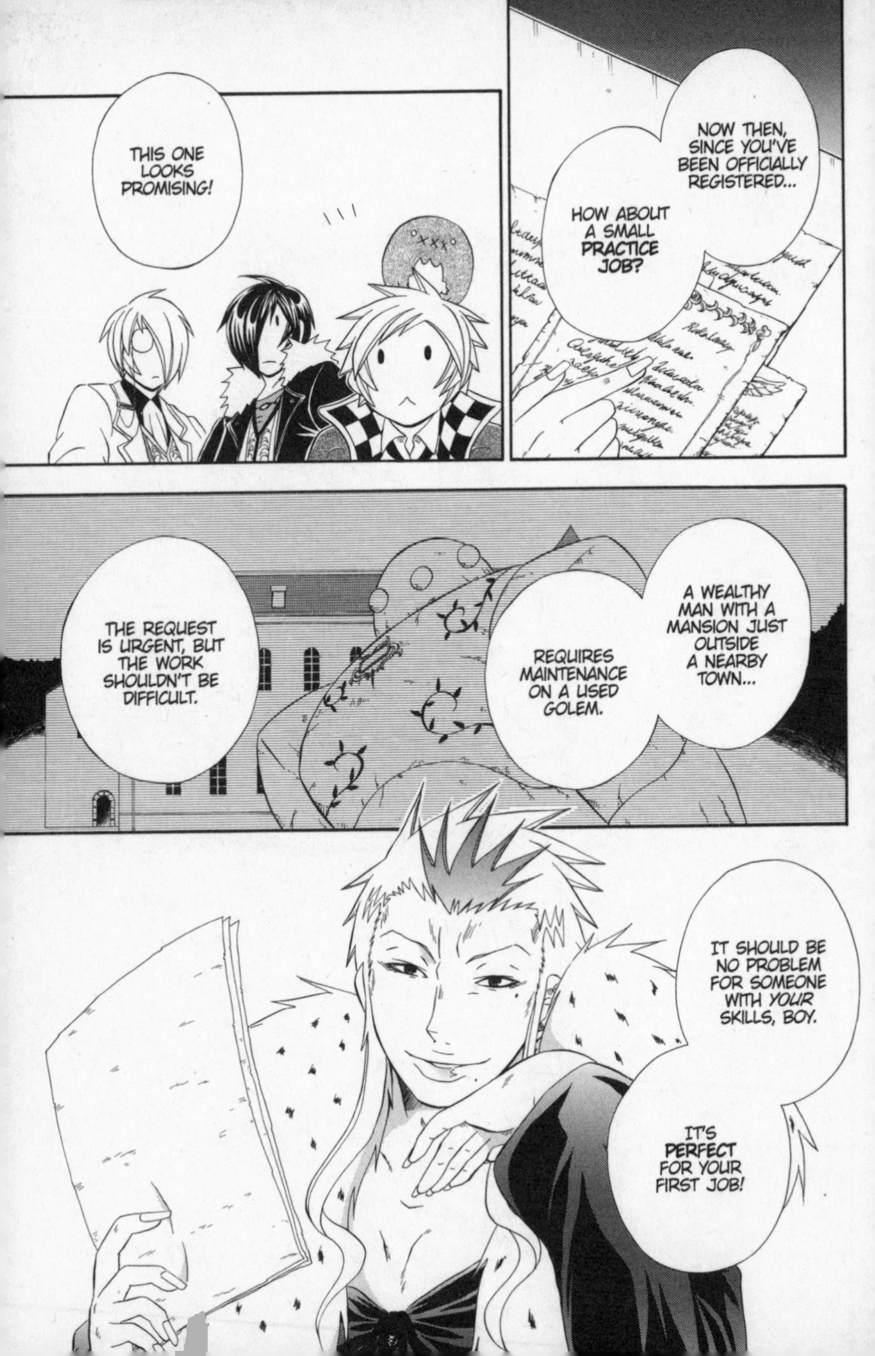
NOW THEN, SINCE YOU'VE BEEN OFFICIALLY REGISTERED...
HOW ABOUT A SMALL PRACTICE JOB?
THIS ONE LOOKS PROMISING!
A WEALTHY MAN WITH A MANSION JUST OUTSIDE A NEARBY TOWN...
REQUIRES MAINTENANCE ON A USED GOLEM.
THE REQUEST IS URGENT, BUT THE WORK SHOULDN'T BE DIFFICULT.
IT SHOULD BE NO PROBLEM FOR SOMEONE WITH YOUR SKILLS, BOY.
IT'S PERFECT FOR YOUR FIRST JOB!

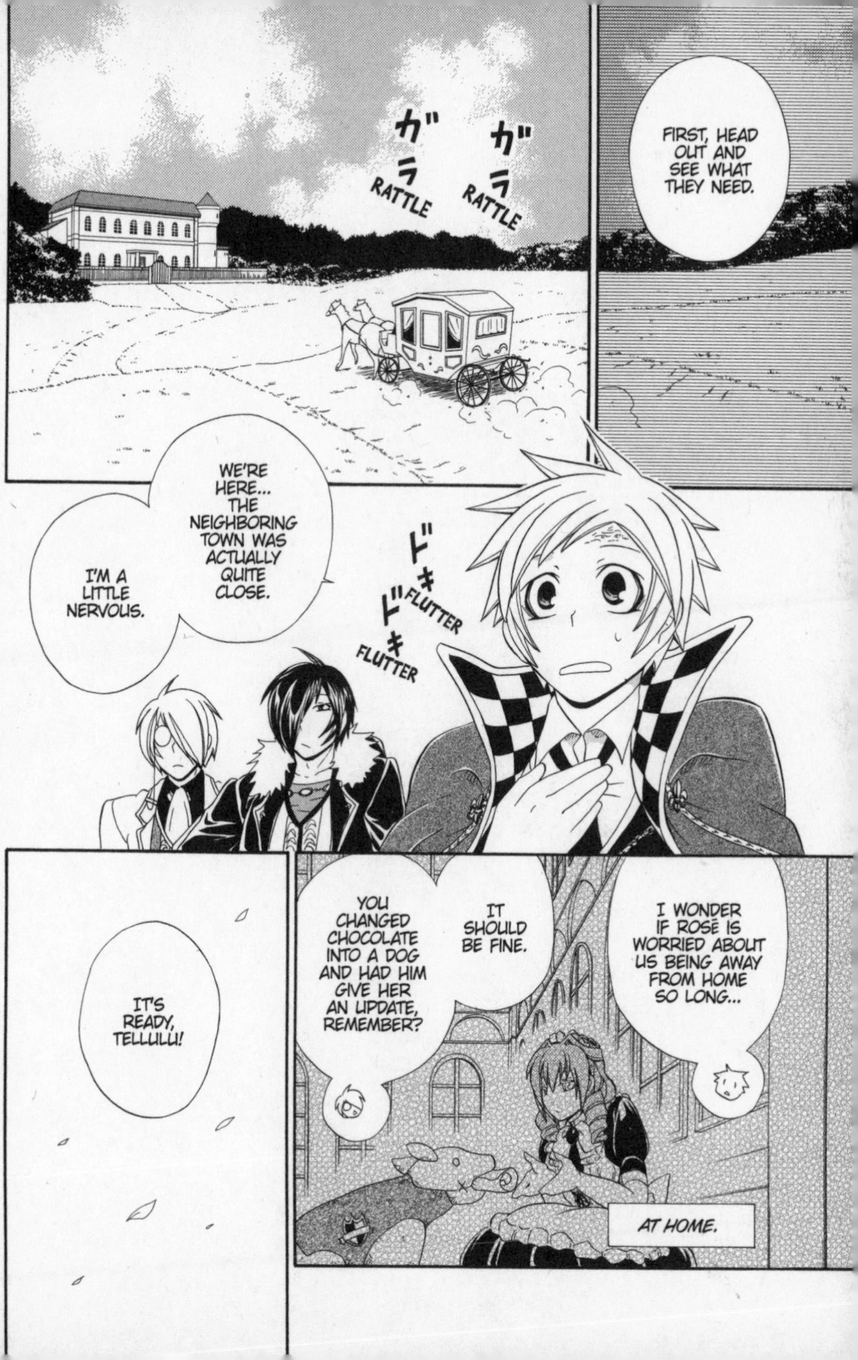
FIRST, HEAD OUT AND SEE WHAT THEY NEED.
ガラ RATTLE
ガラ RATTLE
ドキ FLUTTER
ドキ FLUTTER
WE'RE HERE... THE NEIGHBORING TOWN WAS ACTUALLY QUITE CLOSE.
I'M A LITTLE NERVOUS.
I WONDER IF ROSÉ IS WORRIED ABOUT US BEING AWAY FROM HOME SO LONG...
IT SHOULD BE FINE.
YOU CHANGED CHOCOLATE INTO A DOG AND HAD HIM GIVE HER AN UPDATE, REMEMBER?
AT HOME.
IT'S READY, TELLULU!

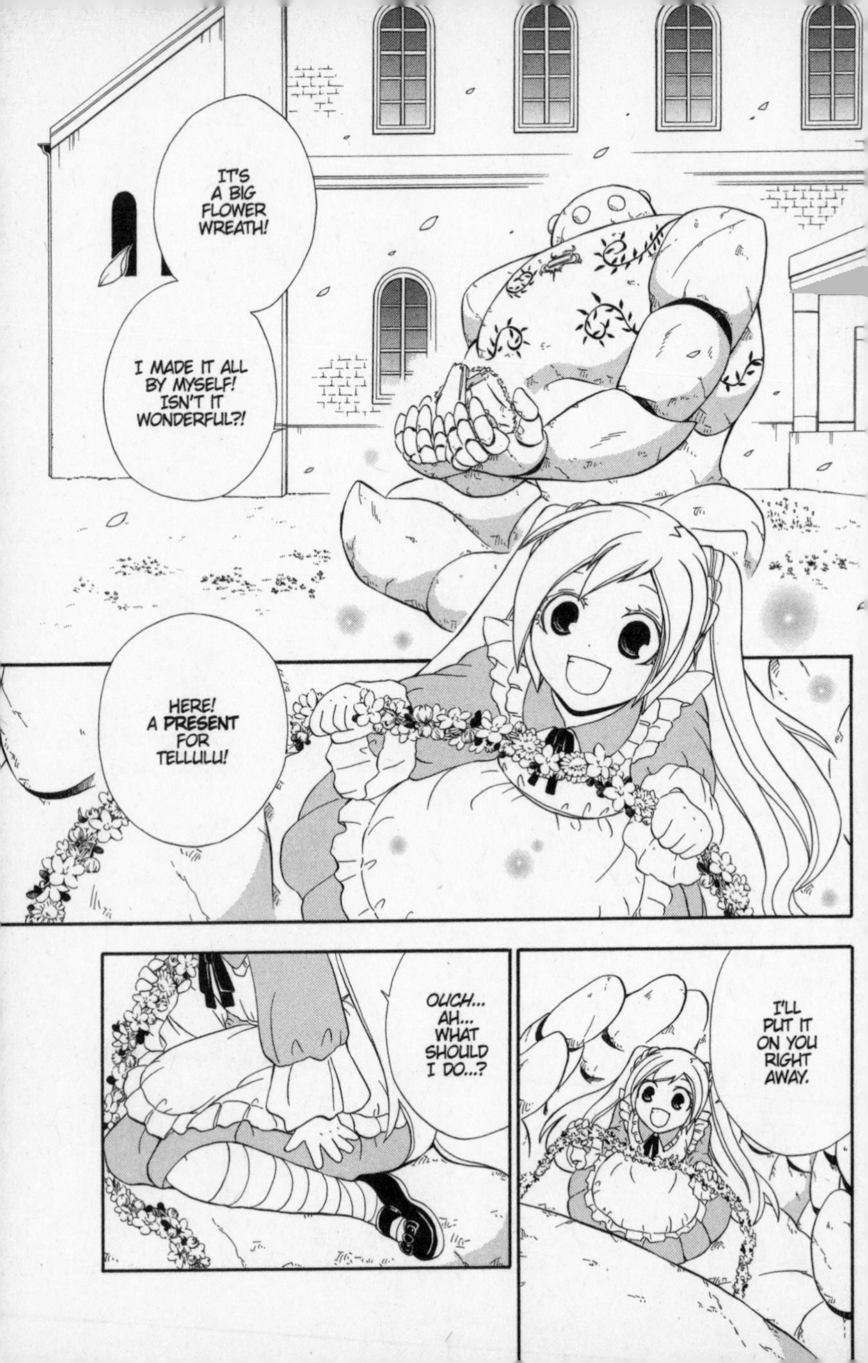
IT'S A BIG FLOWER WREATH!
I MADE IT ALL BY MYSELF! ISN'T IT WONDERFUL?!
HERE! A PRESENT FOR TELLULU!
I'LL PUT IT ON YOU RIGHT AWAY.
OUCH... AH... WHAT SHOULD I DO...?

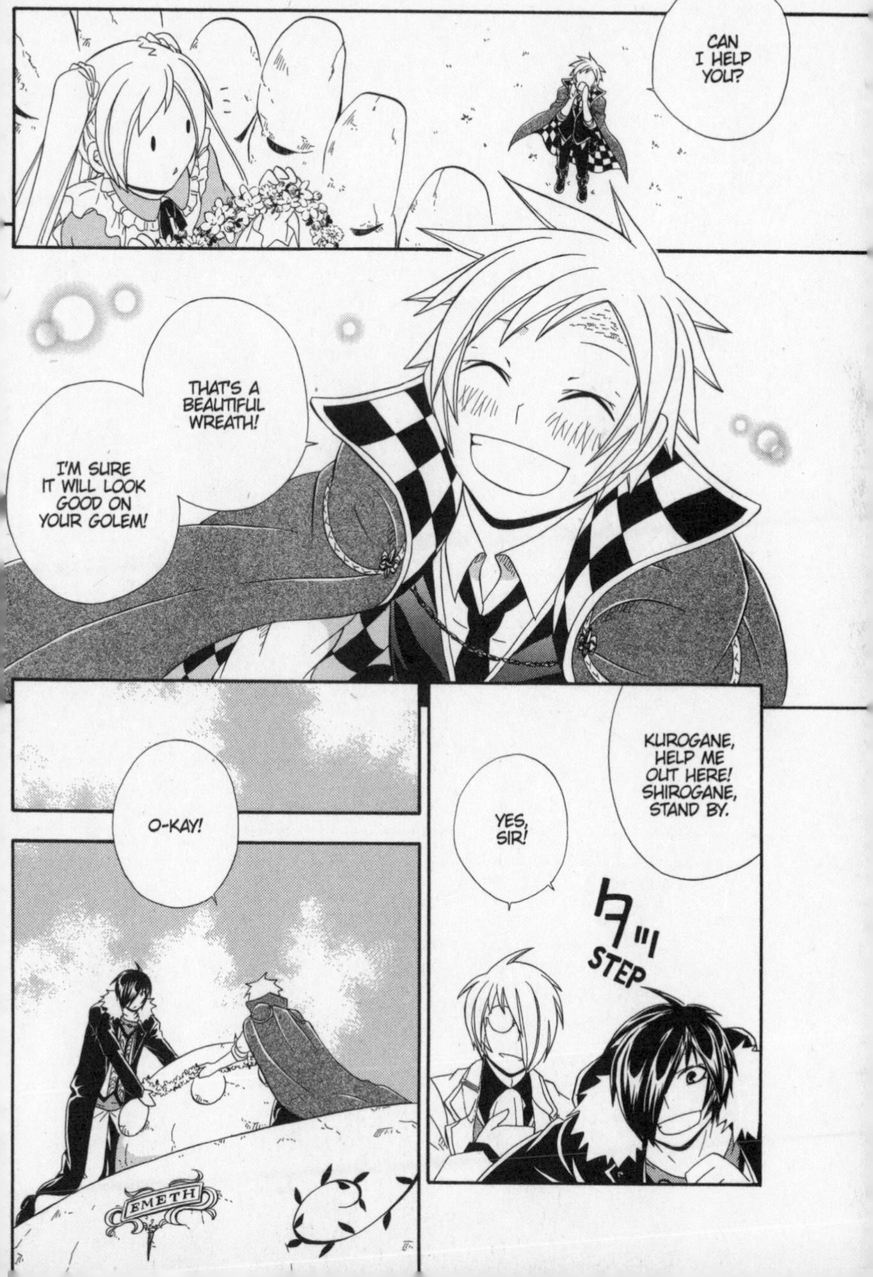
CAN I HELP YOU?
THAT'S A BEAUTIFUL WREATH!
I'M SURE IT WILL LOOK GOOD ON YOUR GOLEM!
KUROGANE, HELP ME OUT HERE! SHIROGANE, STAND BY.
YES, SIR!
タッ
STEP
O-KAY!
EMETH

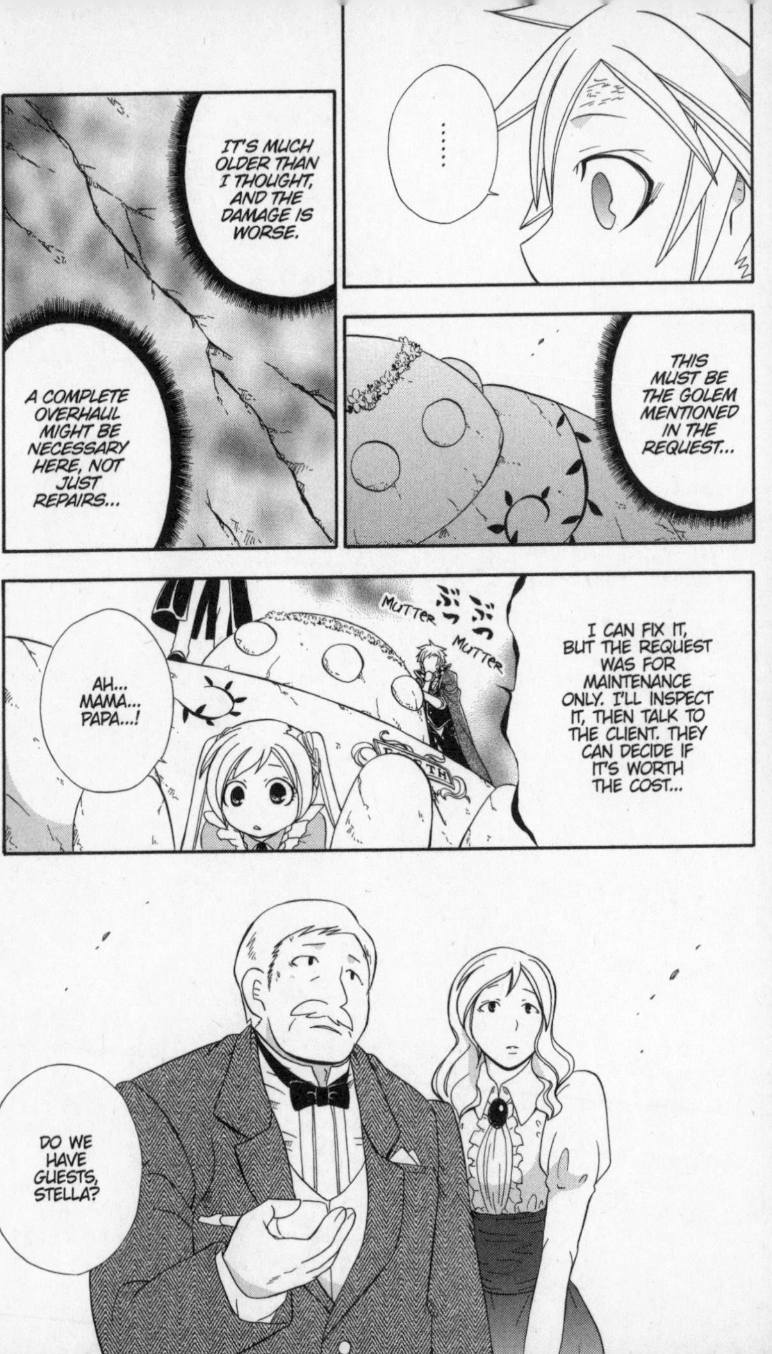
......
THIS MUST BE THE GOLEM MENTIONED IN THE REQUEST...
IT'S MUCH OLDER THAN I THOUGHT, AND THE DAMAGE IS WORSE.
A COMPLETE OVERHAUL MIGHT BE NECESSARY HERE, NOT JUST REPAIRS...
I CAN FIX IT, BUT THE REQUEST WAS FOR MAINTENANCE ONLY. I'LL INSPECT IT, THEN TALK TO THE CLIENT. THEY CAN DECIDE IF IT'S WORTH THE COST...
ぶつぶつ
MUTTER MUTTER
AH... MAMA... PAPA...!
DO WE HAVE GUESTS, STELLA?

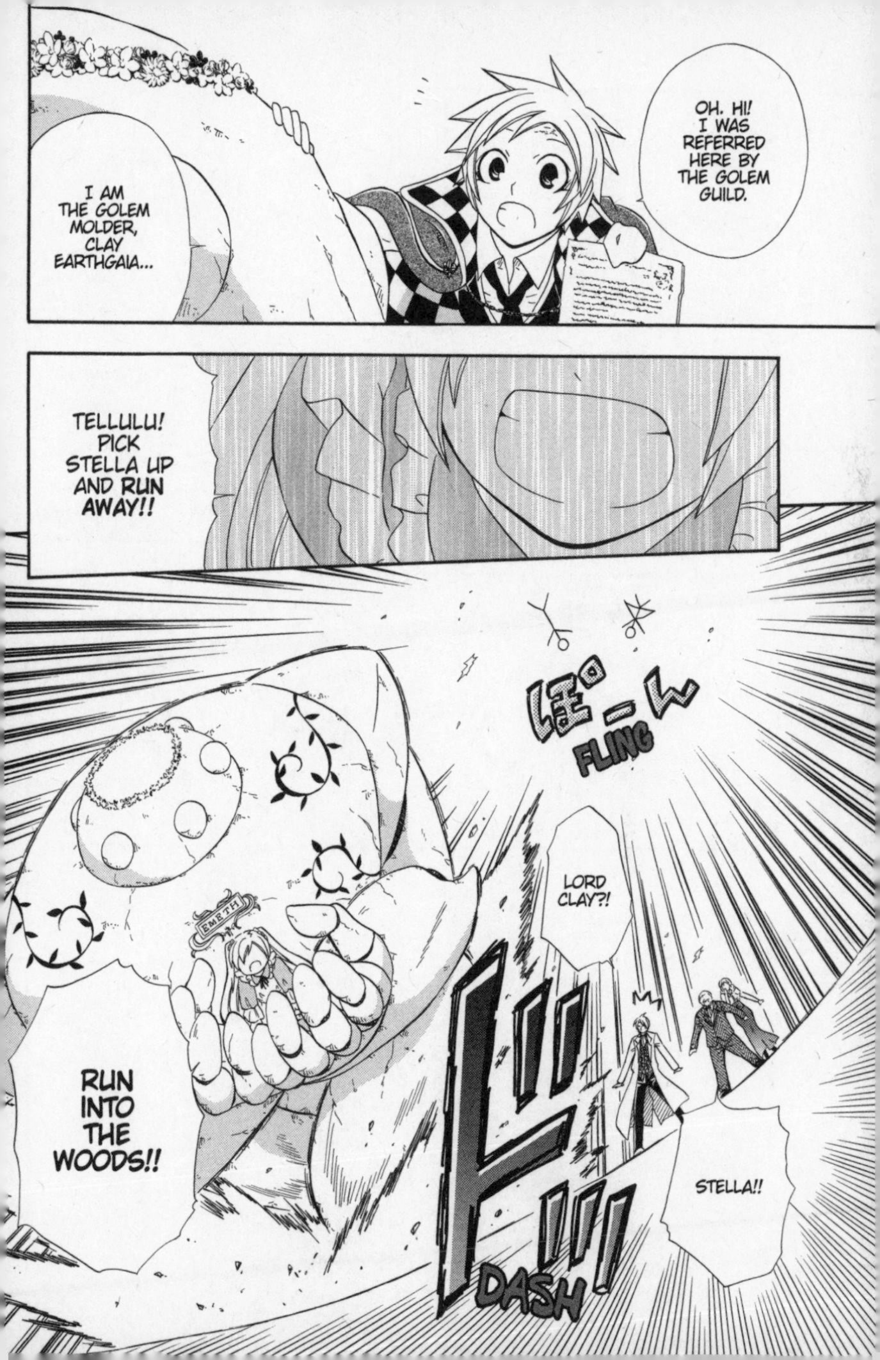
OH. HI! I WAS REFERRED HERE BY THE GOLEM GUILD.
I AM THE GOLEM MOLDER, CLAY EARTHGAIA...
TELLULU! PICK STELLA UP AND RUN AWAY!!
ぽーん
FLING
LORD CLAY?!
STELLA!!
EMETH
DASH
RUN INTO THE WOODS!!

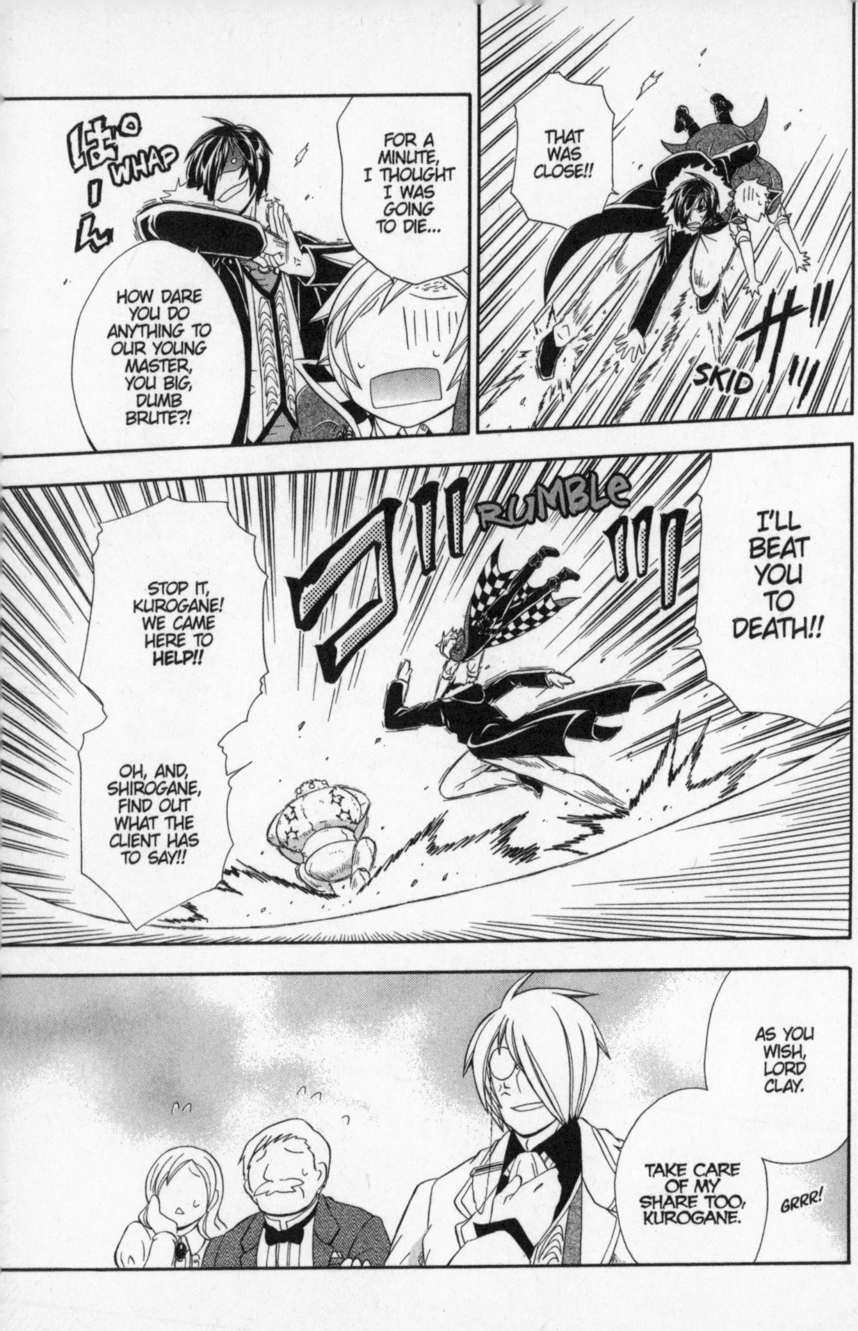
THAT WAS CLOSE!!
SKID
FOR A MINUTE, I THOUGHT I WAS GOING TO DIE...
WHAP
HOW DARE YOU DO ANYTHING TO OUR YOUNG MASTER, YOU BIG, DUMB BRUTE?!
I'LL BEAT YOU TO DEATH!!
RUMBLE
STOP IT, KUROGANE! WE CAME HERE TO HELP!!
OH, AND, SHIROGANE, FIND OUT WHAT THE CLIENT HAS TO SAY!!
AS YOU WISH, LORD CLAY.
GRRR!
TAKE CARE OF MY SHARE TOO, KUROGANE.

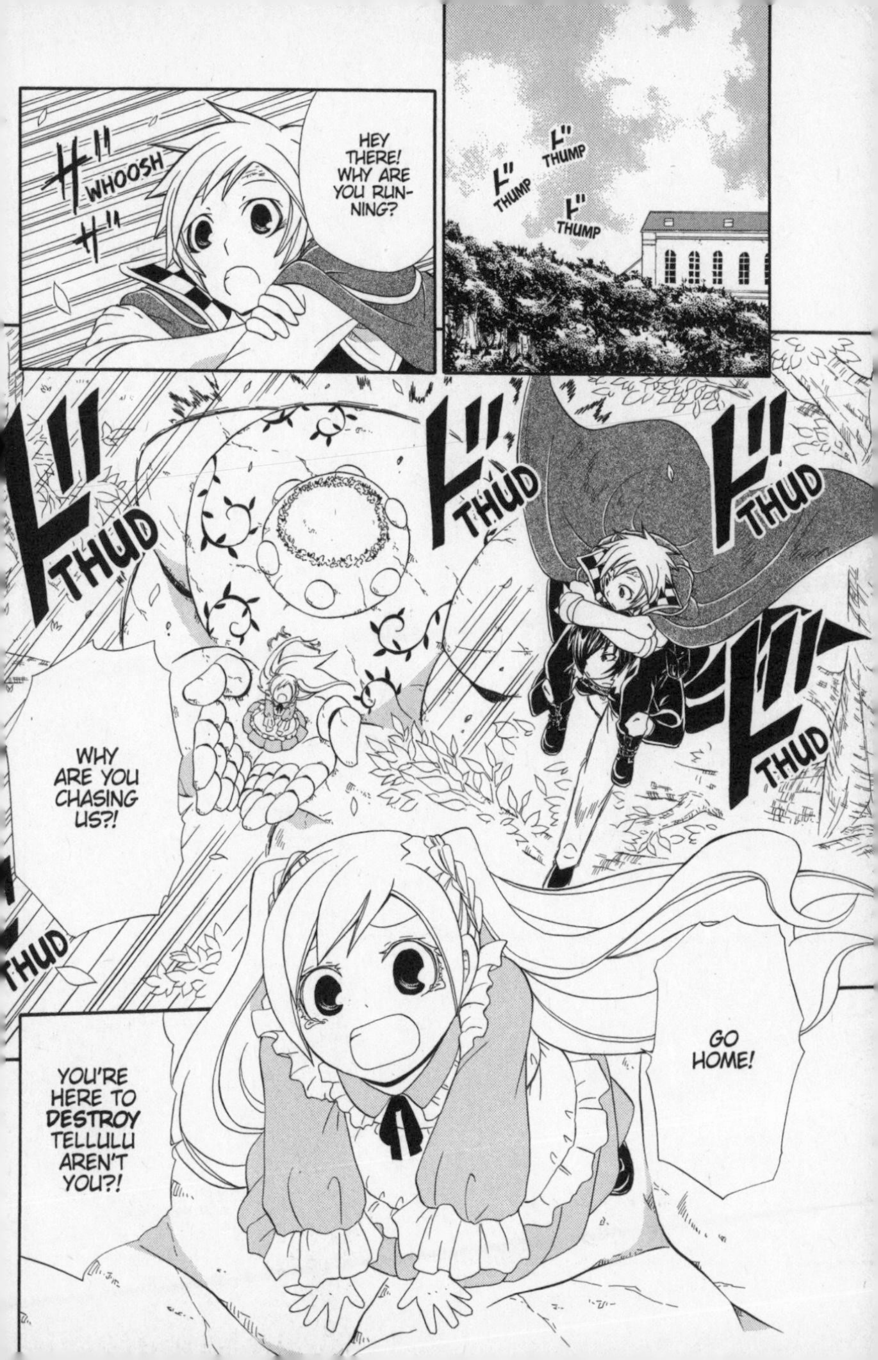
ド THUMP
ド THUMP
ド THUMP
ザッ WHOOSH
ザッ
HEY THERE! WHY ARE YOU RUN-NING?
ド THUD
ド THUD
ドッ THUD
ド THUD
WHY ARE YOU CHASING US?!
THUD
GO HOME!
YOU'RE HERE TO DESTROY TELLULU AREN'T YOU?!

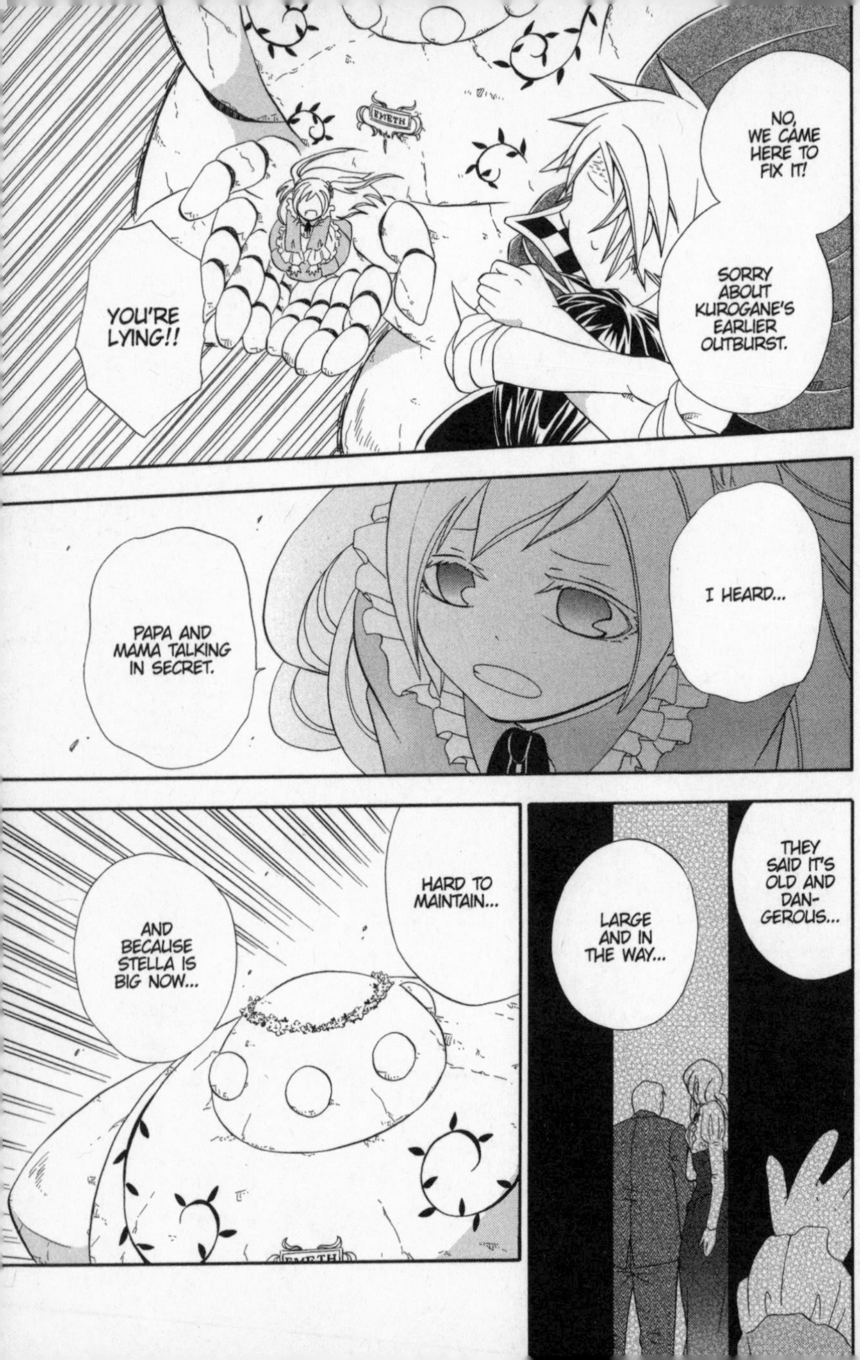
EMETH
NO, WE CAME HERE TO FIX IT!
SORRY ABOUT KUROGANE'S EARLIER OUTBURST.
YOU'RE LYING!!
I HEARD...
PAPA AND MAMA TALKING IN SECRET.
THEY SAID IT'S OLD AND DAN-GEROUS...
LARGE AND IN THE WAY...
HARD TO MAINTAIN...
AND BECAUSE STELLA IS BIG NOW...
EMETH

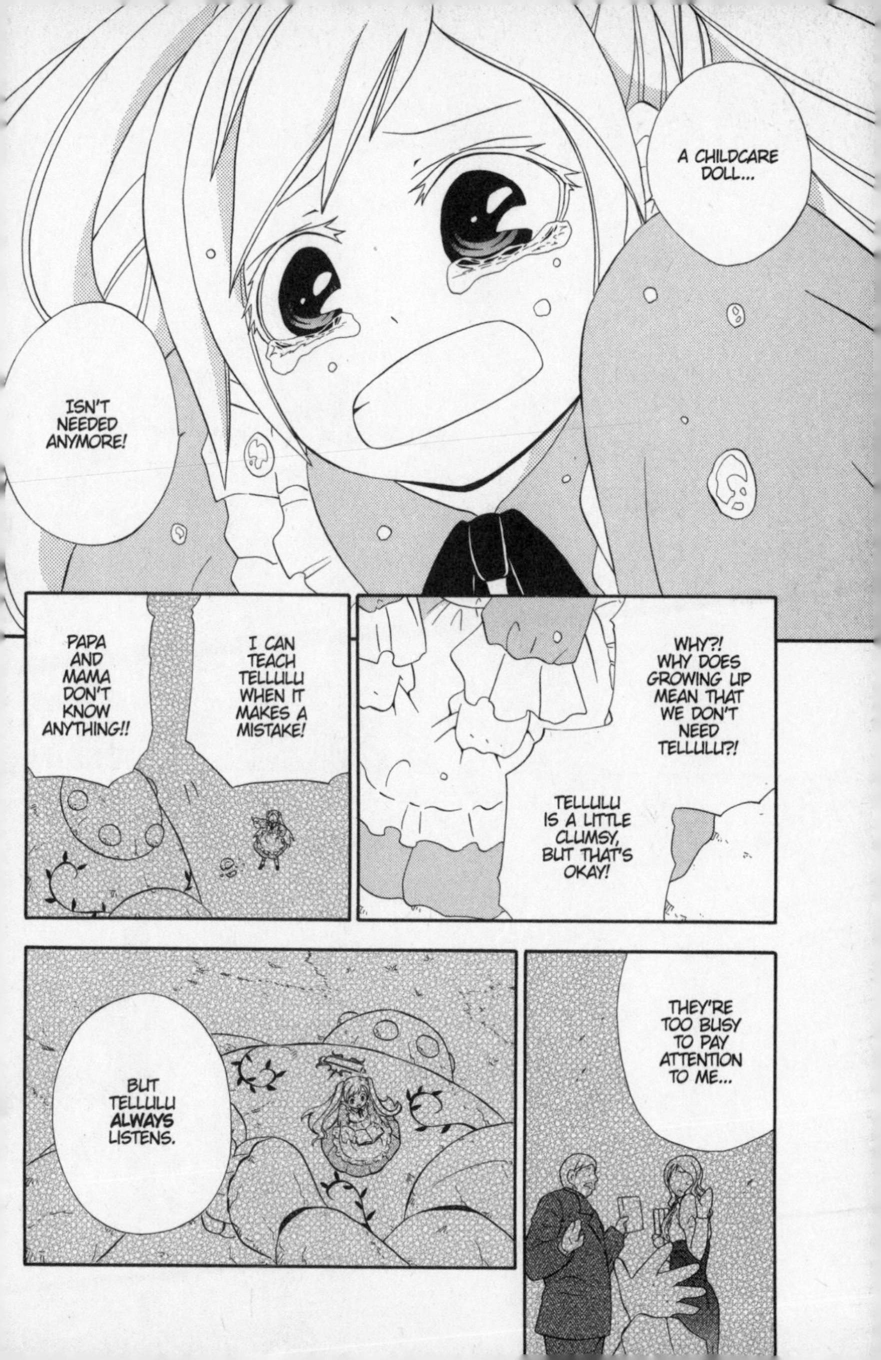
A CHILDCARE DOLL...
ISN'T NEEDED ANYMORE!
WHY?! WHY DOES GROWING UP MEAN THAT WE DON'T NEED TELLULU?!
TELLULU IS A LITTLE CLUMSY, BUT THAT'S OKAY!
I CAN TEACH TELLULU WHEN IT MAKES A MISTAKE!
PAPA AND MAMA DON'T KNOW ANYTHING!!
THEY'RE TOO BUSY TO PAY ATTENTION TO ME...
BUT TELLULU ALWAYS LISTENS.

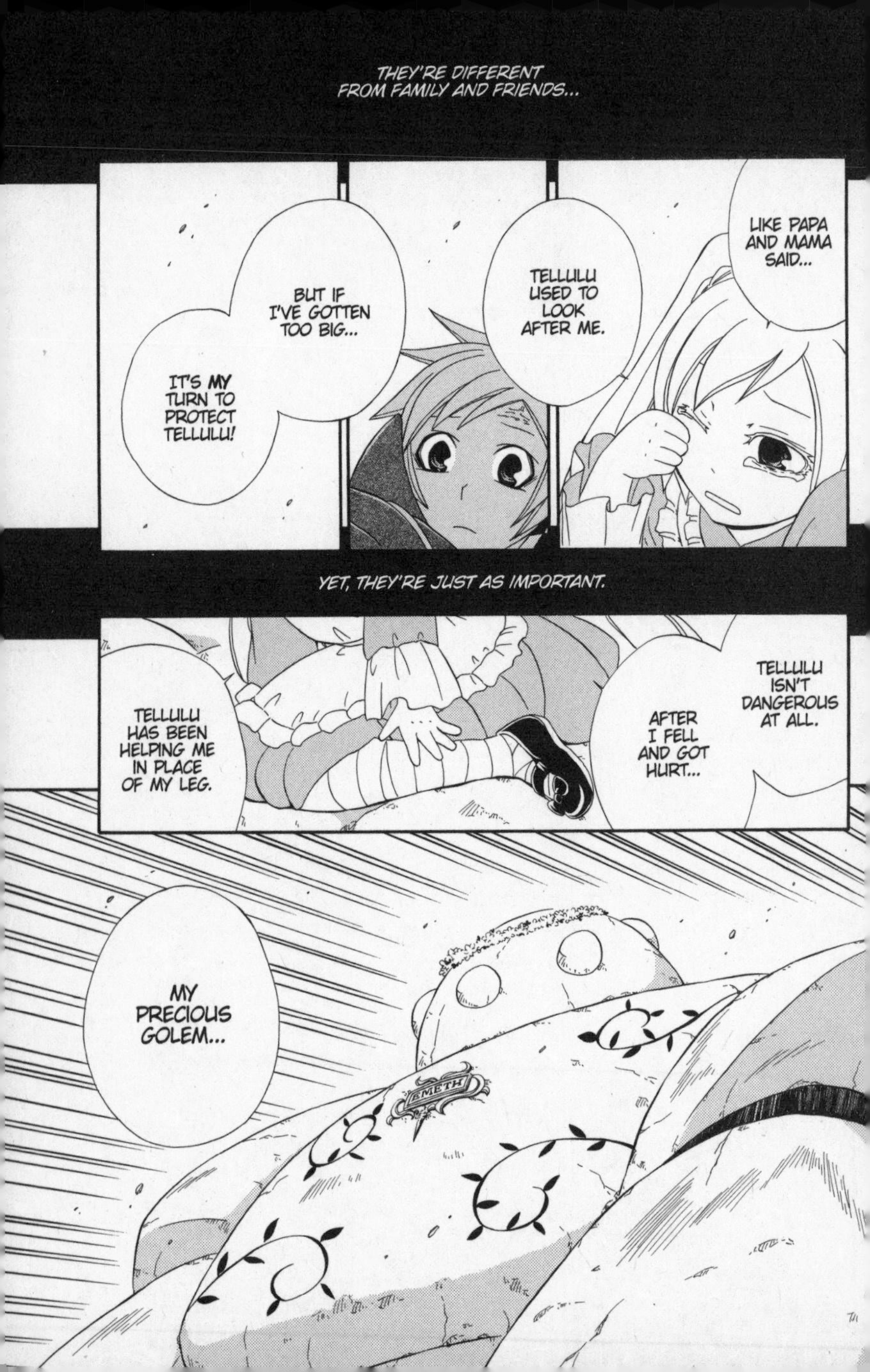
THEY'RE DIFFERENT FROM FAMILY AND FRIENDS...
LIKE PAPA AND MAMA SAID...
TELLULU USED TO LOOK AFTER ME.
BUT IF I'VE GOTTEN TOO BIG...
IT'S MY TURN TO PROTECT TELLULU!
YET, THEY'RE JUST AS IMPORTANT.
TELLULU ISN'T DANGEROUS AT ALL.
AFTER I FELL AND GOT HURT...
TELLULU HAS BEEN HELPING ME IN PLACE OF MY LEG.
MY PRECIOUS GOLEM...
EMETH

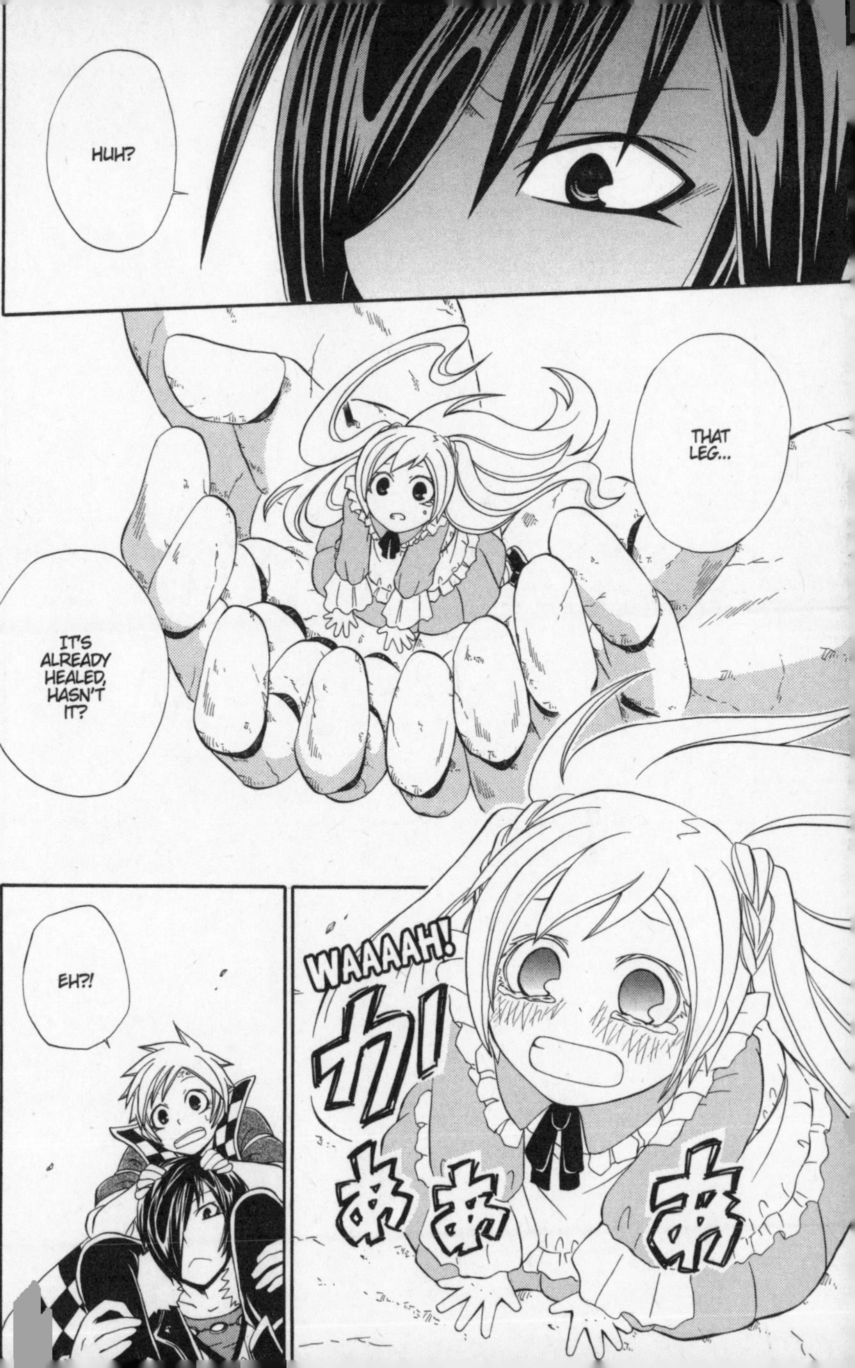
HUH?
THAT LEG...
IT'S ALREADY HEALED, HASN'T IT?
WAAAAH!
わあああ
EH?!

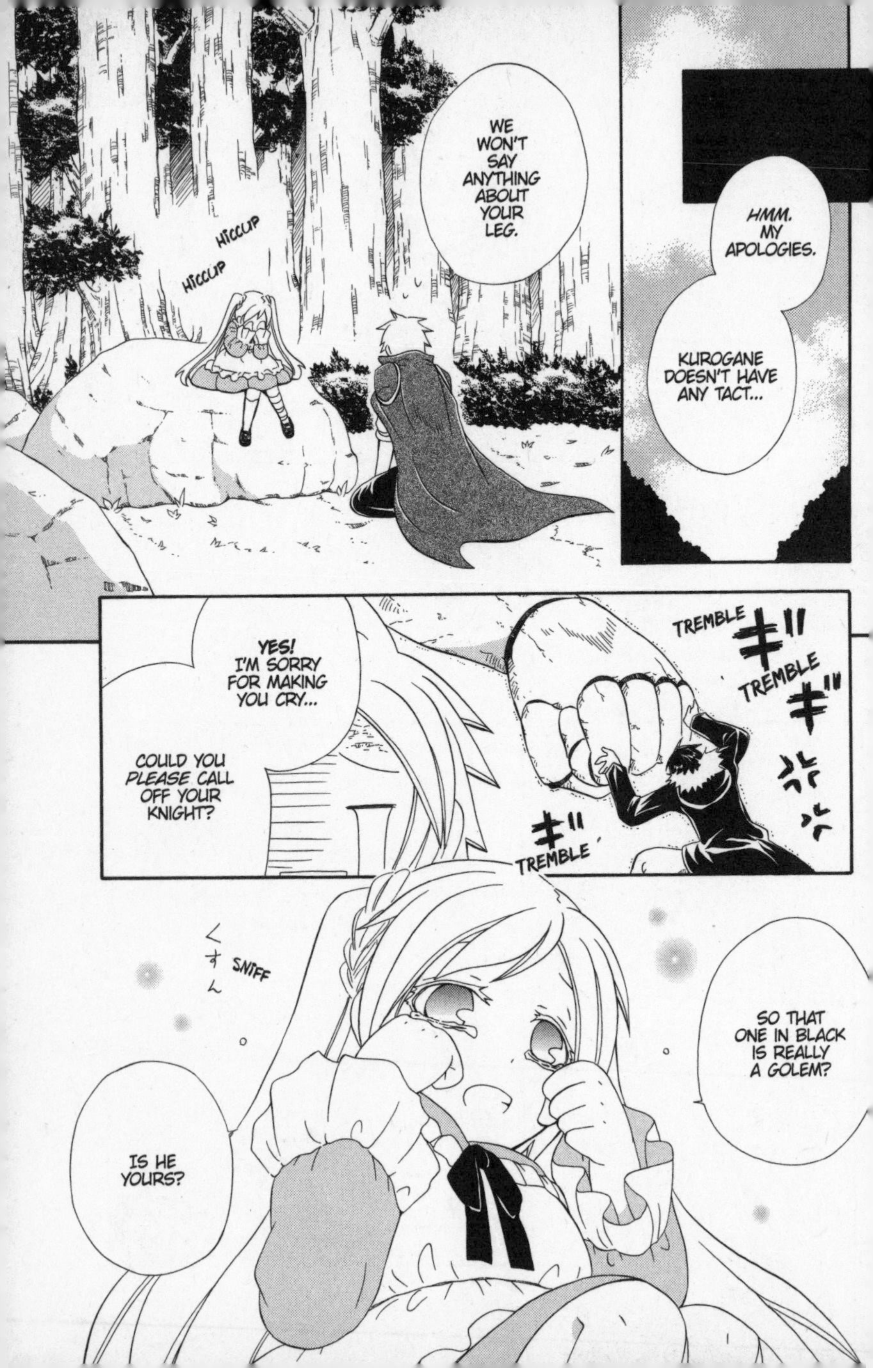
HMM. MY APOLOGIES.
KUROGANE DOESN'T HAVE ANY TACT...
WE WON'T SAY ANYTHING ABOUT YOUR LEG.
HICCUP
HICCUP
TREMBLE
TREMBLE
YES! I'M SORRY FOR MAKING YOU CRY...
COULD YOU PLEASE CALL OFF YOUR KNIGHT?
TREMBLE
SO THAT ONE IN BLACK IS REALLY A GOLEM?
くすん
SNIFF
IS HE YOURS?

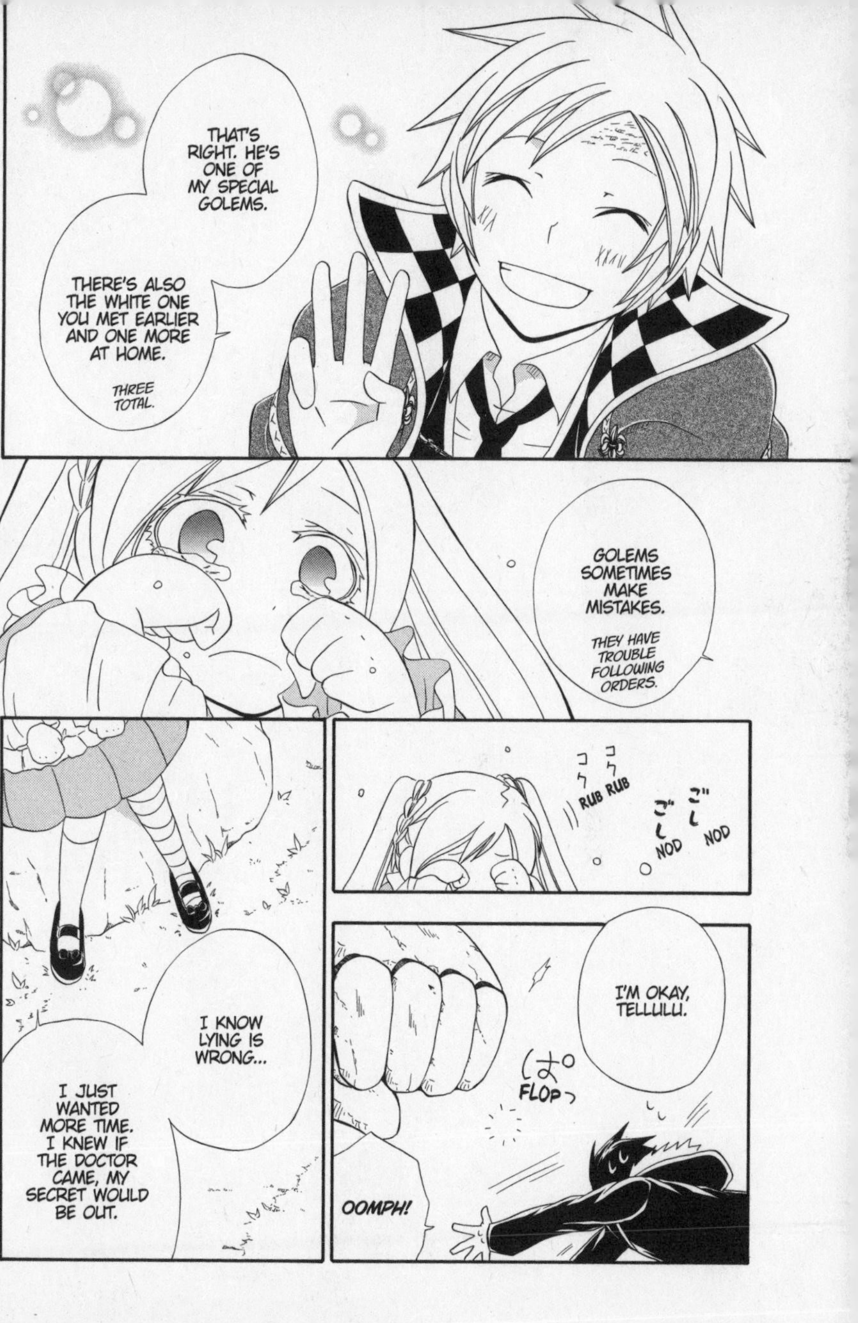
THAT'S RIGHT. HE'S ONE OF MY SPECIAL GOLEMS.
THERE'S ALSO THE WHITE ONE YOU MET EARLIER AND ONE MORE AT HOME.
THREE TOTAL.
GOLEMS SOMETIMES MAKE MISTAKES.
THEY HAVE TROUBLE FOLLOWING ORDERS.
ごし ごし NOD NOD
コク コク RUB RUB
I'M OKAY, TELLULU.
ぱっ FLOP
OOMPH!
I KNOW LYING IS WRONG...
I JUST WANTED MORE TIME. I KNEW IF THE DOCTOR CAME, MY SECRET WOULD BE OUT.

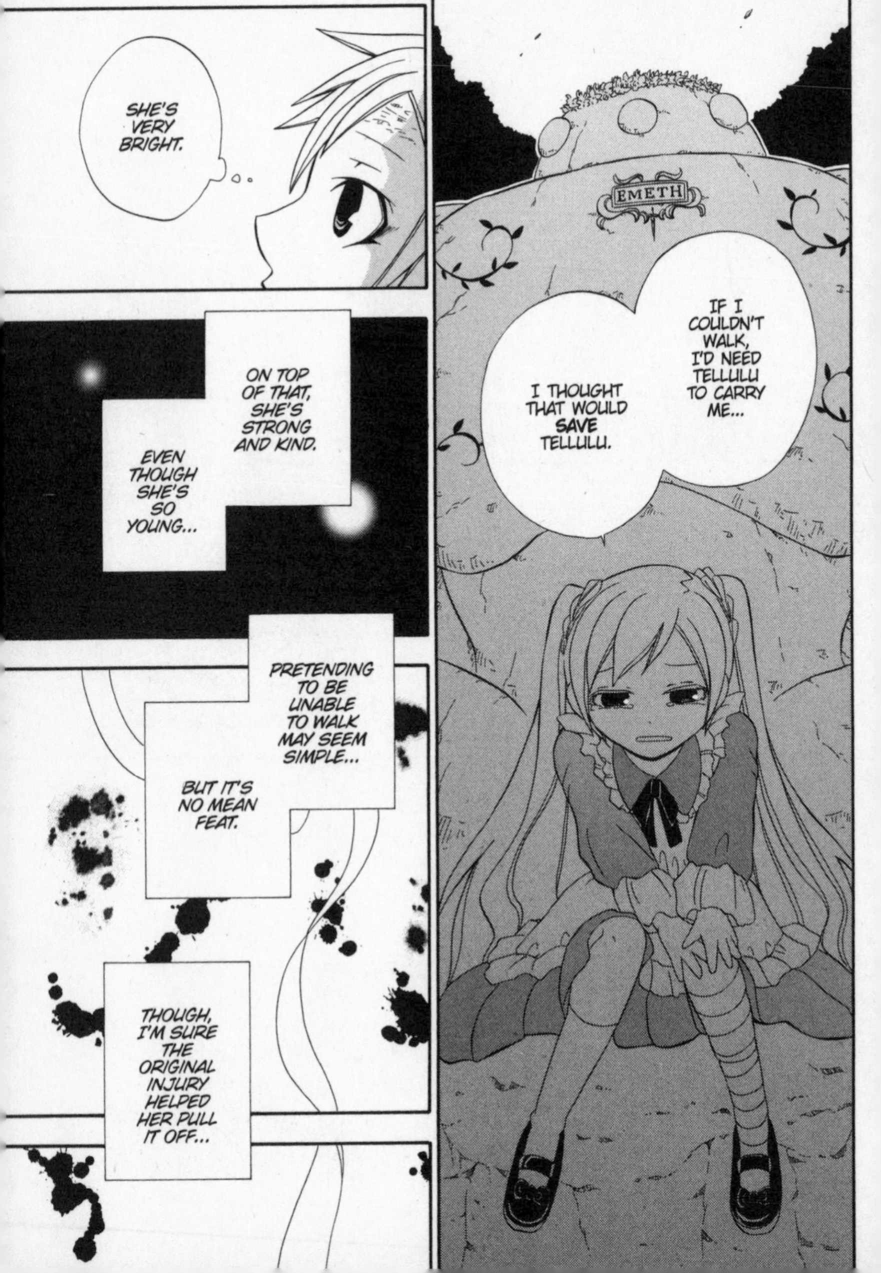
EMETH
IF I COULDN'T WALK, I'D NEED TELLULU TO CARRY ME...
I THOUGHT THAT WOULD SAVE TELLULU.
SHE'S VERY BRIGHT.
ON TOP OF THAT, SHE'S STRONG AND KIND.
EVEN THOUGH SHE'S SO YOUNG...
PRETENDING TO BE UNABLE TO WALK MAY SEEM SIMPLE...
BUT IT'S NO MEAN FEAT.
THOUGH, I'M SURE THE ORIGINAL INJURY HELPED HER PULL IT OFF...

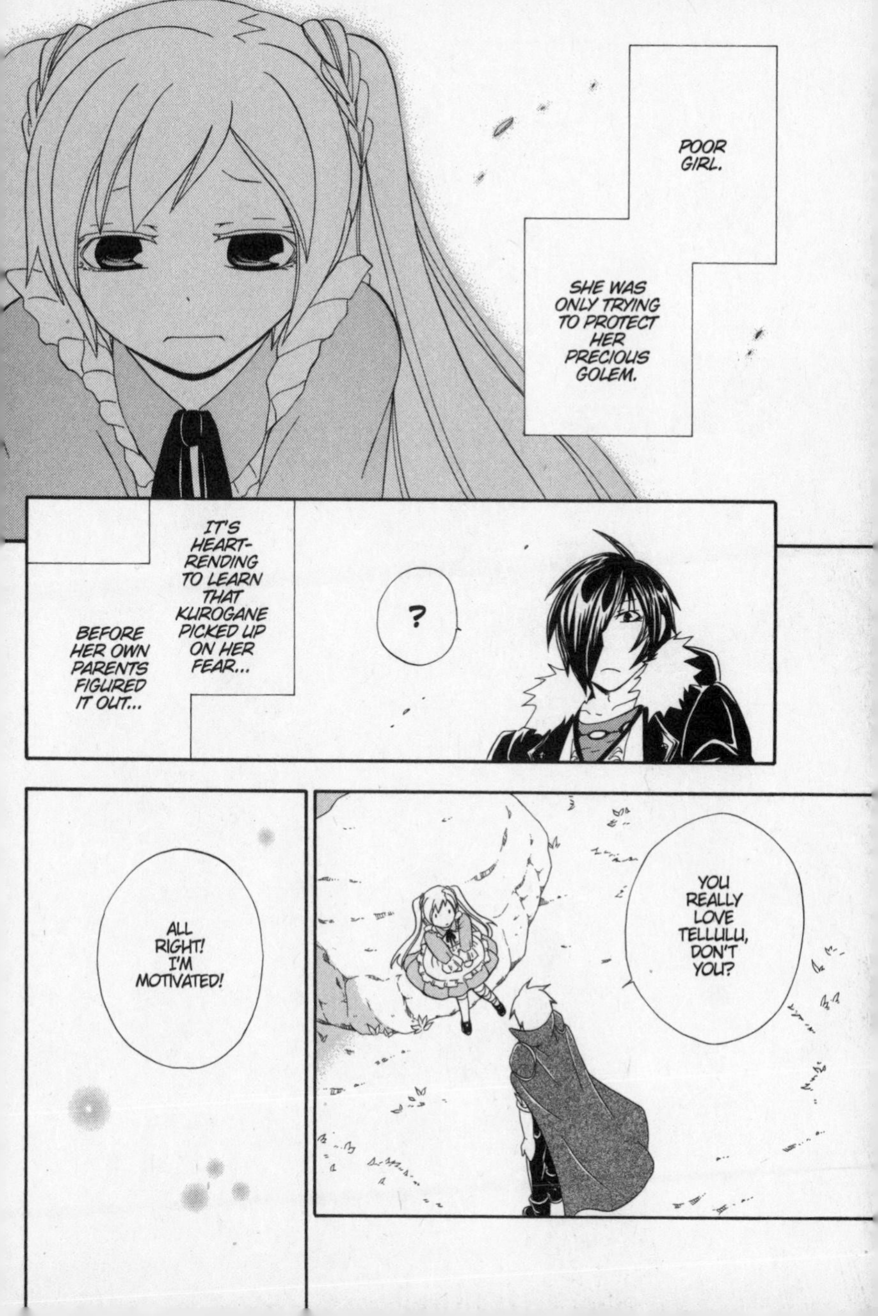
POOR GIRL.
SHE WAS ONLY TRYING TO PROTECT HER PRECIOUS GOLEM.
?
IT'S HEART-RENDING TO LEARN THAT KUROGANE PICKED UP ON HER FEAR...
BEFORE HER OWN PARENTS FIGURED IT OUT...
YOU REALLY LOVE TELLULU, DON'T YOU?
ALL RIGHT! I'M MOTIVATED!

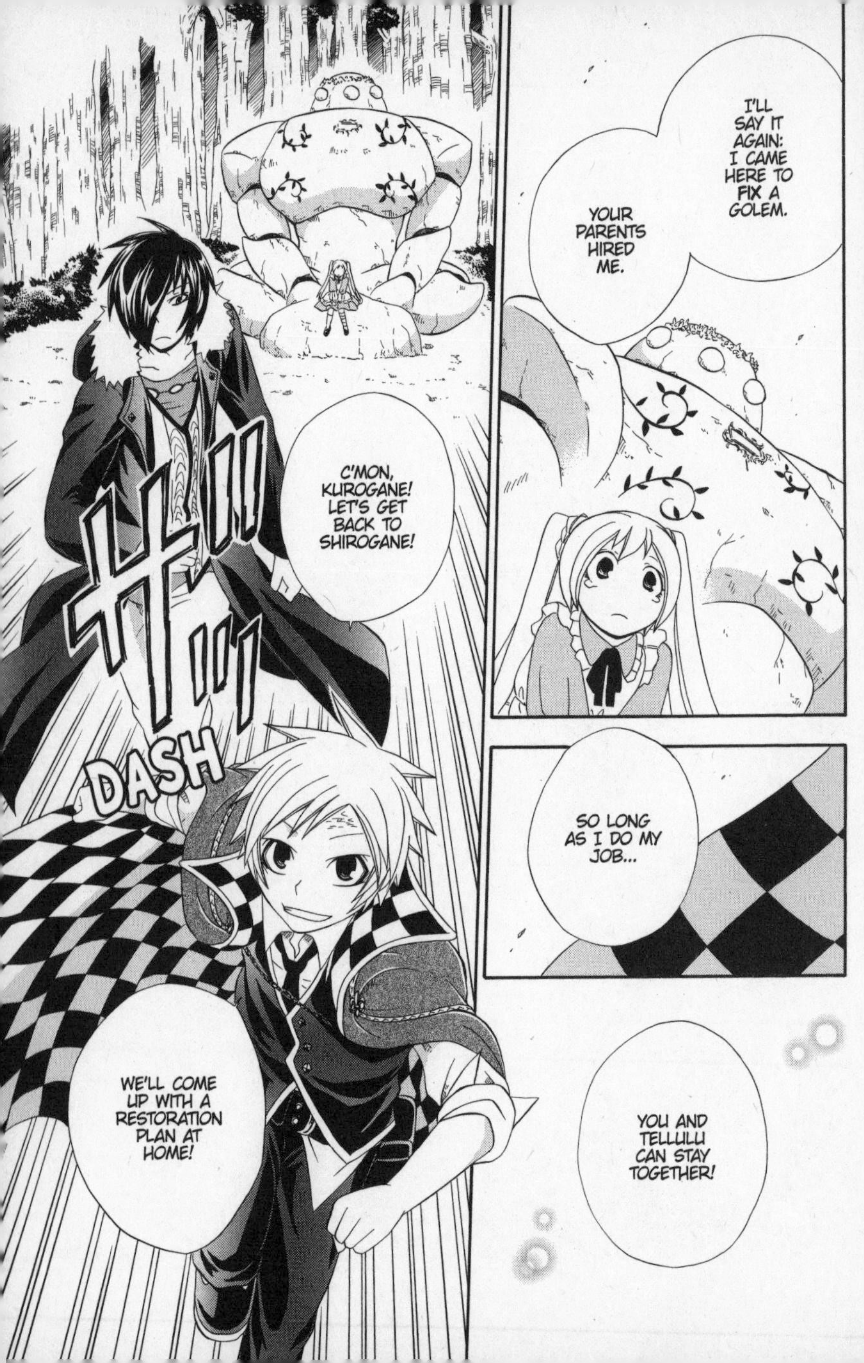
I'LL SAY IT AGAIN: I CAME HERE TO FIX A GOLEM.
YOUR PARENTS HIRED ME.
SO LONG AS I DO MY JOB...
YOU AND TELLULU CAN STAY TOGETHER!
C'MON, KUROGANE! LET'S GET BACK TO SHIROGANE!
DASH
WE'LL COME UP WITH A RESTORATION PLAN AT HOME!

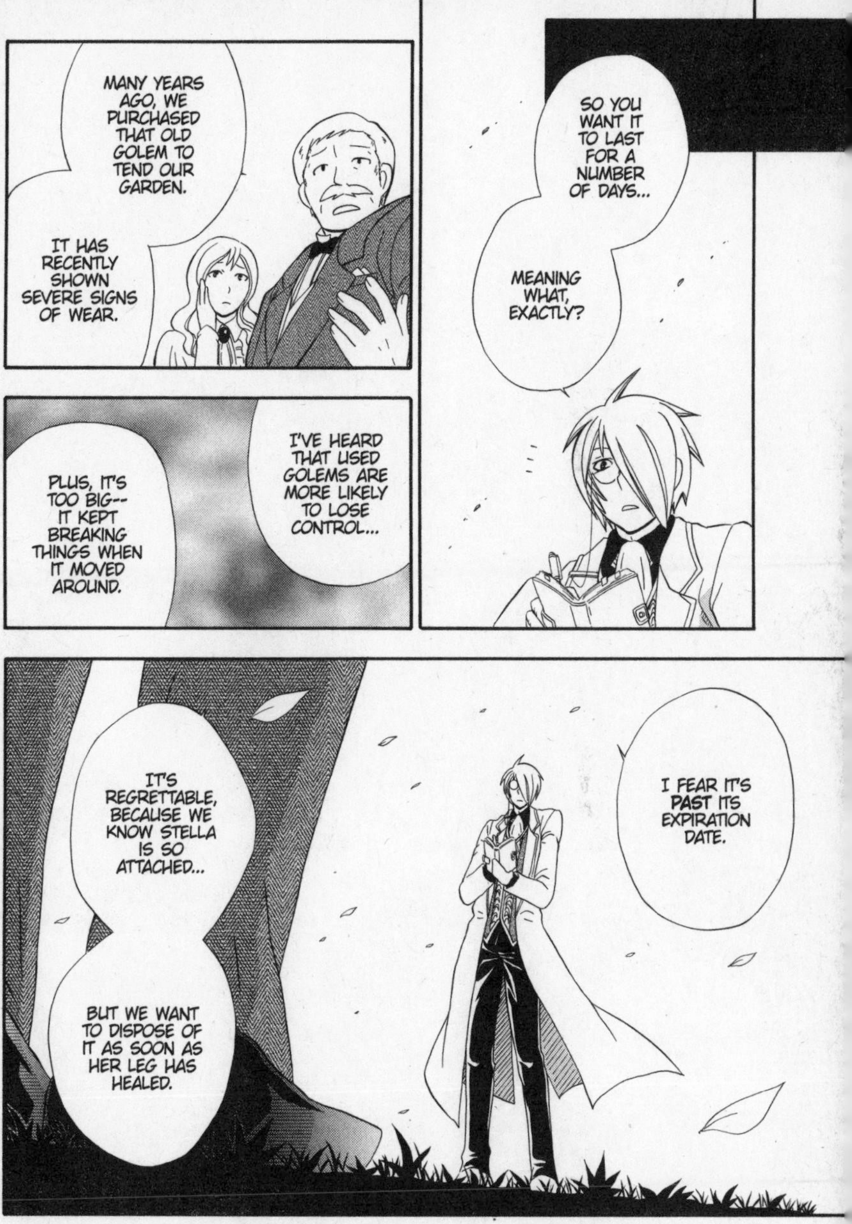
SO YOU WANT IT TO LAST FOR A NUMBER OF DAYS...
MEANING WHAT, EXACTLY?
MANY YEARS AGO, WE PURCHASED THAT OLD GOLEM TO TEND OUR GARDEN.
IT HAS RECENTLY SHOWN SEVERE SIGNS OF WEAR.
I'VE HEARD THAT USED GOLEMS ARE MORE LIKELY TO LOSE CONTROL...
PLUS, IT'S TOO BIG--IT KEPT BREAKING THINGS WHEN IT MOVED AROUND.
I FEAR IT'S PAST ITS EXPIRATION DATE.
IT'S REGRETTABLE, BECAUSE WE KNOW STELLA IS SO ATTACHED...
BUT WE WANT TO DISPOSE OF IT AS SOON AS HER LEG HAS HEALED.

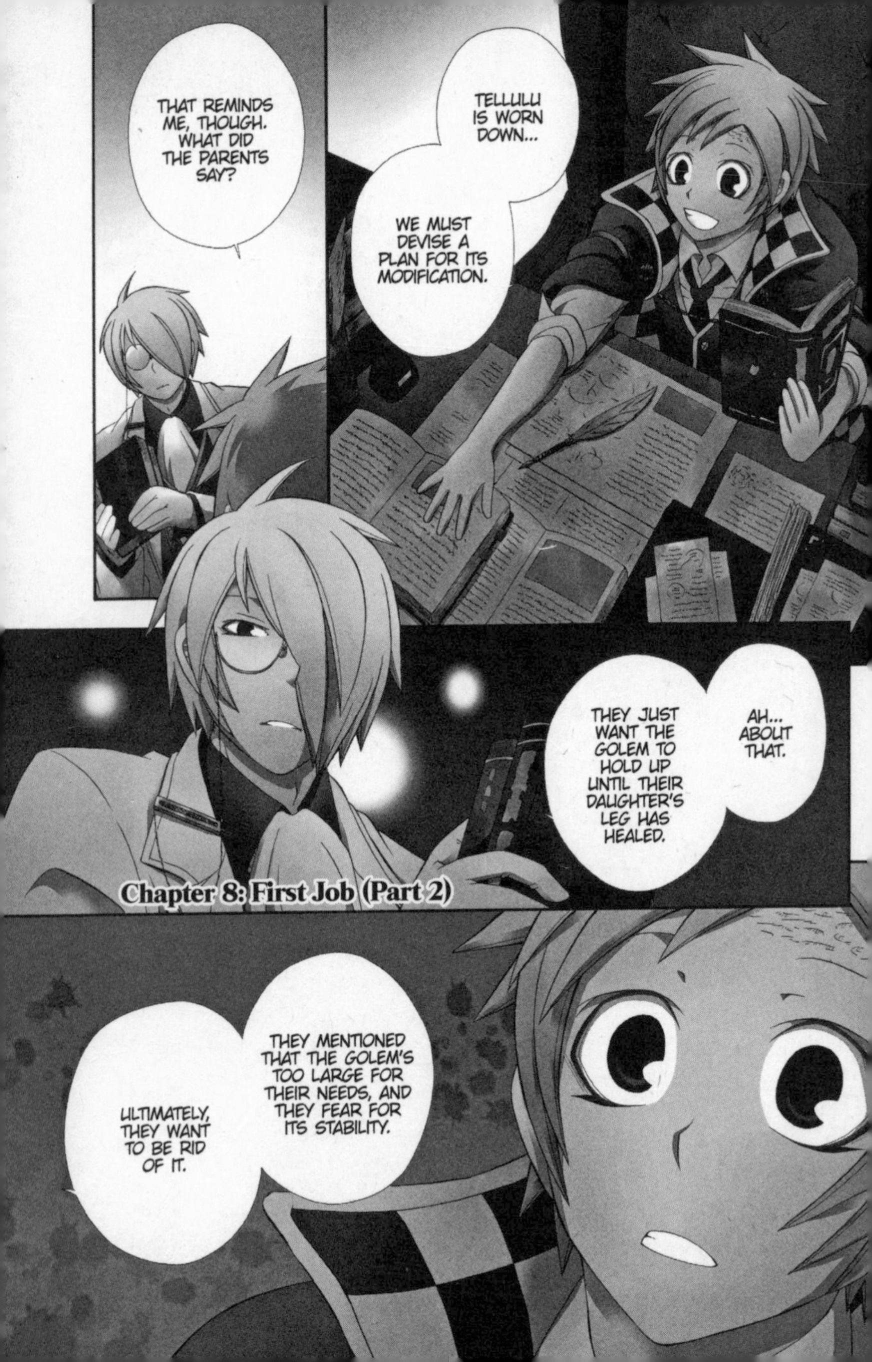
TELLULU IS WORN DOWN...
WE MUST DEVISE A PLAN FOR ITS MODIFICATION.
THAT REMINDS ME, THOUGH. WHAT DID THE PARENTS SAY?
AH... ABOUT THAT.
THEY JUST WANT THE GOLEM TO HOLD UP UNTIL THEIR DAUGHTER'S LEG HAS HEALED.
Chapter 8: First Job (Part 2)
THEY MENTIONED THAT THE GOLEM'S TOO LARGE FOR THEIR NEEDS, AND THEY FEAR FOR ITS STABILITY.
ULTIMATELY, THEY WANT TO BE RID OF IT.

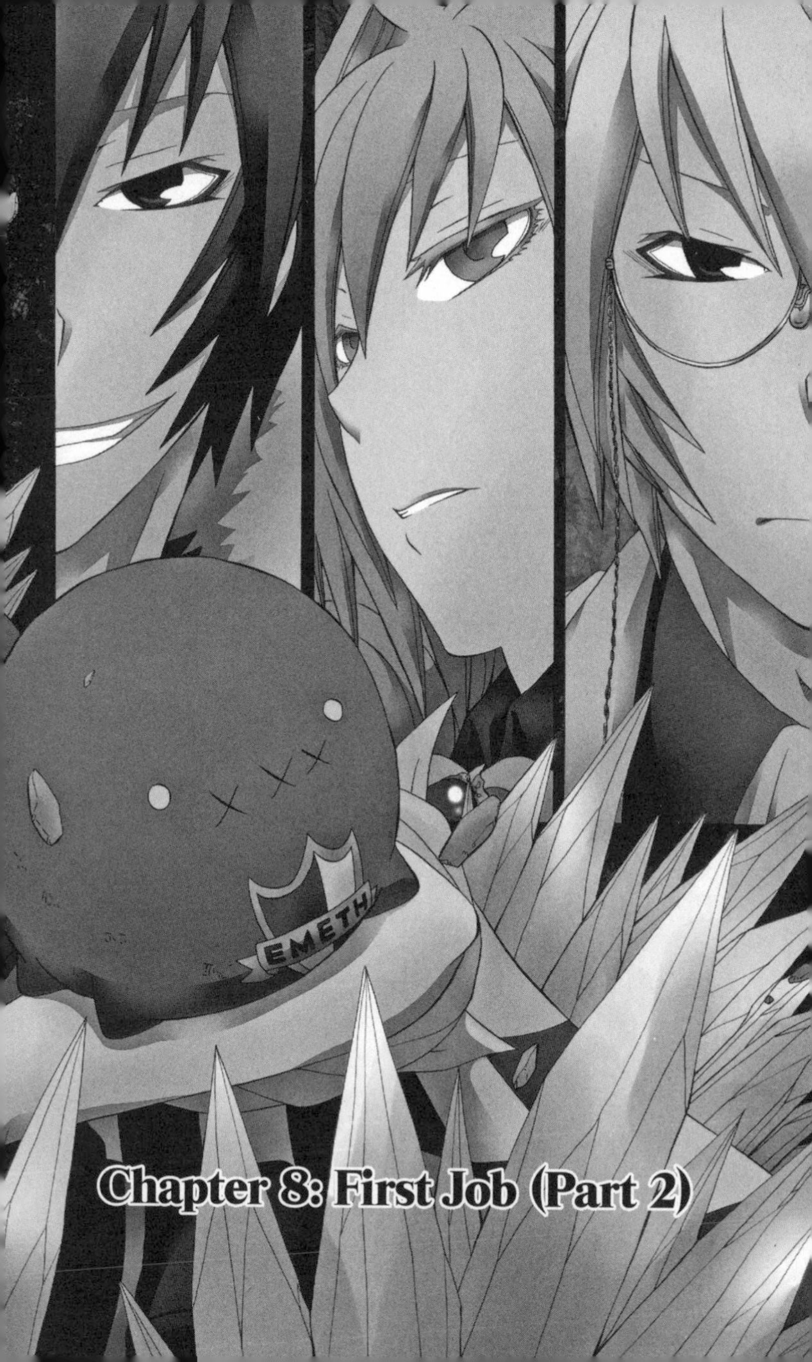
EMETH
Chapter 8: First Job (Part 2)

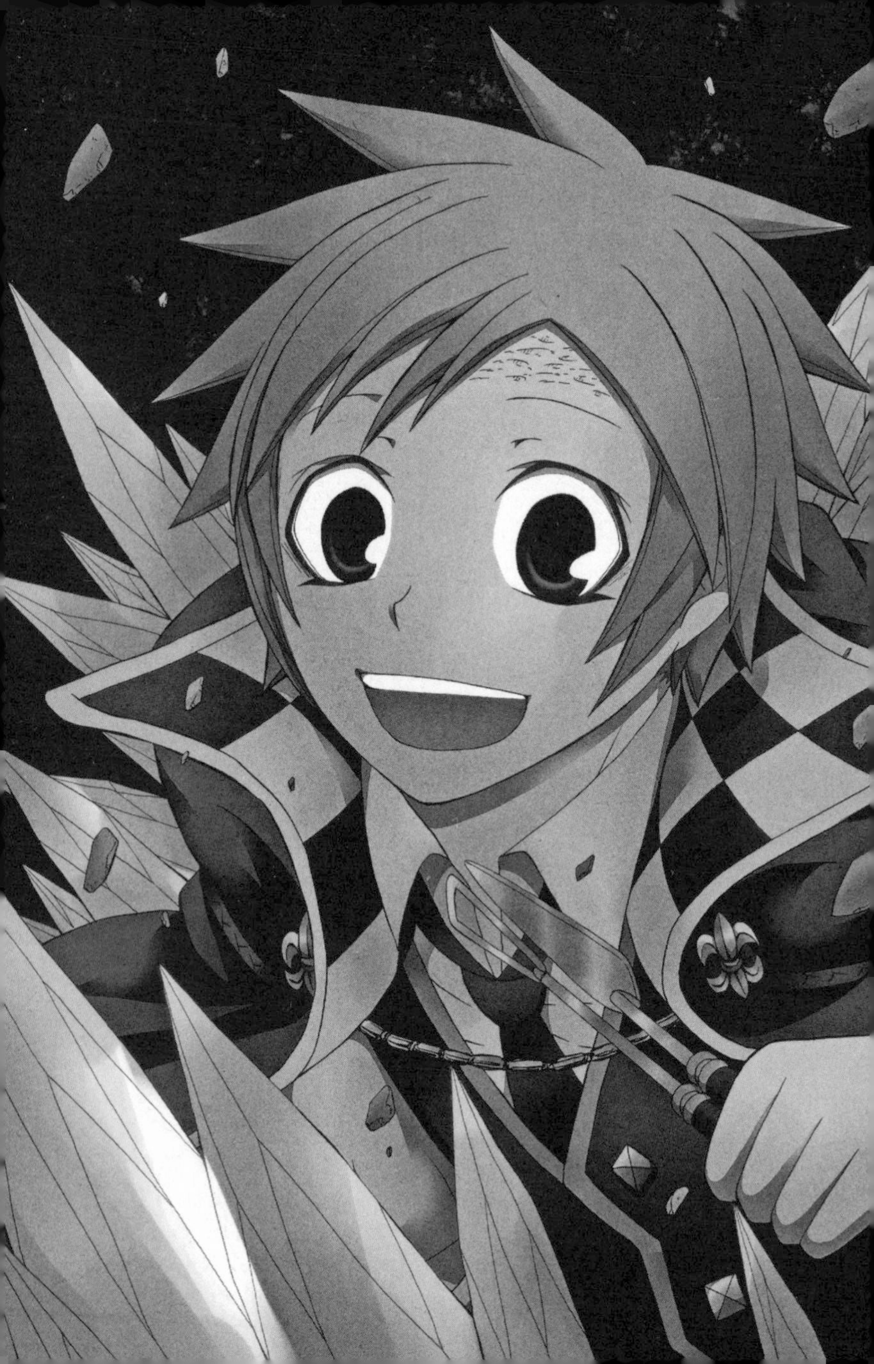

CLAY LORD

MASTER of GOLEMS

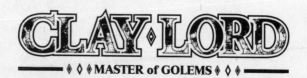

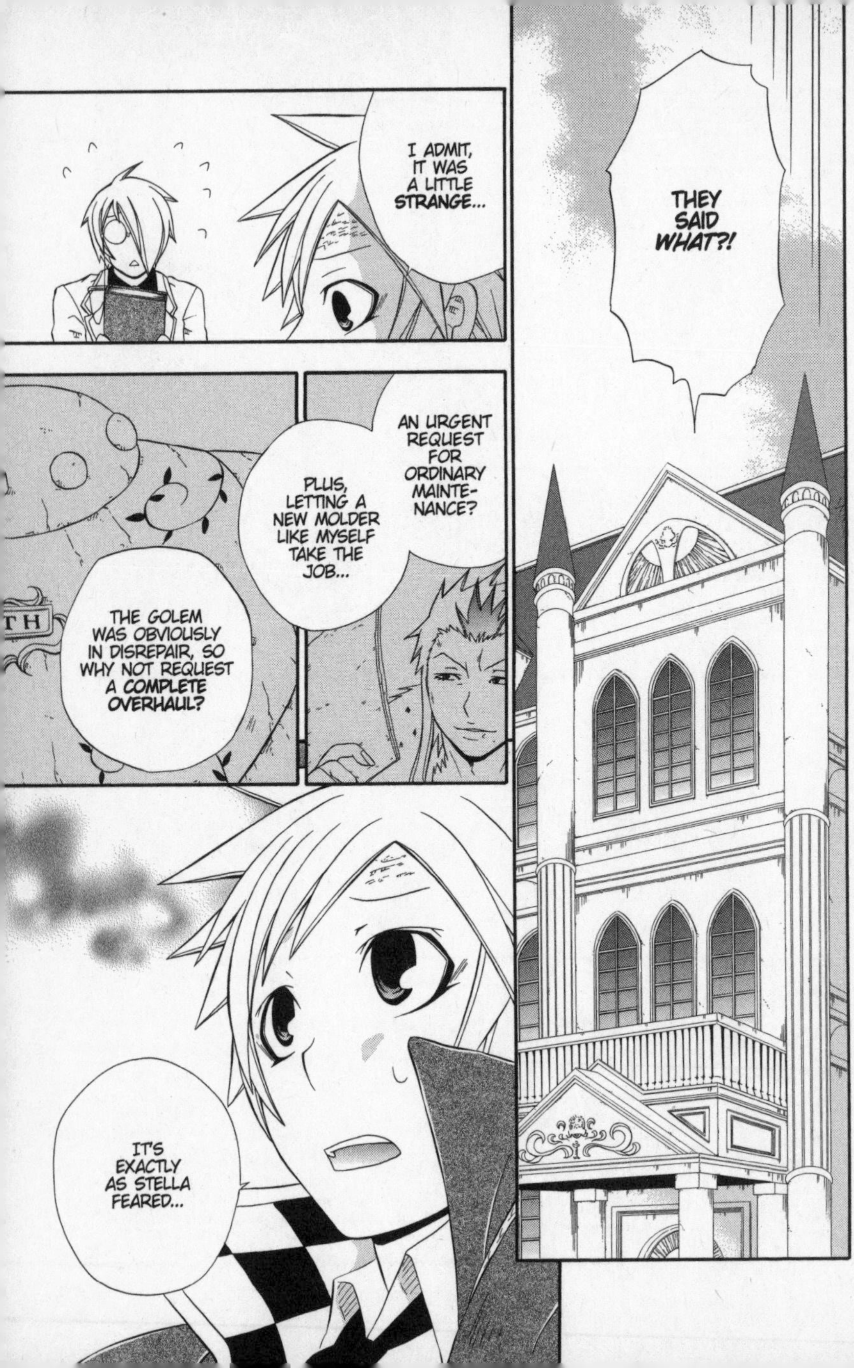
THEY SAID WHAT?!
I ADMIT, IT WAS A LITTLE STRANGE...
AN URGENT REQUEST FOR ORDINARY MAINTE-NANCE?
PLUS, LETTING A NEW MOLDER LIKE MYSELF TAKE THE JOB...
THE GOLEM WAS OBVIOUSLY IN DISREPAIR, SO WHY NOT REQUEST A COMPLETE OVERHAUL?
IT'S EXACTLY AS STELLA FEARED...

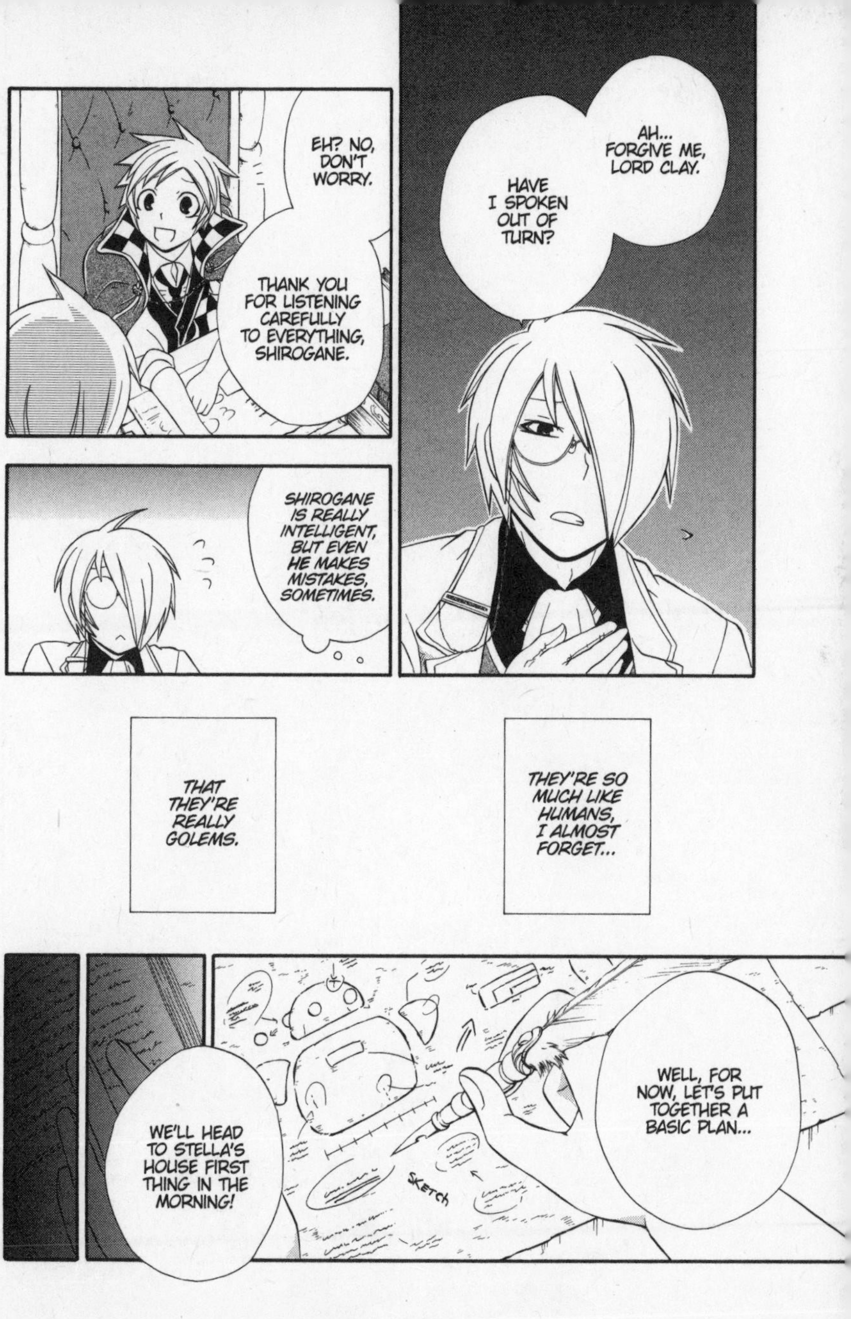
AH... FORGIVE ME, LORD CLAY.
HAVE I SPOKEN OUT OF TURN?
EH? NO, DON'T WORRY.
THANK YOU FOR LISTENING CAREFULLY TO EVERYTHING, SHIROGANE.
SHIROGANE IS REALLY INTELLIGENT, BUT EVEN HE MAKES MISTAKES, SOMETIMES.
THEY'RE SO MUCH LIKE HUMANS, I ALMOST FORGET...
THAT THEY'RE REALLY GOLEMS.
WELL, FOR NOW, LET'S PUT TOGETHER A BASIC PLAN...
SKETCH
WE'LL HEAD TO STELLA'S HOUSE FIRST THING IN THE MORNING!

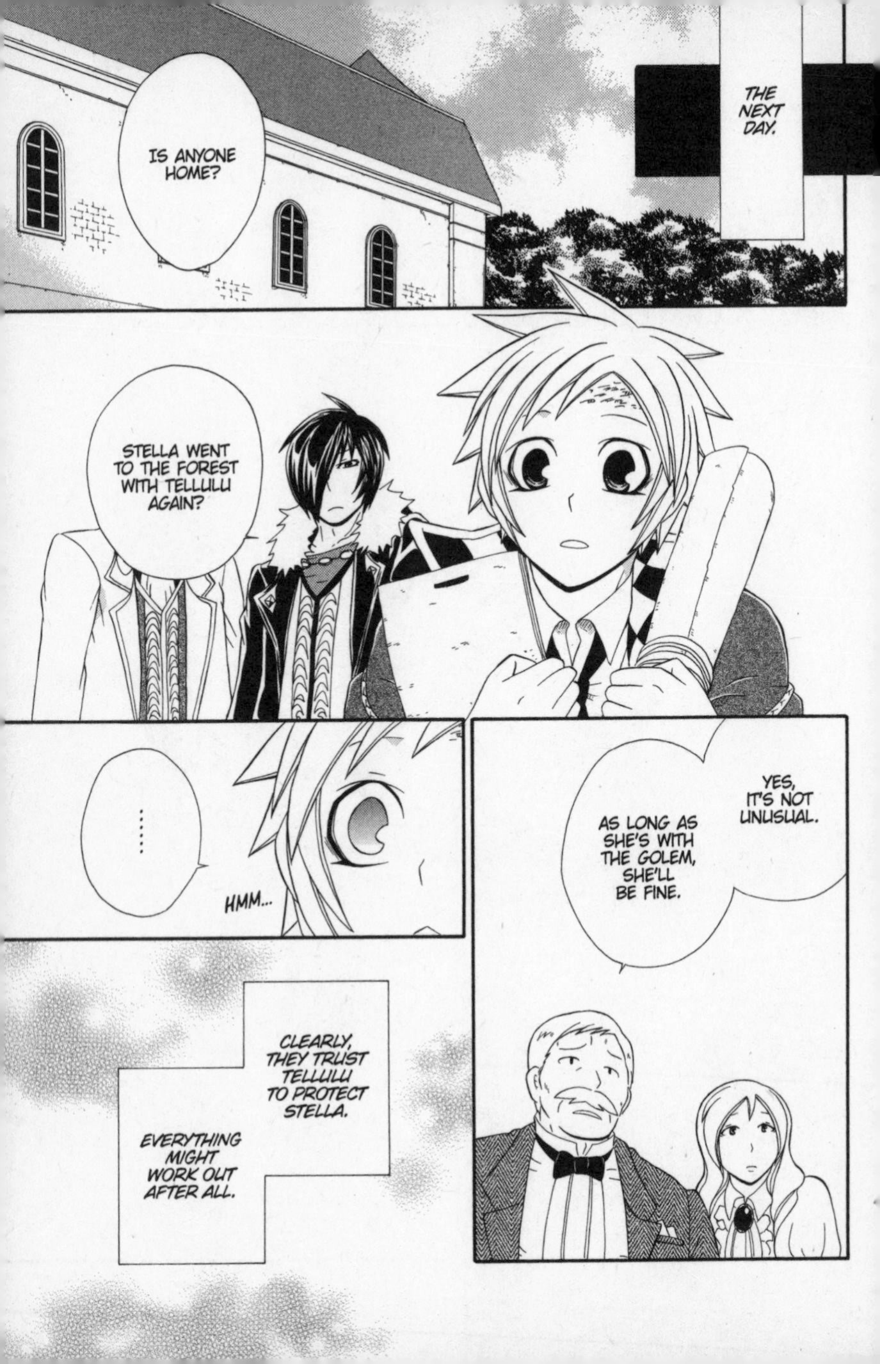
THE NEXT DAY.
IS ANYONE HOME?
STELLA WENT TO THE FOREST WITH TELLULU AGAIN?
YES, IT'S NOT UNUSUAL.
AS LONG AS SHE'S WITH THE GOLEM, SHE'LL BE FINE.
......
HMM...
CLEARLY, THEY TRUST TELLULU TO PROTECT STELLA.
EVERYTHING MIGHT WORK OUT AFTER ALL.

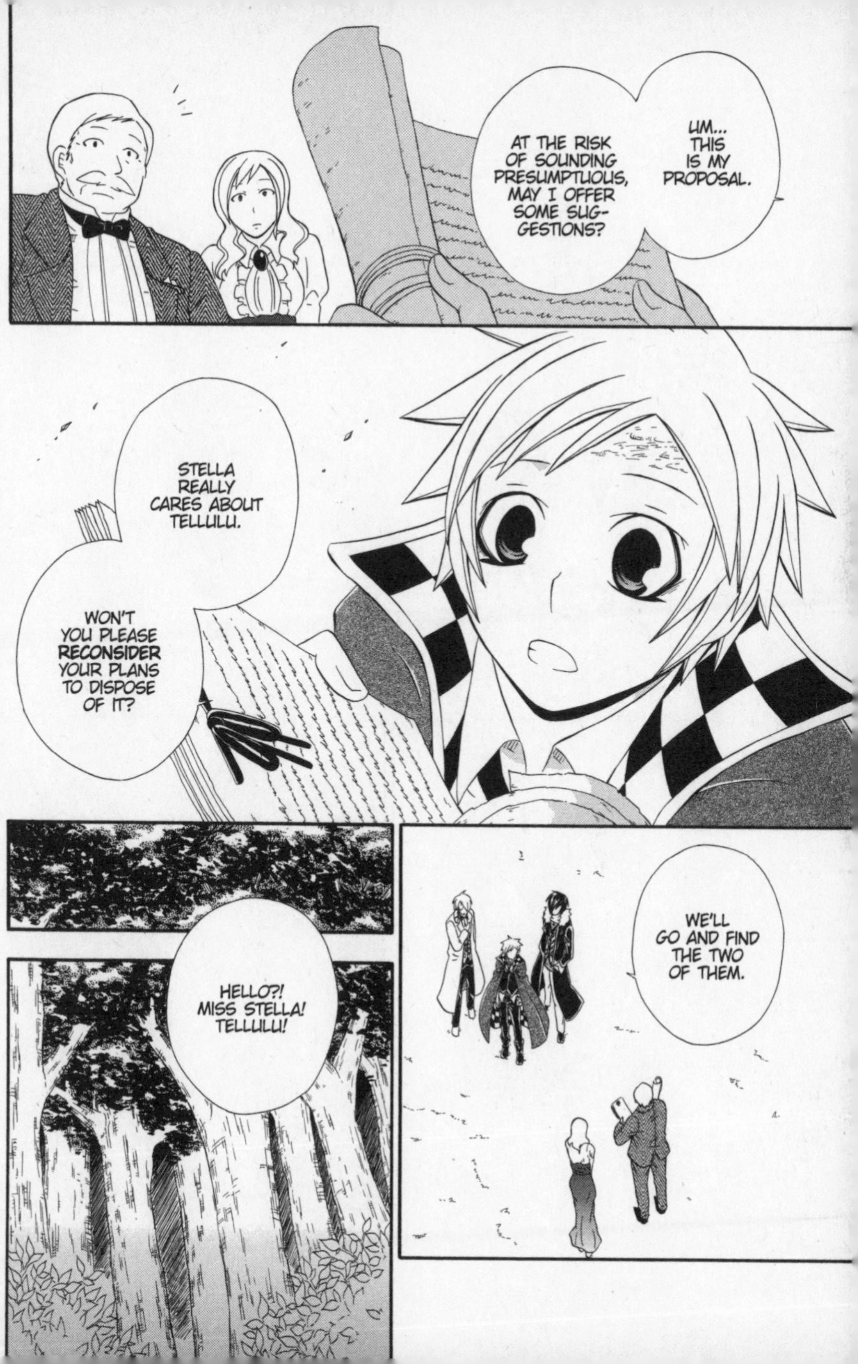
UM... THIS IS MY PROPOSAL.
AT THE RISK OF SOUNDING PRESUMPTUOUS, MAY I OFFER SOME SUG-GESTIONS?
STELLA REALLY CARES ABOUT TELLULU.
WON'T YOU PLEASE RECONSIDER YOUR PLANS TO DISPOSE OF IT?
WE'LL GO AND FIND THE TWO OF THEM.
HELLO?! MISS STELLA! TELLULU!

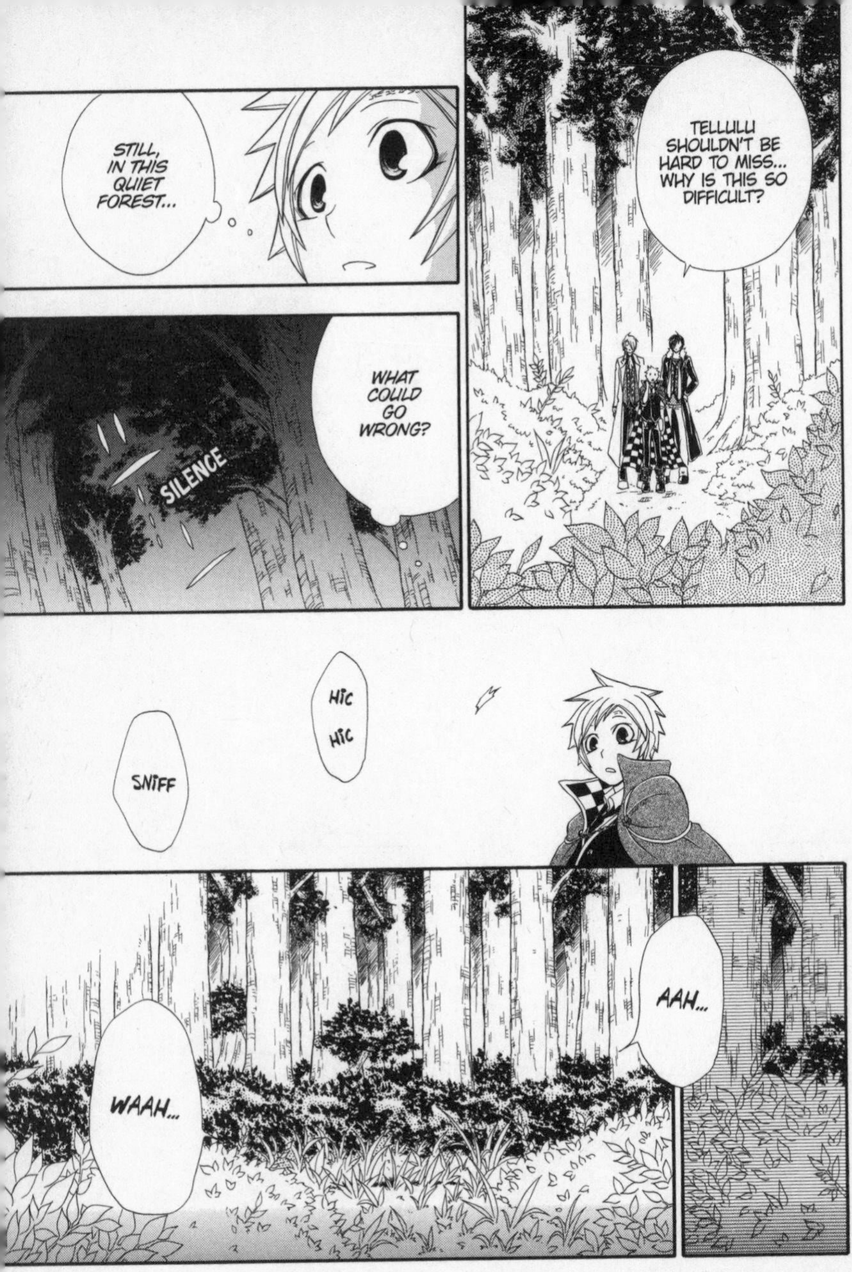
TELLULU SHOULDN'T BE HARD TO MISS... WHY IS THIS SO DIFFICULT?
STILL, IN THIS QUIET FOREST...
WHAT COULD GO WRONG?
SILENCE
HIC
HIC
SNIFF
AAH...
WAAH...

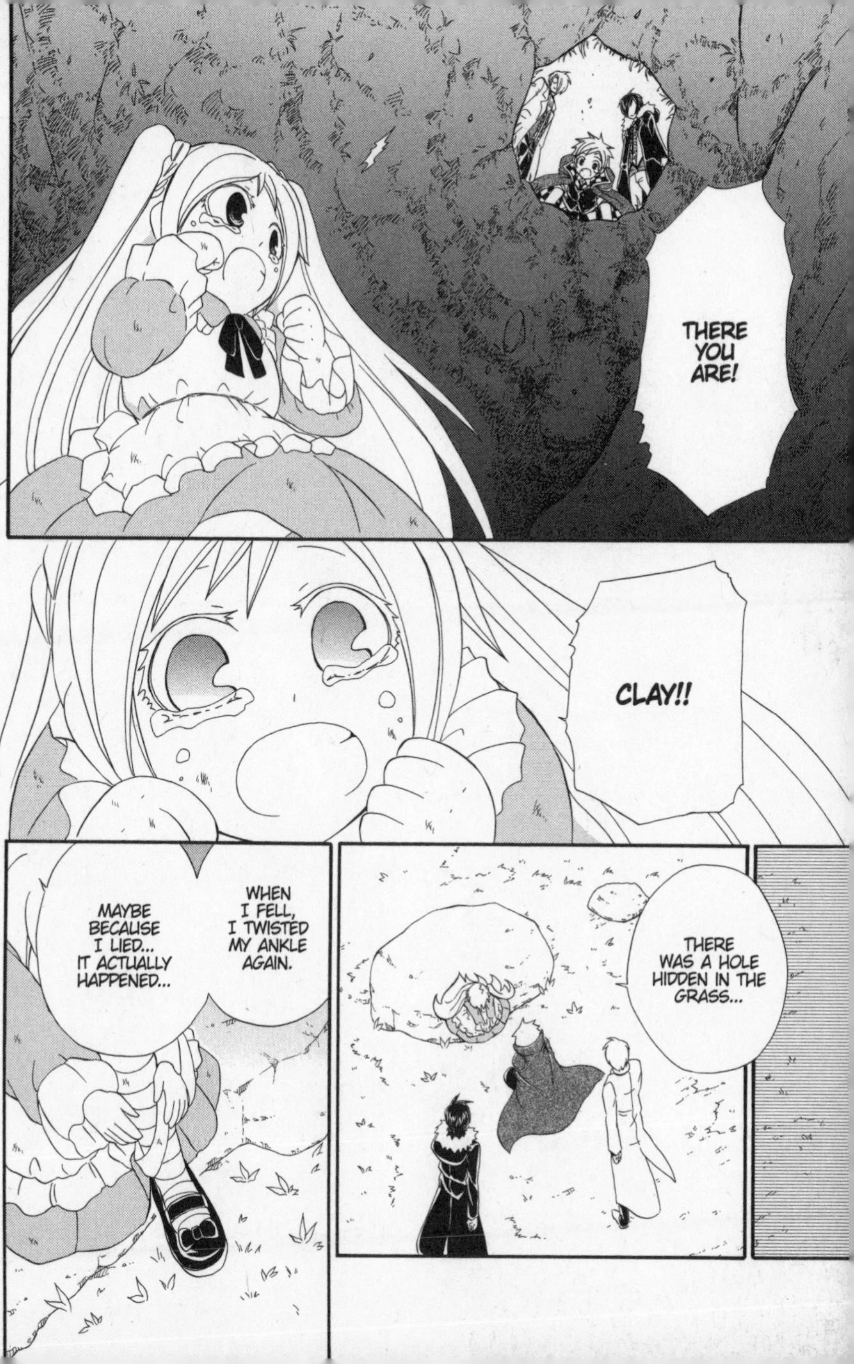
THERE YOU ARE!
CLAY!!
THERE WAS A HOLE HIDDEN IN THE GRASS...
WHEN I FELL, I TWISTED MY ANKLE AGAIN.
MAYBE BECAUSE I LIED... IT ACTUALLY HAPPENED...

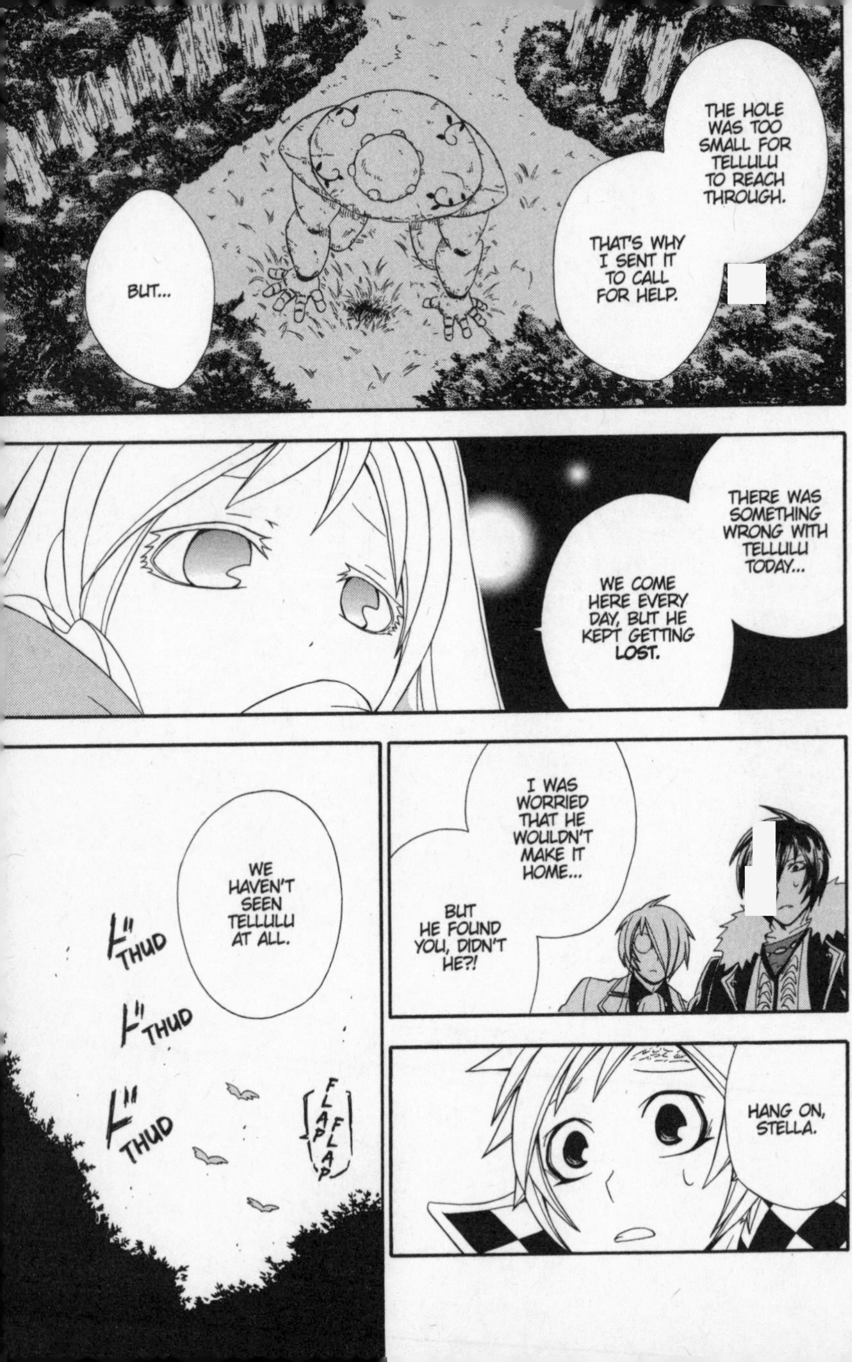
THE HOLE WAS TOO SMALL FOR TELLULU TO REACH THROUGH.
THAT'S WHY I SENT IT TO CALL FOR HELP.
BUT...
THERE WAS SOMETHING WRONG WITH TELLULU TODAY...
WE COME HERE EVERY DAY, BUT HE KEPT GETTING LOST.
I WAS WORRIED THAT HE WOULDN'T MAKE IT HOME...
BUT HE FOUND YOU, DIDN'T HE?!
HANG ON, STELLA.
WE HAVEN'T SEEN TELLULU AT ALL.
ド THUD
ド THUD
ド THUD
FLAP FLAP

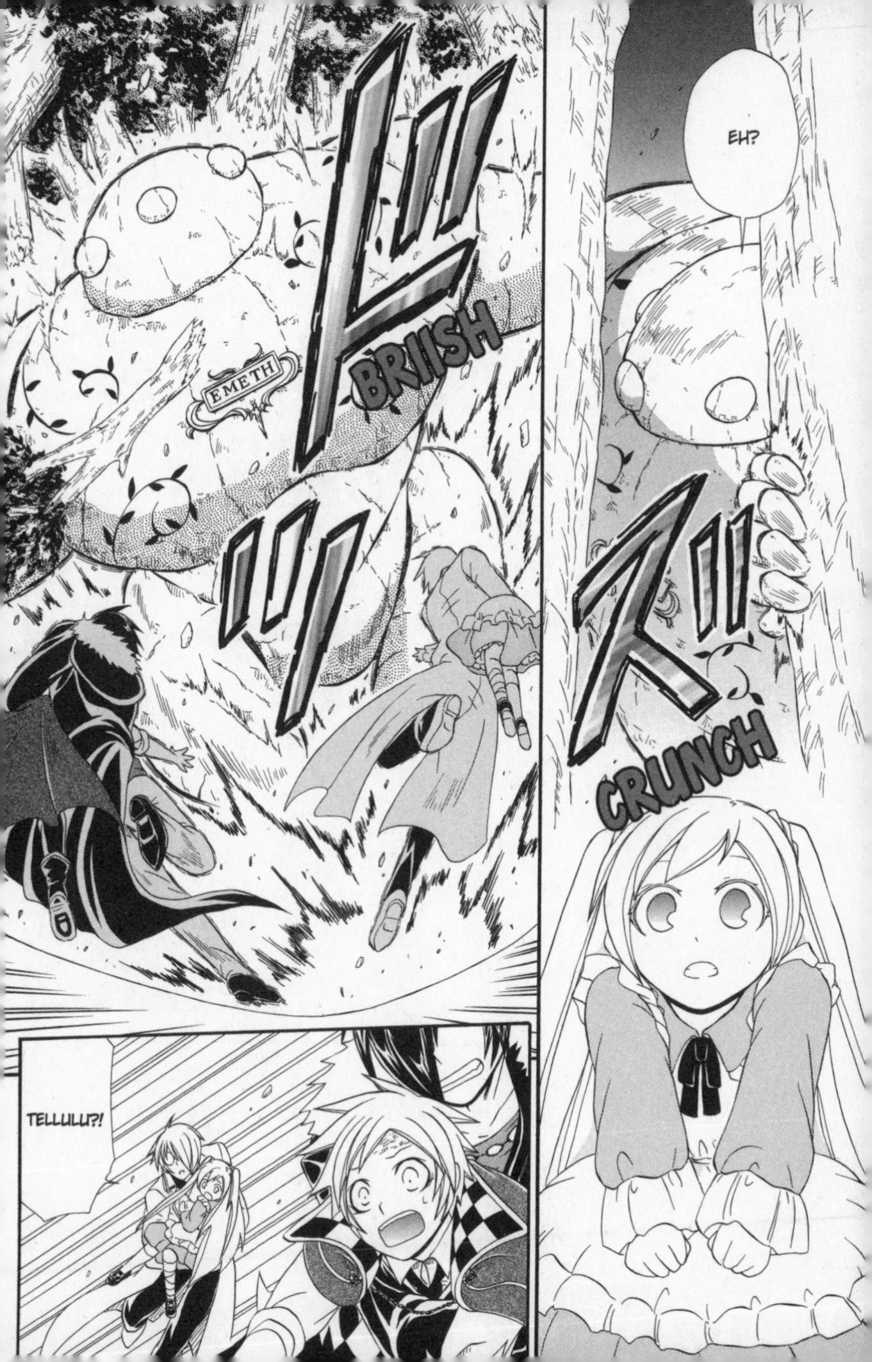
EH?
CRUNCH
EMETH
BRIISH
TELLULU?!

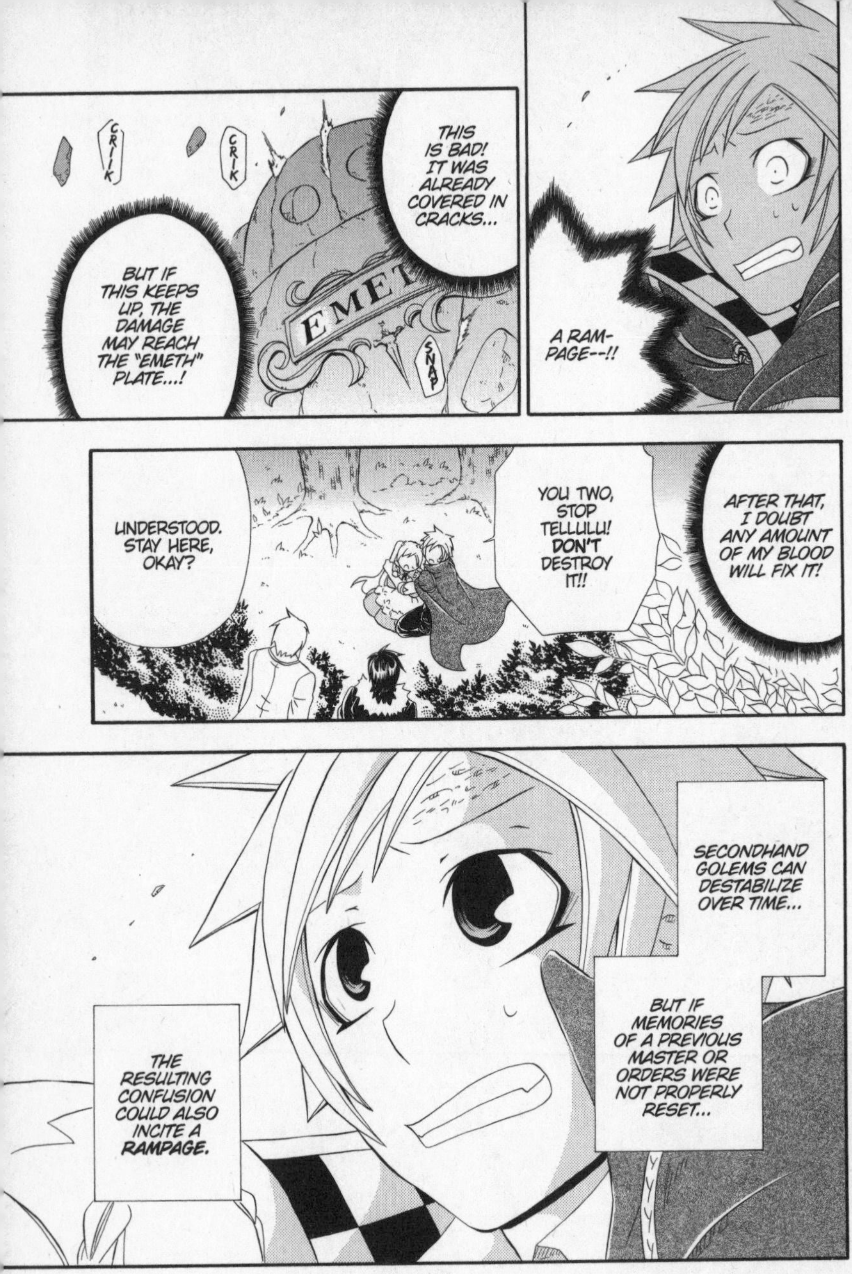
A RAM-PAGE--!!
THIS IS BAD! IT WAS ALREADY COVERED IN CRACKS...
CRIK
CRIK
BUT IF THIS KEEPS UP, THE DAMAGE MAY REACH THE "EMETH" PLATE...!
EMET
SNAP
AFTER THAT, I DOUBT ANY AMOUNT OF MY BLOOD WILL FIX IT!
YOU TWO, STOP TELLULU! DON'T DESTROY IT!!
UNDERSTOOD. STAY HERE, OKAY?
SECONDHAND GOLEMS CAN DESTABILIZE OVER TIME...
BUT IF MEMORIES OF A PREVIOUS MASTER OR ORDERS WERE NOT PROPERLY RESET...
THE RESULTING CONFUSION COULD ALSO INCITE A RAMPAGE.

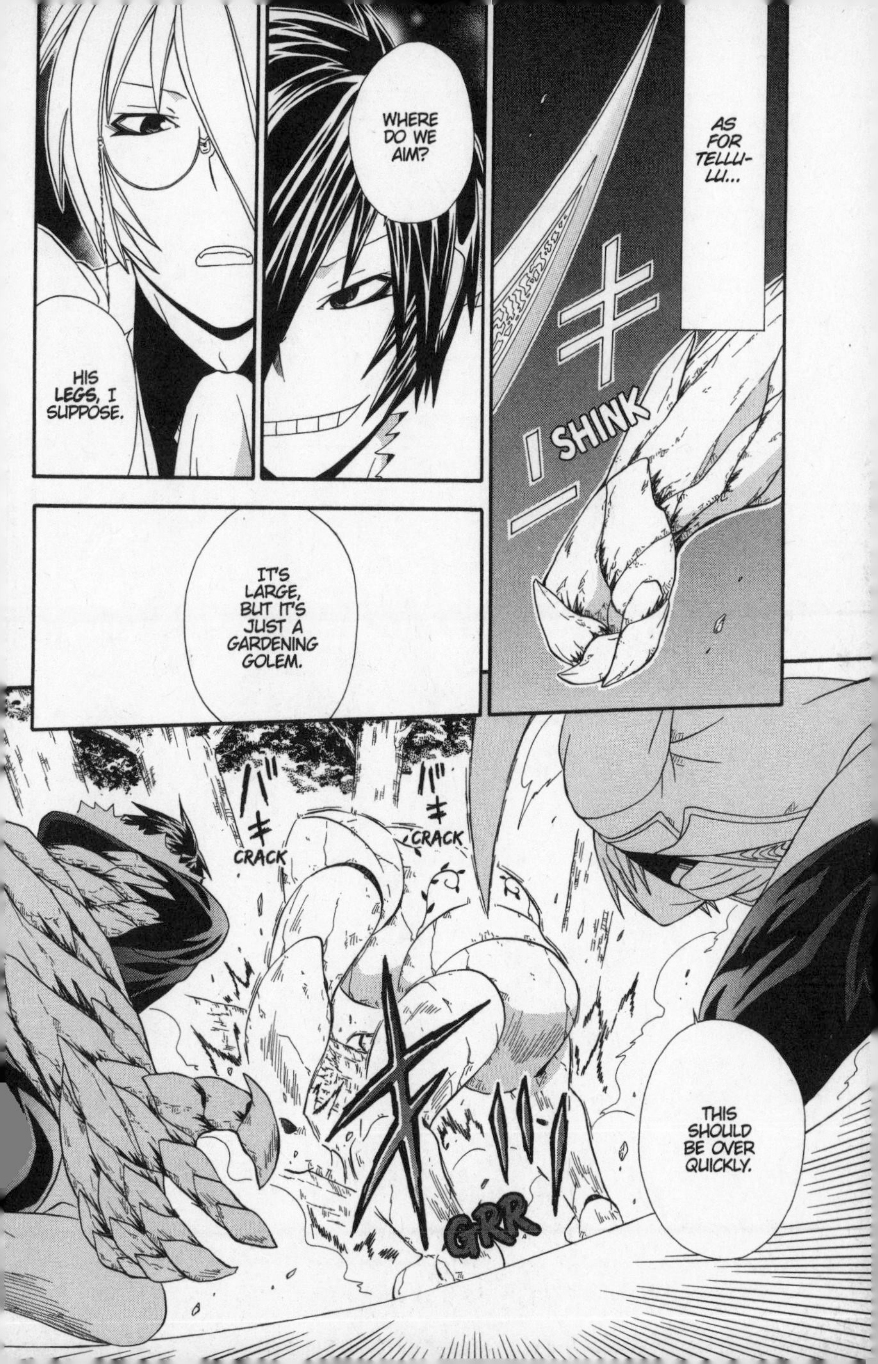
AS FOR TELLULU...
SHINK
WHERE DO WE AIM?
HIS LEGS, I SUPPOSE.
IT'S LARGE, BUT IT'S JUST A GARDENING GOLEM.
バキ
CRACK
バキ
CRACK
THIS SHOULD BE OVER QUICKLY.
GRR

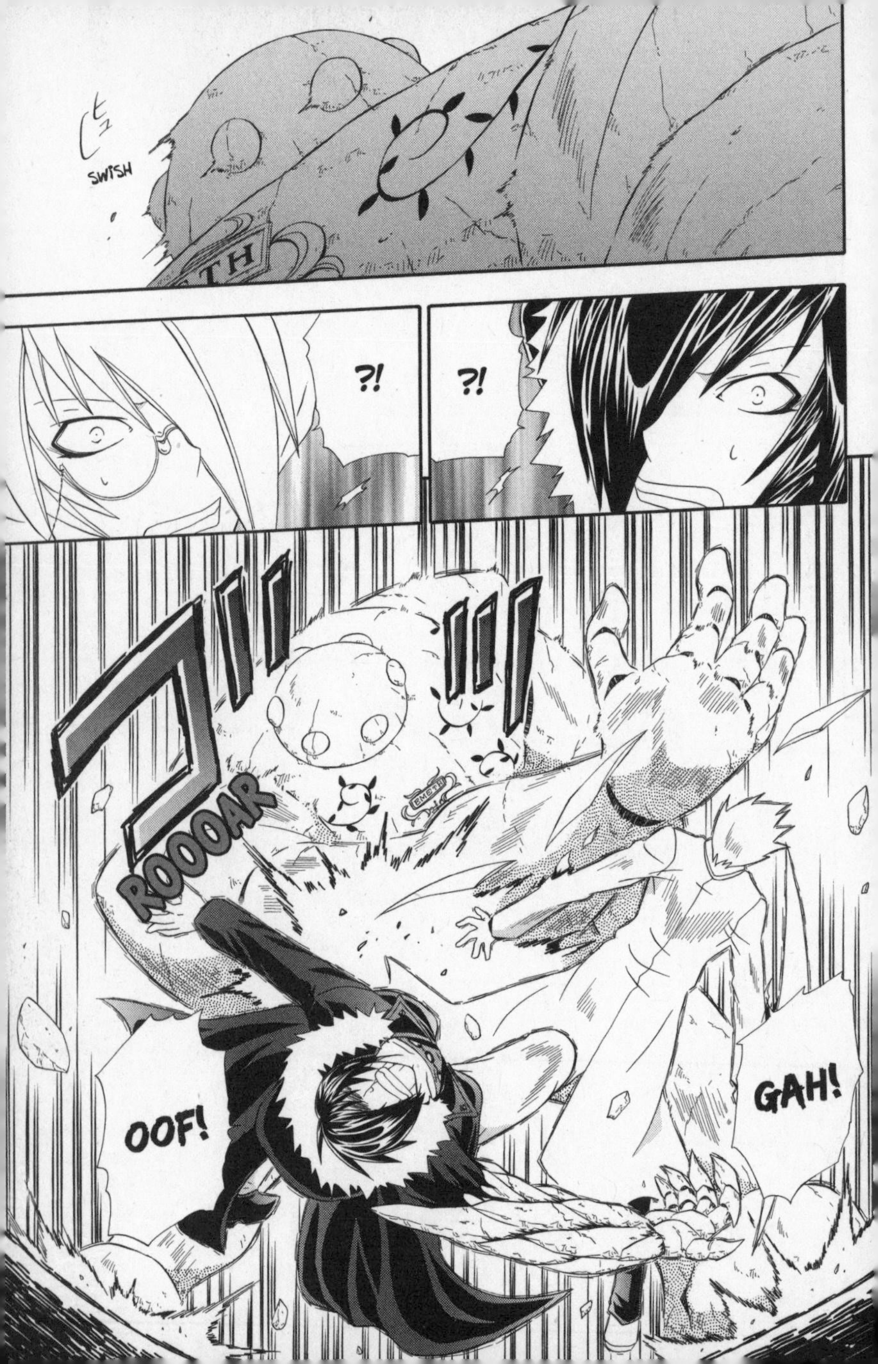
ヒュ
SWISH
?!
?!
ROOOAR
EMETH
GAH!
OOF!

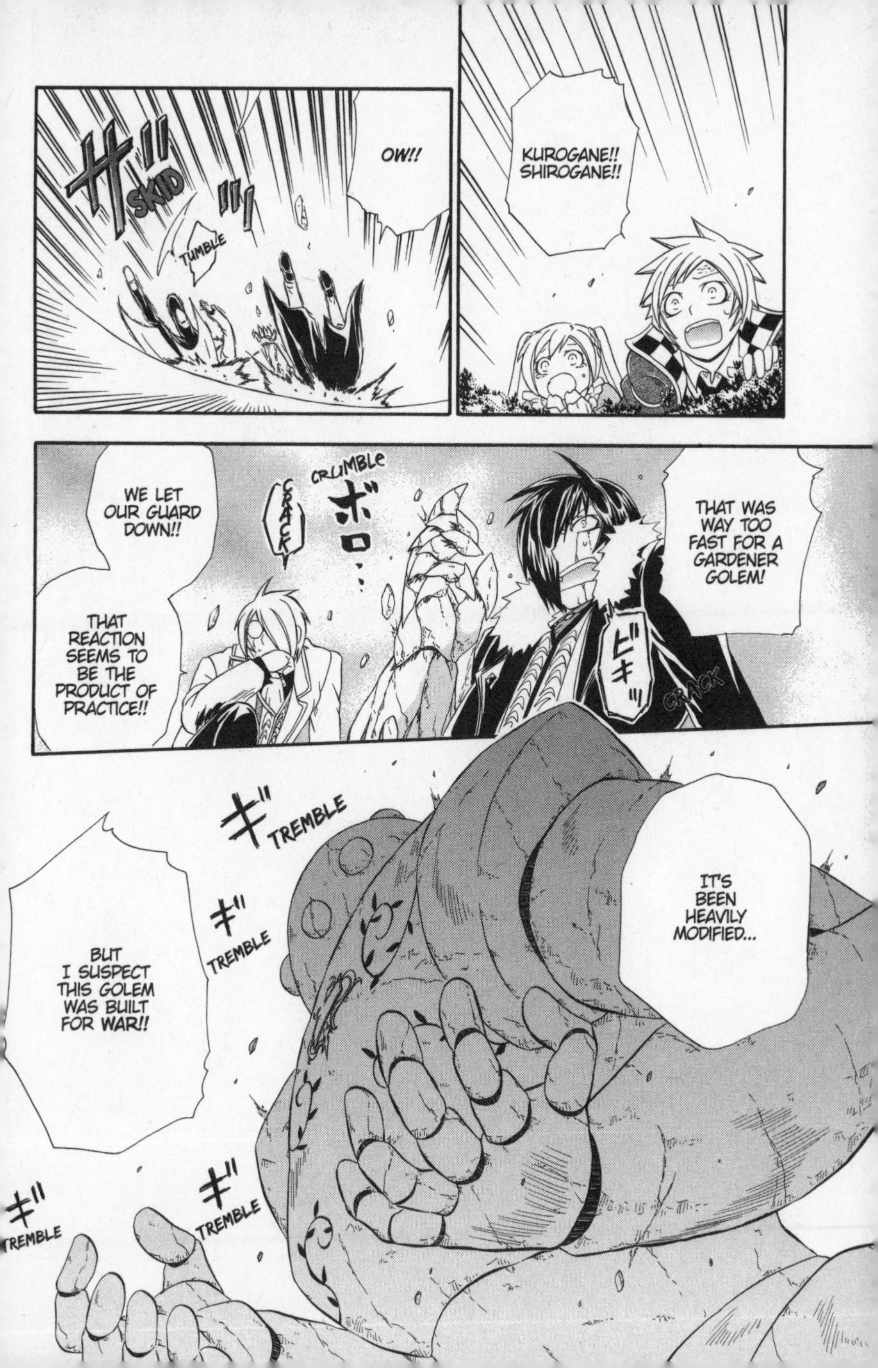
KUROGANE!! SHIROGANE!!
OW!!
ザッ
SKID
TUMBLE
THAT WAS WAY TOO FAST FOR A GARDENER GOLEM!
ビキッ
CRACK
ボロ・・・
CRUMBLE
CRACK
WE LET OUR GUARD DOWN!!
THAT REACTION SEEMS TO BE THE PRODUCT OF PRACTICE!!
IT'S BEEN HEAVILY MODIFIED...
ギ
TREMBLE
ギ
TREMBLE
BUT I SUSPECT THIS GOLEM WAS BUILT FOR WAR!!
ギ
TREMBLE
ギ
TREMBLE

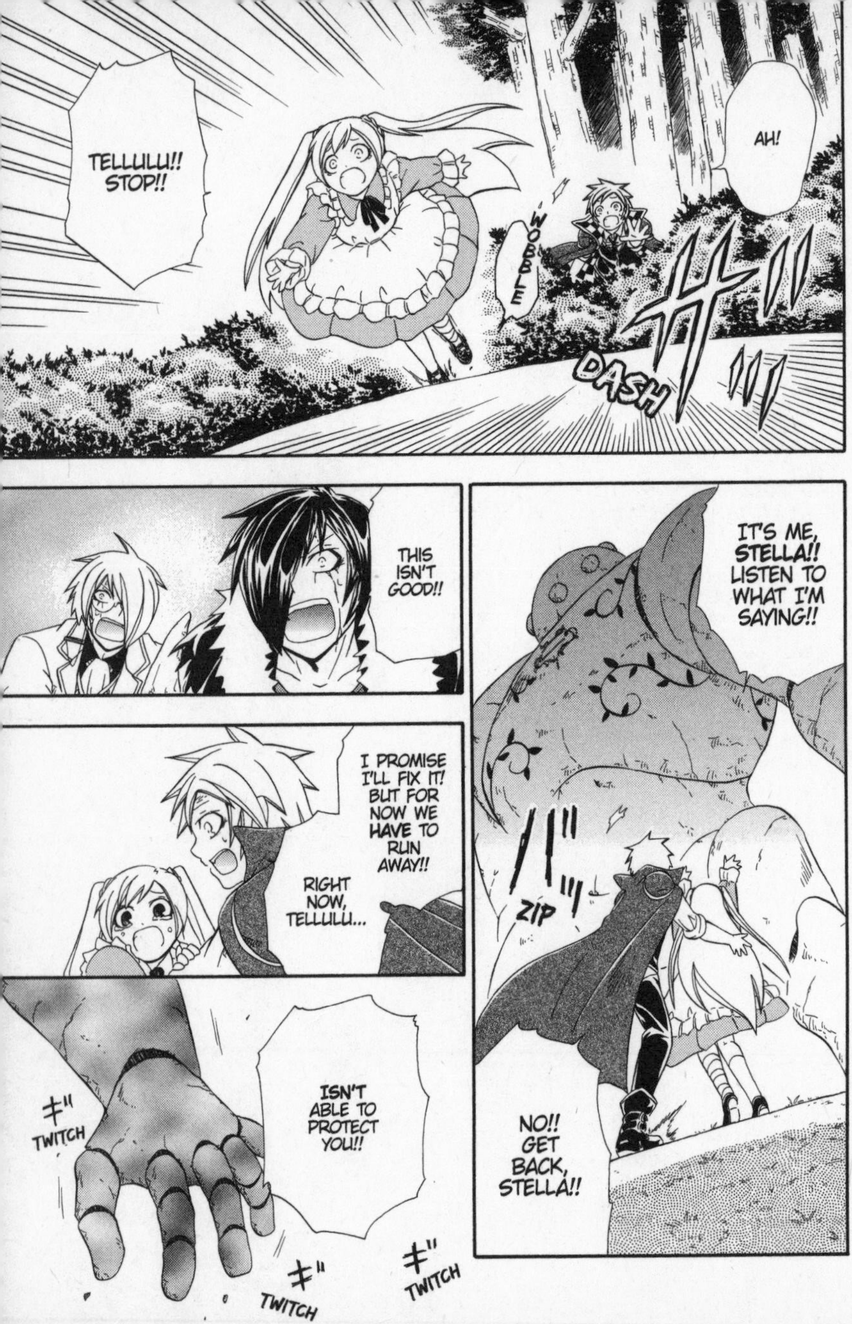
AH!
WOBBLE
DASH
TELLULU!! STOP!!
IT'S ME, STELLA!! LISTEN TO WHAT I'M SAYING!!
ZIP
NO!! GET BACK, STELLA!!
THIS ISN'T GOOD!!
I PROMISE I'LL FIX IT! BUT FOR NOW WE HAVE TO RUN AWAY!!
RIGHT NOW, TELLULU...
ISN'T ABLE TO PROTECT YOU!!
TWITCH
TWITCH
TWITCH

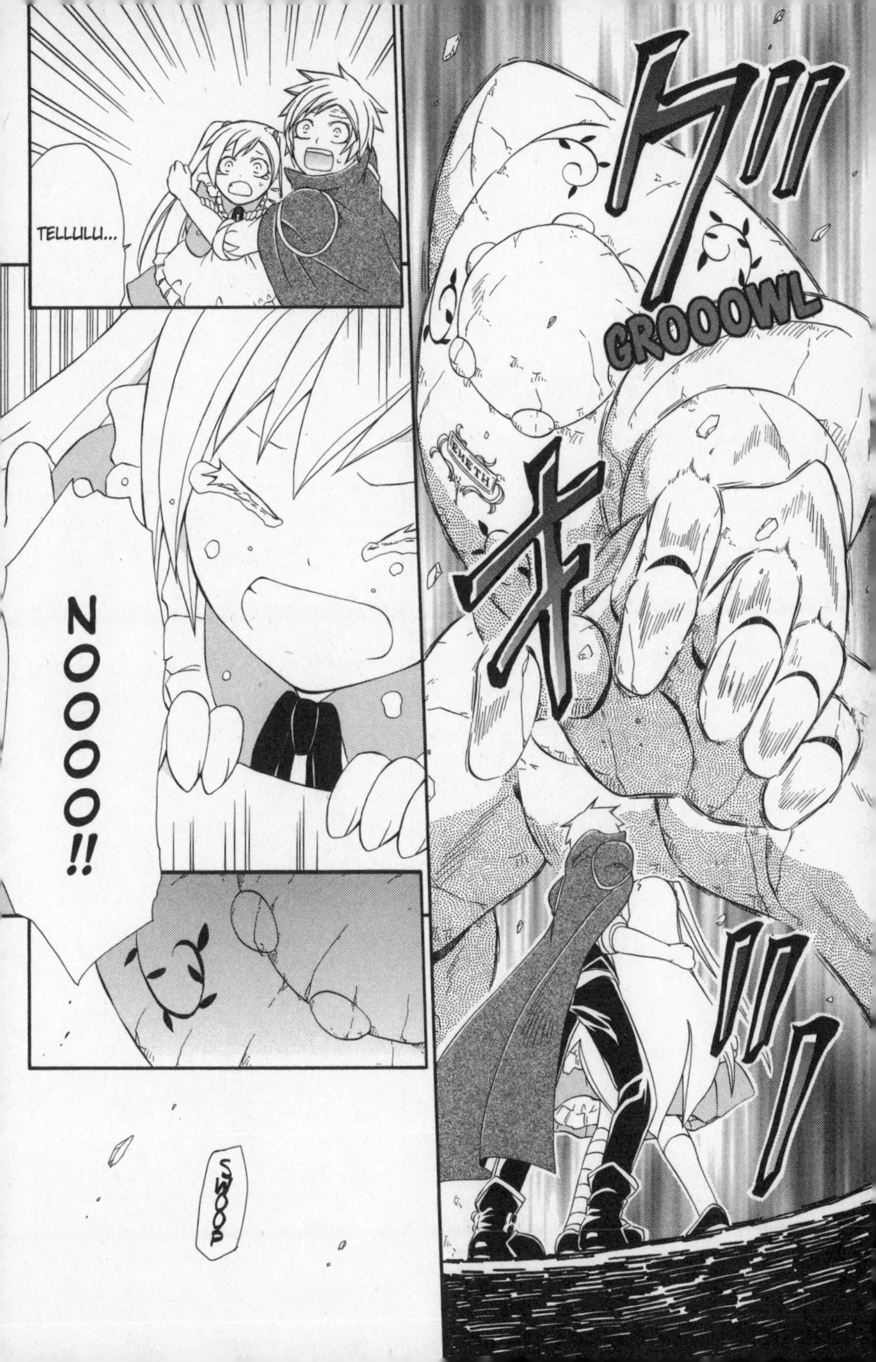
ゴ
GROOOWL
オ
TELLULU...
NOOOOO!!
SWOOP

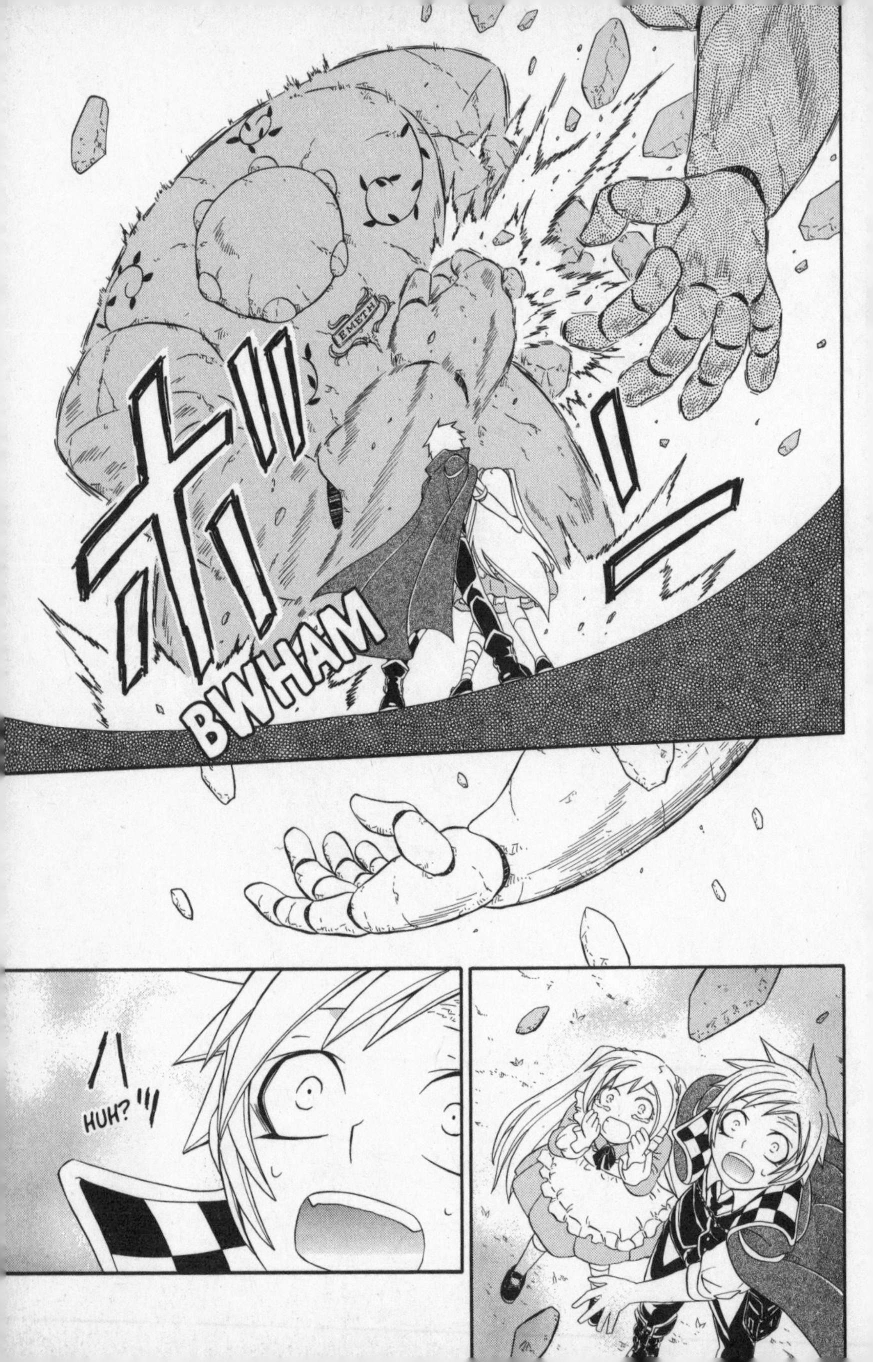
BWHAM
HUH?

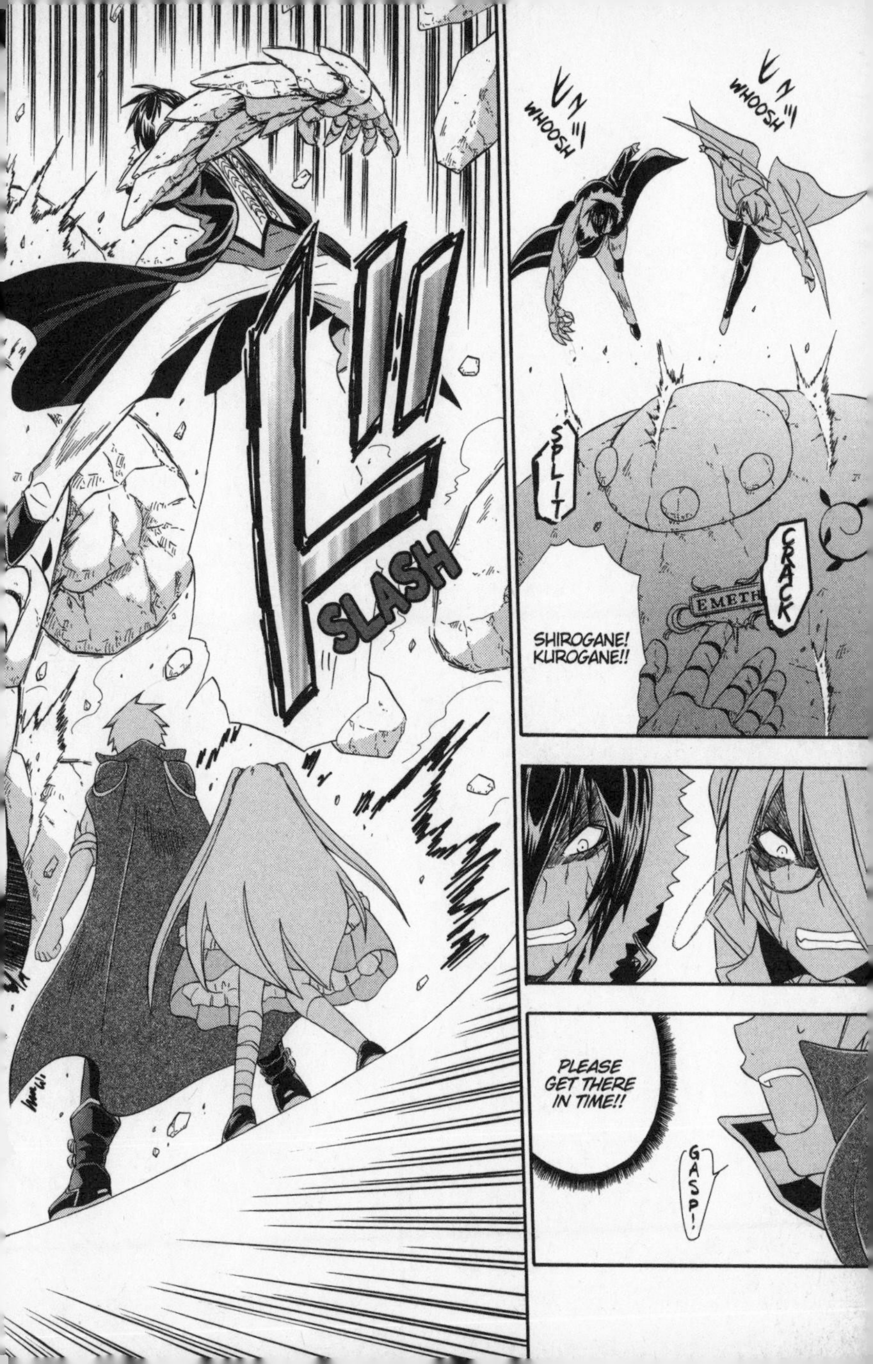

WHOOSH
WHOOSH
CRACK
SPLIT
EMETH
SHIROGANE! KUROGANE!!
PLEASE GET THERE IN TIME!!
GASP!
SLASH

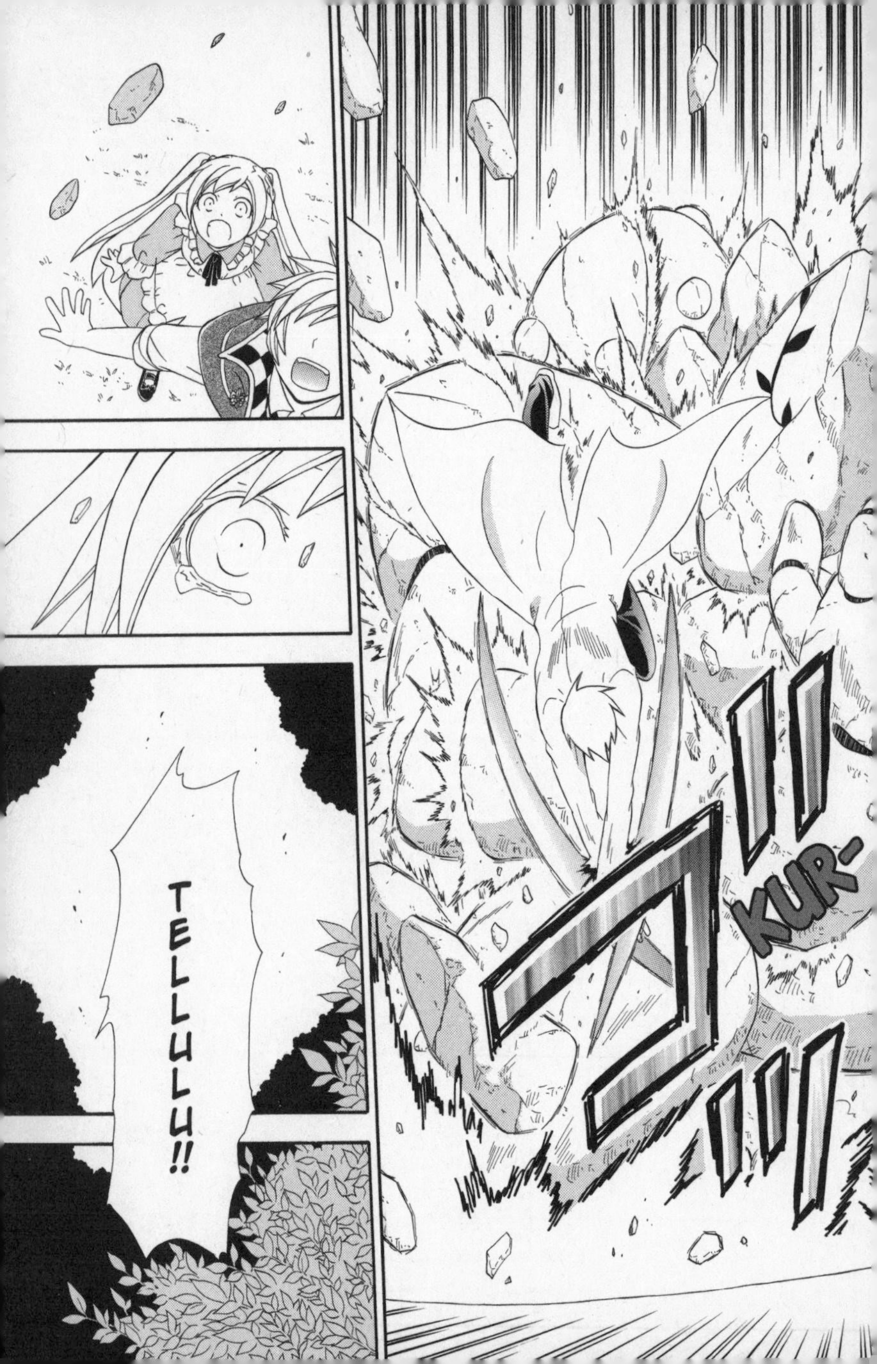
KUR-
TELLLULU!!

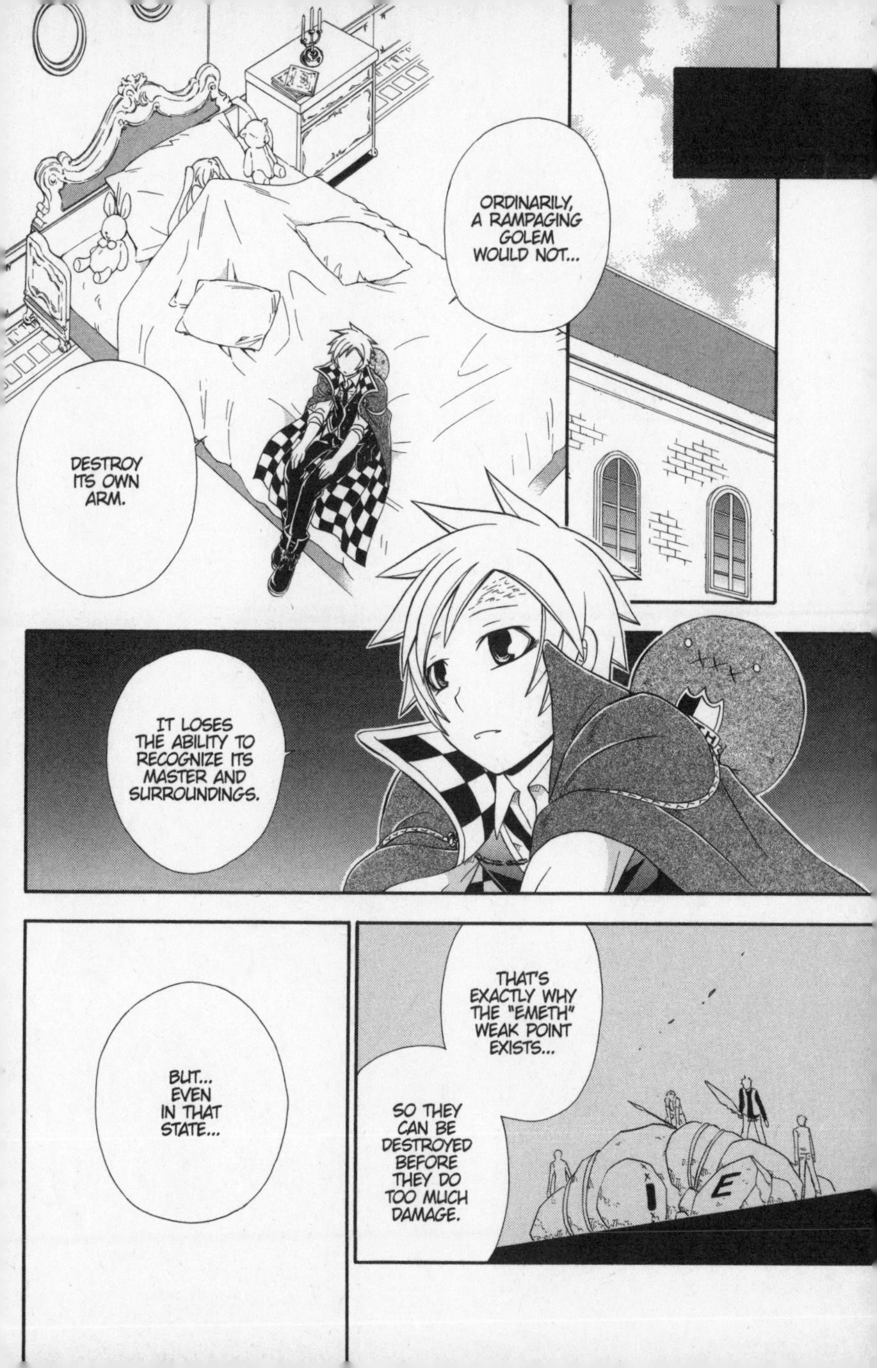
ORDINARILY, A RAMPAGING GOLEM WOULD NOT...
DESTROY ITS OWN ARM.
IT LOSES THE ABILITY TO RECOGNIZE ITS MASTER AND SURROUNDINGS.
THAT'S EXACTLY WHY THE "EMETH" WEAK POINT EXISTS...
SO THEY CAN BE DESTROYED BEFORE THEY DO TOO MUCH DAMAGE.
BUT... EVEN IN THAT STATE...

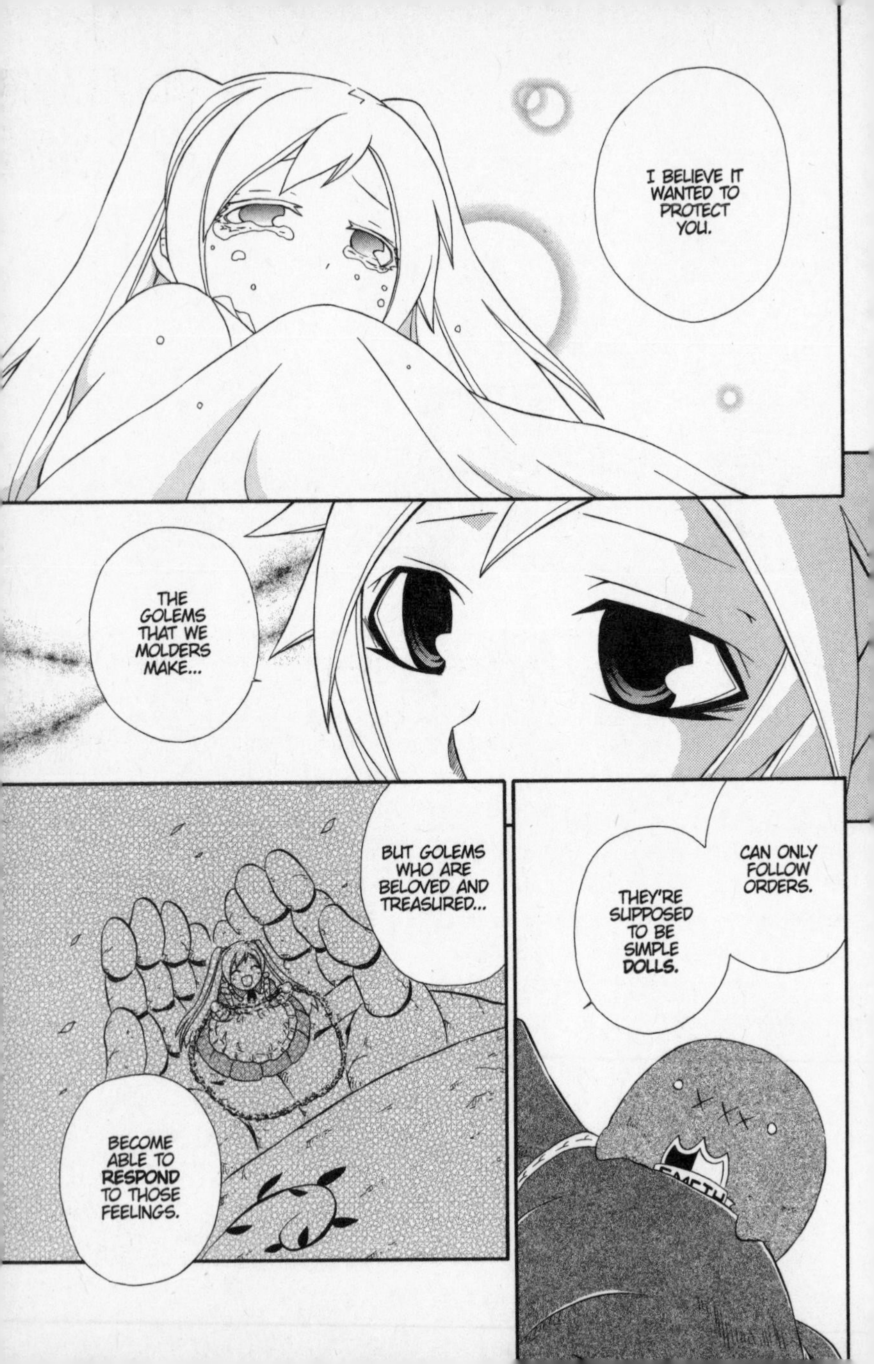
I BELIEVE IT WANTED TO PROTECT YOU.
THE GOLEMS THAT WE MOLDERS MAKE...
CAN ONLY FOLLOW ORDERS.
THEY'RE SUPPOSED TO BE SIMPLE DOLLS.
BUT GOLEMS WHO ARE BELOVED AND TREASURED...
BECOME ABLE TO RESPOND TO THOSE FEELINGS.

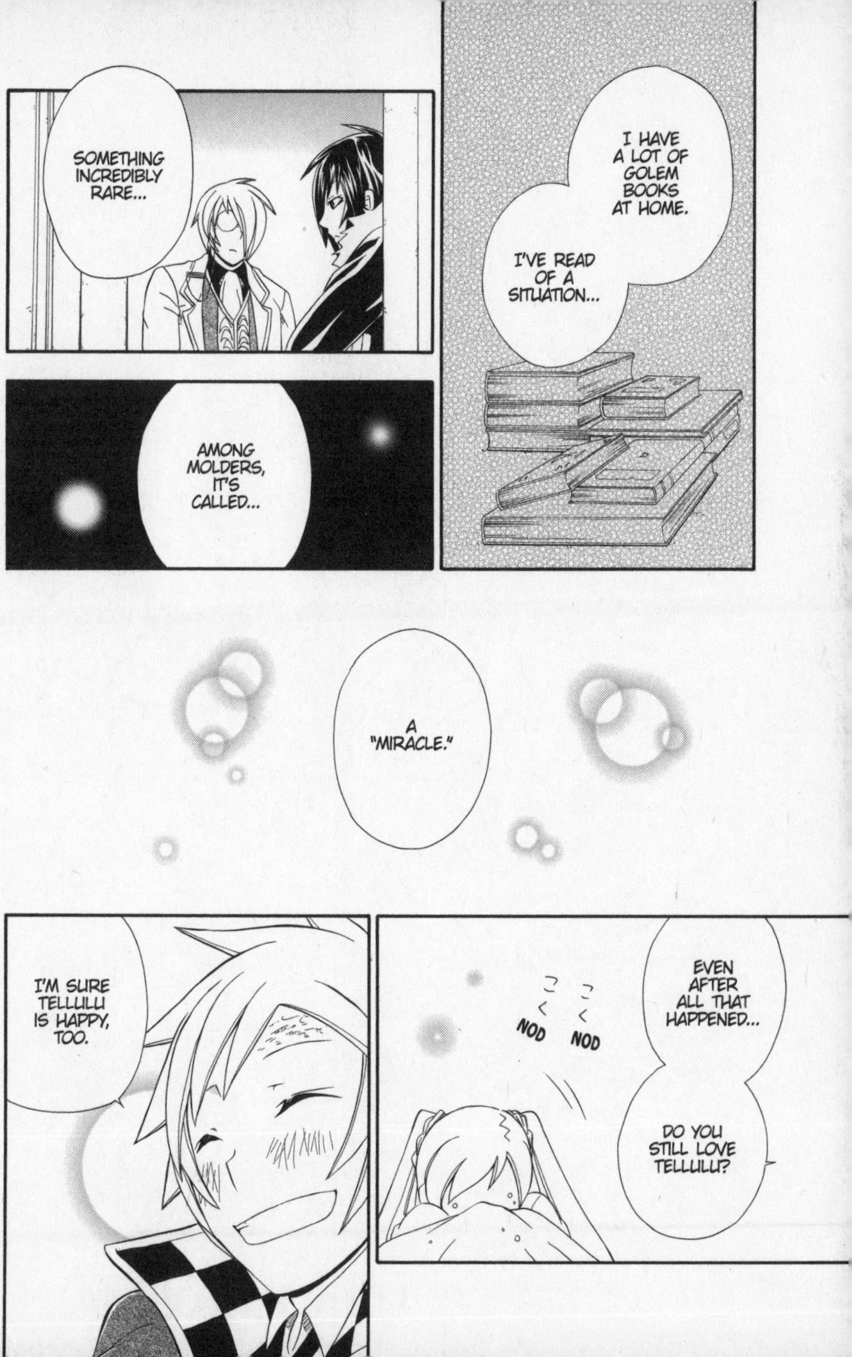
I HAVE A LOT OF GOLEM BOOKS AT HOME.
I'VE READ OF A SITUATION...
SOMETHING INCREDIBLY RARE...
AMONG MOLDERS, IT'S CALLED...
A "MIRACLE."
EVEN AFTER ALL THAT HAPPENED...
DO YOU STILL LOVE TELLULU?
こく こく
NOD NOD
I'M SURE TELLULU IS HAPPY, TOO.

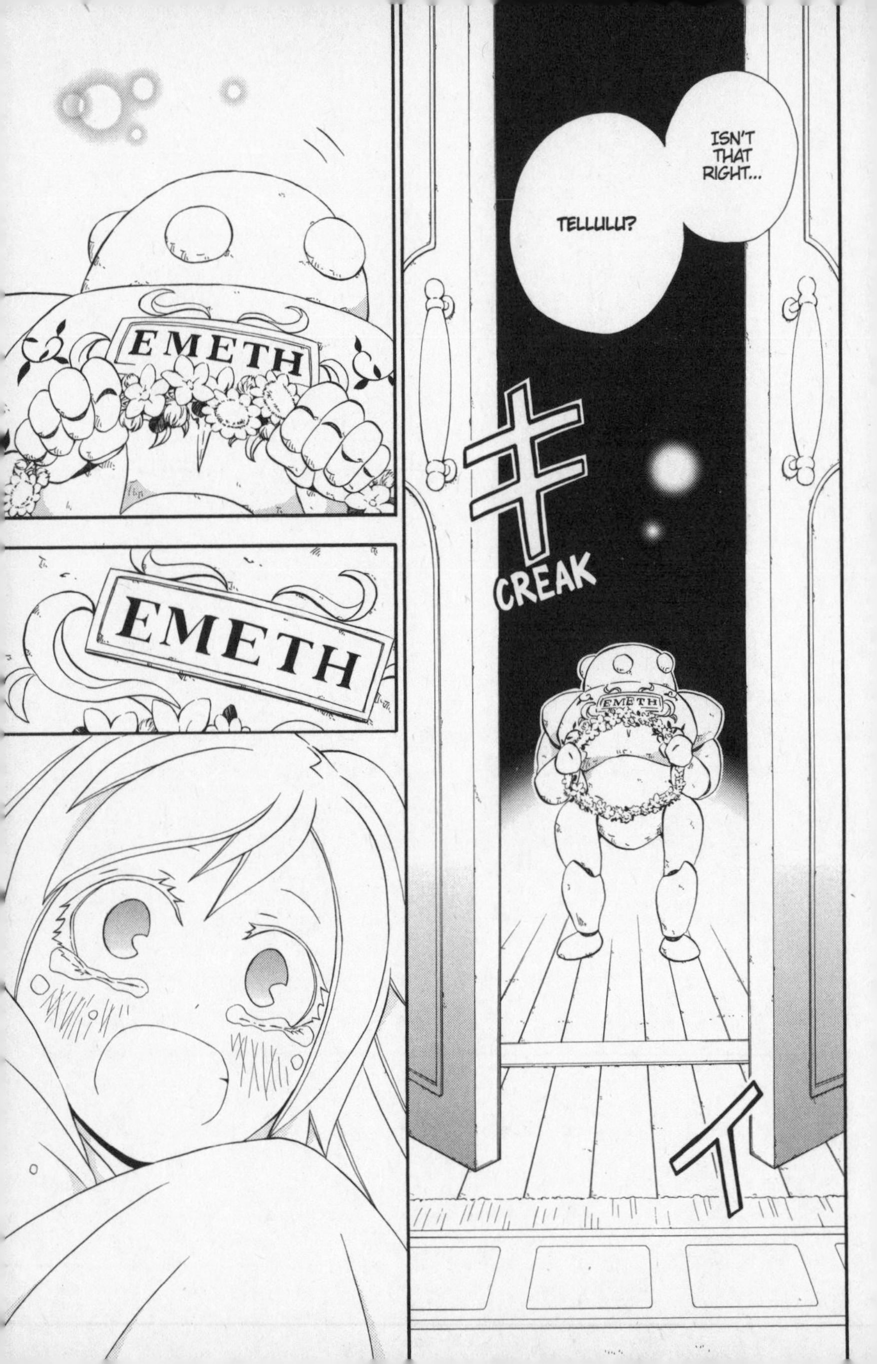
ISN'T THAT RIGHT...
TELLULU?
CREAK
EMETH
EMETH

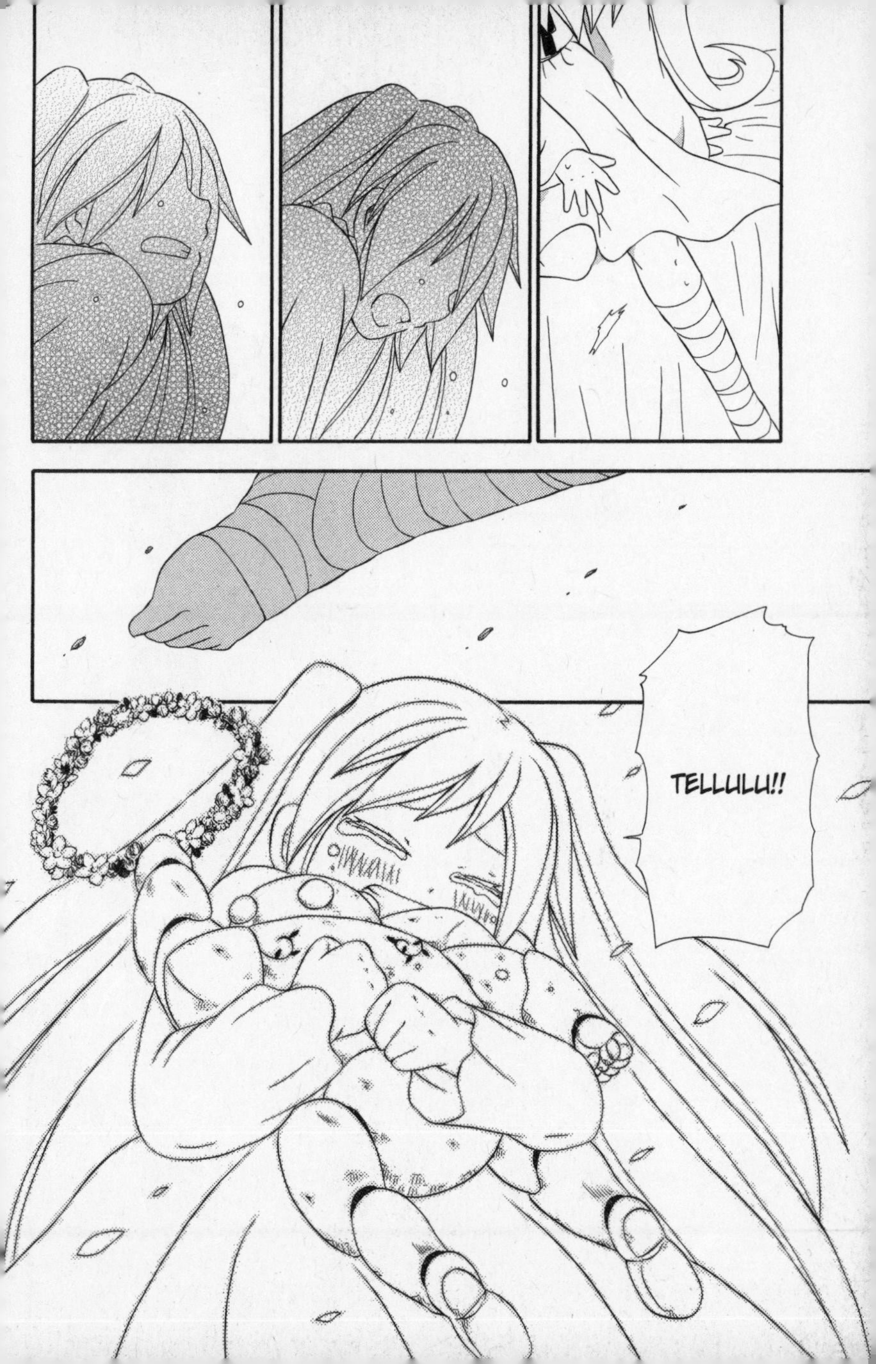
TELLULU!!

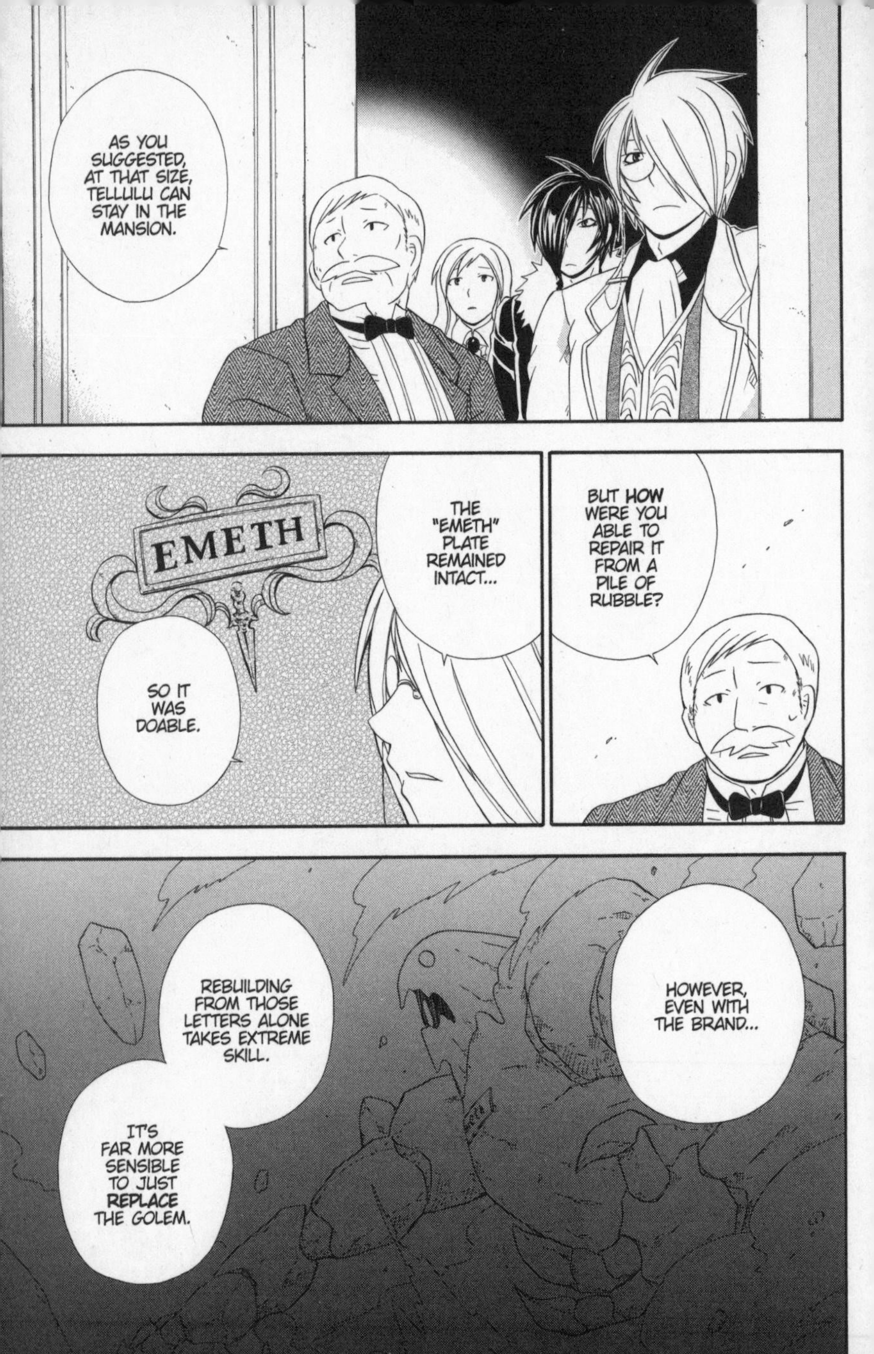
AS YOU SUGGESTED, AT THAT SIZE, TELLULU CAN STAY IN THE MANSION.
BUT **HOW** WERE YOU ABLE TO REPAIR IT FROM A PILE OF RUBBLE?
THE "EMETH" PLATE REMAINED INTACT...
EMETH
SO IT WAS DOABLE.
HOWEVER, EVEN WITH THE BRAND...
REBUILDING FROM THOSE LETTERS ALONE TAKES EXTREME SKILL.
IT'S FAR MORE SENSIBLE TO JUST **REPLACE** THE GOLEM.

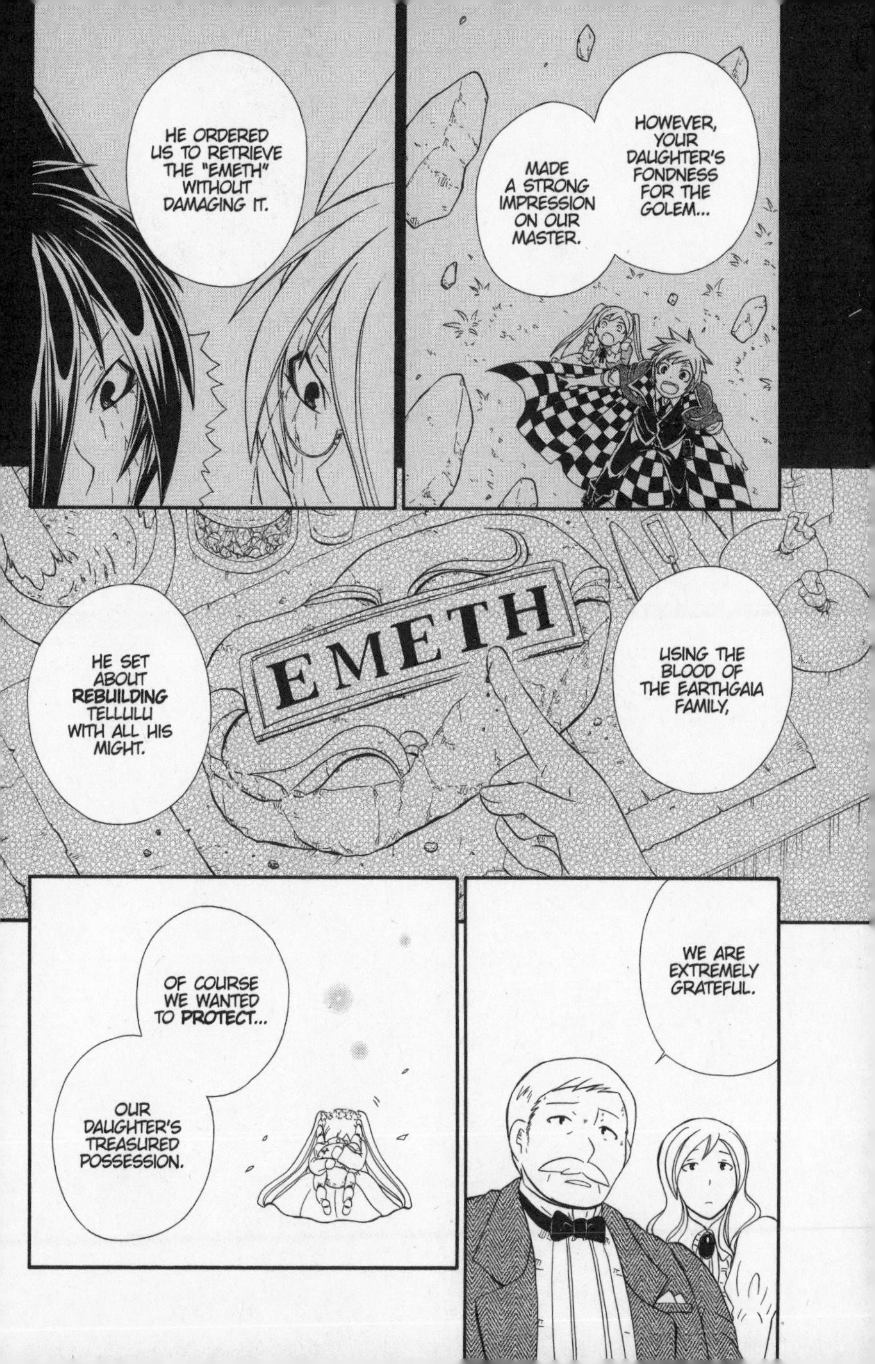
HOWEVER, YOUR DAUGHTER'S FONDNESS FOR THE GOLEM...
MADE A STRONG IMPRESSION ON OUR MASTER.
HE ORDERED US TO RETRIEVE THE "EMETH" WITHOUT DAMAGING IT.
EMETH
USING THE BLOOD OF THE EARTHGAIA FAMILY,
HE SET ABOUT **REBUILDING** TELLULU WITH ALL HIS MIGHT.
WE ARE EXTREMELY GRATEFUL.
OF COURSE WE WANTED TO **PROTECT**...
OUR DAUGHTER'S TREASURED POSSESSION.

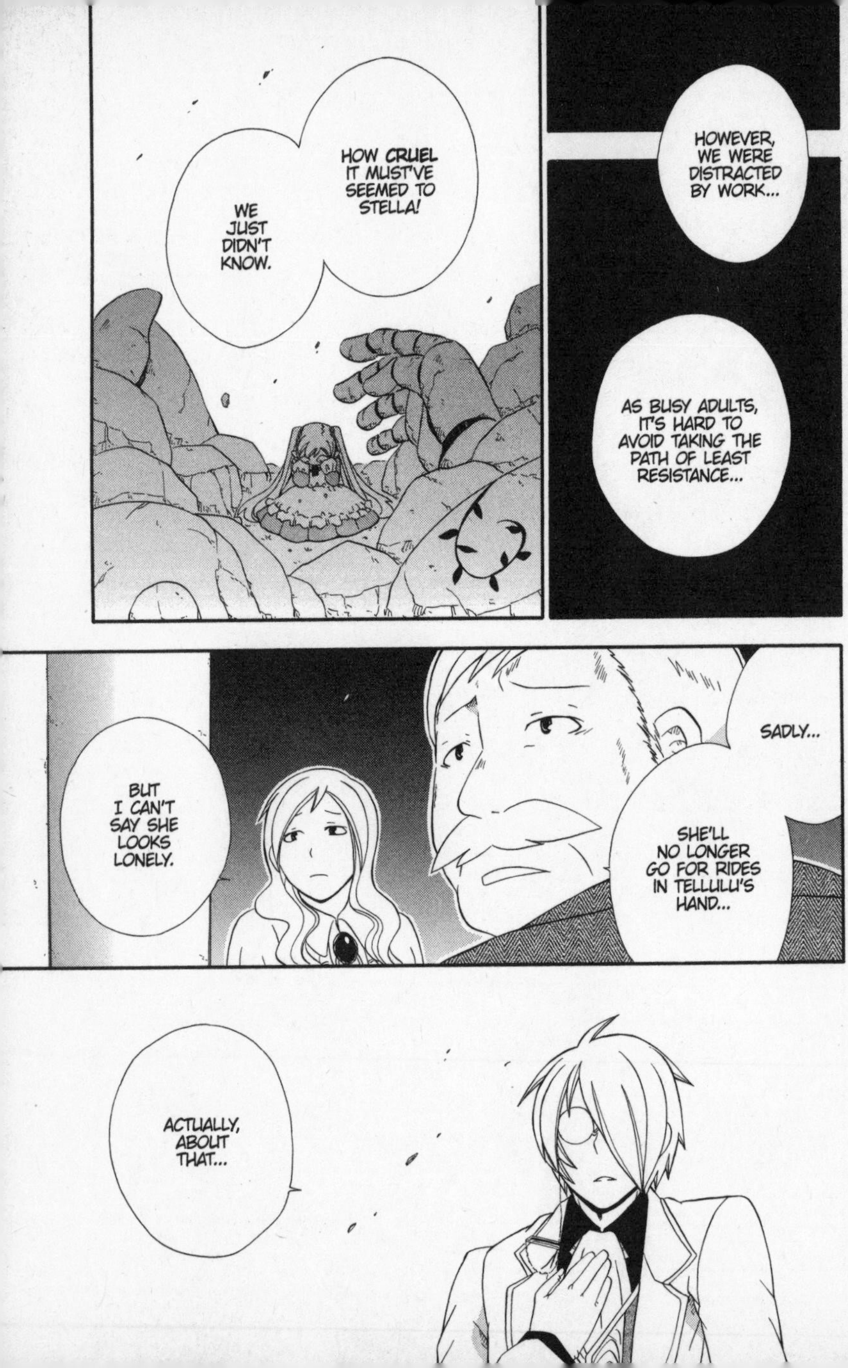
HOWEVER, WE WERE DISTRACTED BY WORK...
AS BUSY ADULTS, IT'S HARD TO AVOID TAKING THE PATH OF LEAST RESISTANCE...
HOW CRUEL IT MUST'VE SEEMED TO STELLA!
WE JUST DIDN'T KNOW.
SADLY...
SHE'LL NO LONGER GO FOR RIDES IN TELLULULI'S HAND...
BUT I CAN'T SAY SHE LOOKS LONELY.
ACTUALLY, ABOUT THAT...

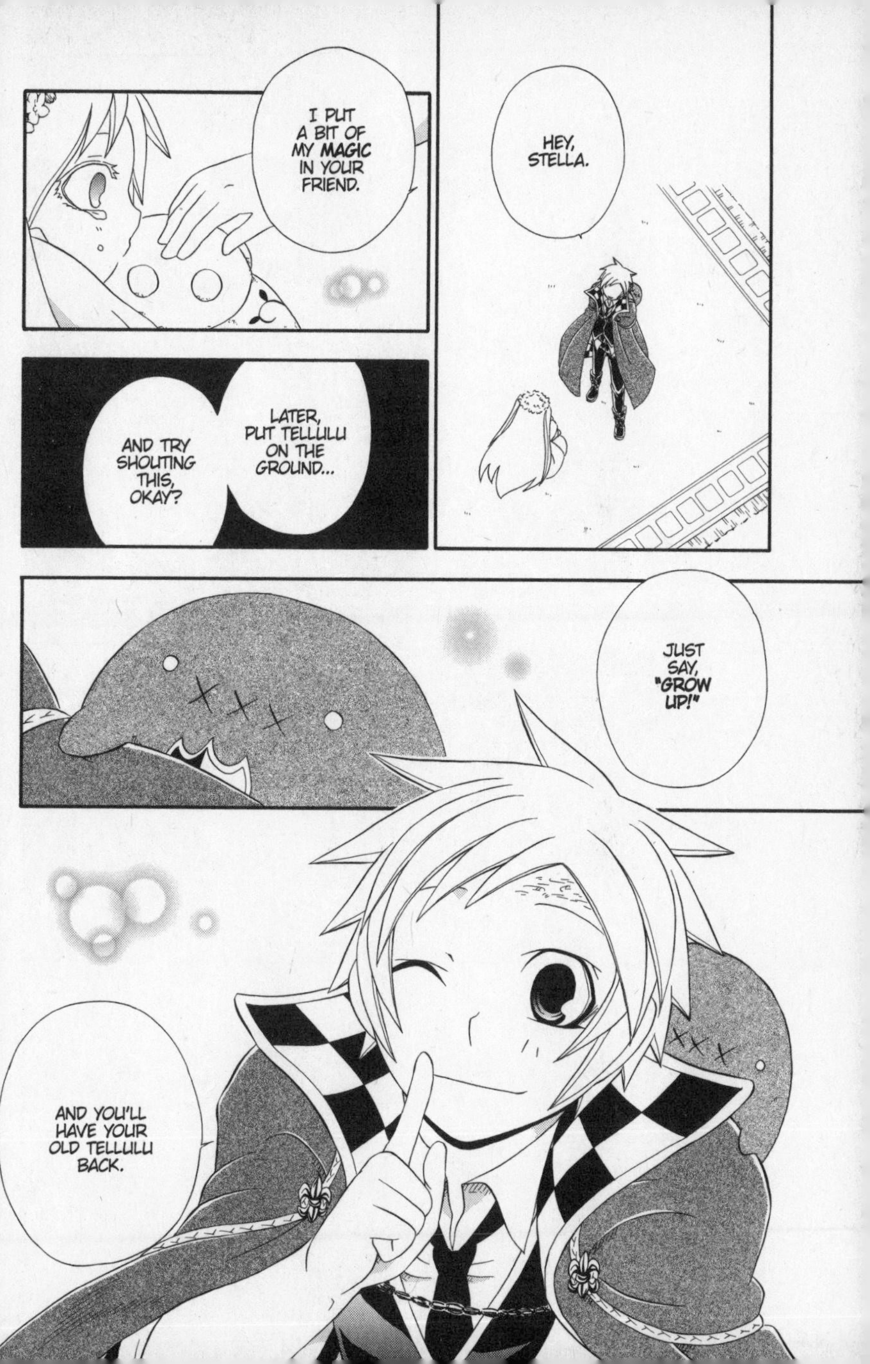
HEY, STELLA.
I PUT A BIT OF MY **MAGIC** IN YOUR FRIEND.
LATER, PUT TELLULU ON THE GROUND...
AND TRY SHOUTING THIS, OKAY?
JUST SAY, "GROW UP!"
AND YOU'LL HAVE YOUR OLD TELLULU BACK.

Chapter 9: Secret

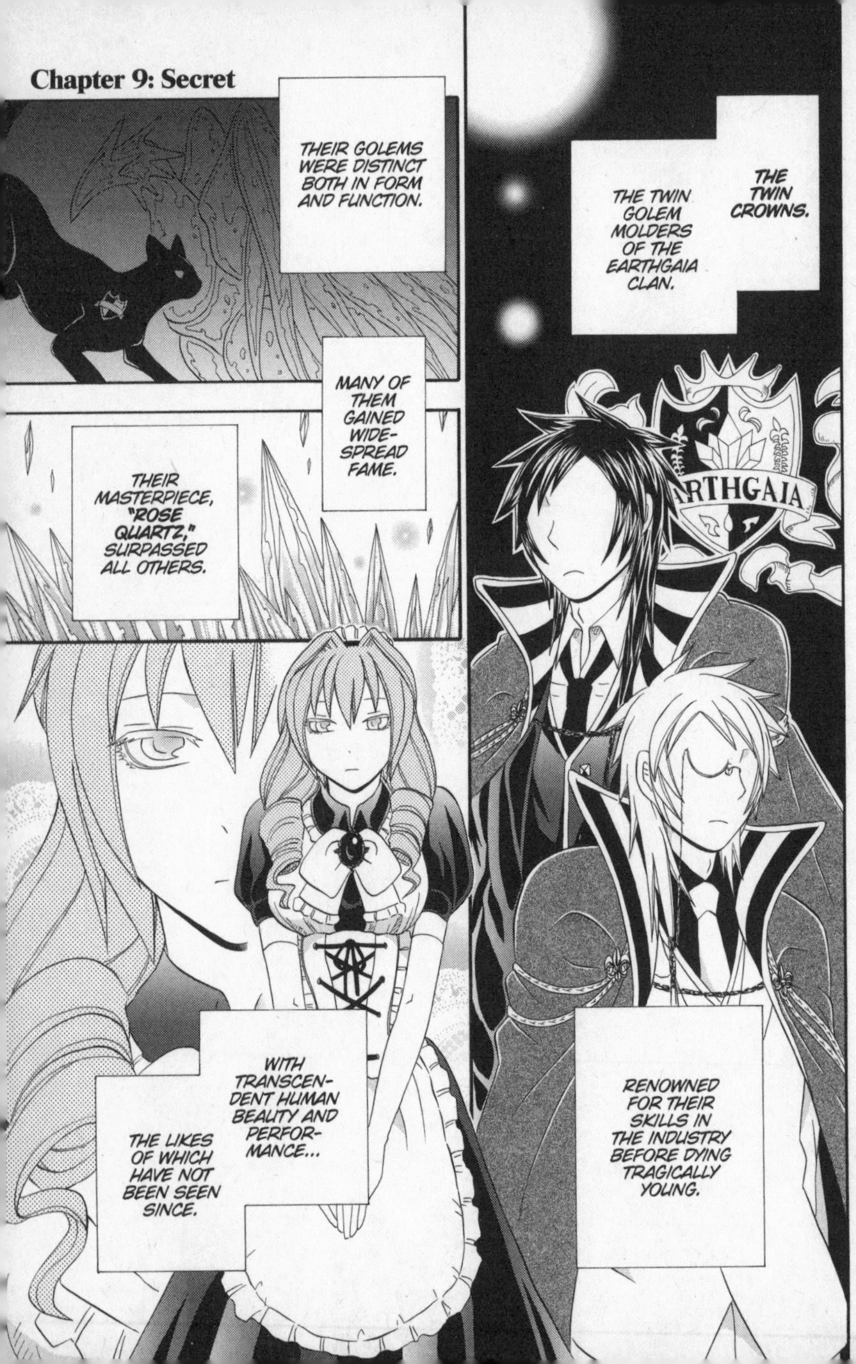
THE TWIN CROWNS.
THE TWIN GOLEM MOLDERS OF THE EARTHGAIA CLAN.
EARTHGAIA
RENOWNED FOR THEIR SKILLS IN THE INDUSTRY BEFORE DYING TRAGICALLY YOUNG.
THEIR GOLEMS WERE DISTINCT BOTH IN FORM AND FUNCTION.
MANY OF THEM GAINED WIDE-SPREAD FAME.
THEIR MASTERPIECE, "ROSE QUARTZ," SURPASSED ALL OTHERS.
WITH TRANSCEN-DENT HUMAN BEAUTY AND PERFOR-MANCE...
THE LIKES OF WHICH HAVE NOT BEEN SEEN SINCE.

Chapter 9: Secret

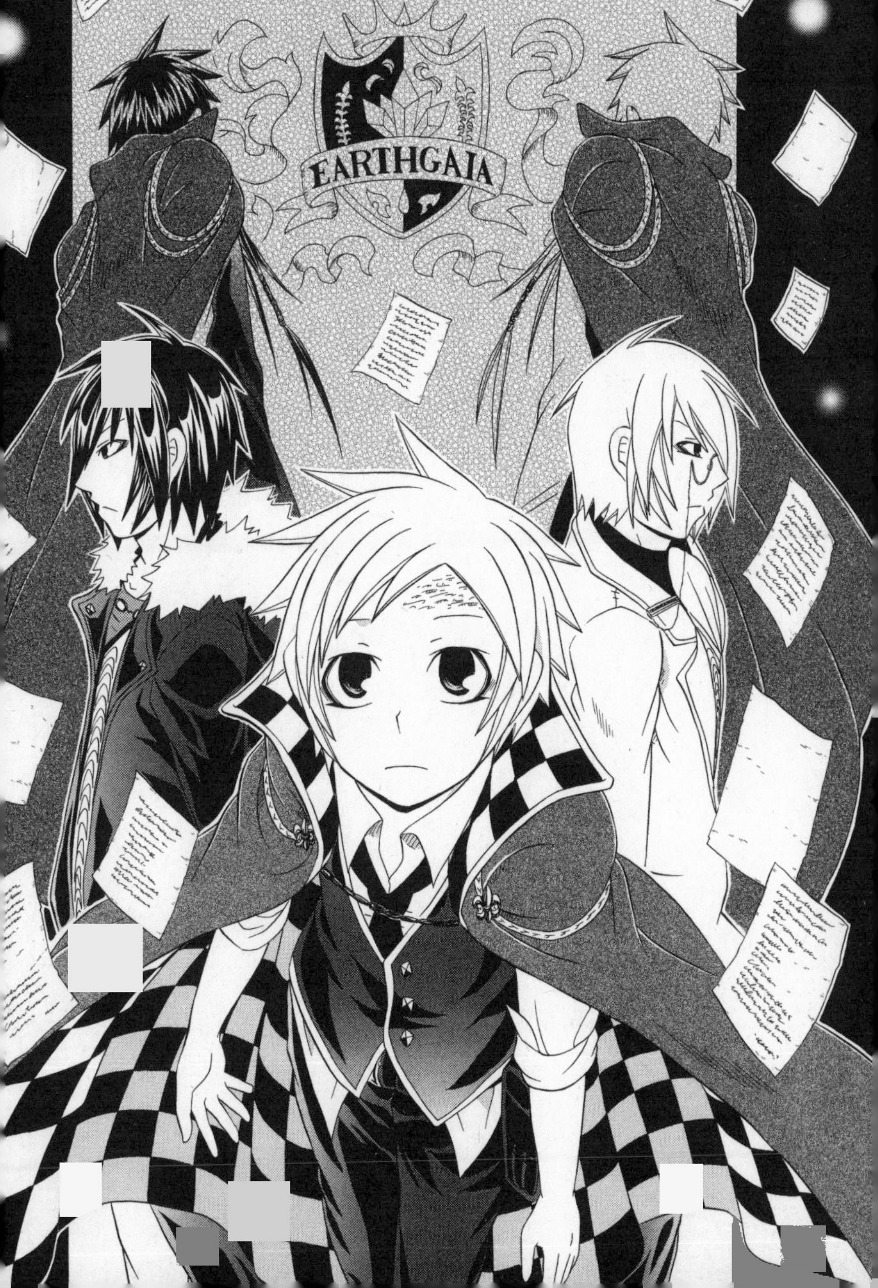
EARTHGAIA

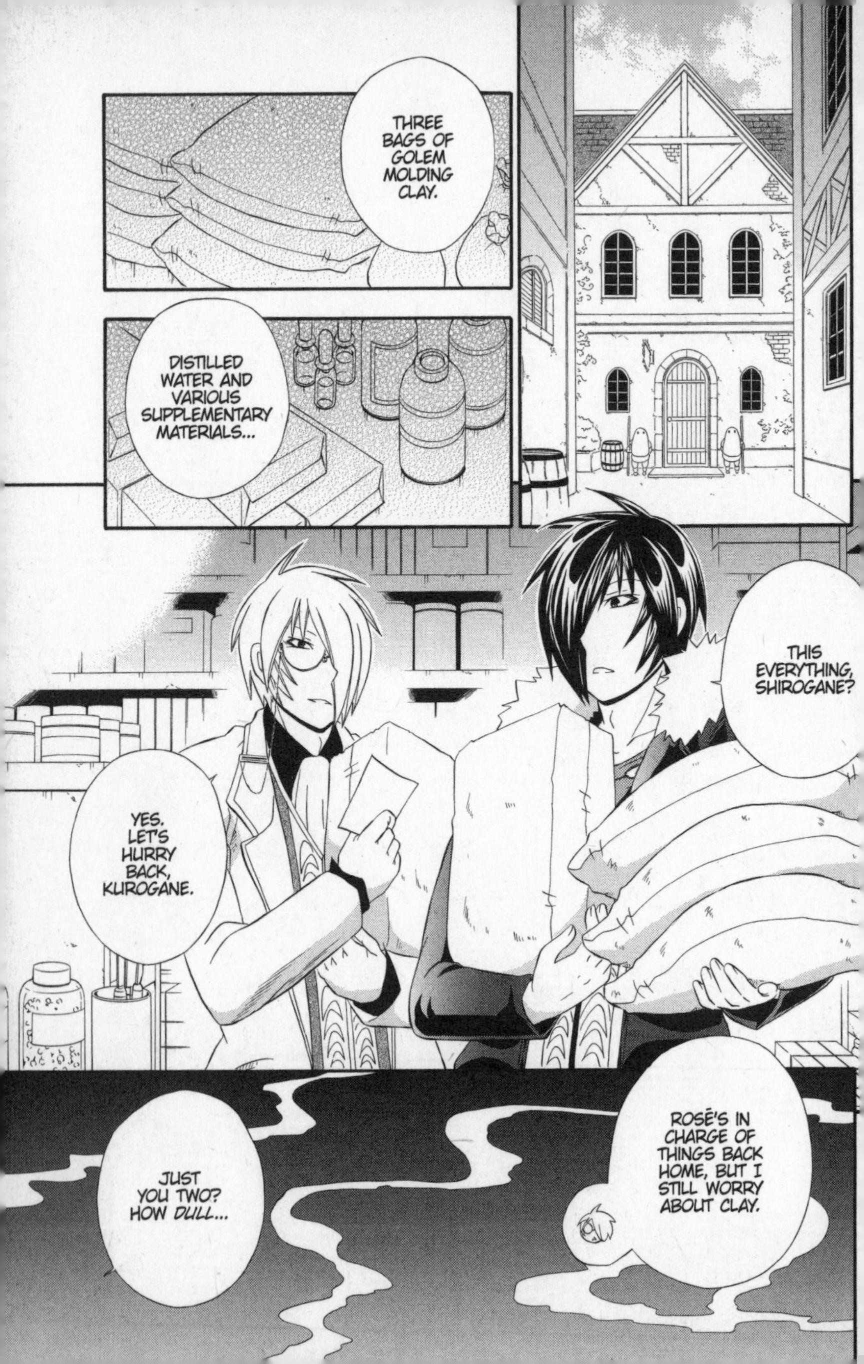
THREE BAGS OF GOLEM MOLDING CLAY.
DISTILLED WATER AND VARIOUS SUPPLEMENTARY MATERIALS...
THIS EVERYTHING, SHIROGANE?
YES. LET'S HURRY BACK, KUROGANE.
ROSÉ'S IN CHARGE OF THINGS BACK HOME, BUT I STILL WORRY ABOUT CLAY.
JUST YOU TWO? HOW *DULL*...

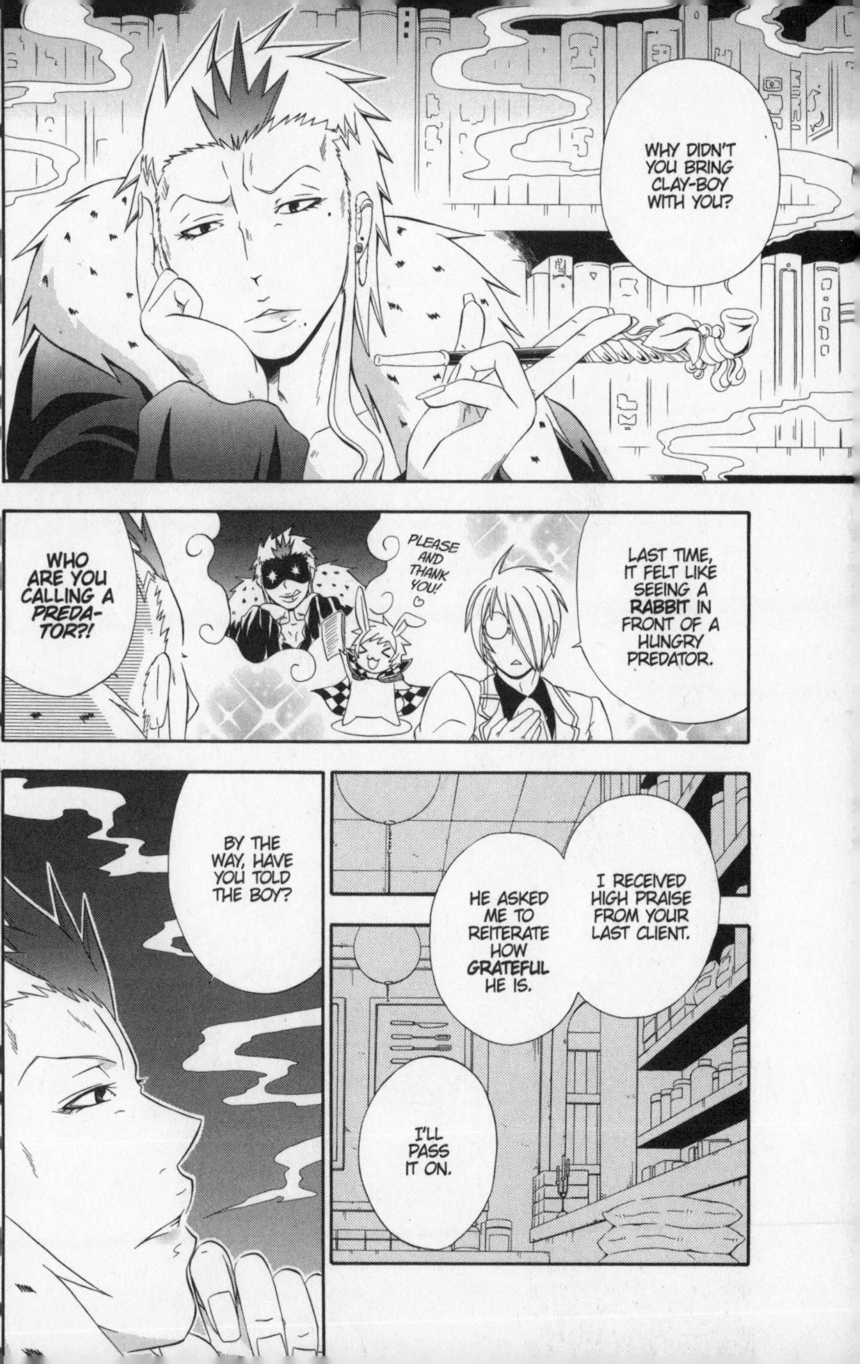
WHY DIDN'T YOU BRING CLAY-BOY WITH YOU?
LAST TIME, IT FELT LIKE SEEING A RABBIT IN FRONT OF A HUNGRY PREDATOR.
PLEASE AND THANK YOU!
WHO ARE YOU CALLING A PREDA-TOR?!
I RECEIVED HIGH PRAISE FROM YOUR LAST CLIENT.
HE ASKED ME TO REITERATE HOW GRATEFUL HE IS.
I'LL PASS IT ON.
BY THE WAY, HAVE YOU TOLD THE BOY?

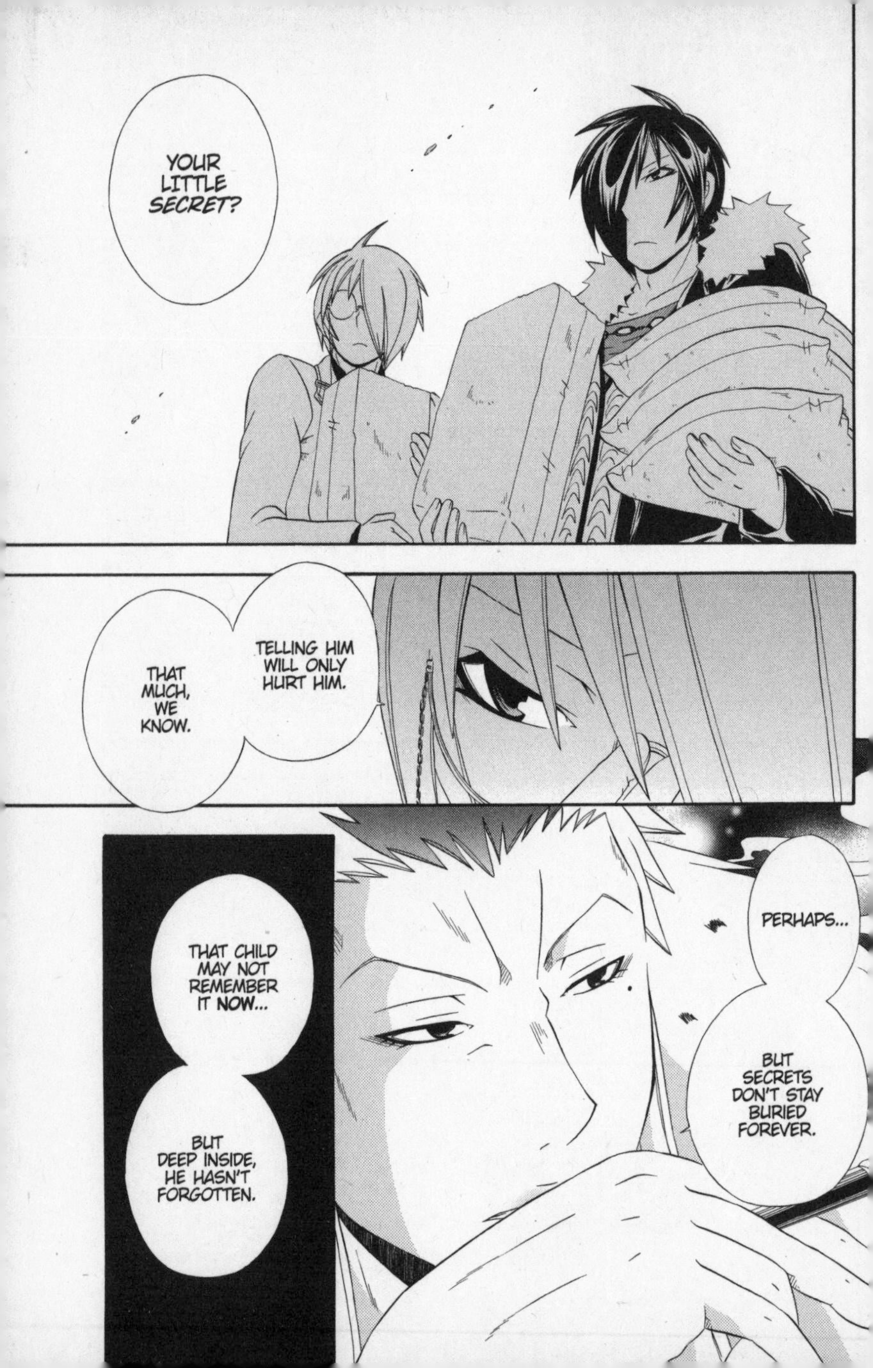
YOUR LITTLE SECRET?
TELLING HIM WILL ONLY HURT HIM.
THAT MUCH, WE KNOW.
PERHAPS...
BUT SECRETS DON'T STAY BURIED FOREVER.
THAT CHILD MAY NOT REMEMBER IT NOW...
BUT DEEP INSIDE, HE HASN'T FORGOTTEN.

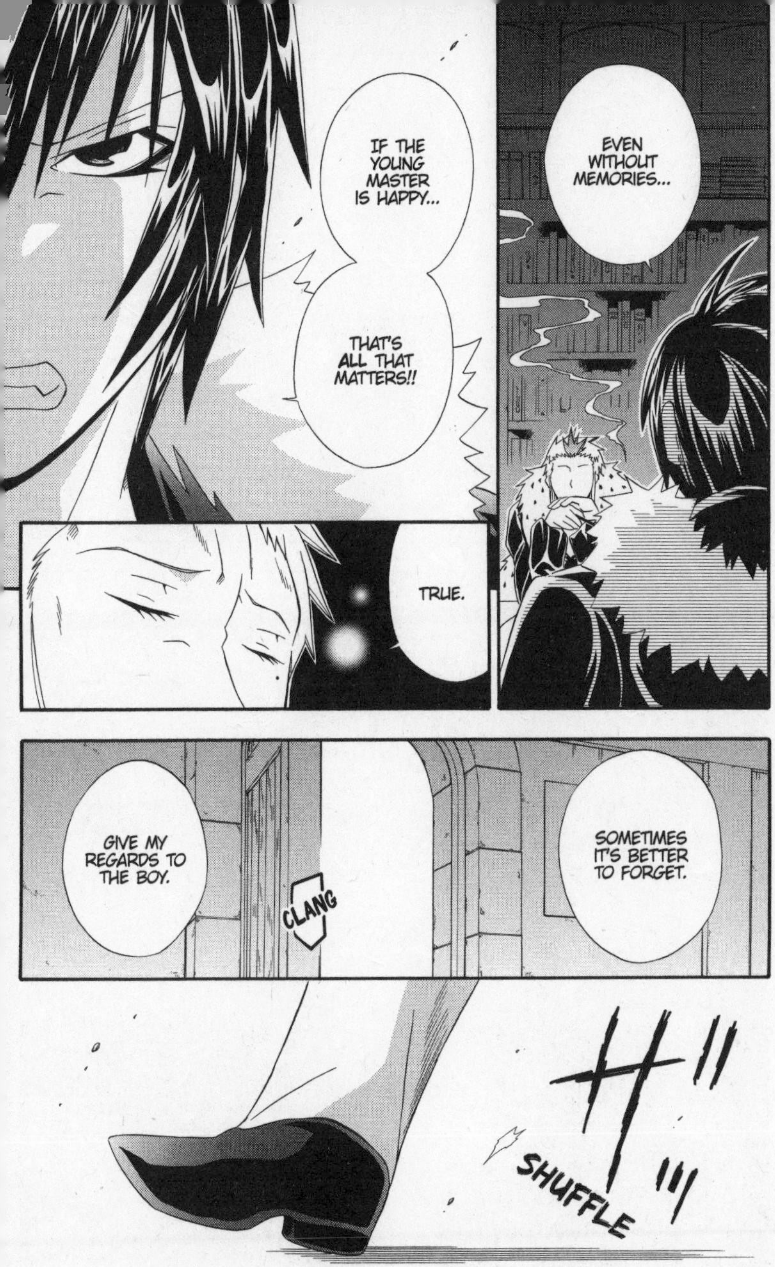
EVEN WITHOUT MEMORIES...
IF THE YOUNG MASTER IS HAPPY...
THAT'S ALL THAT MATTERS!!
TRUE.
SOMETIMES IT'S BETTER TO FORGET.
CLANG
GIVE MY REGARDS TO THE BOY.
SHUFFLE

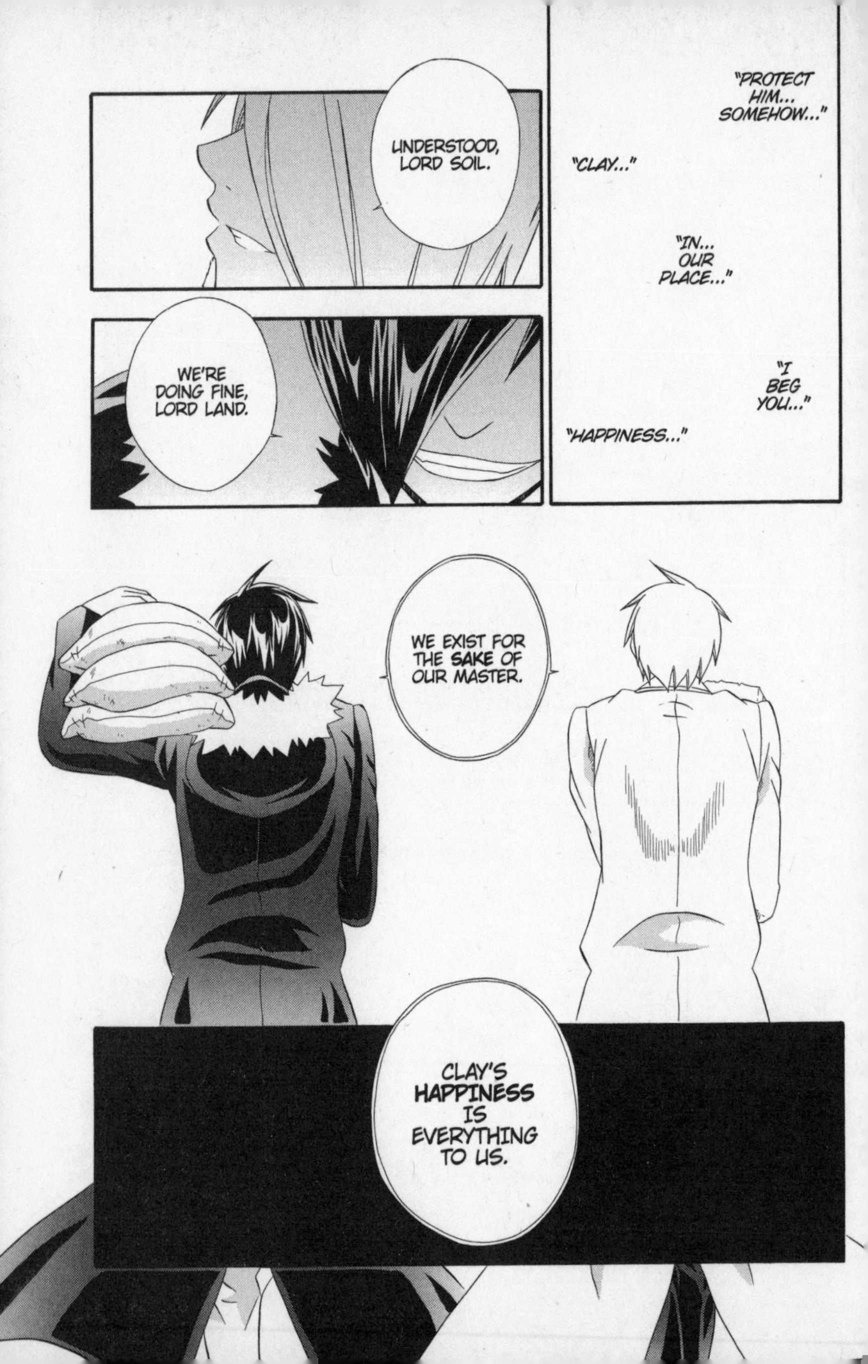
"PROTECT HIM... SOMEHOW..."
"CLAY..."
"IN... OUR PLACE..."
"I BEG YOU..."
"HAPPINESS..."
UNDERSTOOD, LORD SOIL.
WE'RE DOING FINE, LORD LAND.
WE EXIST FOR THE SAKE OF OUR MASTER.
CLAY'S HAPPINESS IS EVERYTHING TO US.

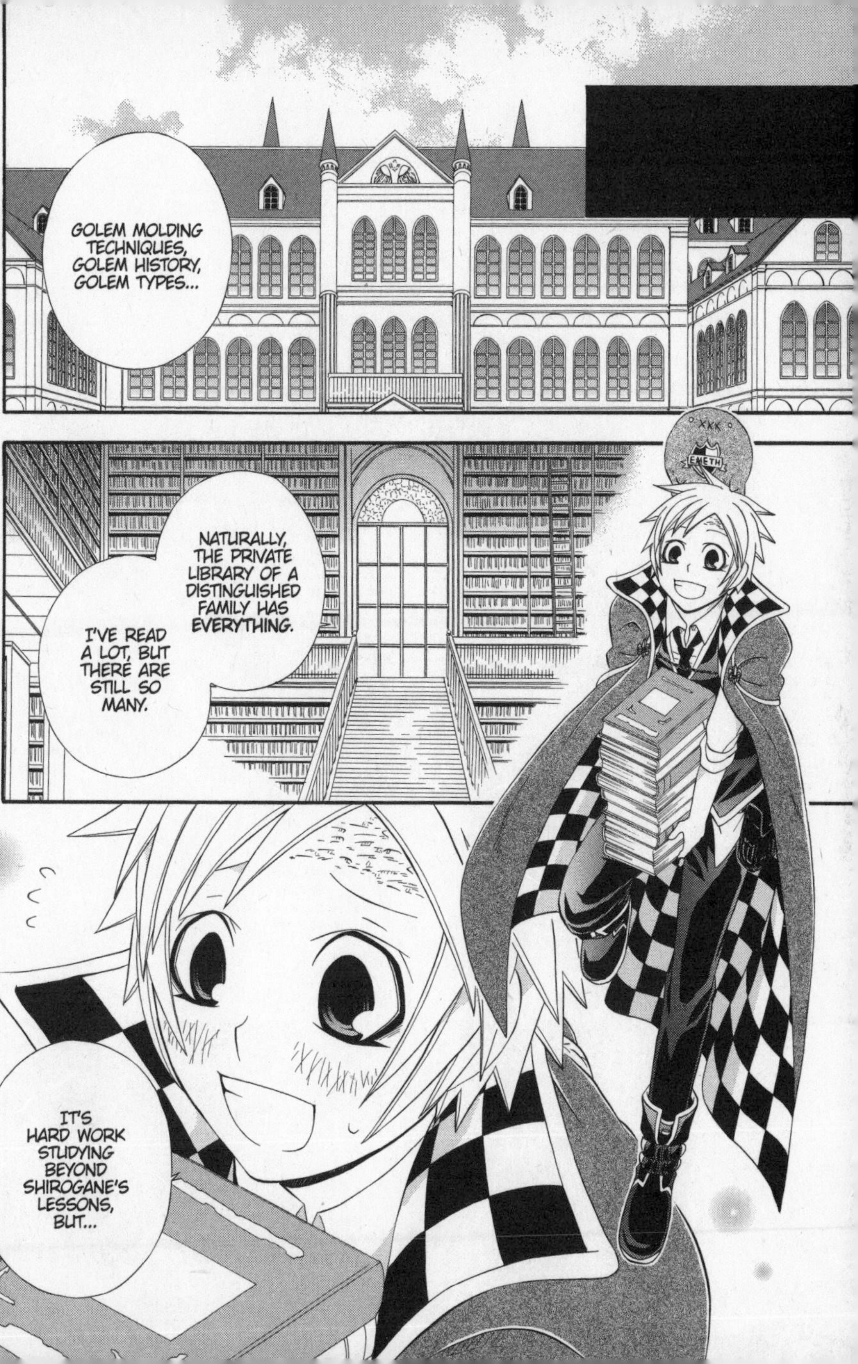
[redacted]
GOLEM MOLDING TECHNIQUES, GOLEM HISTORY, GOLEM TYPES...
EMETH
NATURALLY, THE PRIVATE LIBRARY OF A DISTINGUISHED FAMILY HAS EVERYTHING.
I'VE READ A LOT, BUT THERE ARE STILL SO MANY.
IT'S HARD WORK STUDYING BEYOND SHIROGANE'S LESSONS, BUT...

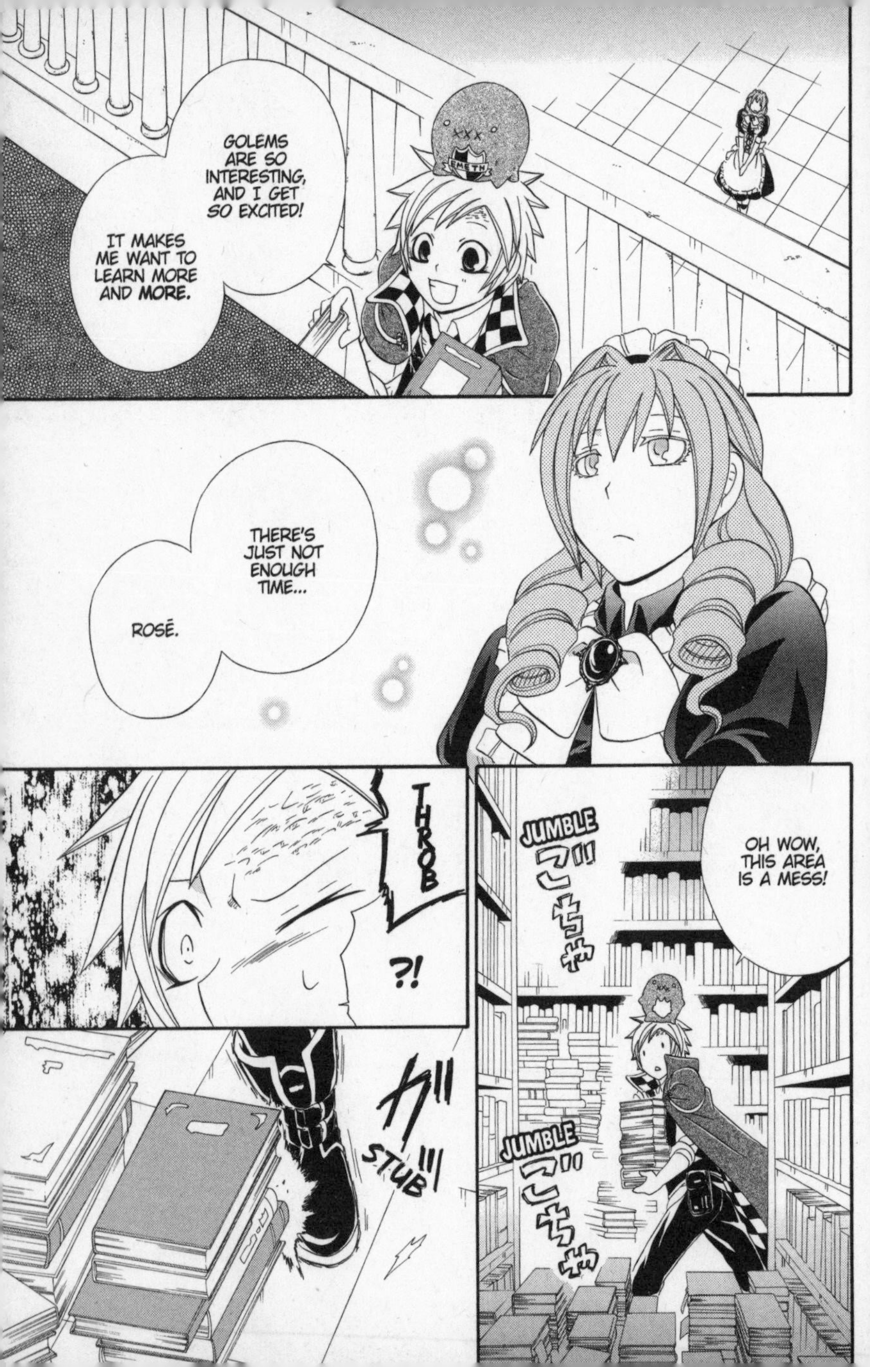
GOLEMS ARE SO INTERESTING, AND I GET SO EXCITED!
IT MAKES ME WANT TO LEARN MORE AND MORE.
THERE'S JUST NOT ENOUGH TIME...
ROSÉ.
OH WOW, THIS AREA IS A MESS!
JUMBLE
ごちゃ
JUMBLE
ごちゃ
THROB
?!
ガ
STUB
!!!

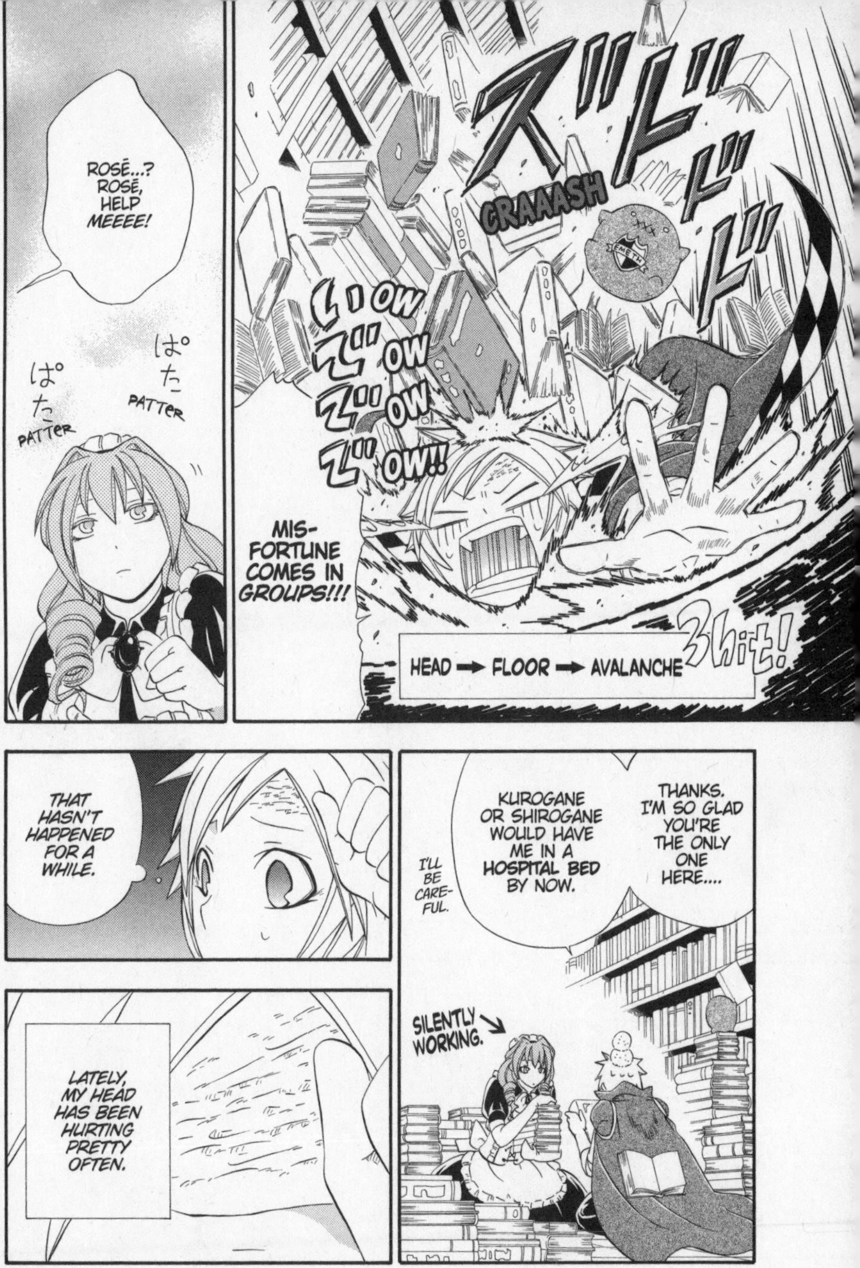
スドドド
CRAAASH
OW
OW
OW
OW!!
MIS-FORTUNE COMES IN GROUPS!!!
HEAD → FLOOR → AVALANCHE
ROSÉ...? ROSÉ, HELP MEEEE!
ぱた
PATTER
ぱた
PATTER
THANKS. I'M SO GLAD YOU'RE THE ONLY ONE HERE....
KUROGANE OR SHIROGANE WOULD HAVE ME IN A HOSPITAL BED BY NOW.
I'LL BE CAREFUL.
SILENTLY WORKING.
THAT HASN'T HAPPENED FOR A WHILE.
LATELY, MY HEAD HAS BEEN HURTING PRETTY OFTEN.

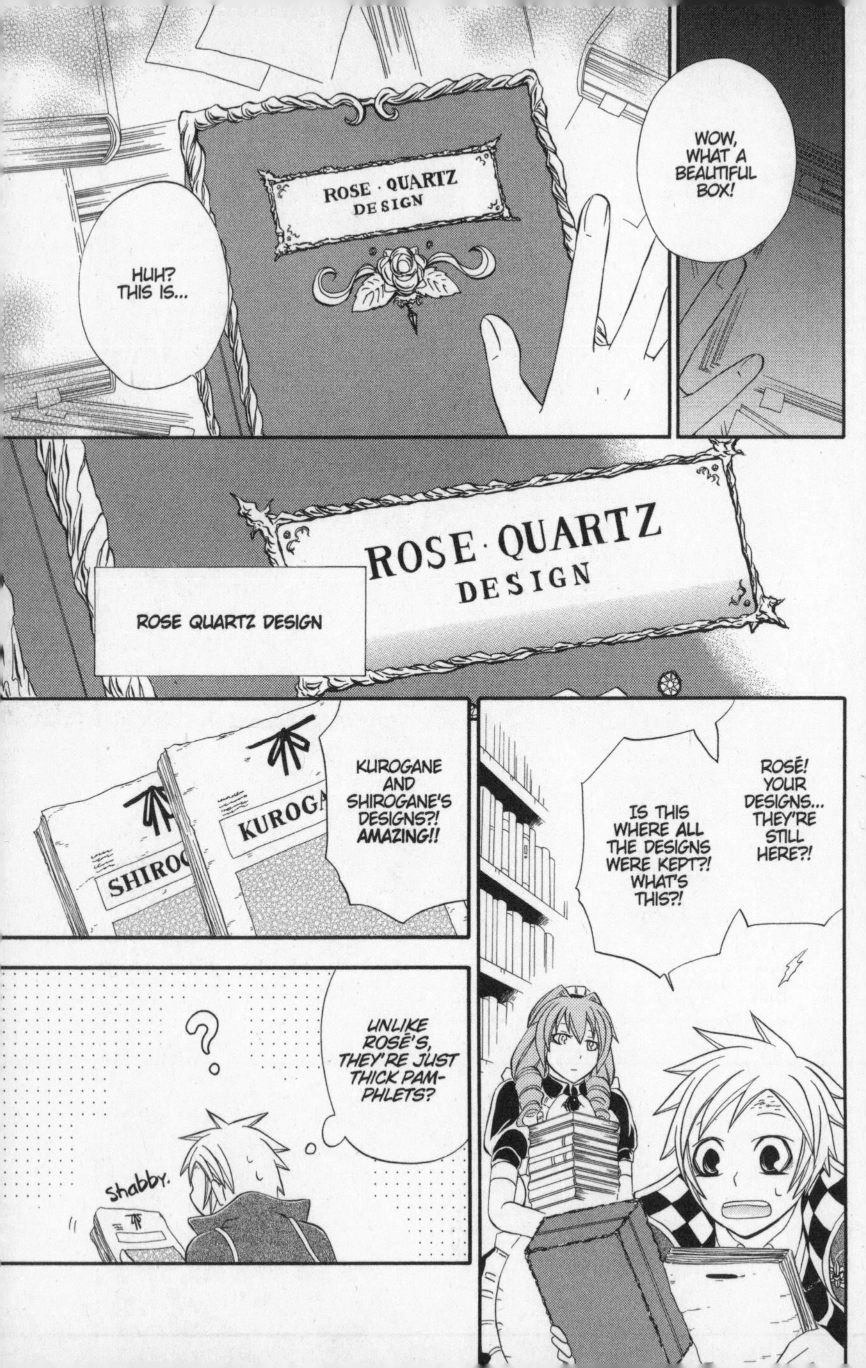
WOW, WHAT A BEAUTIFUL BOX!
ROSE · QUARTZ DESIGN
HUH? THIS IS...
ROSE · QUARTZ DESIGN
ROSE QUARTZ DESIGN
ROSÉ! YOUR DESIGNS... THEY'RE STILL HERE?!
IS THIS WHERE ALL THE DESIGNS WERE KEPT?! WHAT'S THIS?!
KUROGANE AND SHIROGANE'S DESIGNS?! AMAZING!!
UNLIKE ROSÉ'S, THEY'RE JUST THICK PAMPHLETS?
Shabby.

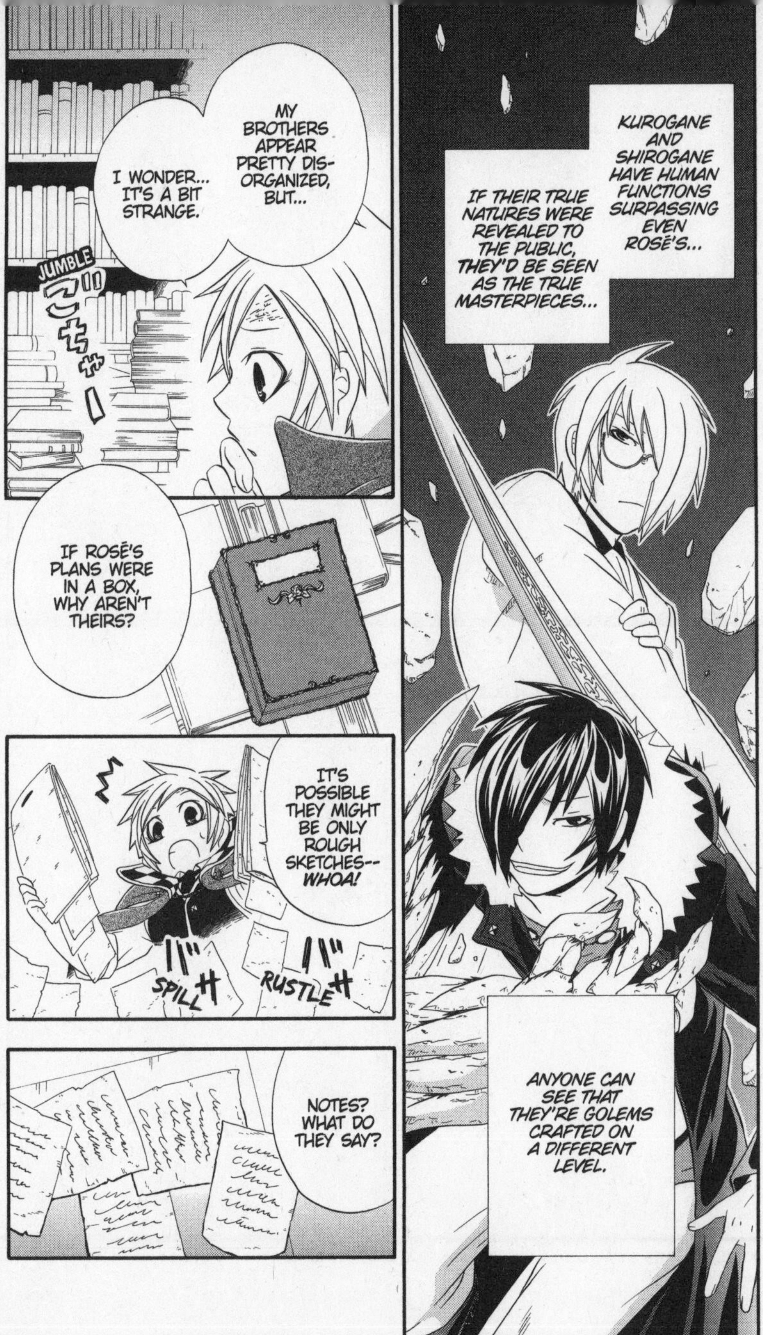
KUROGANE AND SHIROGANE HAVE HUMAN FUNCTIONS SURPASSING EVEN ROSÉ'S...
IF THEIR TRUE NATURES WERE REVEALED TO THE PUBLIC, THEY'D BE SEEN AS THE TRUE MASTERPIECES...
ANYONE CAN SEE THAT THEY'RE GOLEMS CRAFTED ON A DIFFERENT LEVEL.
MY BROTHERS APPEAR PRETTY DIS-ORGANIZED, BUT...
I WONDER... IT'S A BIT STRANGE.
JUMBLE
IF ROSÉ'S PLANS WERE IN A BOX, WHY AREN'T THEIRS?
IT'S POSSIBLE THEY MIGHT BE ONLY ROUGH SKETCHES--*WHOA!*
SPILL
RUSTLE
NOTES? WHAT DO THEY SAY?

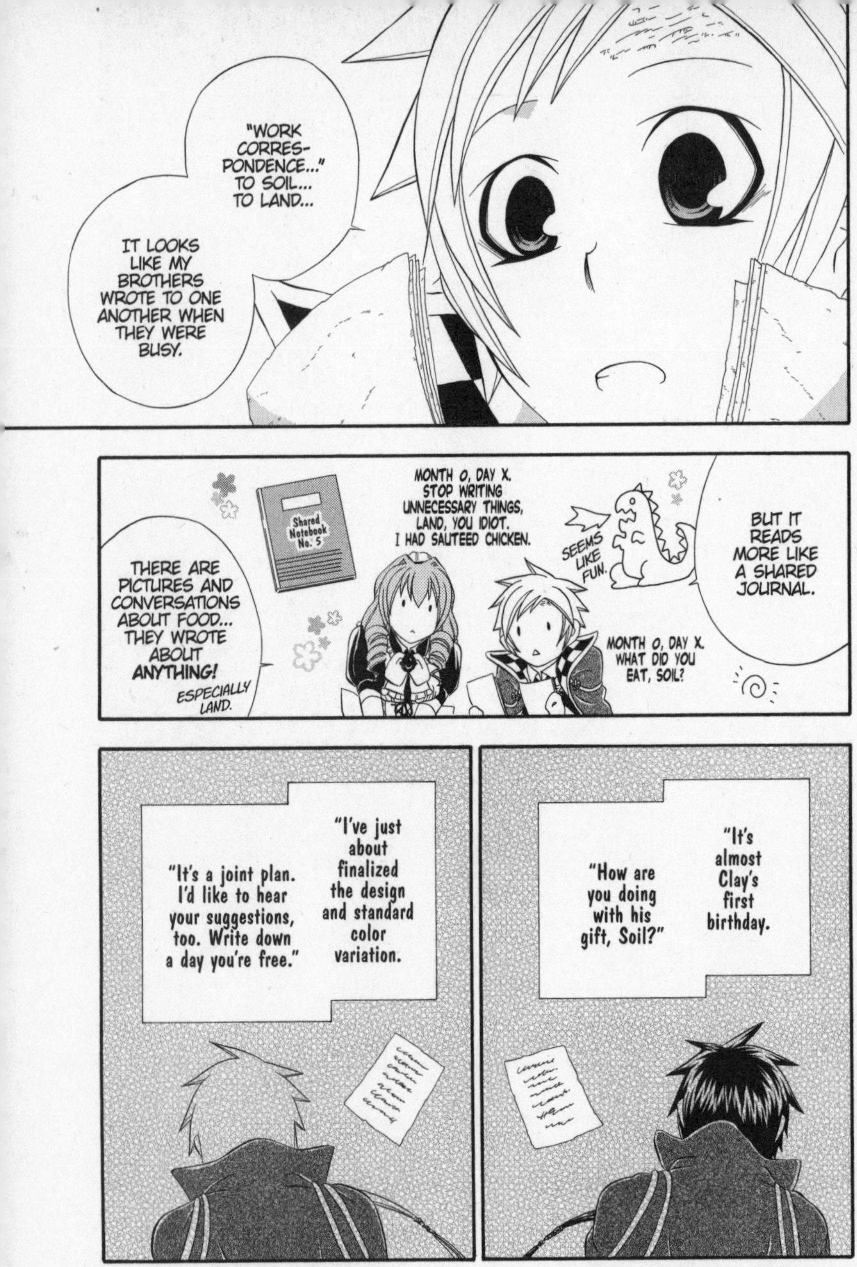
"WORK CORRES-PONDENCE..." TO SOIL... TO LAND...
IT LOOKS LIKE MY BROTHERS WROTE TO ONE ANOTHER WHEN THEY WERE BUSY.
BUT IT READS MORE LIKE A SHARED JOURNAL.
SEEMS LIKE FUN.
MONTH O, DAY X. STOP WRITING UNNECESSARY THINGS, LAND, YOU IDIOT. I HAD SAUTEED CHICKEN.
Shared Notebook No. 5
THERE ARE PICTURES AND CONVERSATIONS ABOUT FOOD... THEY WROTE ABOUT ANYTHING!
MONTH O, DAY X. WHAT DID YOU EAT, SOIL?
ESPECIALLY LAND.
"It's almost Clay's first birthday.
"How are you doing with his gift, Soil?"
"I've just about finalized the design and standard color variation.
"It's a joint plan. I'd like to hear your suggestions, too. Write down a day you're free."

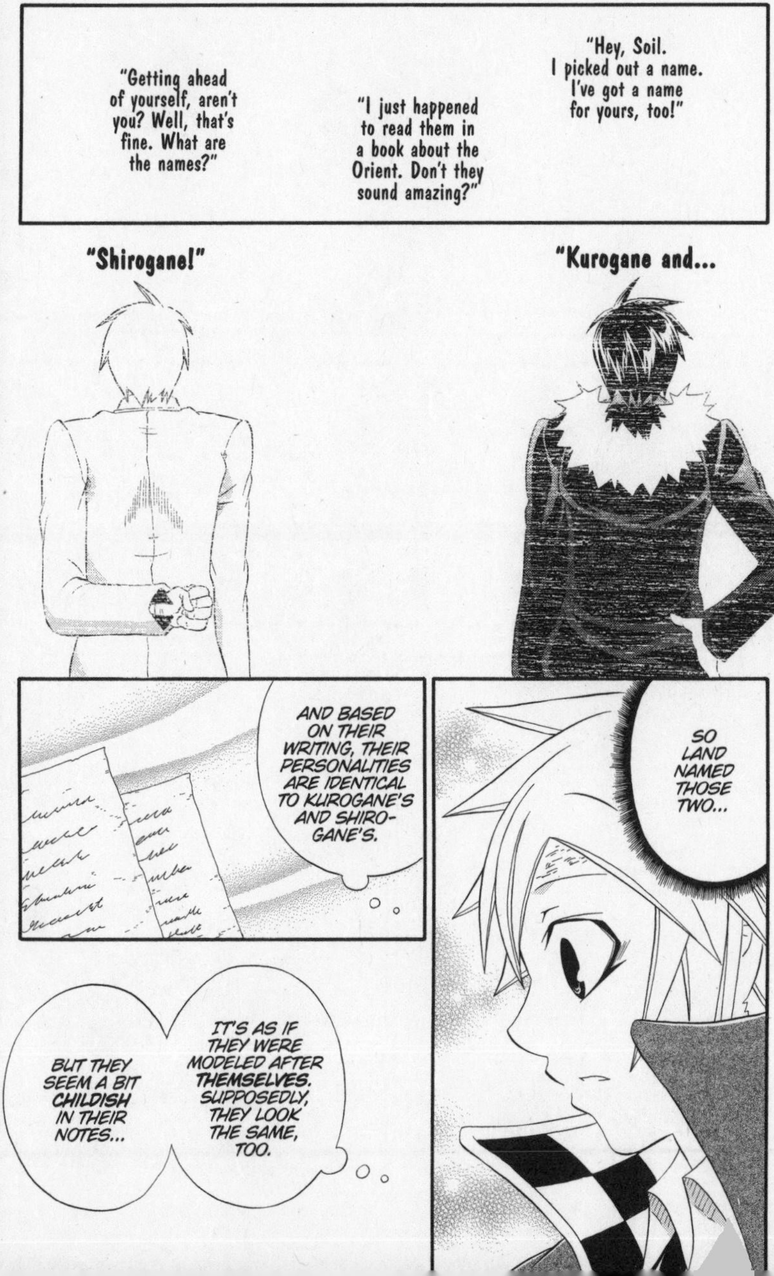
"Hey, Soil. I picked out a name. I've got a name for yours, too!"
"I just happened to read them in a book about the Orient. Don't they sound amazing?"
"Getting ahead of yourself, aren't you? Well, that's fine. What are the names?"
"Kurogane and...
"Shirogane!"
SO LAND NAMED THOSE TWO...
AND BASED ON THEIR WRITING, THEIR PERSONALITIES ARE IDENTICAL TO KUROGANE'S AND SHIRO-GANE'S.
IT'S AS IF THEY WERE MODELED AFTER THEMSELVES. SUPPOSEDLY, THEY LOOK THE SAME, TOO.
BUT THEY SEEM A BIT CHILDISH IN THEIR NOTES...

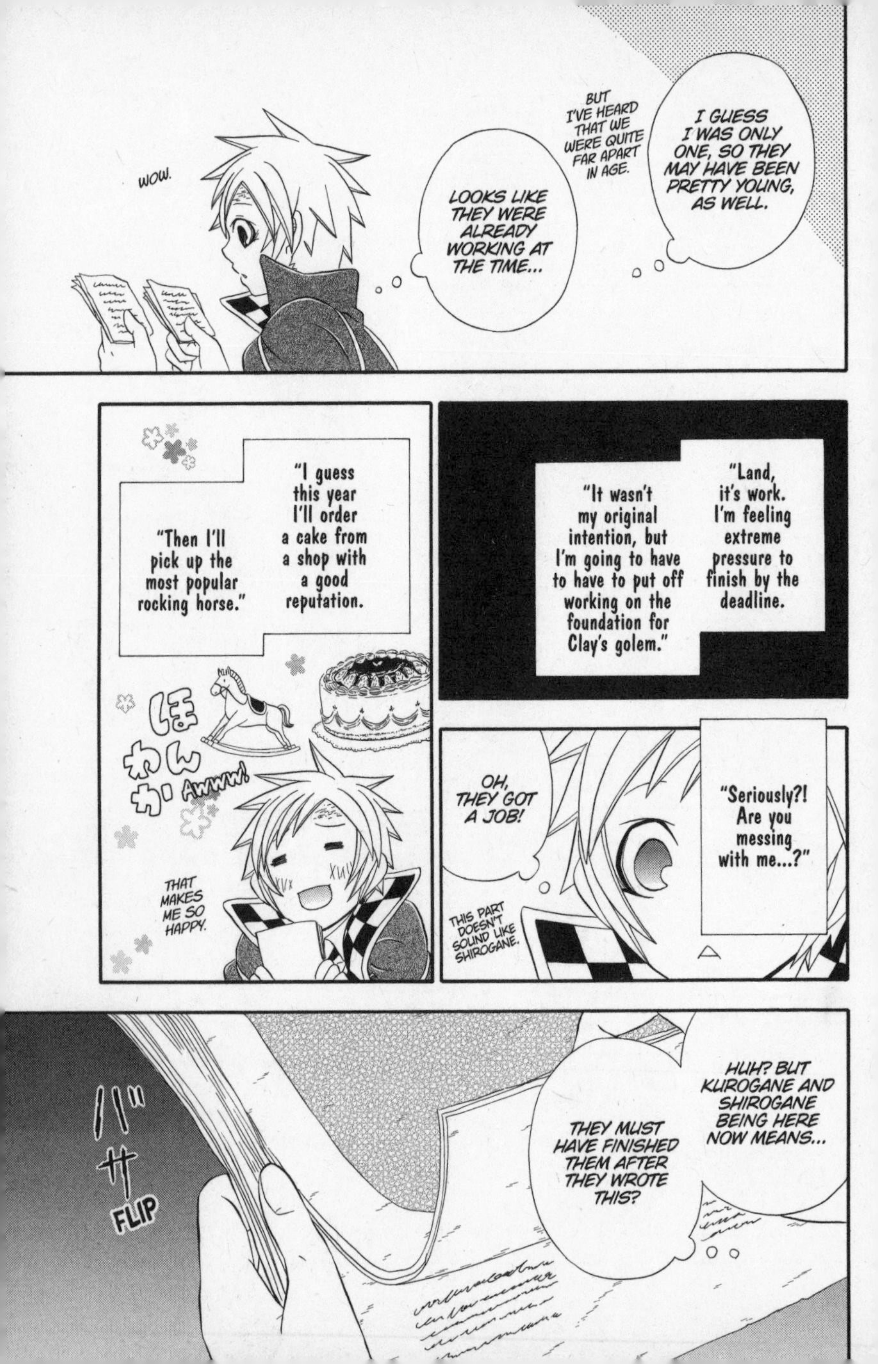
I GUESS I WAS ONLY ONE, SO THEY MAY HAVE BEEN PRETTY YOUNG, AS WELL.
BUT I'VE HEARD THAT WE WERE QUITE FAR APART IN AGE.
LOOKS LIKE THEY WERE ALREADY WORKING AT THE TIME...
WOW.
"Land, it's work. I'm feeling extreme pressure to finish by the deadline.
"It wasn't my original intention, but I'm going to have to have to put off working on the foundation for Clay's golem."
"Seriously?! Are you messing with me...?"
OH, THEY GOT A JOB!
THIS PART DOESN'T SOUND LIKE SHIROGANE.
"I guess this year I'll order a cake from a shop with a good reputation.
"Then I'll pick up the most popular rocking horse."
ほわんか
AWWW!
THAT MAKES ME SO HAPPY.
HUH? BUT KUROGANE AND SHIROGANE BEING HERE NOW MEANS...
THEY MUST HAVE FINISHED THEM AFTER THEY WROTE THIS?
バサ
FLIP

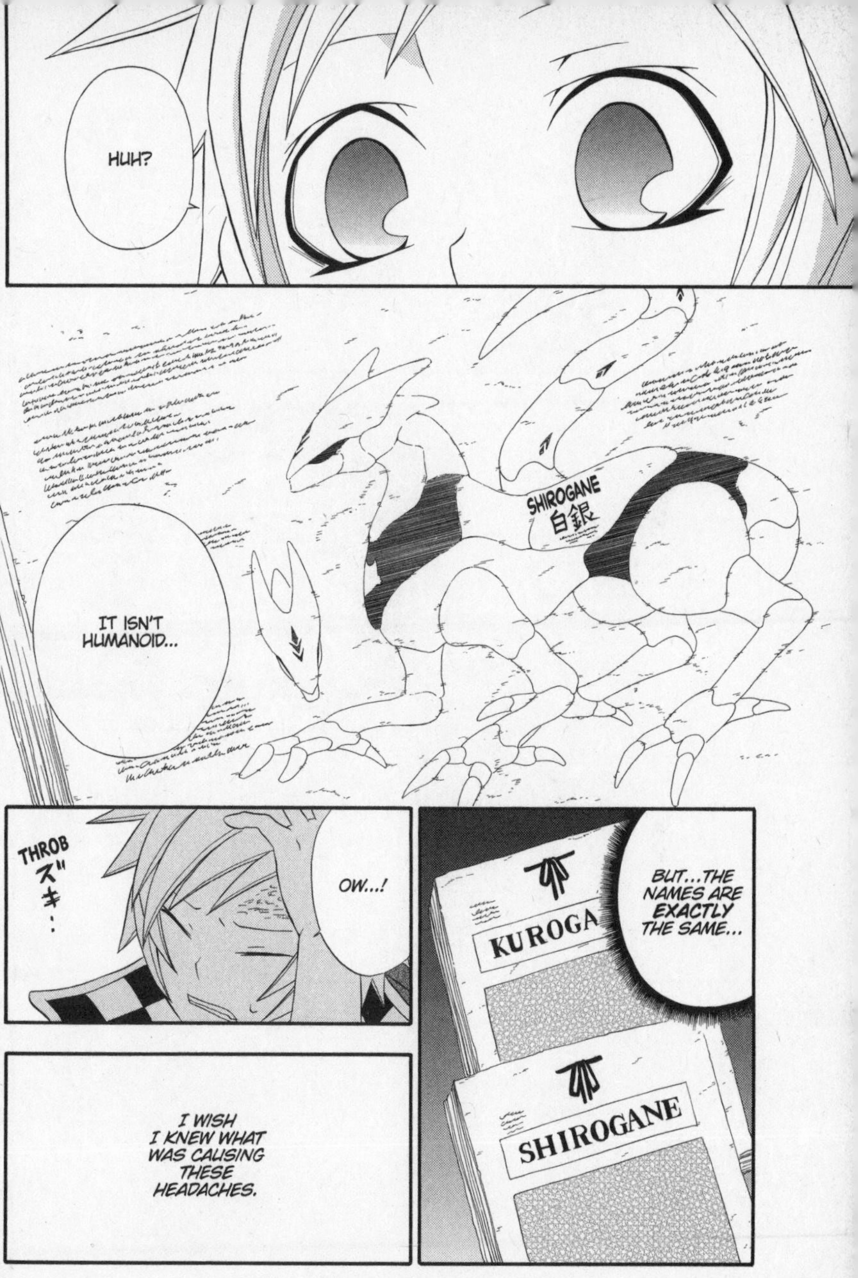
HUH?
SHIROGANE
白銀
IT ISN'T HUMANOID...
BUT...THE NAMES ARE EXACTLY THE SAME...
KUROGA
SHIROGANE
THROB
ズキ..
OW...!
I WISH I KNEW WHAT WAS CAUSING THESE HEADACHES.

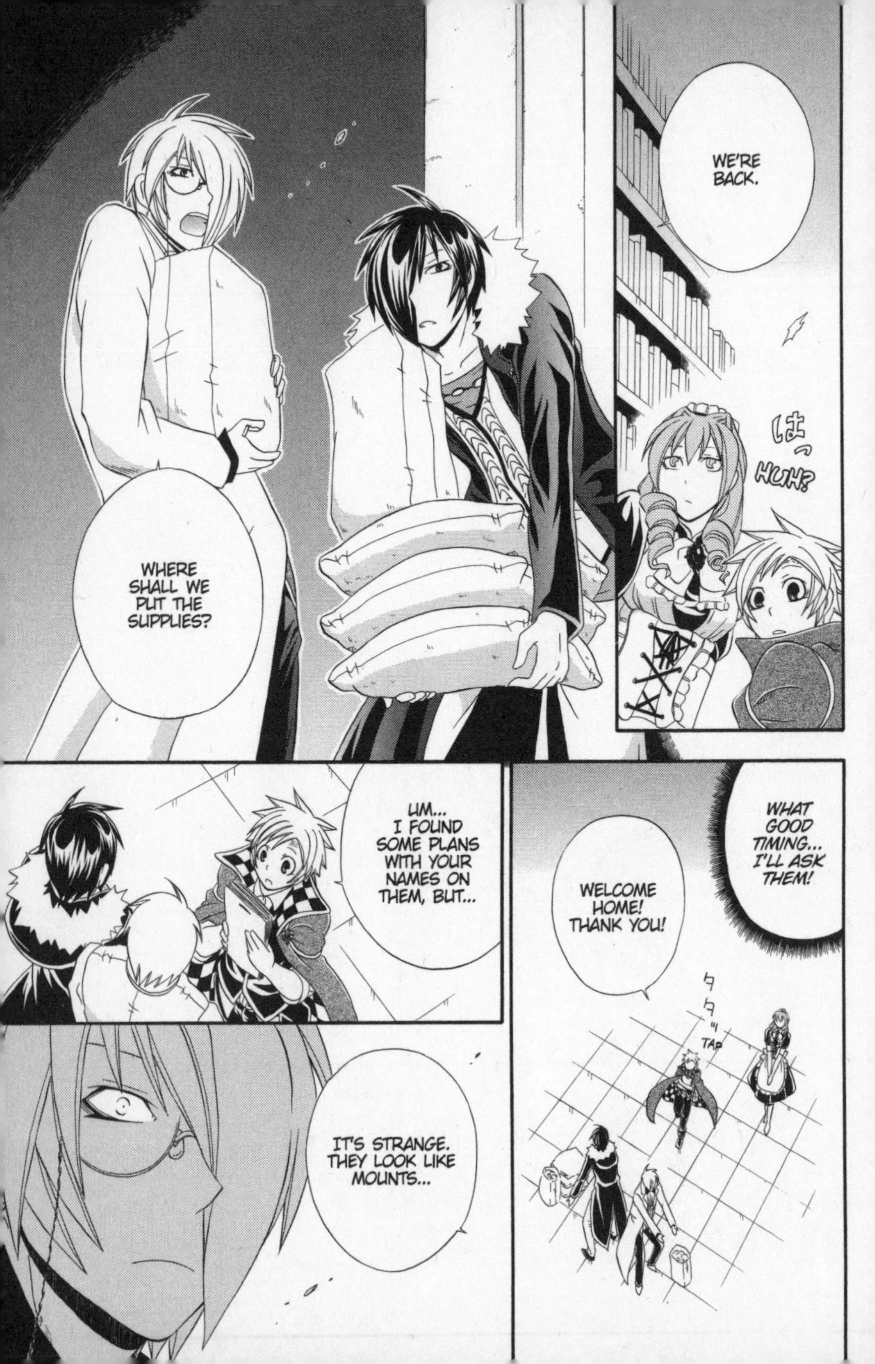
WE'RE BACK.
はっ
HUH?
WHERE SHALL WE PUT THE SUPPLIES?
WHAT GOOD TIMING... I'LL ASK THEM!
WELCOME HOME! THANK YOU!
タタッ
TAP
UM... I FOUND SOME PLANS WITH YOUR NAMES ON THEM, BUT...
IT'S STRANGE. THEY LOOK LIKE MOUNTS...

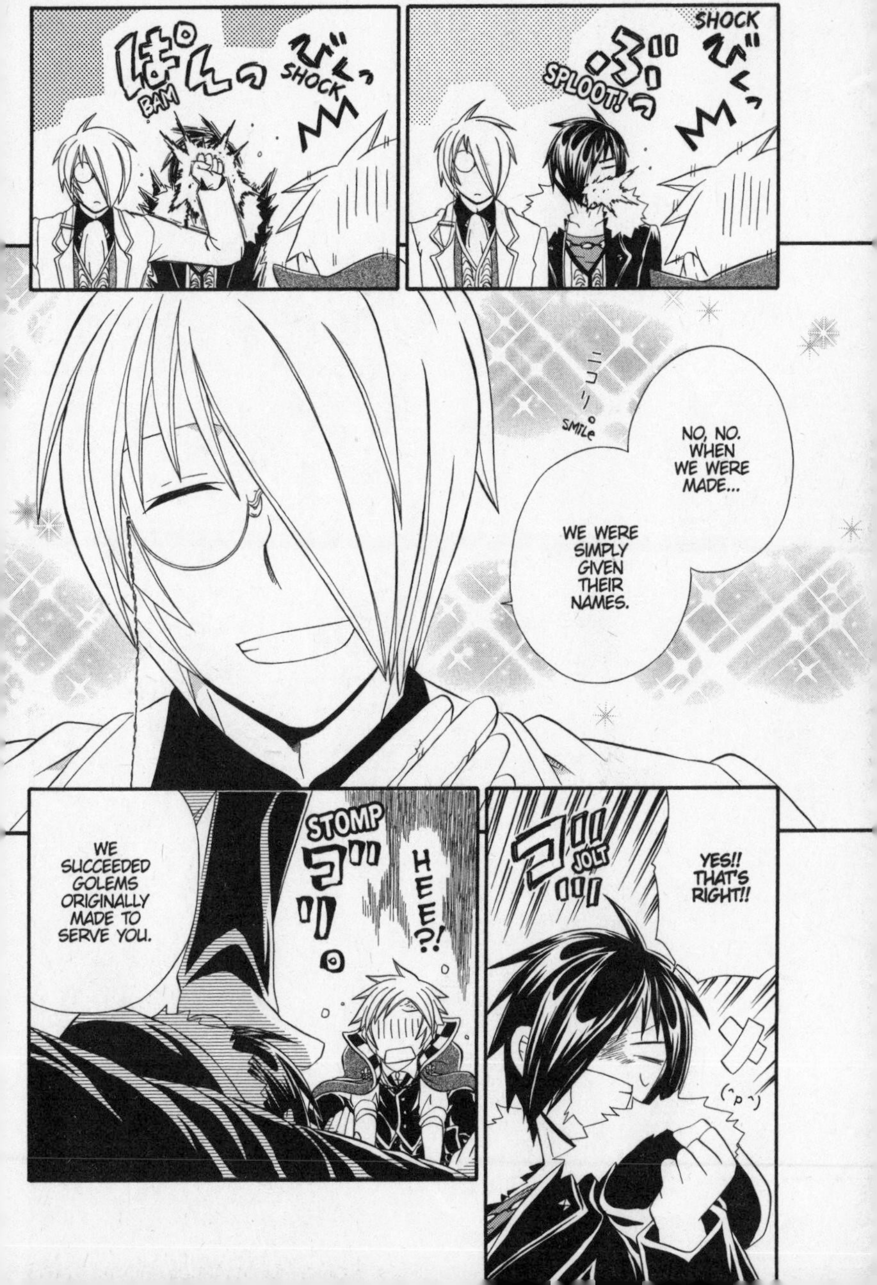
SHOCK
SPLOOT!
BAM
SHOCK
SMILE
NO, NO. WHEN WE WERE MADE...
WE WERE SIMPLY GIVEN THEIR NAMES.
JOLT
YES!! THAT'S RIGHT!!
(^p^)
WE SUCCEEDED GOLEMS ORIGINALLY MADE TO SERVE YOU.
STOMP
HEE?!

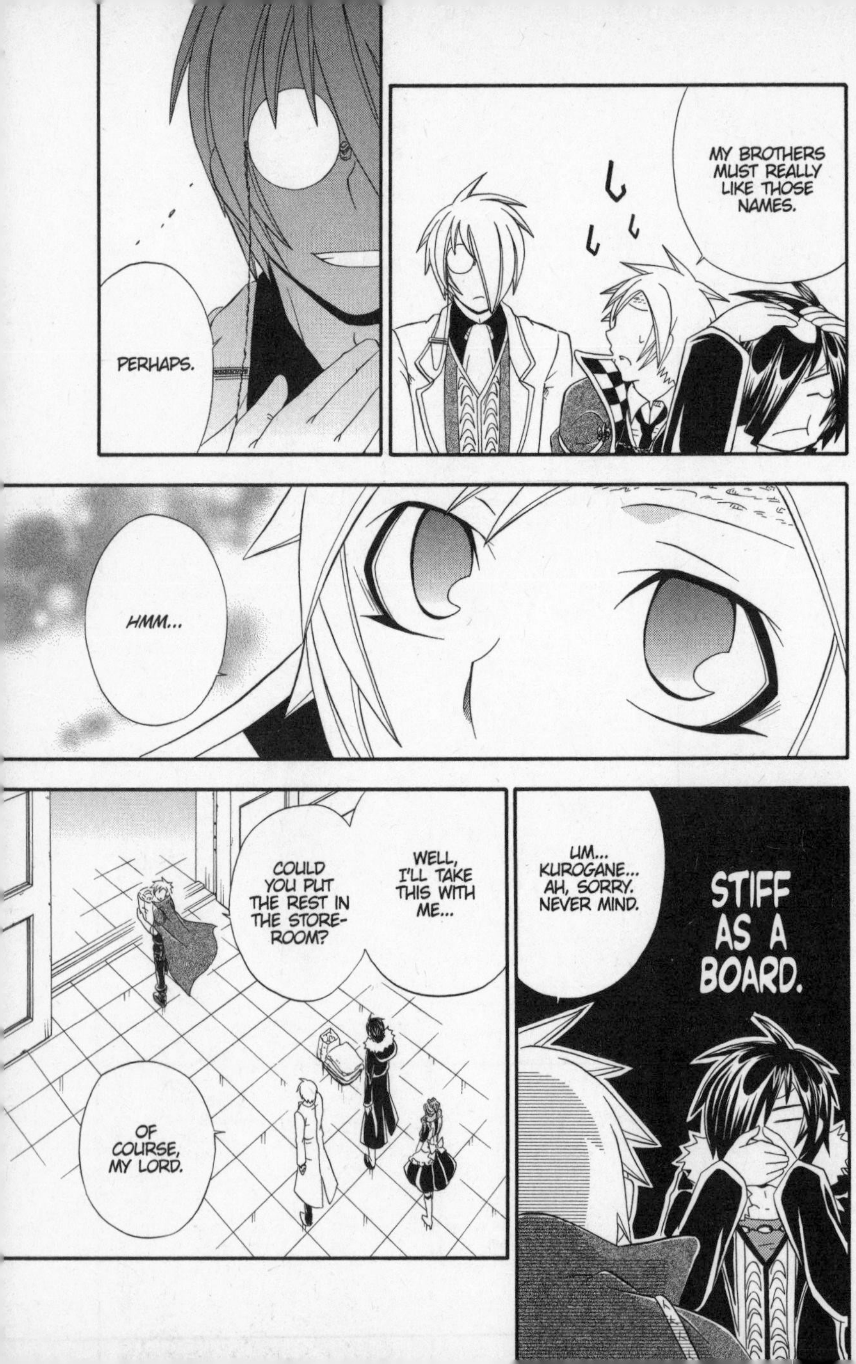
MY BROTHERS MUST REALLY LIKE THOSE NAMES.
PERHAPS.
HMM...
STIFF AS A BOARD.
UM... KUROGANE... AH, SORRY. NEVER MIND.
WELL, I'LL TAKE THIS WITH ME...
COULD YOU PUT THE REST IN THE STORE-ROOM?
OF COURSE, MY LORD.

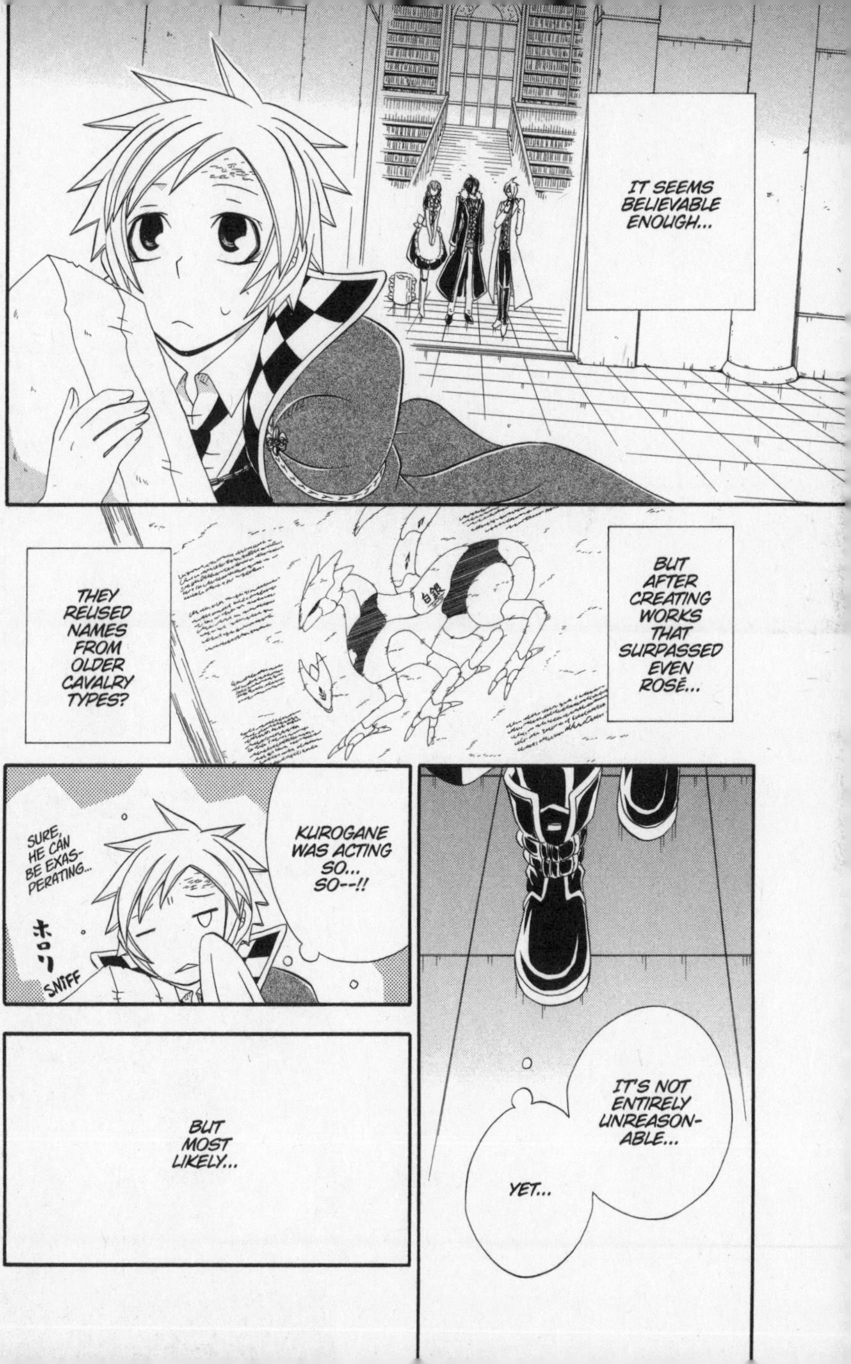
IT SEEMS BELIEVABLE ENOUGH...
BUT AFTER CREATING WORKS THAT SURPASSED EVEN ROSÉ...
THEY REUSED NAMES FROM OLDER CAVALRY TYPES?
IT'S NOT ENTIRELY UNREASON-ABLE...
YET...
KUROGANE WAS ACTING SO... SO--!!
SURE, HE CAN BE EXAS-PERATING...
ホロリ
SNIFF
BUT MOST LIKELY...

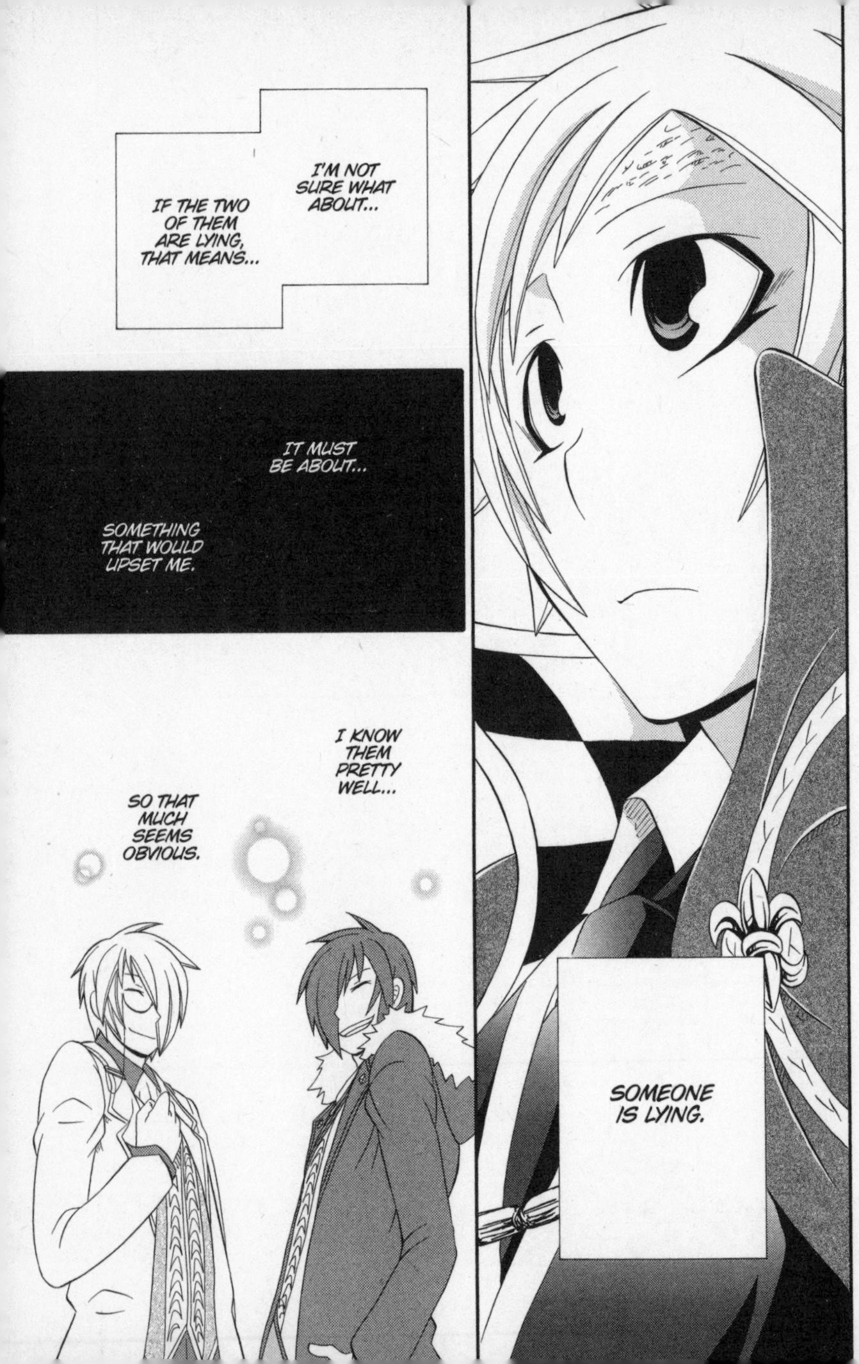
SOMEONE IS LYING.
I'M NOT SURE WHAT ABOUT...
IF THE TWO OF THEM ARE LYING, THAT MEANS...
IT MUST BE ABOUT...
SOMETHING THAT WOULD UPSET ME.
I KNOW THEM PRETTY WELL...
SO THAT MUCH SEEMS OBVIOUS.

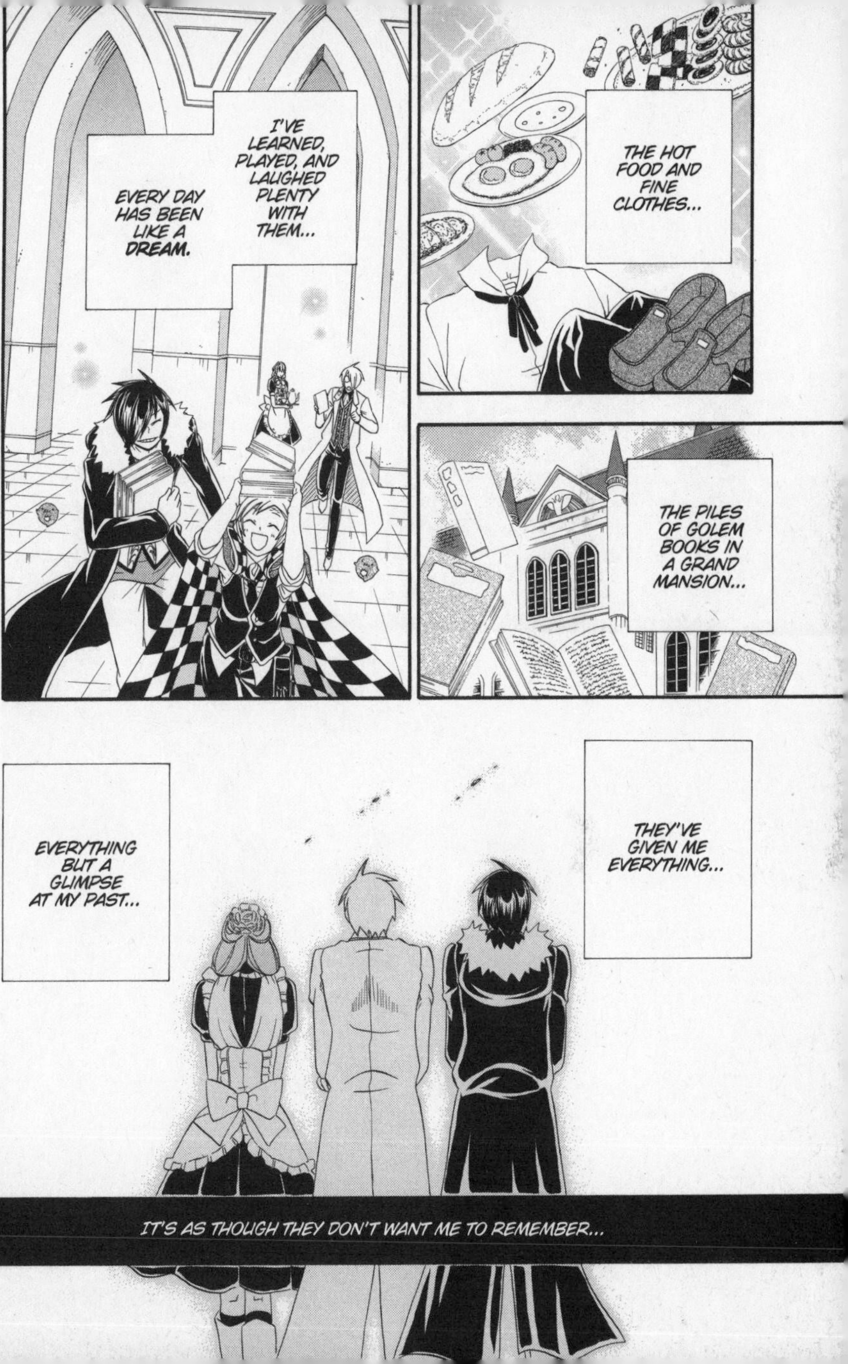
THE HOT FOOD AND FINE CLOTHES...
THE PILES OF GOLEM BOOKS IN A GRAND MANSION...
I'VE LEARNED, PLAYED, AND LAUGHED PLENTY WITH THEM...
EVERY DAY HAS BEEN LIKE A DREAM.
THEY'VE GIVEN ME EVERYTHING...
EVERYTHING BUT A GLIMPSE AT MY PAST...
IT'S AS THOUGH THEY DON'T WANT ME TO REMEMBER...

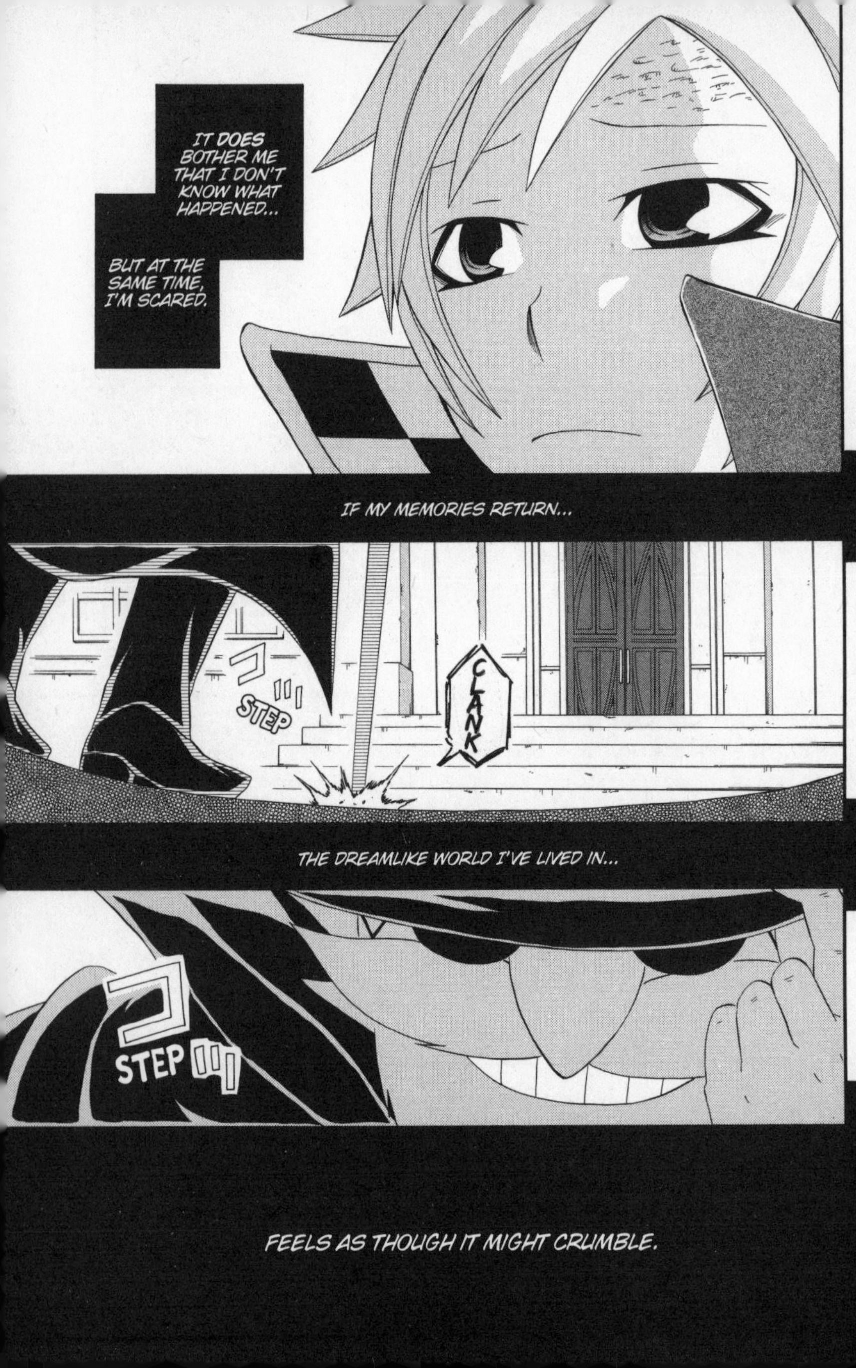
IT DOES BOTHER ME THAT I DON'T KNOW WHAT HAPPENED...
BUT AT THE SAME TIME, I'M SCARED.
IF MY MEMORIES RETURN...
CLANK
STEP
THE DREAMLIKE WORLD I'VE LIVED IN...
STEP
FEELS AS THOUGH IT MIGHT CRUMBLE.

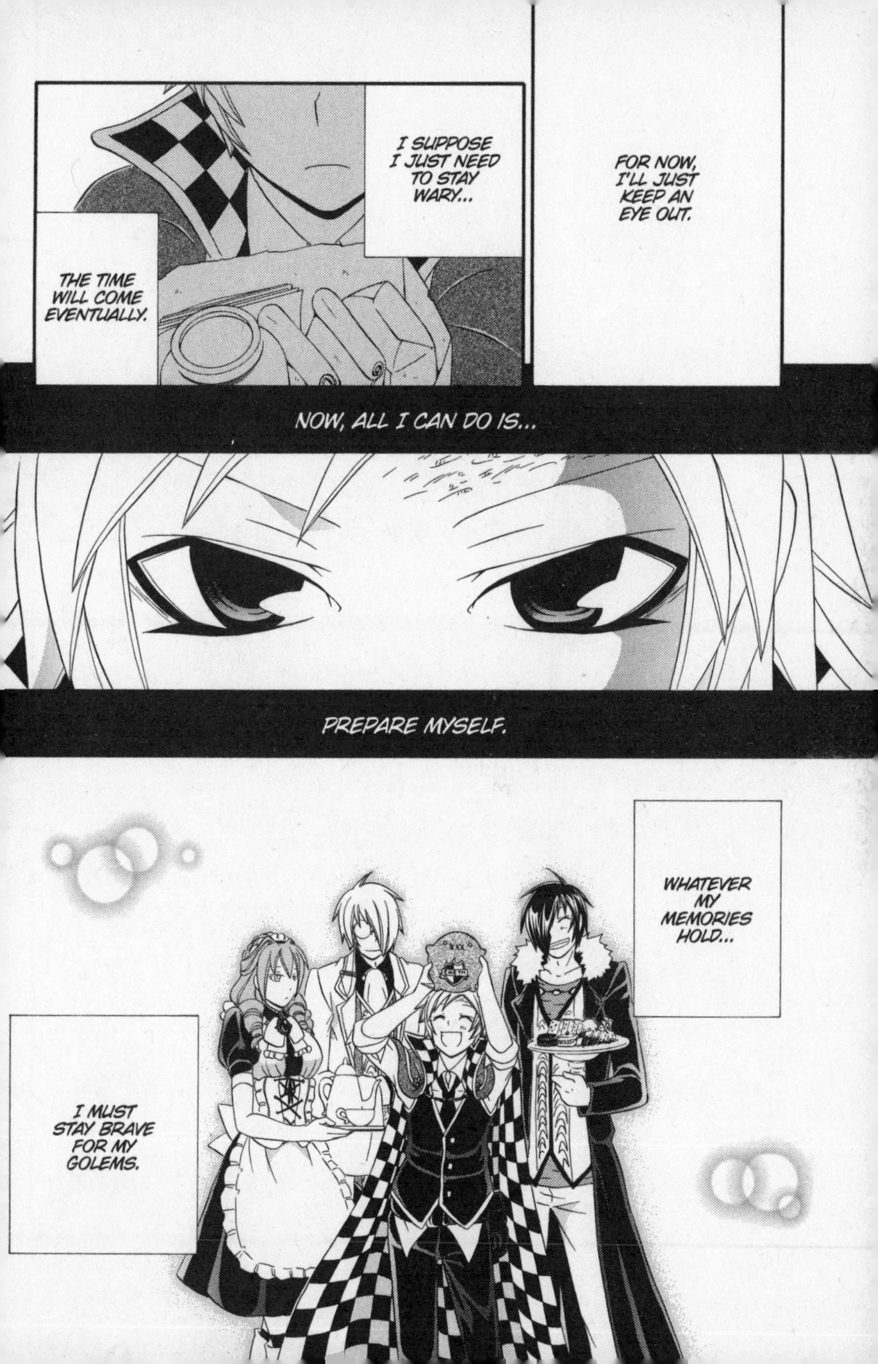
FOR NOW, I'LL JUST KEEP AN EYE OUT.
I SUPPOSE I JUST NEED TO STAY WARY...
THE TIME WILL COME EVENTUALLY.
NOW, ALL I CAN DO IS...
PREPARE MYSELF.
WHATEVER MY MEMORIES HOLD...
I MUST STAY BRAVE FOR MY GOLEMS.

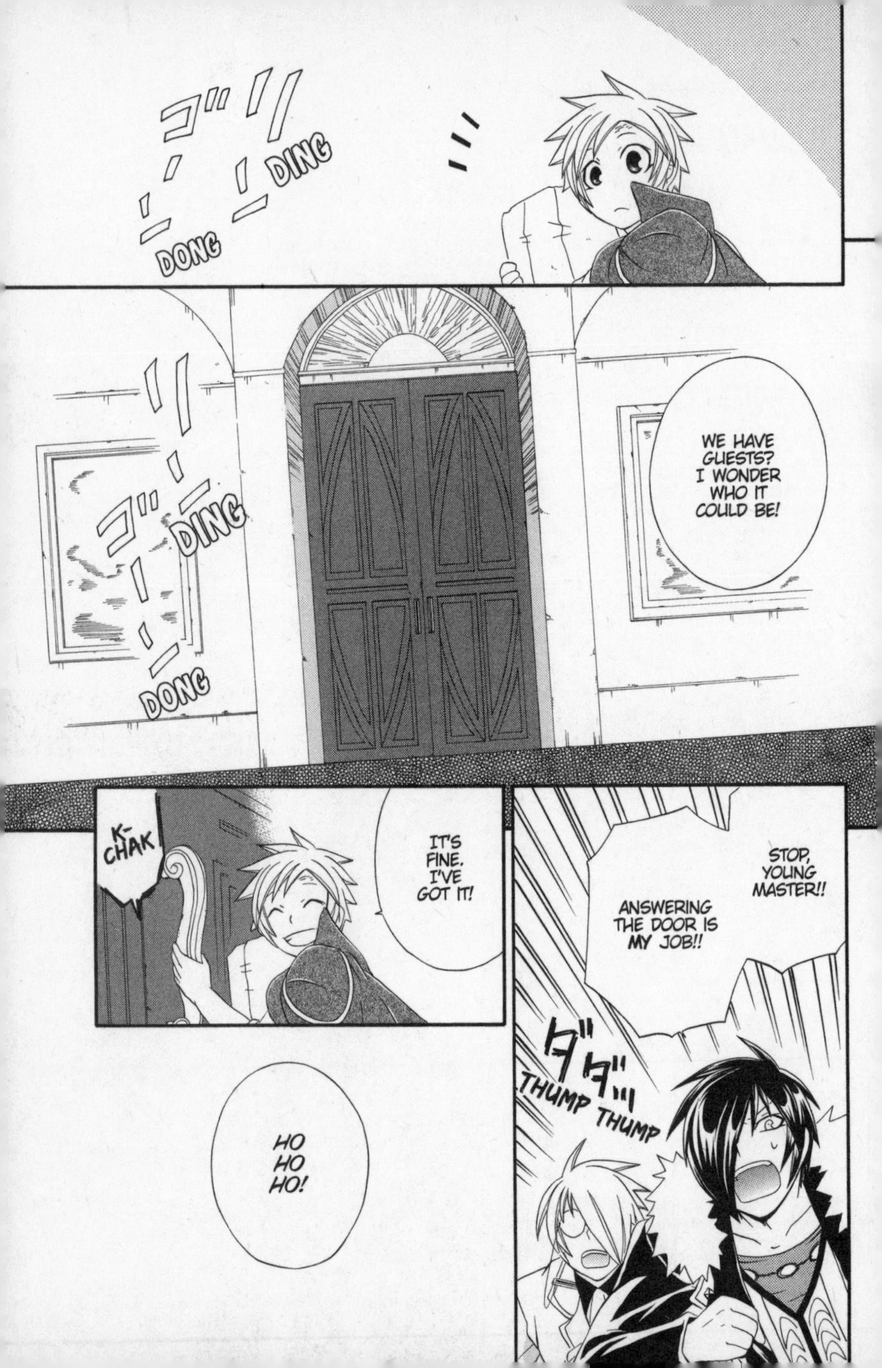
DING
DONG
WE HAVE GUESTS? I WONDER WHO IT COULD BE!
DING
DONG
STOP, YOUNG MASTER!!
ANSWERING THE DOOR IS MY JOB!!
THUMP THUMP
IT'S FINE. I'VE GOT IT!
K-CHAK
HO HO HO!

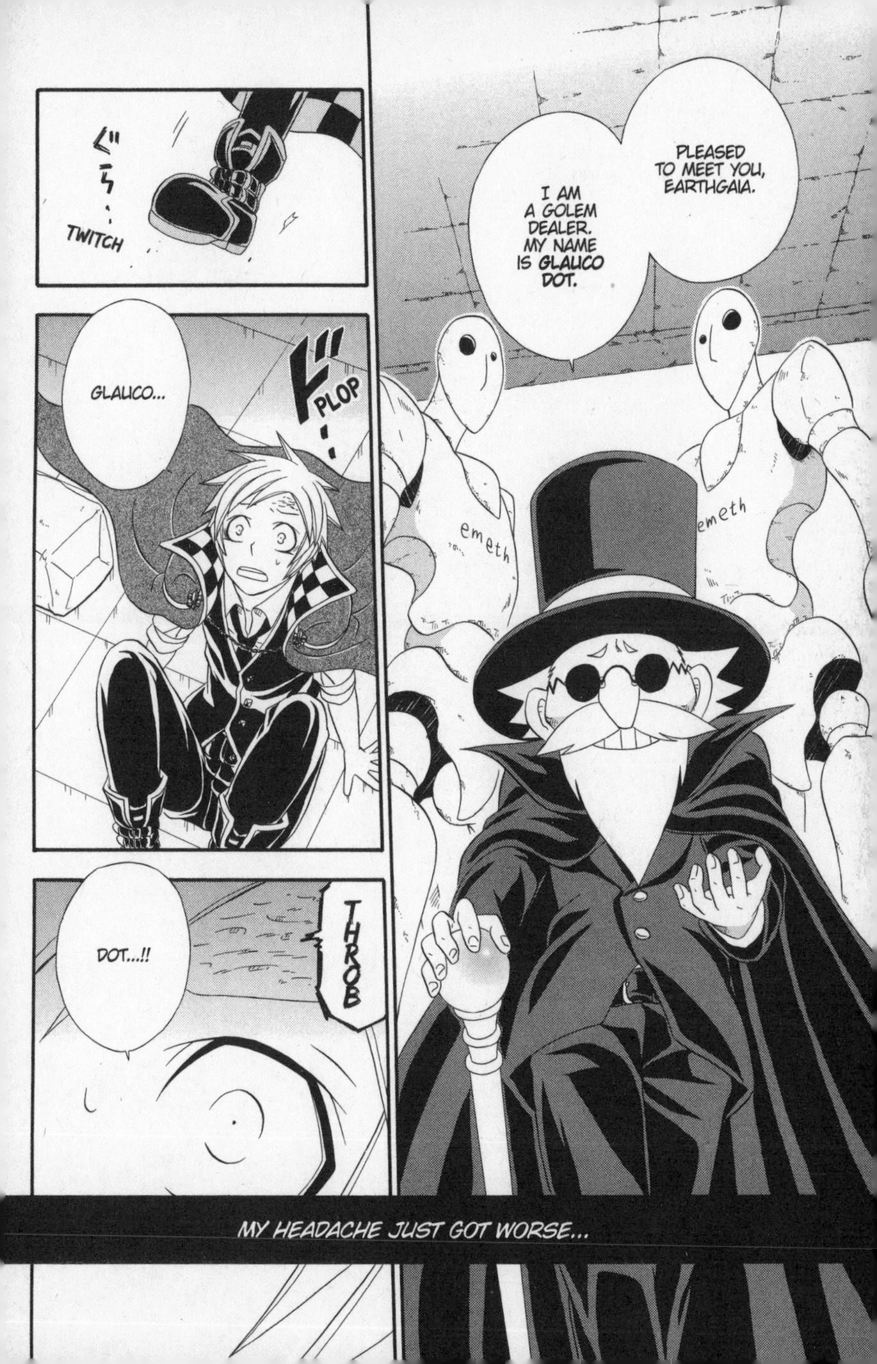
PLEASED TO MEET YOU, EARTHGAIA.
I AM A GOLEM DEALER. MY NAME IS GLAUCO DOT.
emeth
emeth
TWITCH
PLOP
GLAUCO...
THROB
DOT...!!
MY HEADACHE JUST GOT WORSE...

Chapter 10: Memories

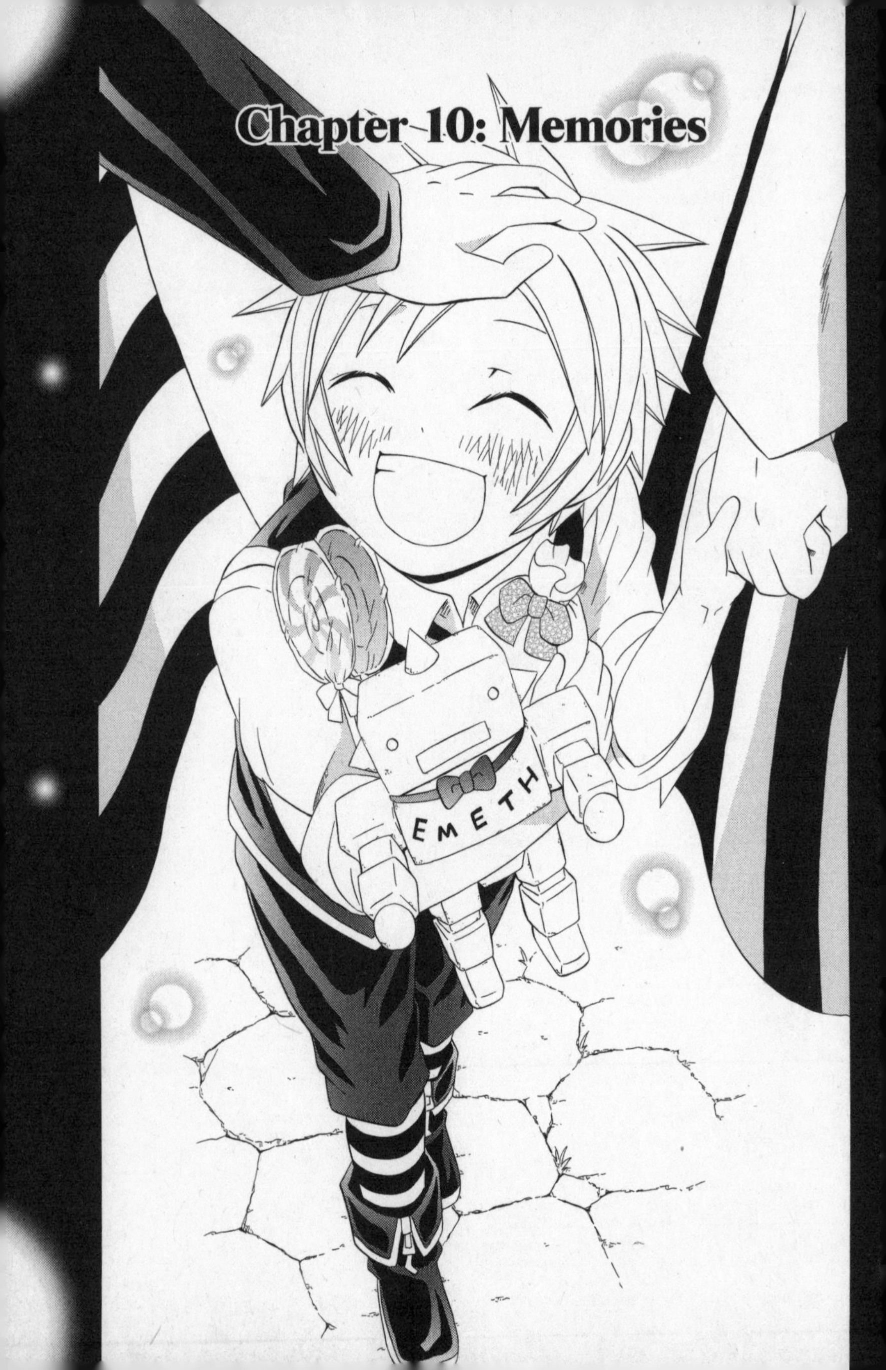
EMETH

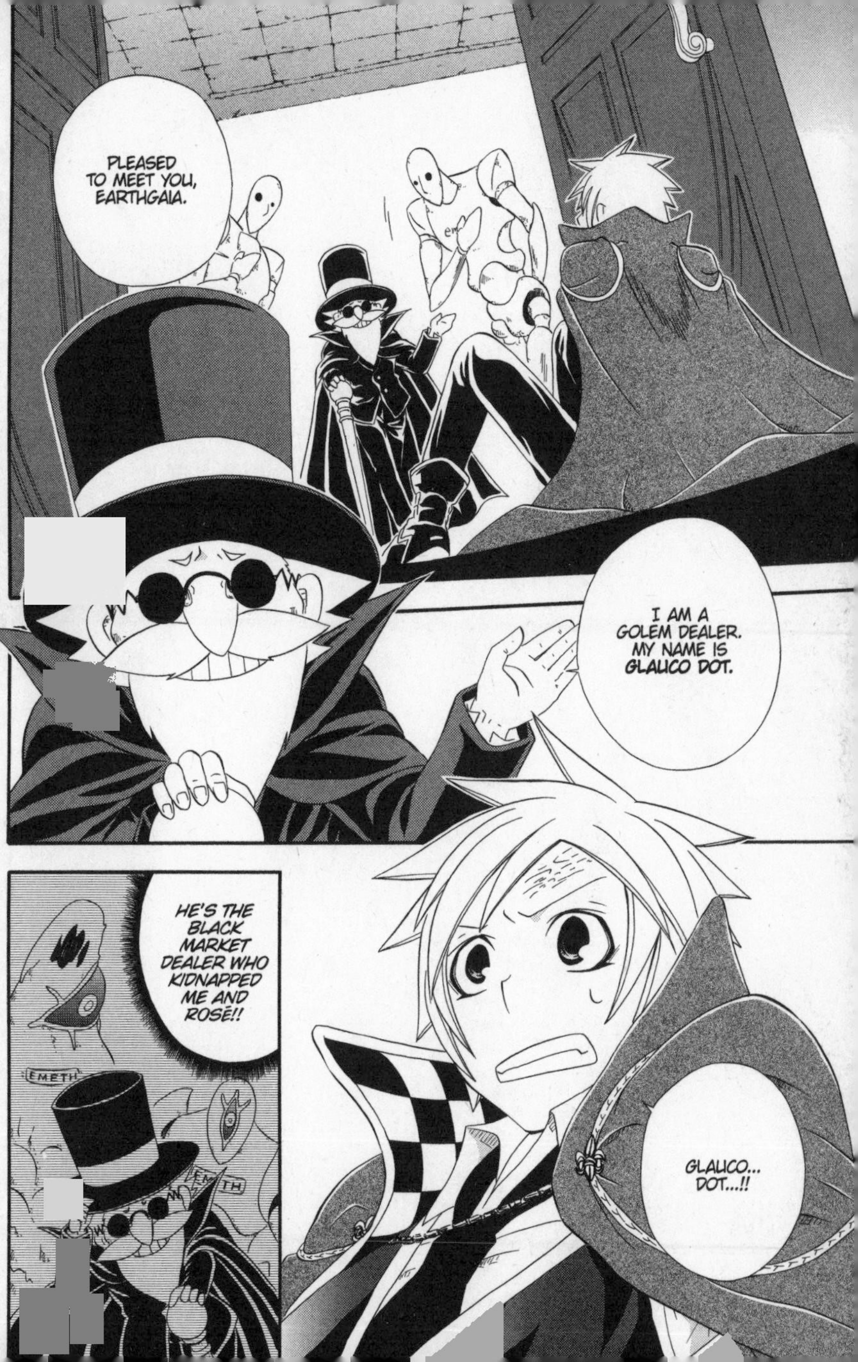
PLEASED TO MEET YOU, EARTHGAIA.
I AM A GOLEM DEALER. MY NAME IS GLAUCO DOT.
GLAUCO... DOT...!!
HE'S THE BLACK MARKET DEALER WHO KIDNAPPED ME AND ROSÉ!!
EMETH

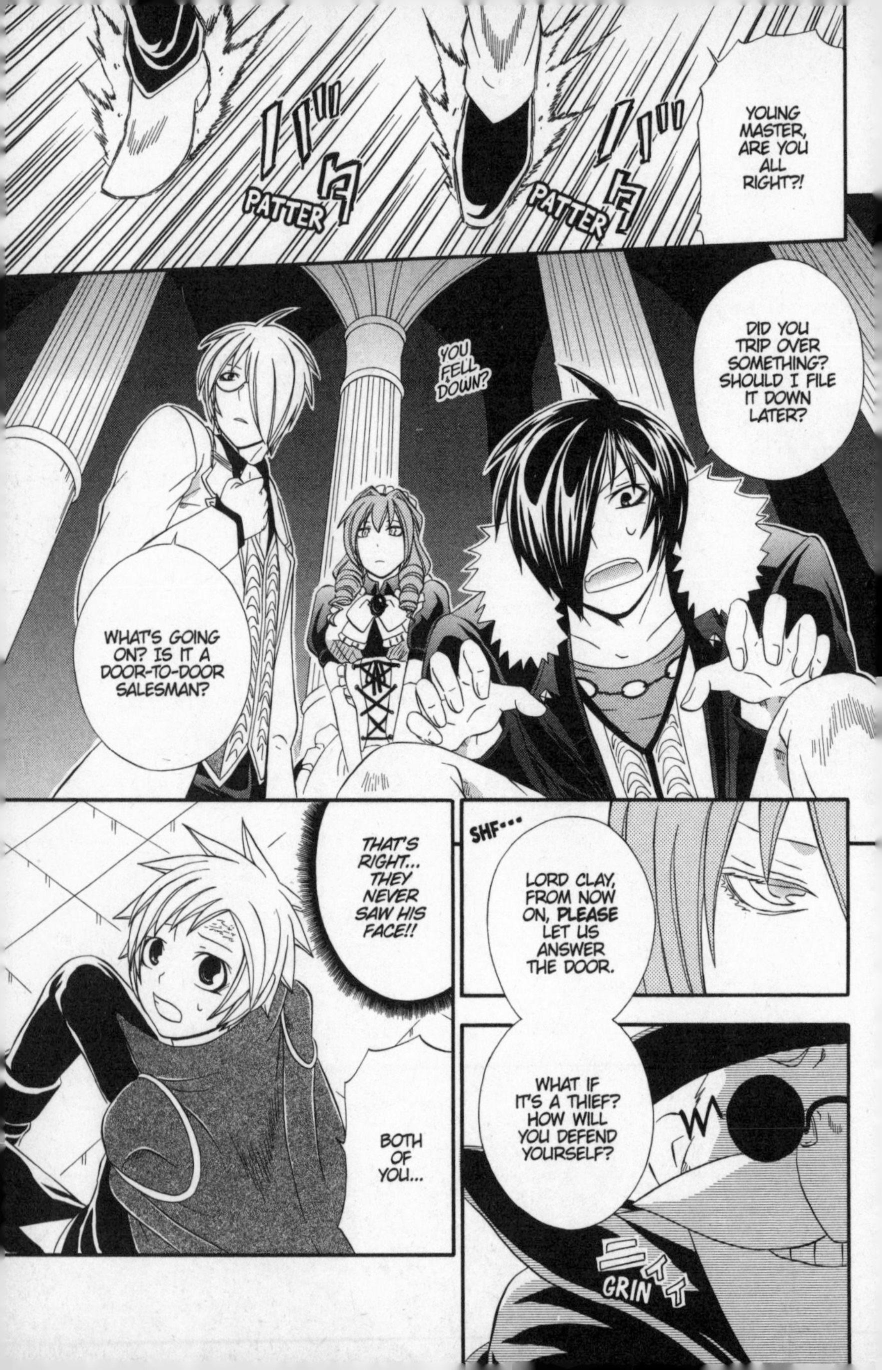
YOUNG MASTER, ARE YOU ALL RIGHT?!
PATTER
PATTER
DID YOU TRIP OVER SOMETHING? SHOULD I FILE IT DOWN LATER?
YOU FELL DOWN?
WHAT'S GOING ON? IS IT A DOOR-TO-DOOR SALESMAN?
SHF...
LORD CLAY, FROM NOW ON, PLEASE LET US ANSWER THE DOOR.
WHAT IF IT'S A THIEF? HOW WILL YOU DEFEND YOURSELF?
GRIN
THAT'S RIGHT... THEY NEVER SAW HIS FACE!!
BOTH OF YOU...

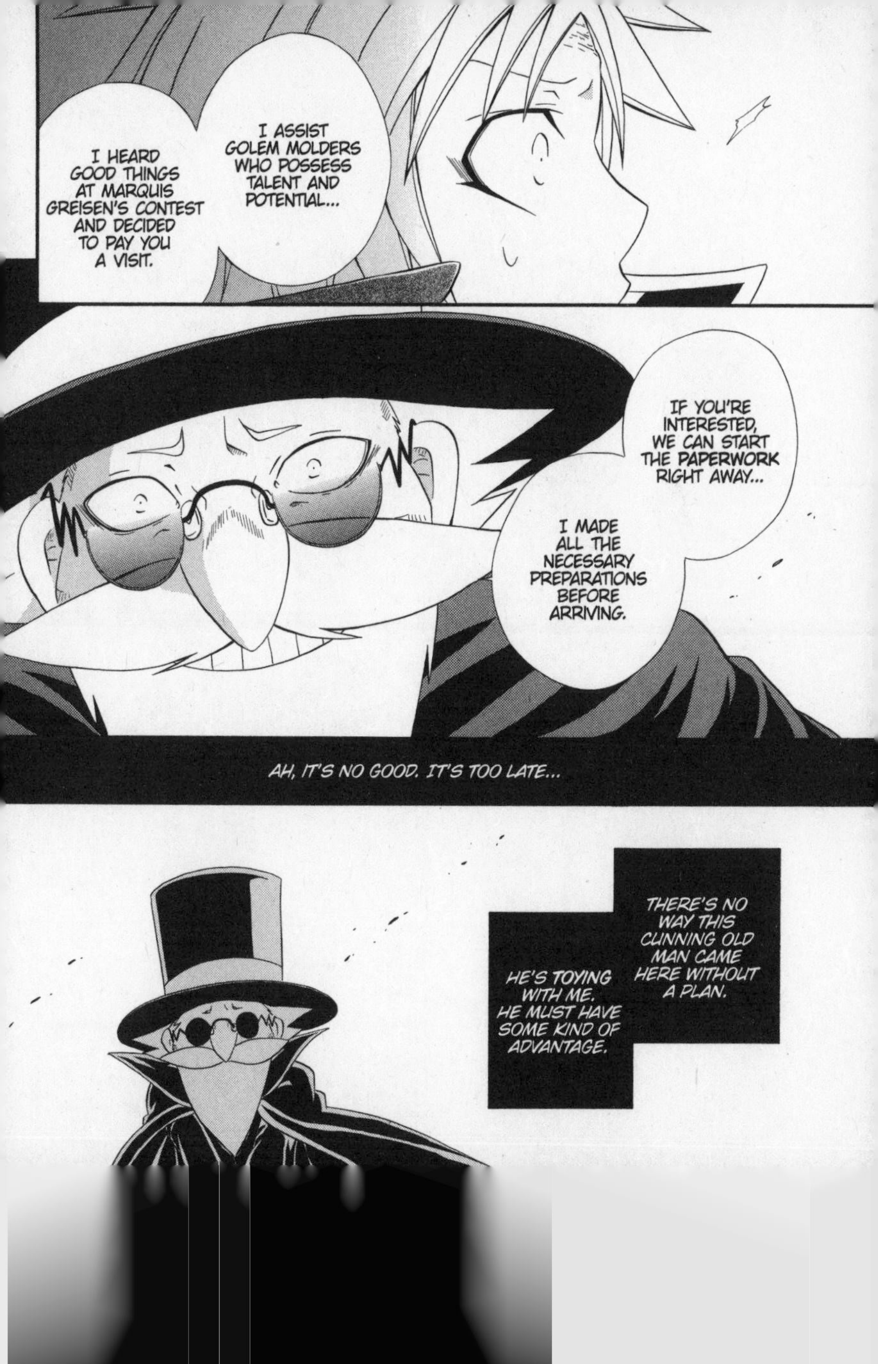
I ASSIST GOLEM MOLDERS WHO POSSESS TALENT AND POTENTIAL...
I HEARD GOOD THINGS AT MARQUIS GREISEN'S CONTEST AND DECIDED TO PAY YOU A VISIT.
IF YOU'RE INTERESTED, WE CAN START THE PAPERWORK RIGHT AWAY...
I MADE ALL THE NECESSARY PREPARATIONS BEFORE ARRIVING.
AH, IT'S NO GOOD. IT'S TOO LATE...
THERE'S NO WAY THIS CUNNING OLD MAN CAME HERE WITHOUT A PLAN.
HE'S TOYING WITH ME. HE MUST HAVE SOME KIND OF ADVANTAGE.

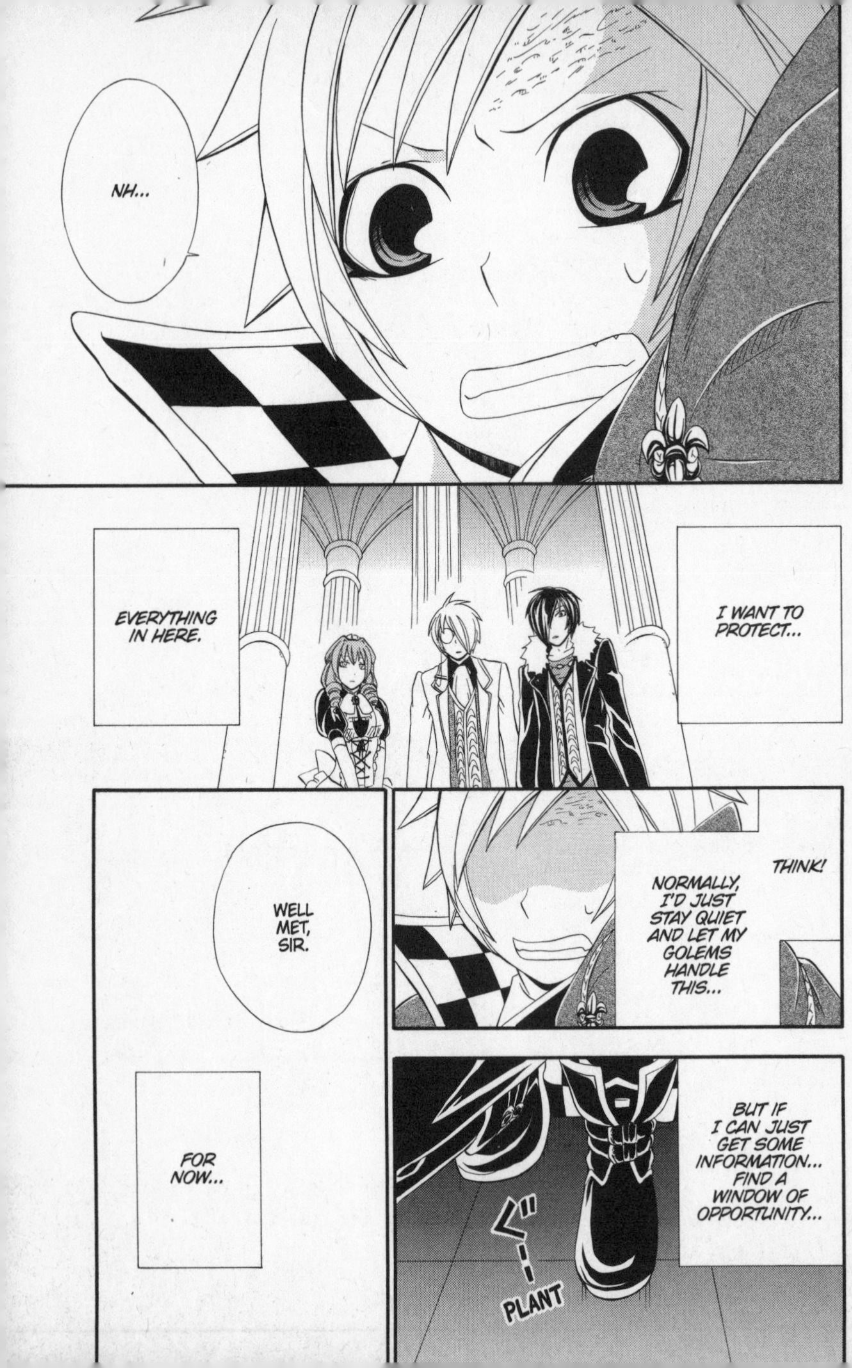
NH...
I WANT TO PROTECT...
EVERYTHING IN HERE.
THINK!
NORMALLY, I'D JUST STAY QUIET AND LET MY GOLEMS HANDLE THIS...
BUT IF I CAN JUST GET SOME INFORMATION... FIND A WINDOW OF OPPORTUNITY...
PLANT
WELL MET, SIR.
FOR NOW...

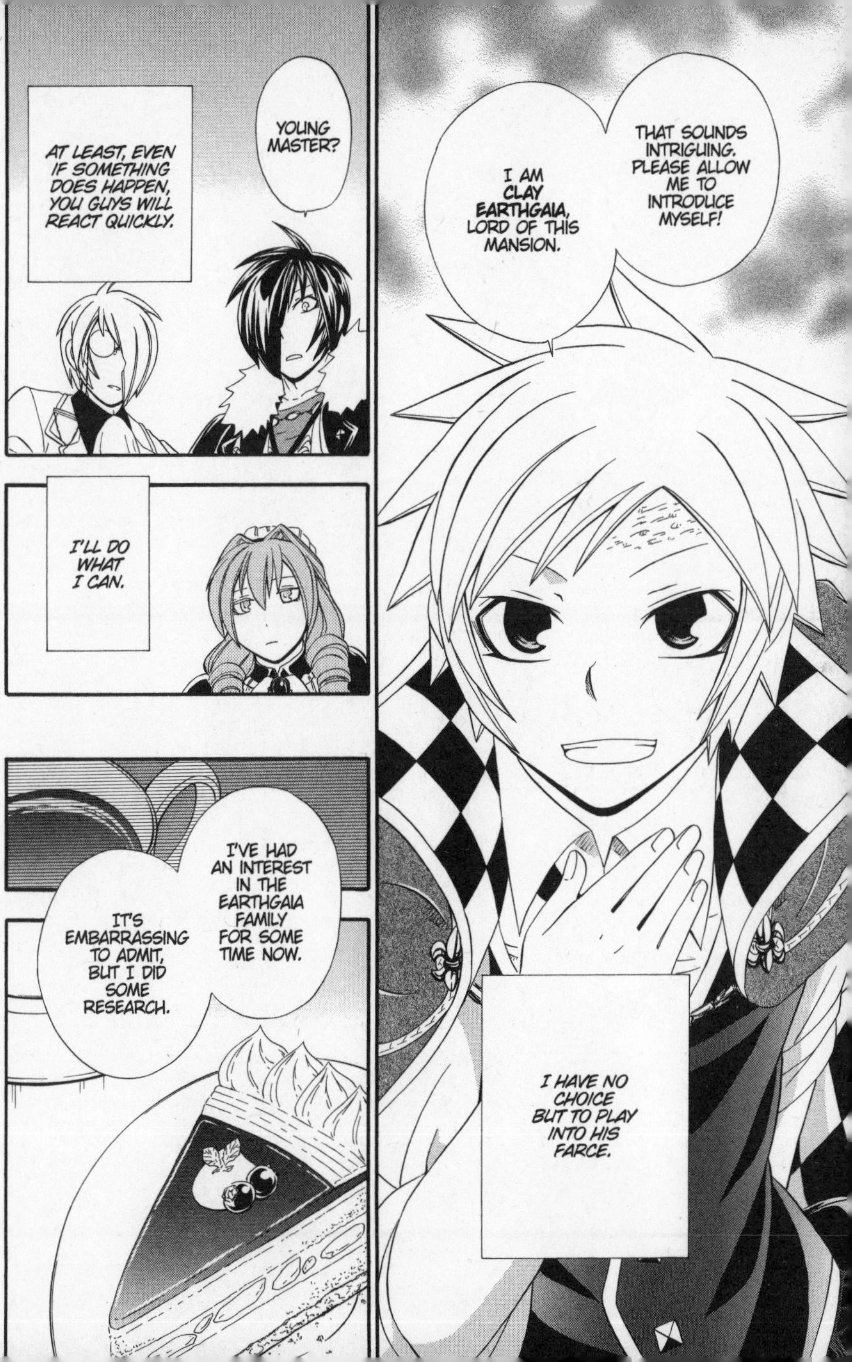
THAT SOUNDS INTRIGUING. PLEASE ALLOW ME TO INTRODUCE MYSELF!
I AM CLAY EARTHGAIA, LORD OF THIS MANSION.
I HAVE NO CHOICE BUT TO PLAY INTO HIS FARCE.
YOUNG MASTER?
AT LEAST, EVEN IF SOMETHING DOES HAPPEN, YOU GUYS WILL REACT QUICKLY.
I'LL DO WHAT I CAN.
I'VE HAD AN INTEREST IN THE EARTHGAIA FAMILY FOR SOME TIME NOW.
IT'S EMBARRASSING TO ADMIT, BUT I DID SOME RESEARCH.

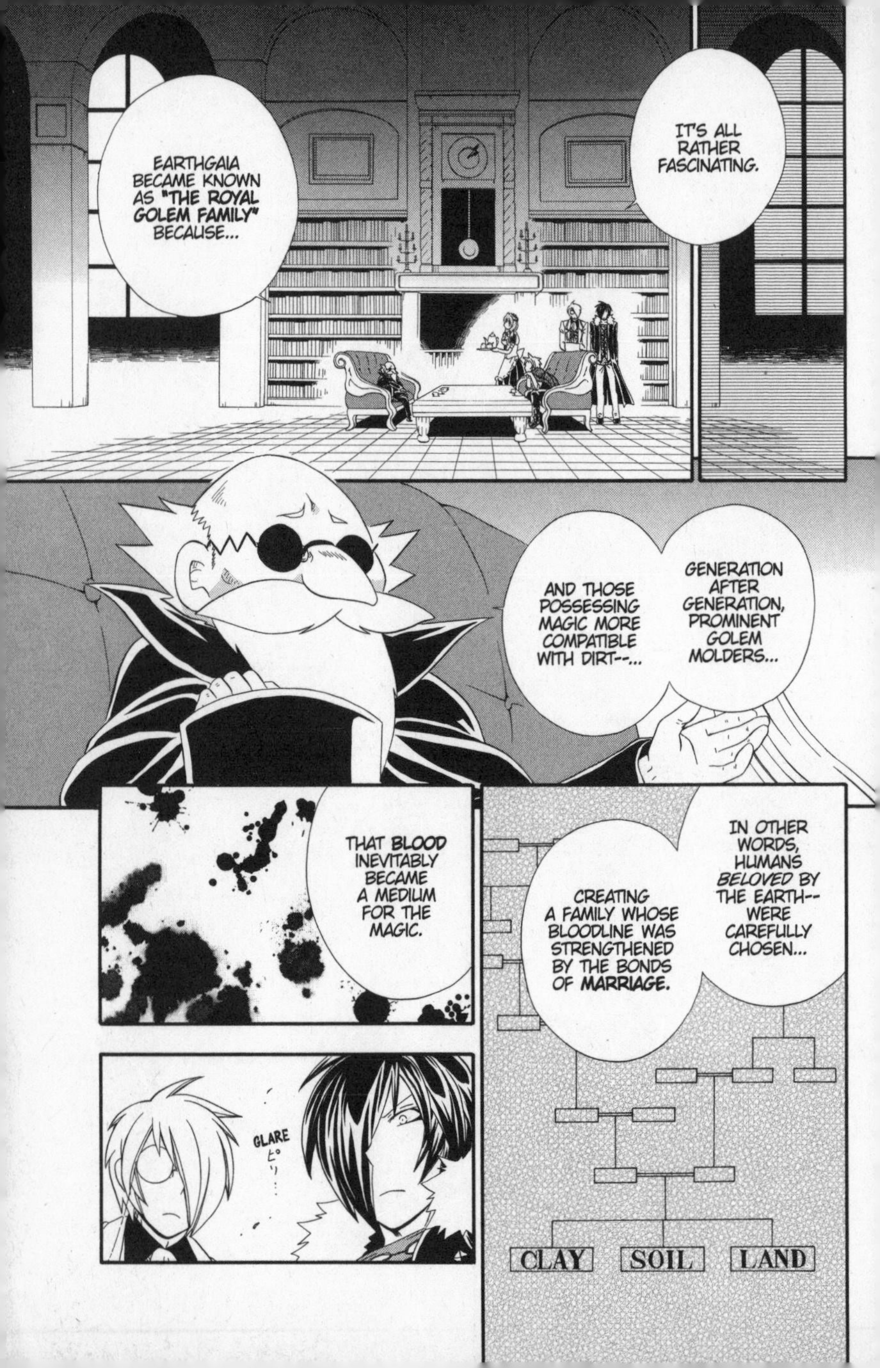
IT'S ALL RATHER FASCINATING.
EARTHGAIA BECAME KNOWN AS "THE ROYAL GOLEM FAMILY" BECAUSE...
GENERATION AFTER GENERATION, PROMINENT GOLEM MOLDERS...
AND THOSE POSSESSING MAGIC MORE COMPATIBLE WITH DIRT--...
IN OTHER WORDS, HUMANS *BELOVED* BY THE EARTH--WERE CAREFULLY CHOSEN...
CREATING A FAMILY WHOSE BLOODLINE WAS STRENGTHENED BY THE BONDS OF **MARRIAGE.**
CLAY
SOIL
LAND
THAT **BLOOD** INEVITABLY BECAME A MEDIUM FOR THE MAGIC.
GLARE
ピリ

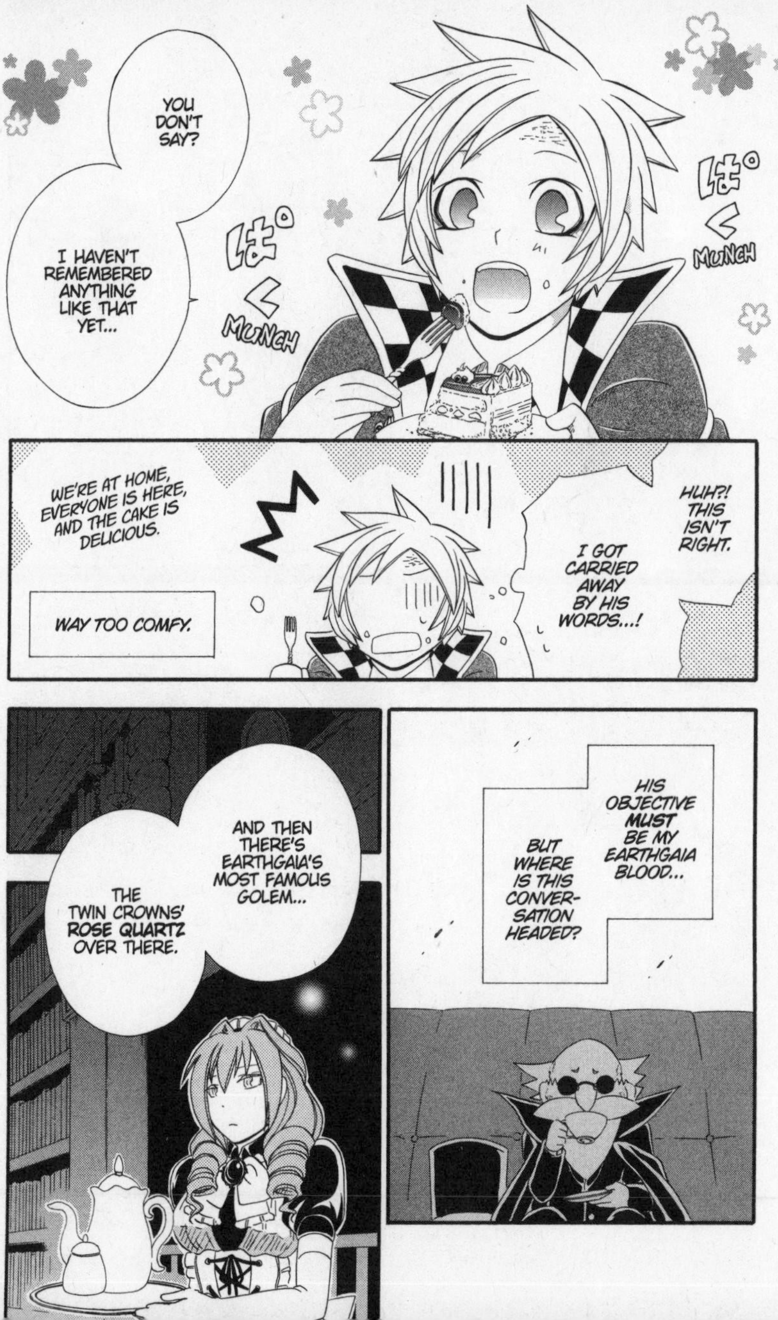
YOU DON'T SAY?
I HAVEN'T REMEMBERED ANYTHING LIKE THAT YET...
はぐ MUNCH
はぐ MUNCH
HUH?! THIS ISN'T RIGHT.
I GOT CARRIED AWAY BY HIS WORDS...!
WE'RE AT HOME, EVERYONE IS HERE, AND THE CAKE IS DELICIOUS.
WAY TOO COMFY.
HIS OBJECTIVE MUST BE MY EARTHGAIA BLOOD...
BUT WHERE IS THIS CONVERSATION HEADED?
AND THEN THERE'S EARTHGAIA'S MOST FAMOUS GOLEM...
THE TWIN CROWNS' ROSE QUARTZ OVER THERE.

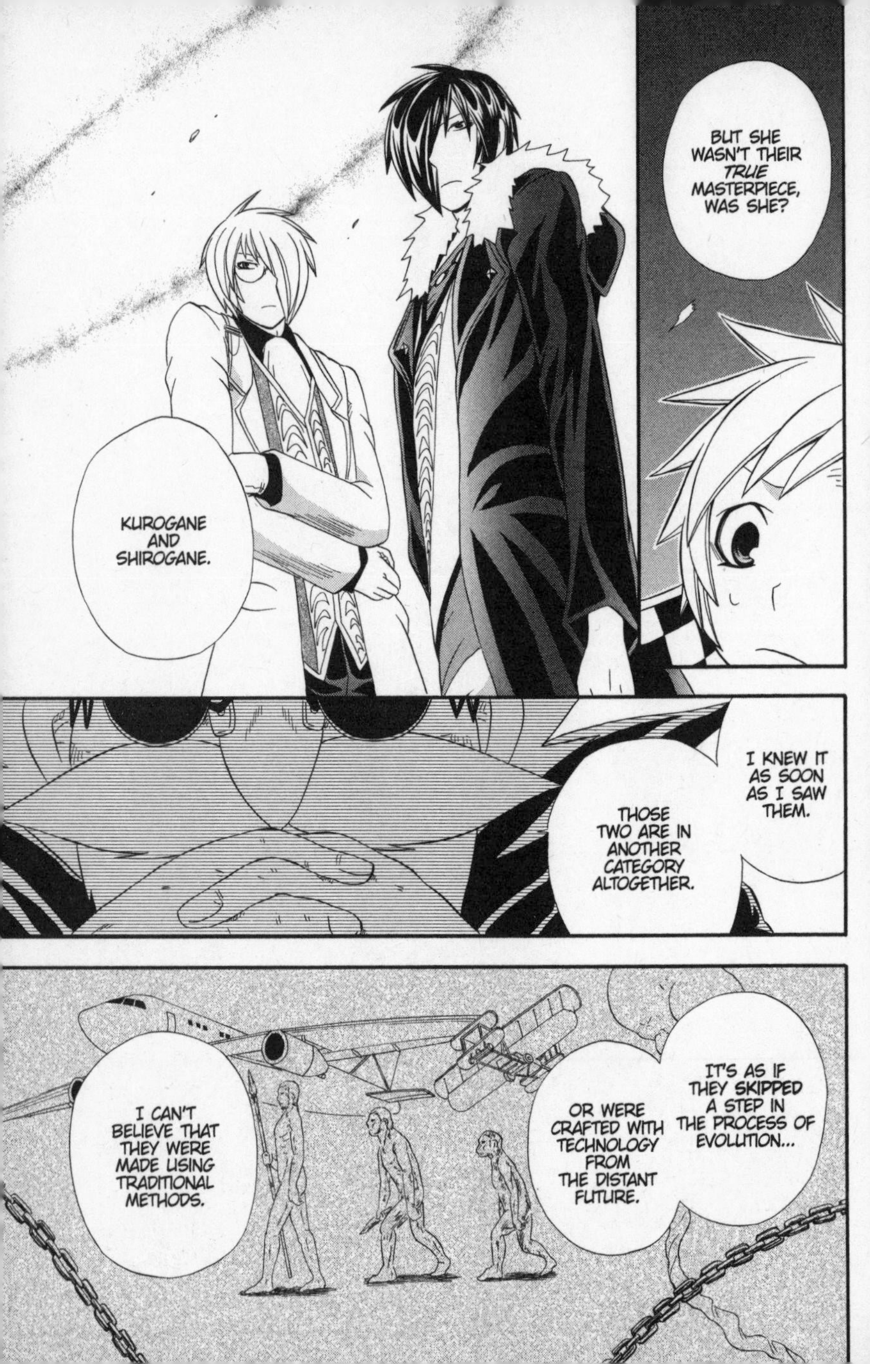
BUT SHE WASN'T THEIR TRUE MASTERPIECE, WAS SHE?
KUROGANE AND SHIROGANE.
I KNEW IT AS SOON AS I SAW THEM.
THOSE TWO ARE IN ANOTHER CATEGORY ALTOGETHER.
IT'S AS IF THEY SKIPPED A STEP IN THE PROCESS OF EVOLUTION...
OR WERE CRAFTED WITH TECHNOLOGY FROM THE DISTANT FUTURE.
I CAN'T BELIEVE THAT THEY WERE MADE USING TRADITIONAL METHODS.

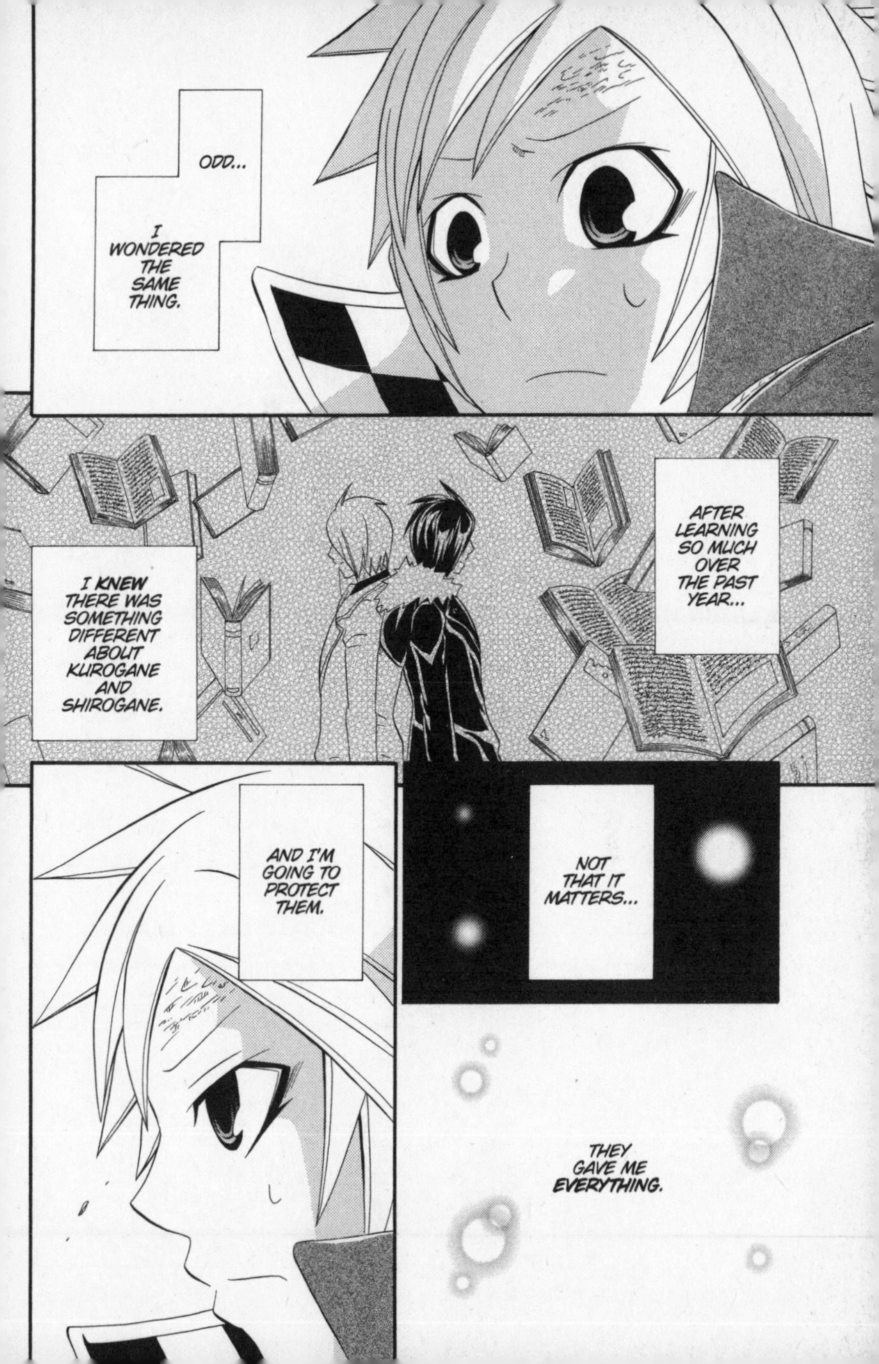
ODD...
I WONDERED THE SAME THING.
AFTER LEARNING SO MUCH OVER THE PAST YEAR...
I KNEW THERE WAS SOMETHING DIFFERENT ABOUT KUROGANE AND SHIROGANE.
NOT THAT IT MATTERS...
THEY GAVE ME EVERYTHING.
AND I'M GOING TO PROTECT THEM.

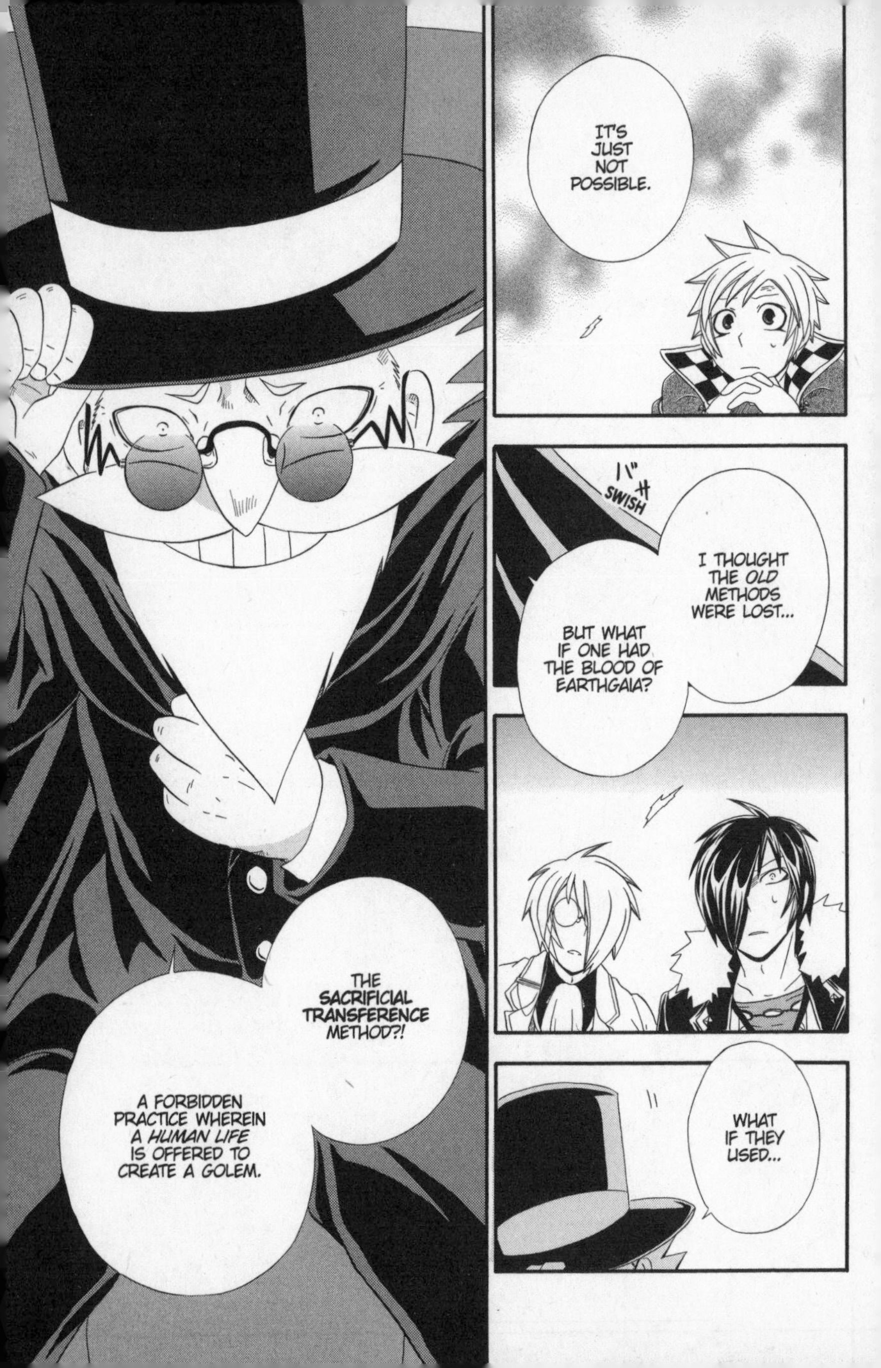
IT'S JUST NOT POSSIBLE.
バッ
SWISH
I THOUGHT THE *OLD* METHODS WERE LOST...
BUT WHAT IF ONE HAD THE BLOOD OF EARTHGAIA?
WHAT IF THEY USED...
THE SACRIFICIAL TRANSFERENCE METHOD?!
A FORBIDDEN PRACTICE WHEREIN A *HUMAN LIFE* IS OFFERED TO CREATE A GOLEM.

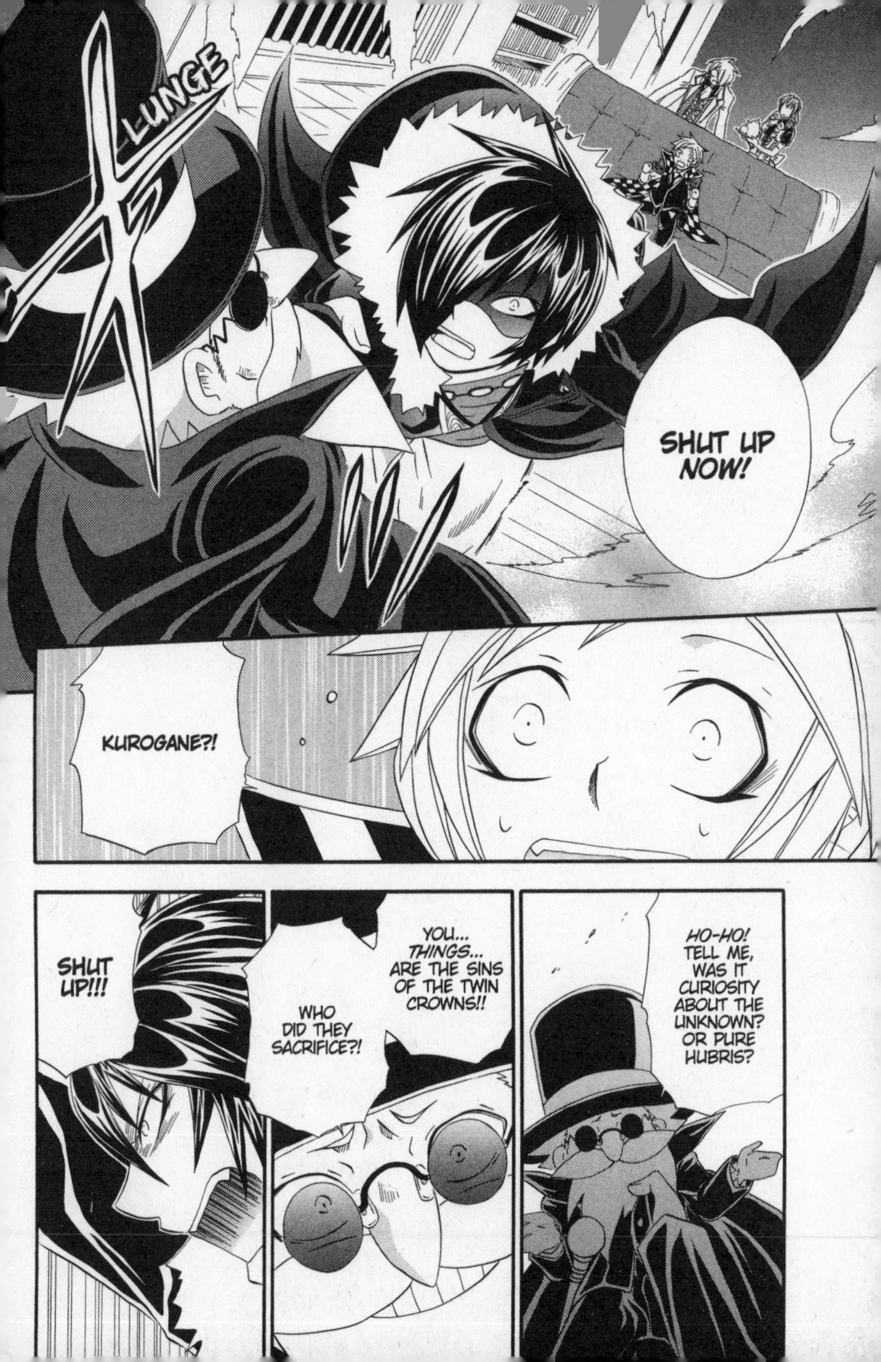
SHUT UP NOW!
LUNGE
KUROGANE?!
HO-HO! TELL ME, WAS IT CURIOSITY ABOUT THE UNKNOWN? OR PURE HUBRIS?
YOU... THINGS... ARE THE SINS OF THE TWIN CROWNS!!
WHO DID THEY SACRIFICE?!
SHUT UP!!!

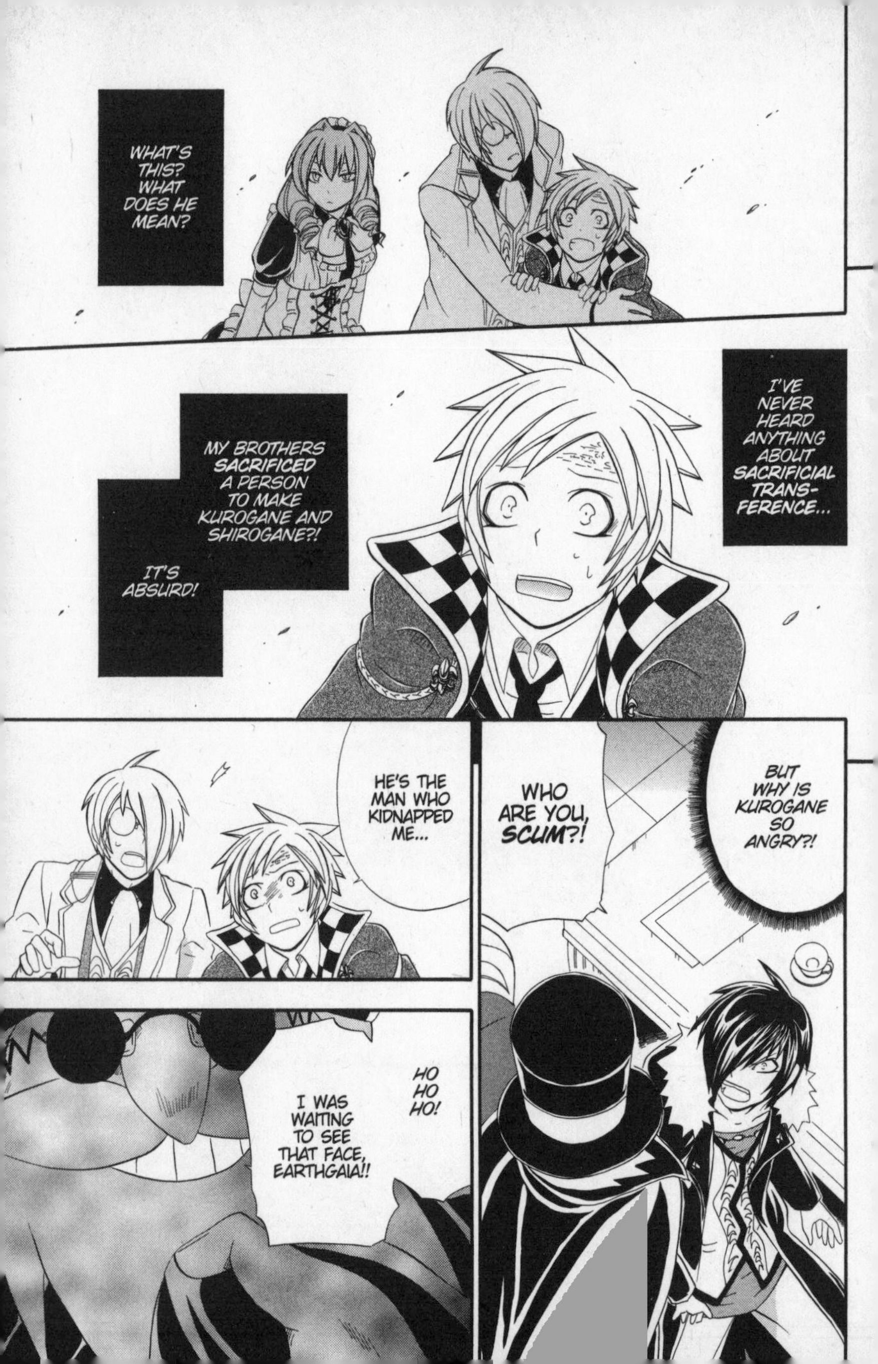
WHAT'S THIS? WHAT DOES HE MEAN?
I'VE NEVER HEARD ANYTHING ABOUT SACRIFICIAL TRANS-FERENCE...
MY BROTHERS SACRIFICED A PERSON TO MAKE KUROGANE AND SHIROGANE?!
IT'S ABSURD!
BUT WHY IS KUROGANE SO ANGRY?!
WHO ARE YOU, SCUM?!
HE'S THE MAN WHO KIDNAPPED ME...
HO HO HO!
I WAS WAITING TO SEE THAT FACE, EARTHGAIA!!

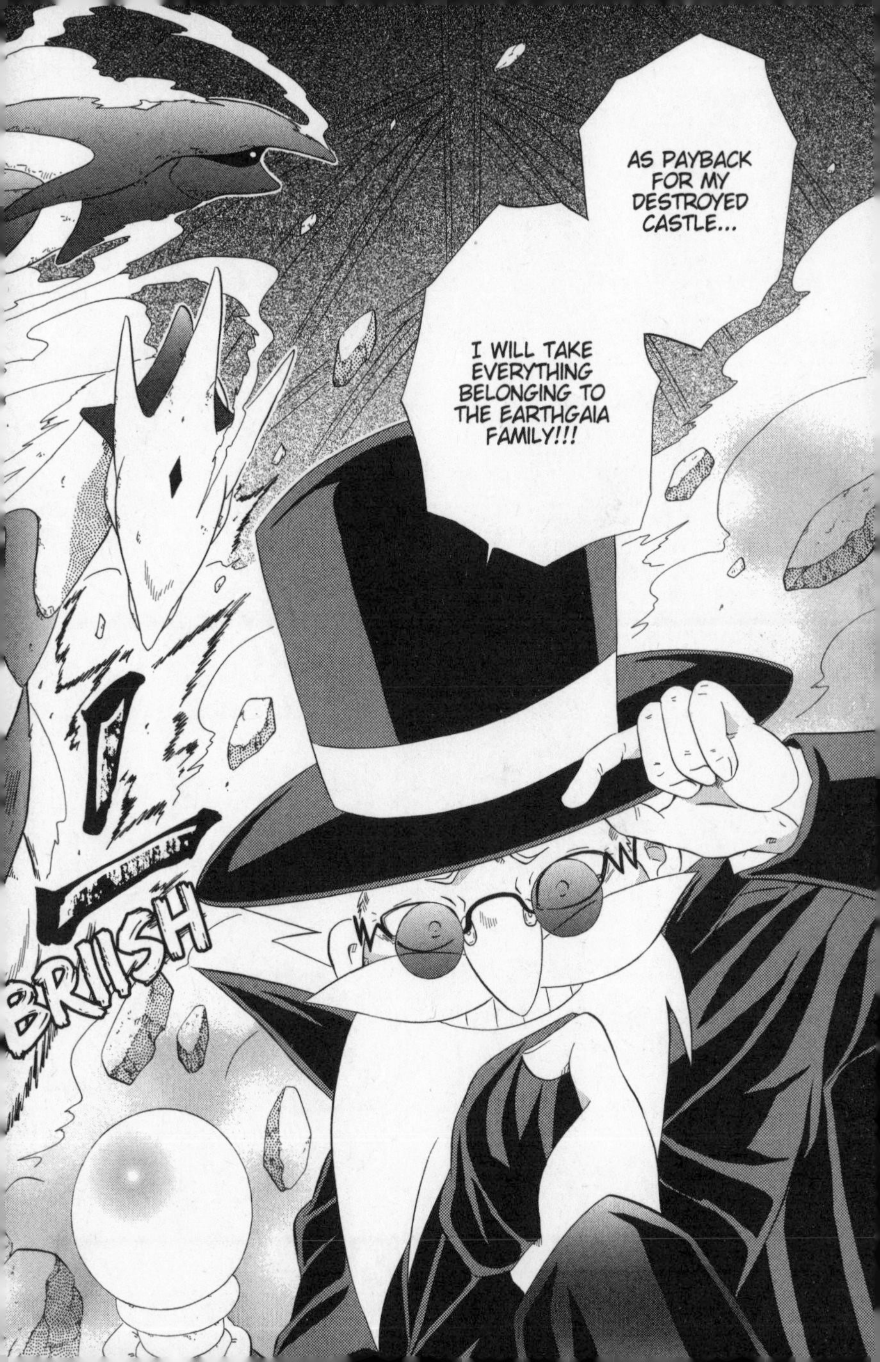
AS PAYBACK FOR MY DESTROYED CASTLE...
I WILL TAKE EVERYTHING BELONGING TO THE EARTHGAIA FAMILY!!!
BRIIISH

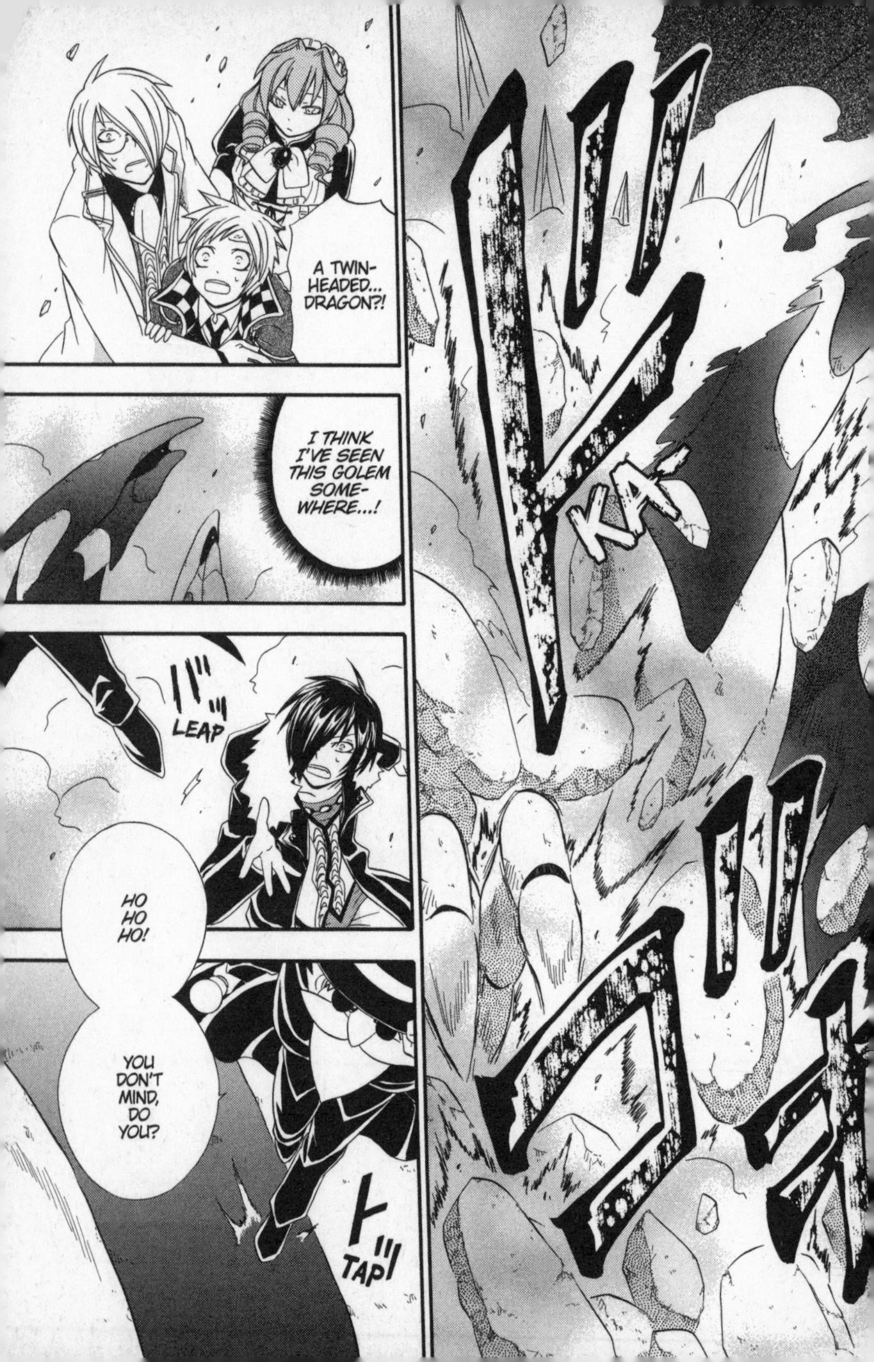
KA
A TWIN-HEADED... DRAGON?!
I THINK I'VE SEEN THIS GOLEM SOME-WHERE...!
LEAP
HO HO HO!
YOU DON'T MIND, DO YOU?
TAP

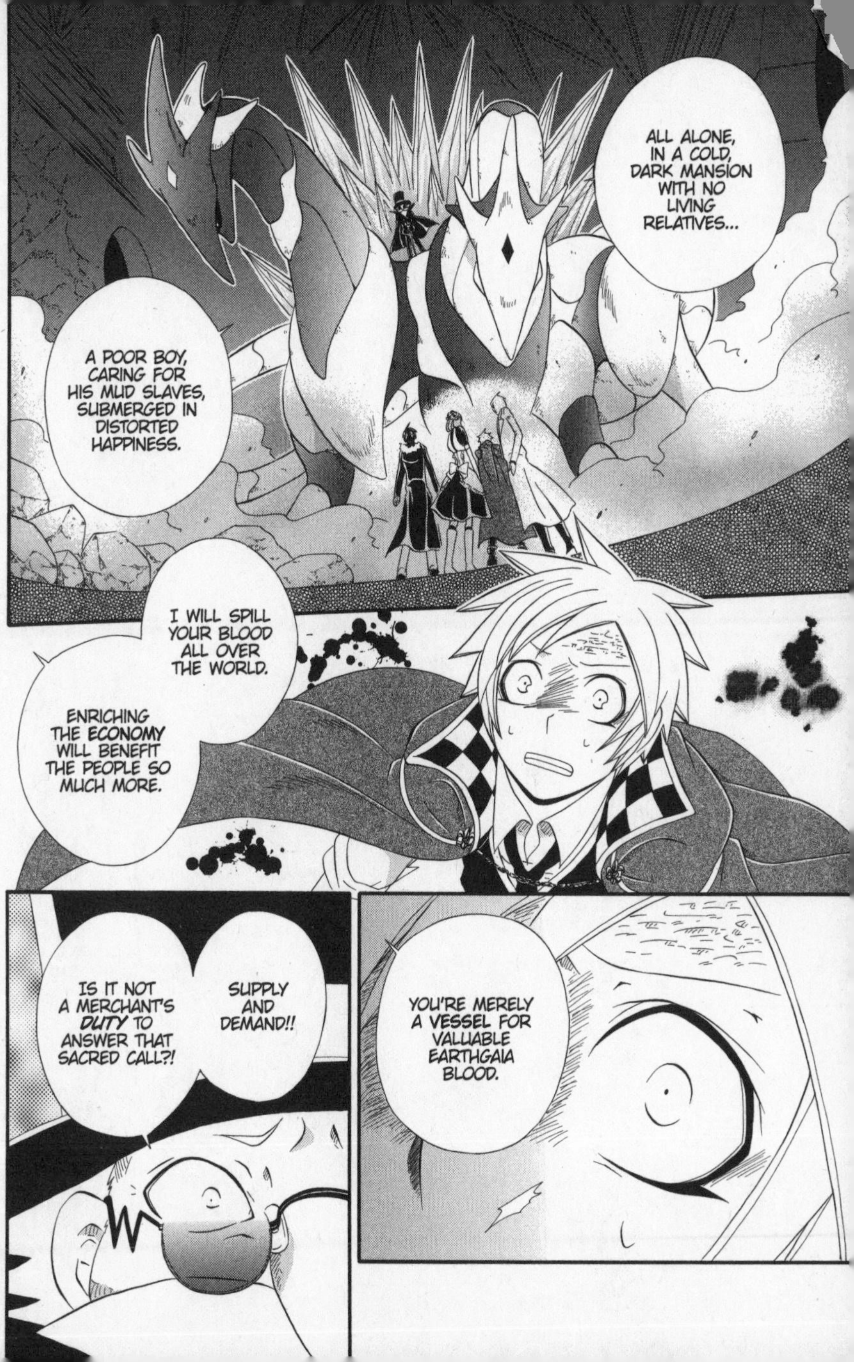
ALL ALONE, IN A COLD, DARK MANSION WITH NO LIVING RELATIVES...
A POOR BOY, CARING FOR HIS MUD SLAVES, SUBMERGED IN DISTORTED HAPPINESS.
I WILL SPILL YOUR BLOOD ALL OVER THE WORLD.
ENRICHING THE ECONOMY WILL BENEFIT THE PEOPLE SO MUCH MORE.
YOU'RE MERELY A VESSEL FOR VALUABLE EARTHGAIA BLOOD.
SUPPLY AND DEMAND!!
IS IT NOT A MERCHANT'S DUTY TO ANSWER THAT SACRED CALL?!

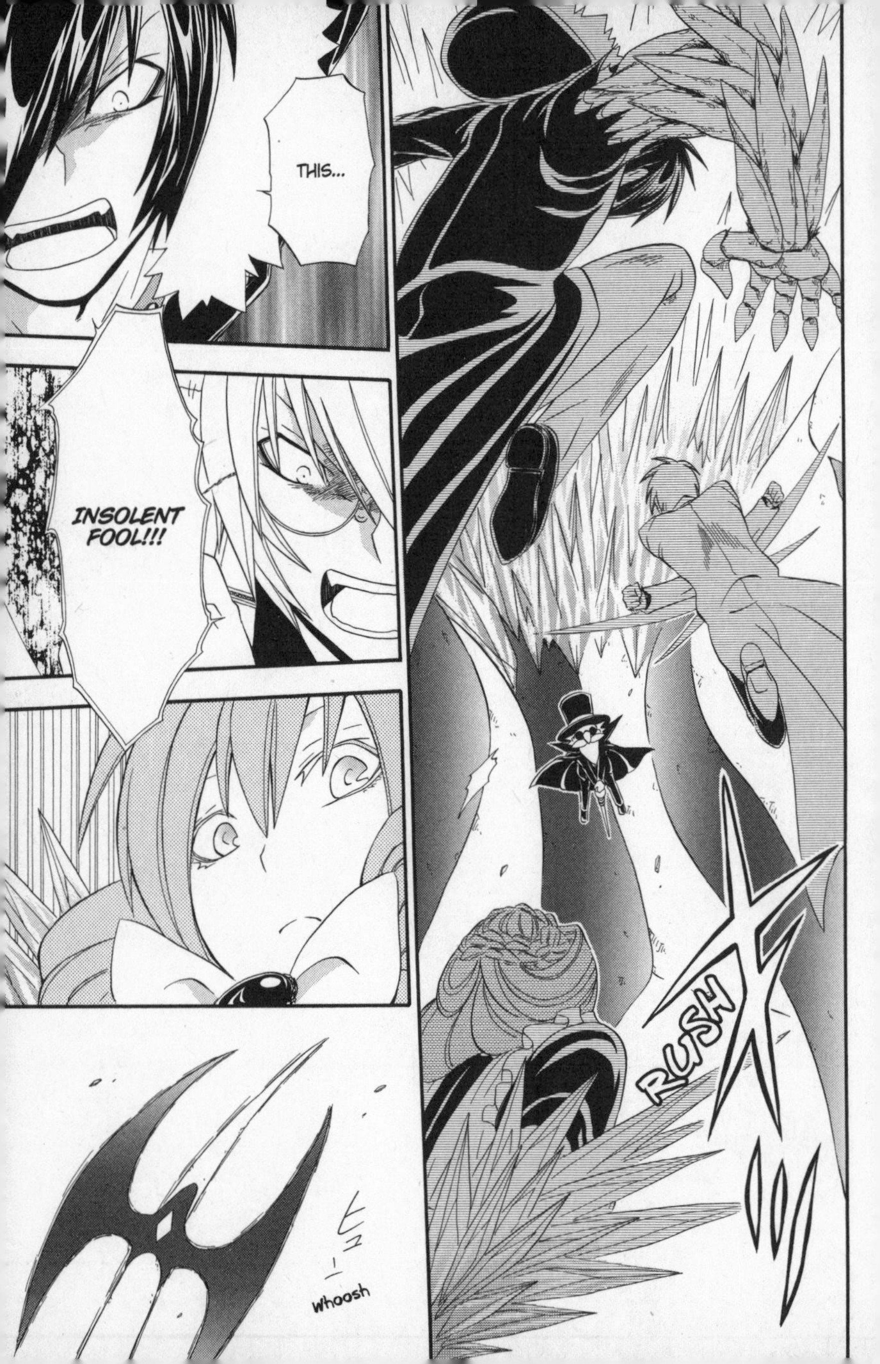
RUSH
THIS...
INSOLENT FOOL!!!
Whoosh

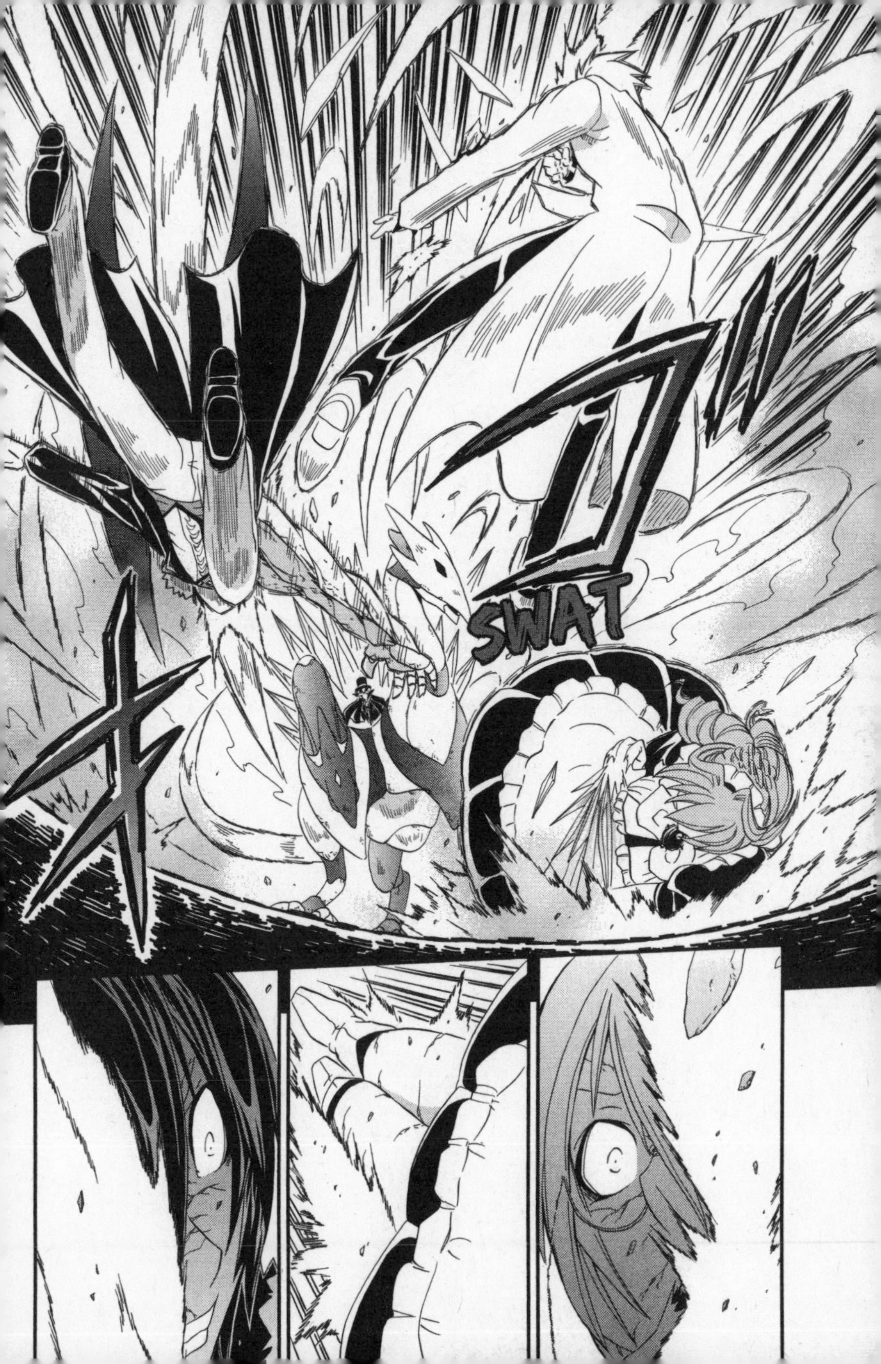
SWAT

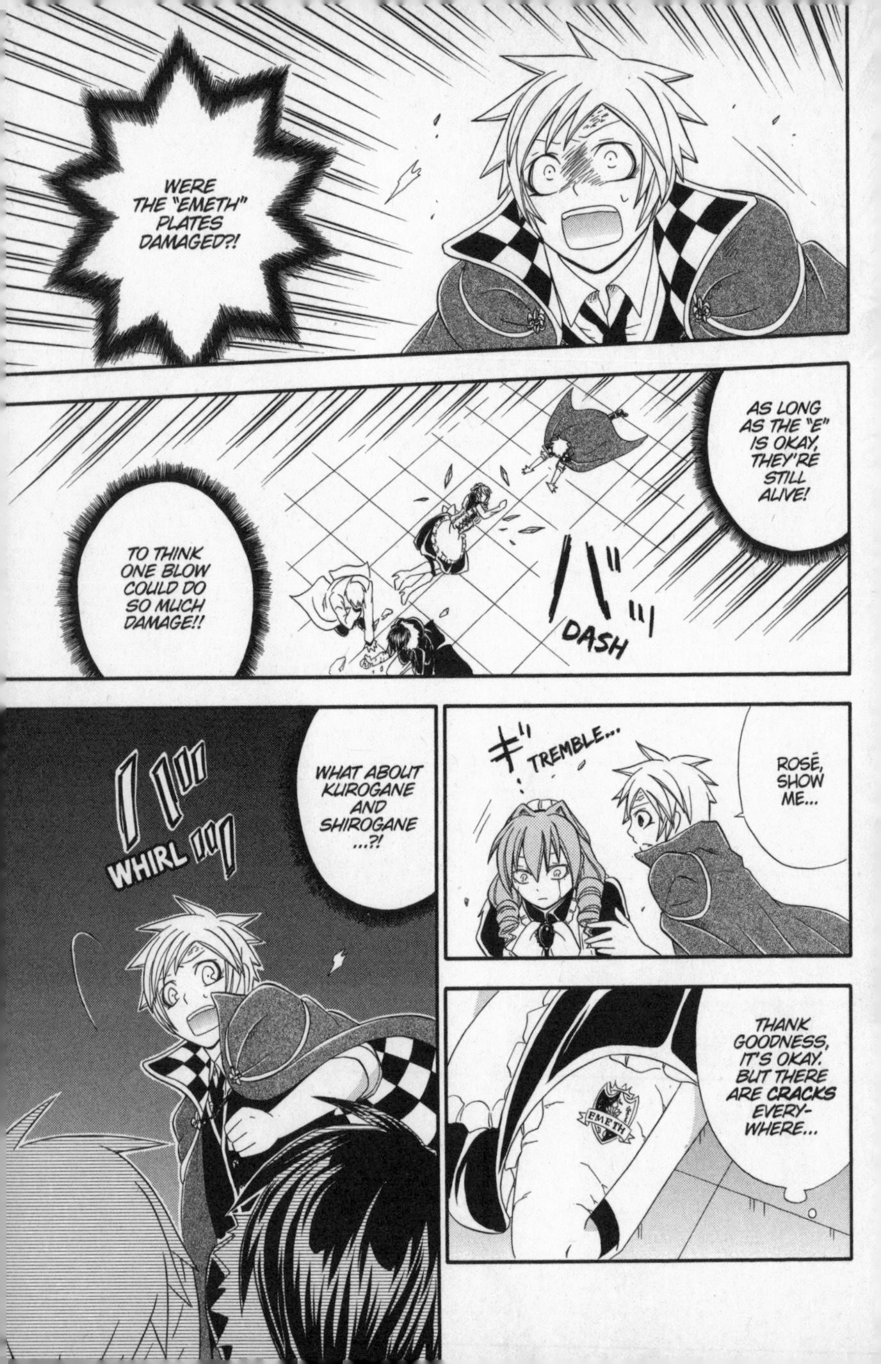
WERE THE "EMETH" PLATES DAMAGED?!
AS LONG AS THE "E" IS OKAY, THEY'RE STILL ALIVE!
DASH
TO THINK ONE BLOW COULD DO SO MUCH DAMAGE!!
ROSÉ, SHOW ME...
TREMBLE...
THANK GOODNESS, IT'S OKAY. BUT THERE ARE CRACKS EVERY-WHERE...
EMETH
WHAT ABOUT KUROGANE AND SHIROGANE ...?!
WHIRL

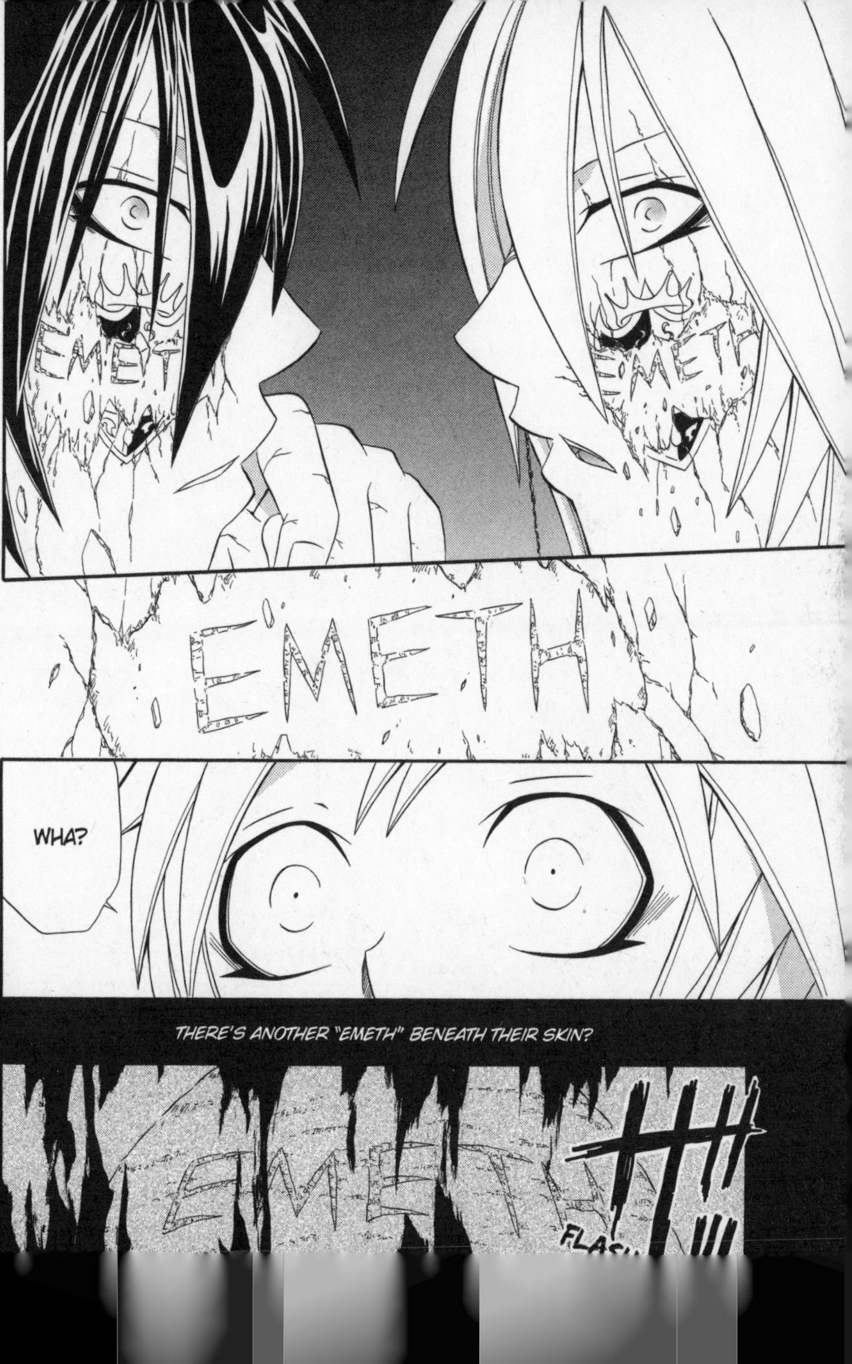
EMETH
EMETH
EMETH
WHA?
THERE'S ANOTHER "EMETH" BENEATH THEIR SKIN?
EMETH!!

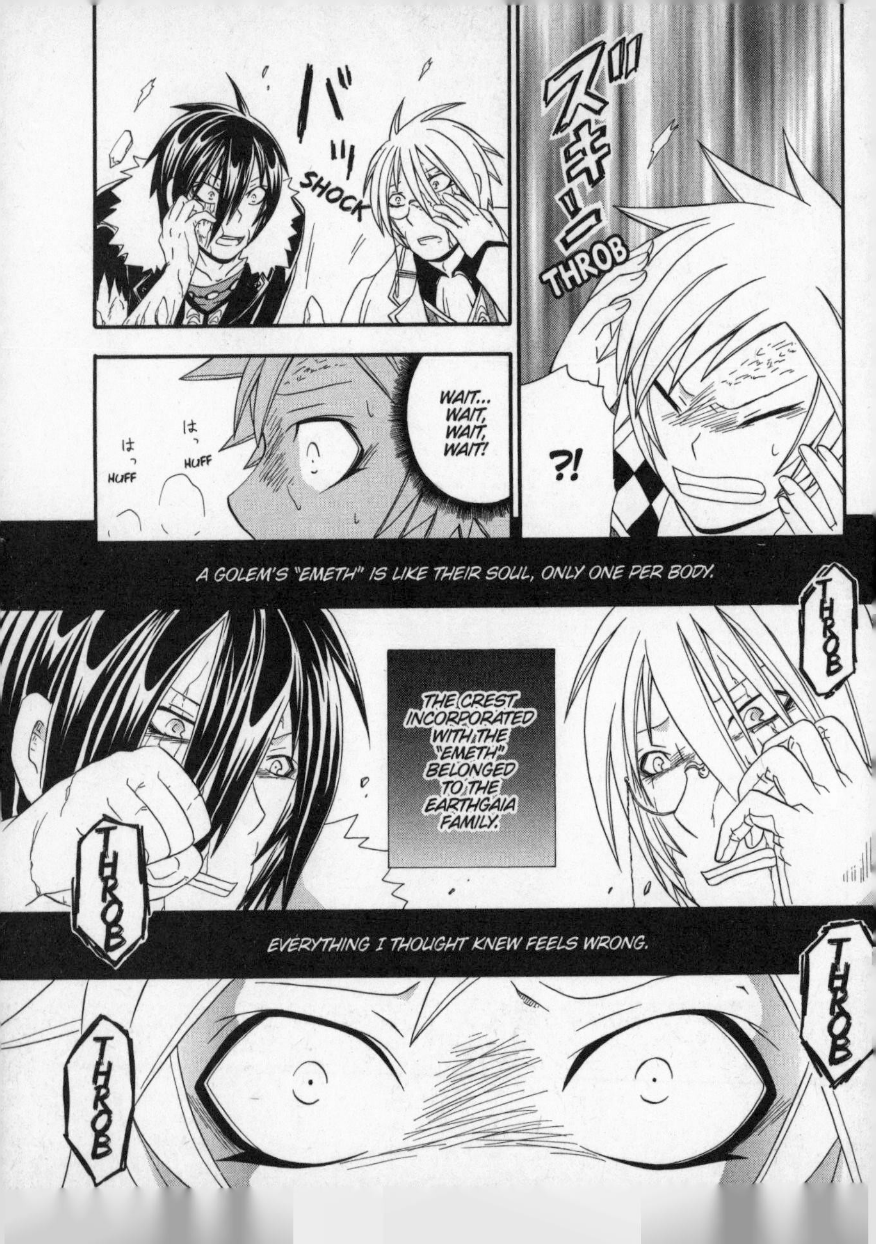
THROB
?!
バッ
SHOCK
WAIT... WAIT, WAIT, WAIT!
はっ HUFF
はっ HUFF
A GOLEM'S "EMETH" IS LIKE THEIR SOUL, ONLY ONE PER BODY.
THROB
THE CREST INCORPORATED WITH THE "EMETH" BELONGED TO THE EARTHGAIA FAMILY.
THROB
EVERYTHING I THOUGHT KNEW FEELS WRONG.
THROB
THROB

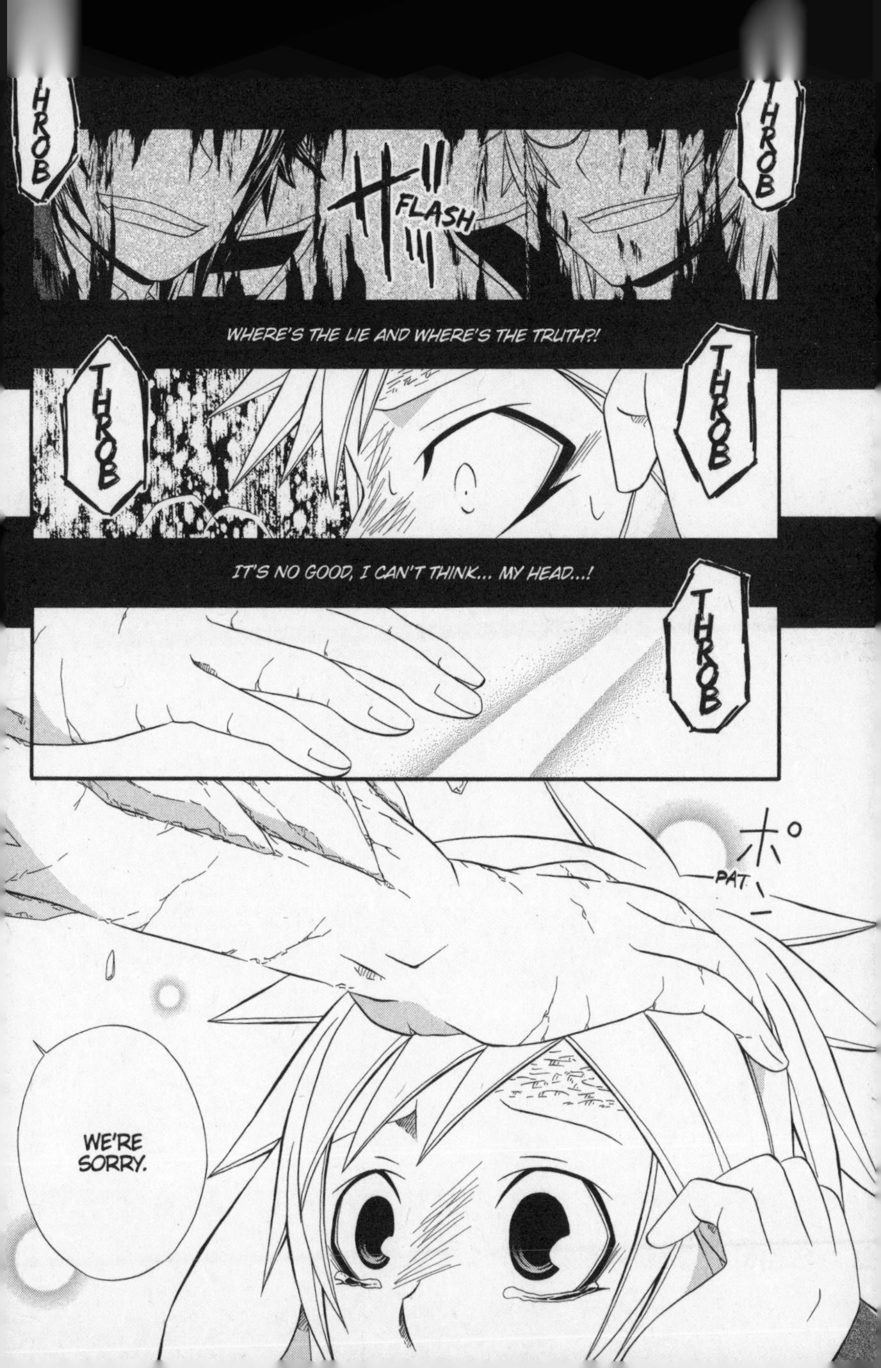
THROB
HROB
FLASH
WHERE'S THE LIE AND WHERE'S THE TRUTH?!
THROB
THROB
IT'S NO GOOD, I CAN'T THINK... MY HEAD...!
THROB
ポ
PAT
WE'RE SORRY.

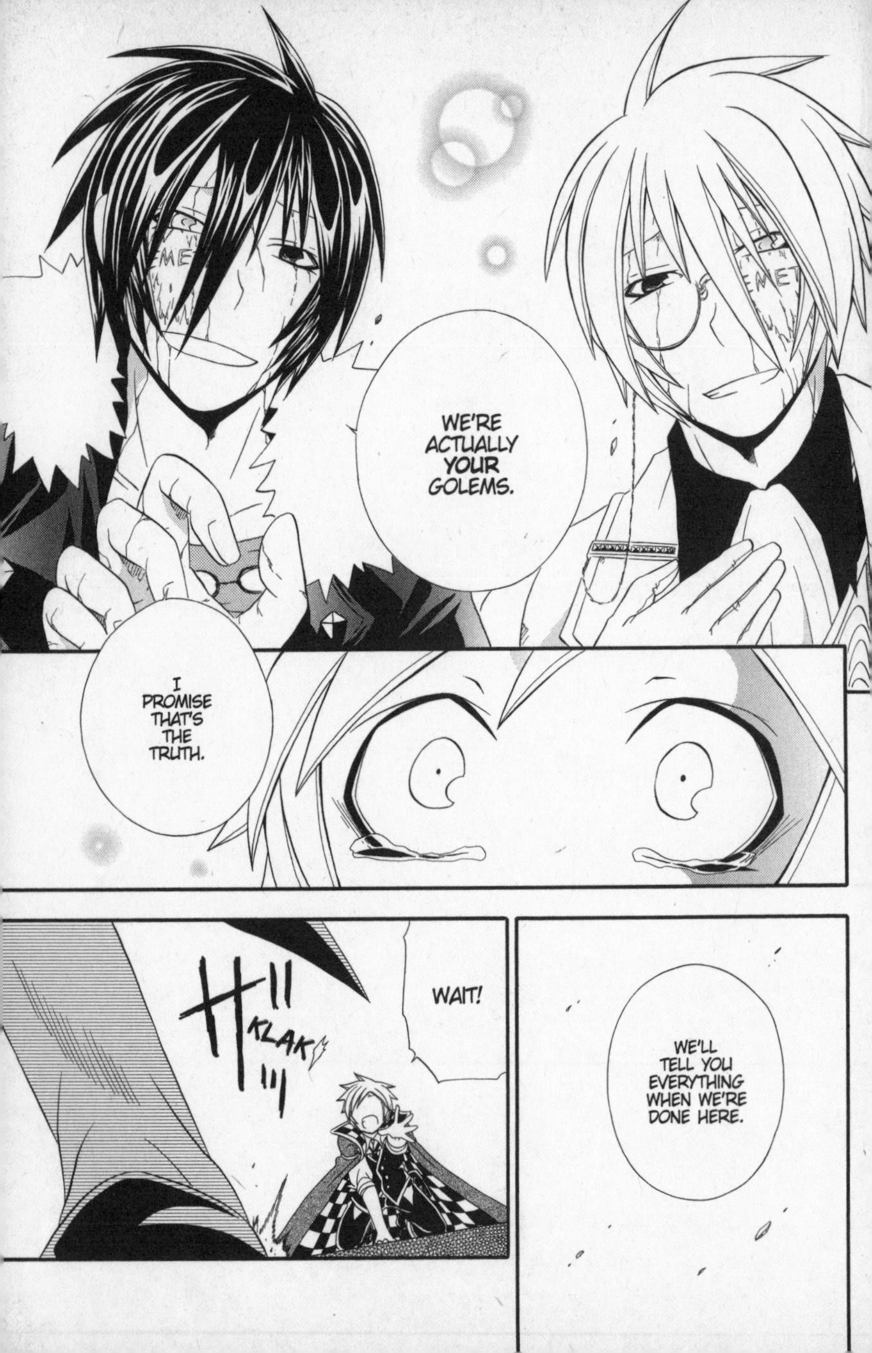
WE'RE ACTUALLY YOUR GOLEMS.
I PROMISE THAT'S THE TRUTH.
WE'LL TELL YOU EVERYTHING WHEN WE'RE DONE HERE.
WAIT!
KLAK

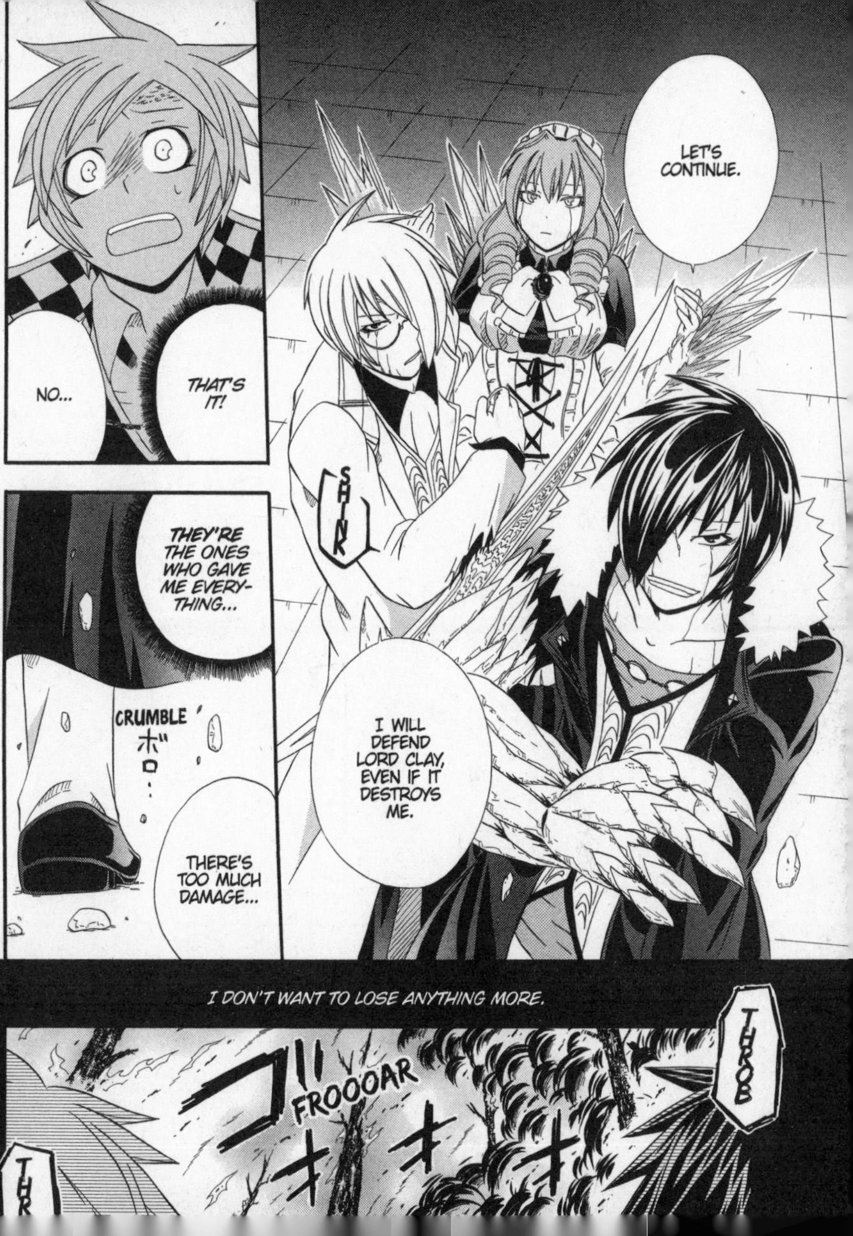
LET'S CONTINUE.
SHINK
I WILL DEFEND LORD CLAY, EVEN IF IT DESTROYS ME.
THAT'S IT!
NO...
THEY'RE THE ONES WHO GAVE ME EVERY-THING...
CRUMBLE
ボロ・・・
THERE'S TOO MUCH DAMAGE...
I DON'T WANT TO LOSE ANYTHING MORE.
THROB
FROOOAR
ゴオオ
THR

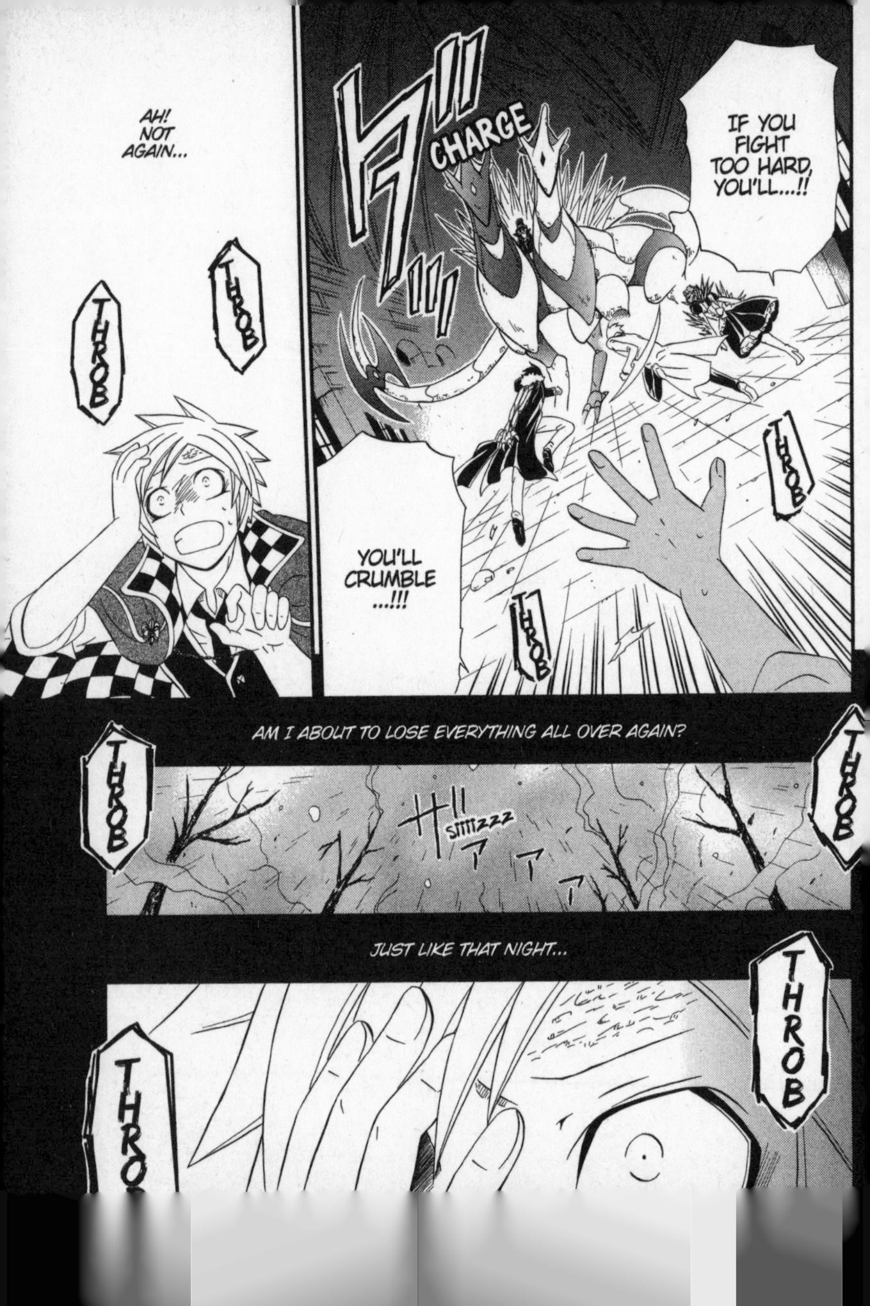
IF YOU FIGHT TOO HARD, YOU'LL...!!
CHARGE
THROB
YOU'LL CRUMBLE ...!!!
THROB
THROB
THROB
AH! NOT AGAIN...
AM I ABOUT TO LOSE EVERYTHING ALL OVER AGAIN?
THROB
SIIIIZZZ
THROB
JUST LIKE THAT NIGHT...
THROB

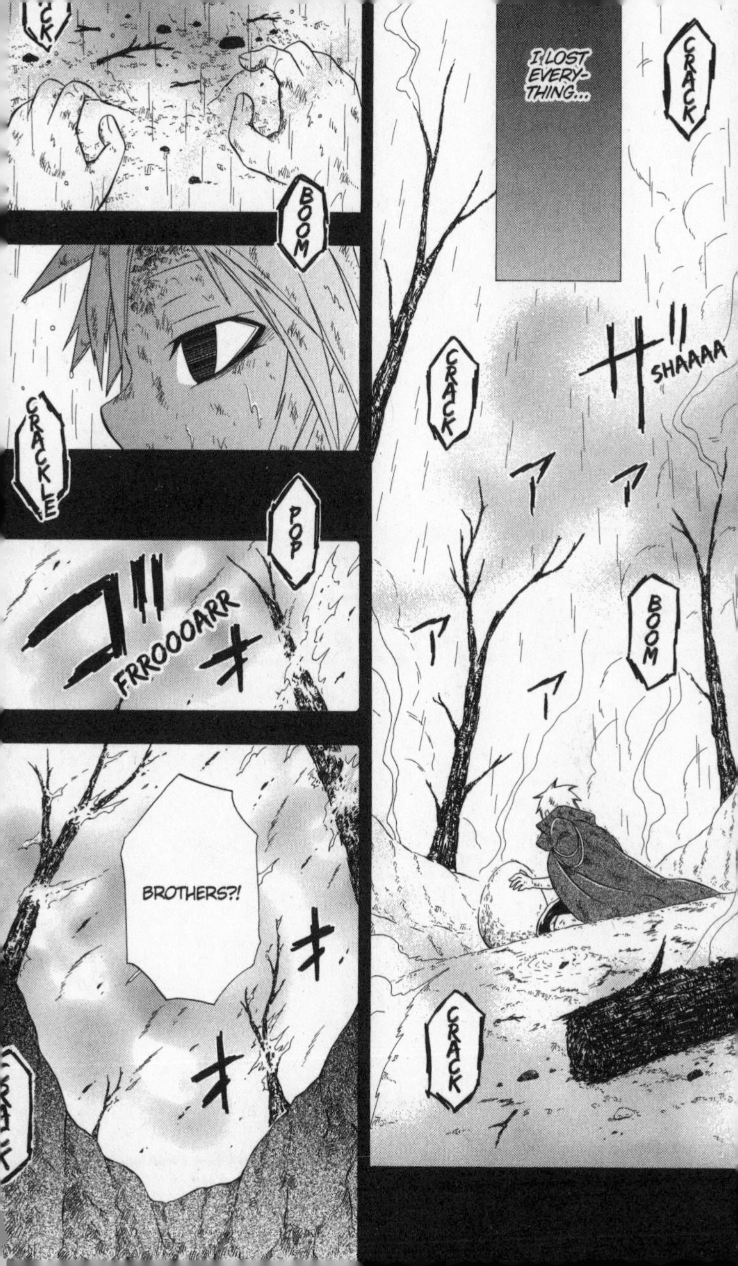
I LOST EVERY-THING...
CRACK
SHAAAA
CRACK
BOOM
CRACK
BOOM
CRACKLE
POP
FRROOOARR
BROTHERS?!

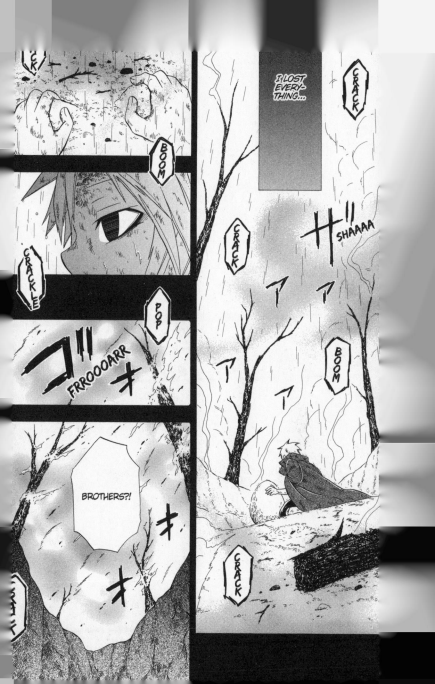

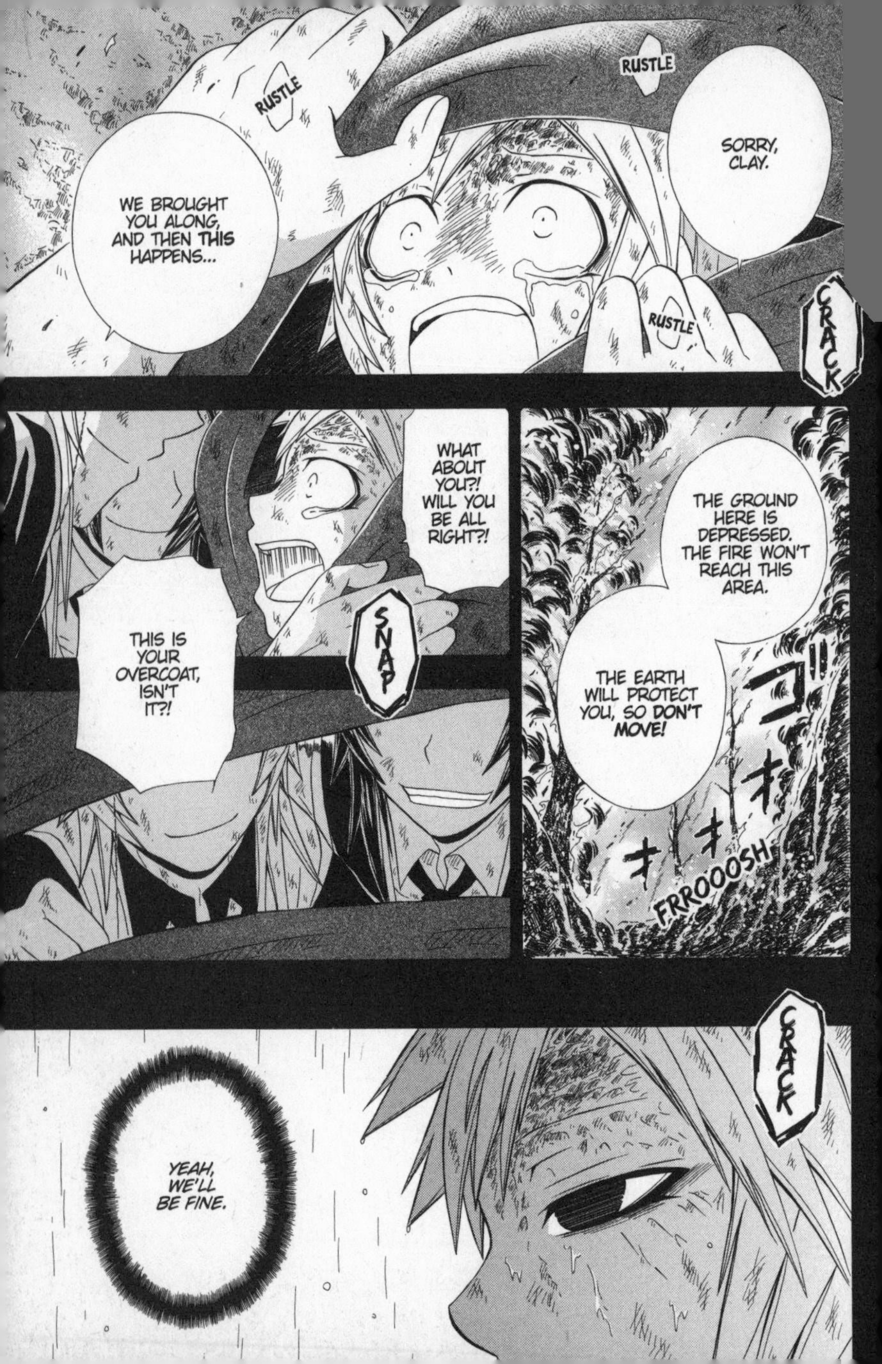
RUSTLE
SORRY, CLAY.
RUSTLE
WE BROUGHT YOU ALONG, AND THEN THIS HAPPENS...
RUSTLE
CRACK
THE GROUND HERE IS DEPRESSED. THE FIRE WON'T REACH THIS AREA.
THE EARTH WILL PROTECT YOU, SO DON'T MOVE!
FRROOOSH
WHAT ABOUT YOU?! WILL YOU BE ALL RIGHT?!
SNAP
THIS IS YOUR OVERCOAT, ISN'T IT?!
CRACK
YEAH, WE'LL BE FINE.

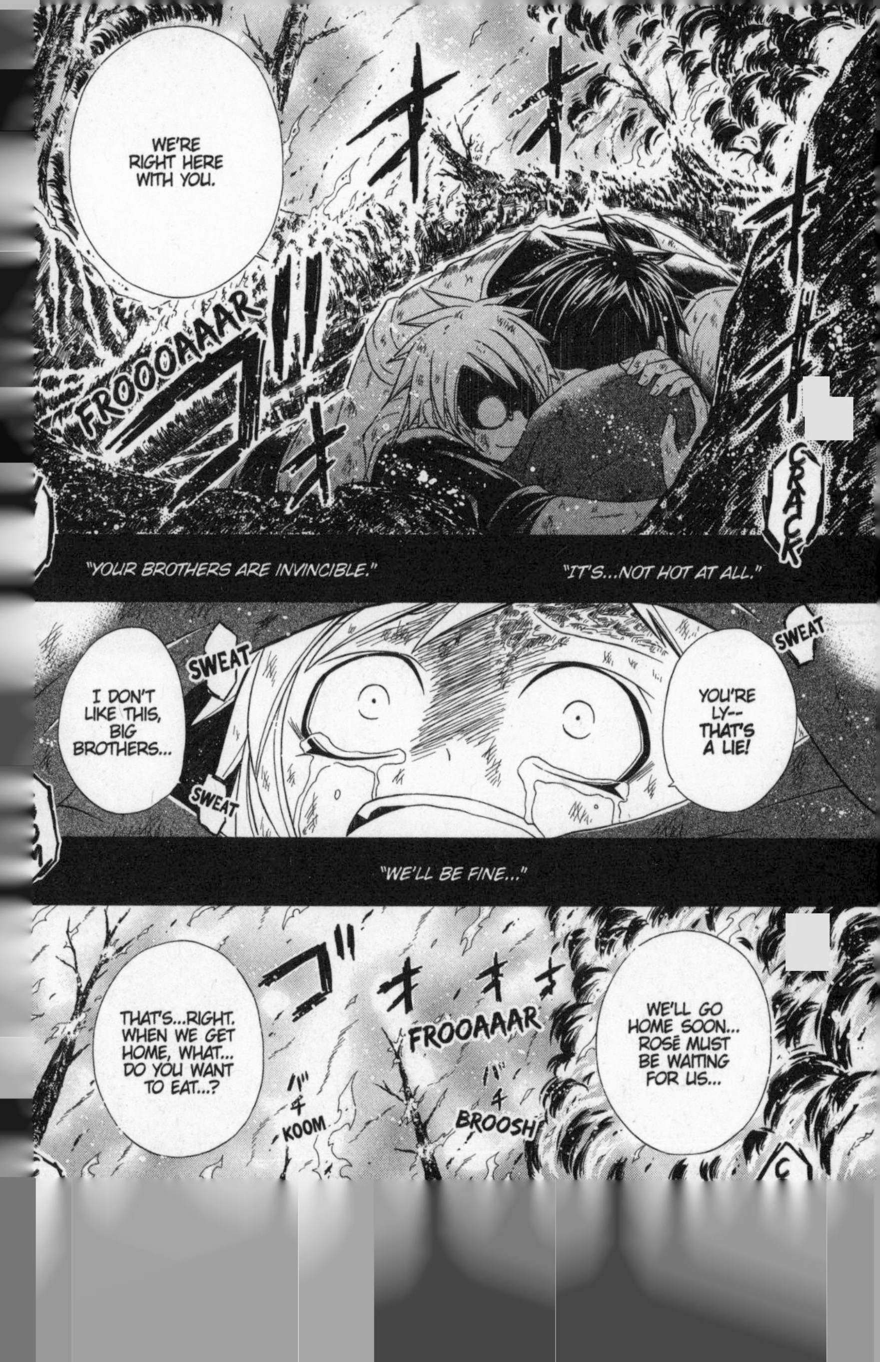
WE'RE RIGHT HERE WITH YOU.
FROOOAAAR
CRACK
"IT'S...NOT HOT AT ALL."
"YOUR BROTHERS ARE INVINCIBLE."
SWEAT
YOU'RE LY-- THAT'S A LIE!
SWEAT
I DON'T LIKE THIS, BIG BROTHERS...
SWEAT
"WE'LL BE FINE..."
WE'LL GO HOME SOON... ROSÉ MUST BE WAITING FOR US...
FROOAAAR
BROOSH
THAT'S...RIGHT. WHEN WE GET HOME, WHAT... DO YOU WANT TO EAT...?
KOOM

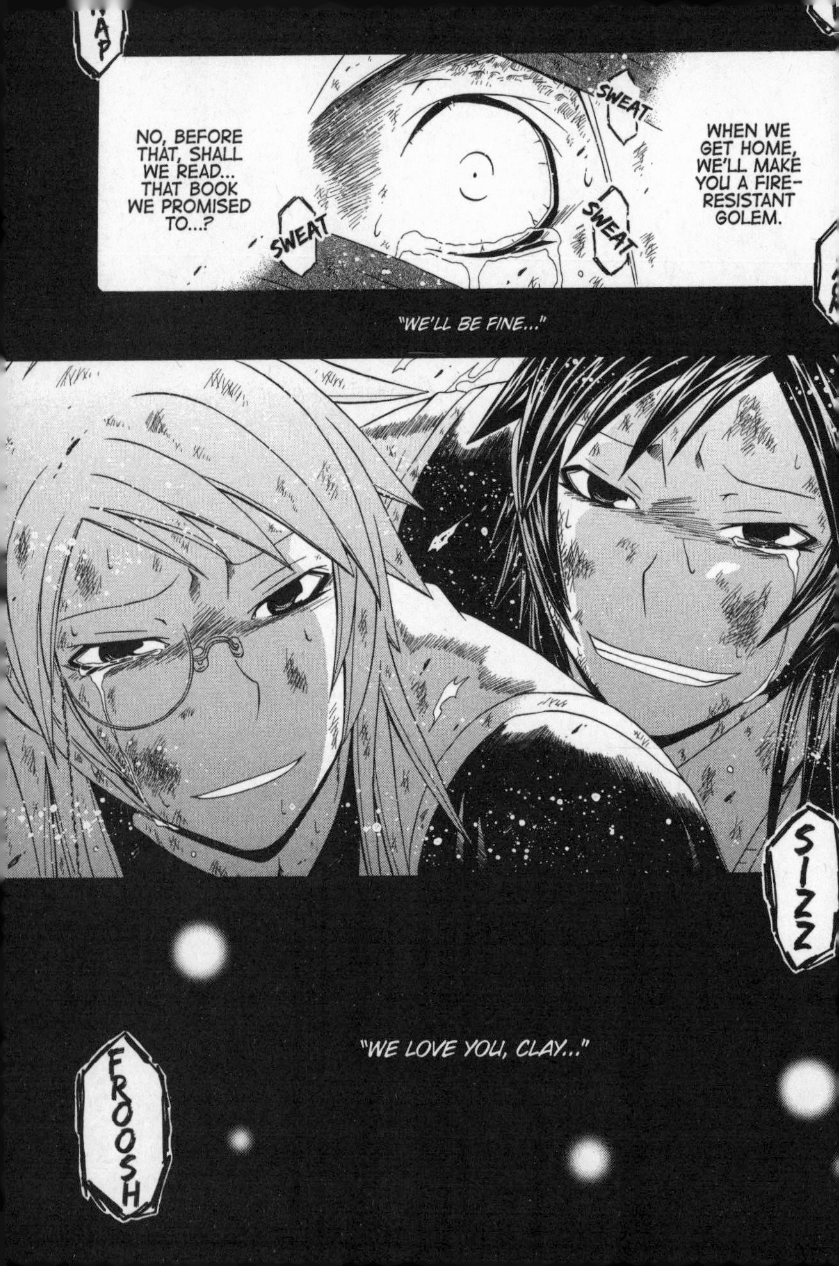

WHEN WE GET HOME, WE'LL MAKE YOU A FIRE-RESISTANT GOLEM.
SWEAT
SWEAT
NO, BEFORE THAT, SHALL WE READ... THAT BOOK WE PROMISED TO...?
SWEAT
"WE'LL BE FINE..."
SIZZ
"WE LOVE YOU, CLAY..."
FROOSH

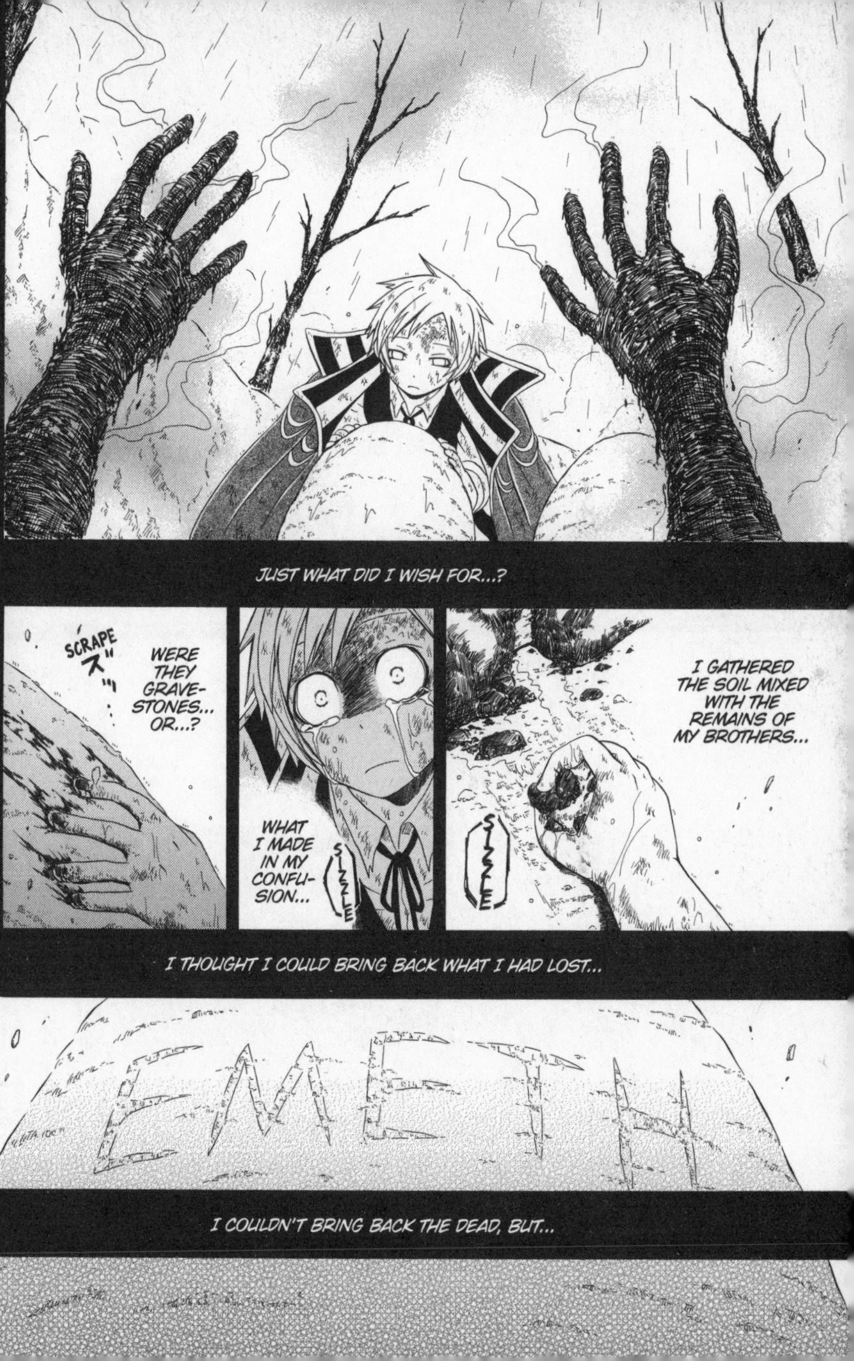
JUST WHAT DID I WISH FOR...?
I GATHERED THE SOIL MIXED WITH THE REMAINS OF MY BROTHERS...
SIZZLE
WHAT I MADE IN MY CONFUSION...
SIZZLE
WERE THEY GRAVESTONES... OR...?
SCRAPE
ズ"
I THOUGHT I COULD BRING BACK WHAT I HAD LOST...
EMETH
I COULDN'T BRING BACK THE DEAD, BUT...

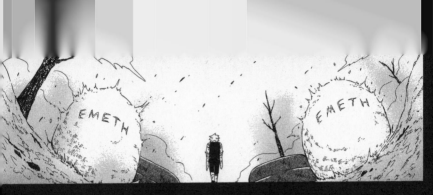

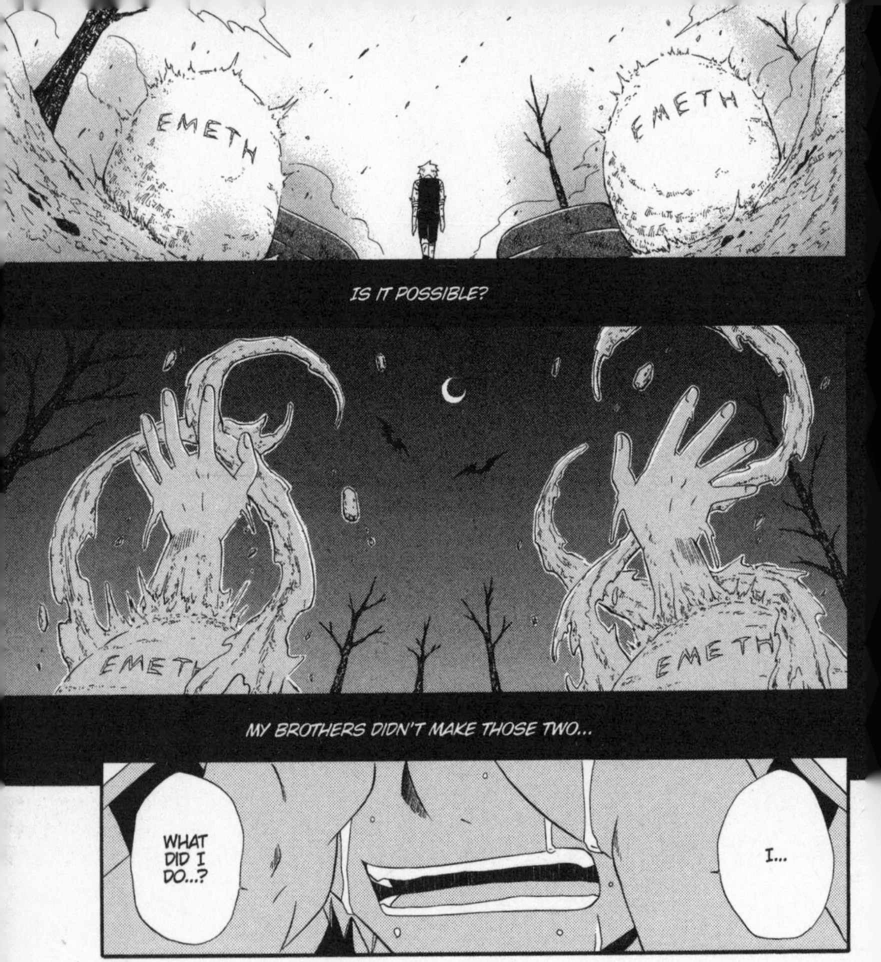
EMETH
EMETH
IS IT POSSIBLE?
EMETH
EMETH
MY BROTHERS DIDN'T MAKE THOSE TWO...
I...
WHAT DID I DO...?
THE ONE WHO MADE THEM...

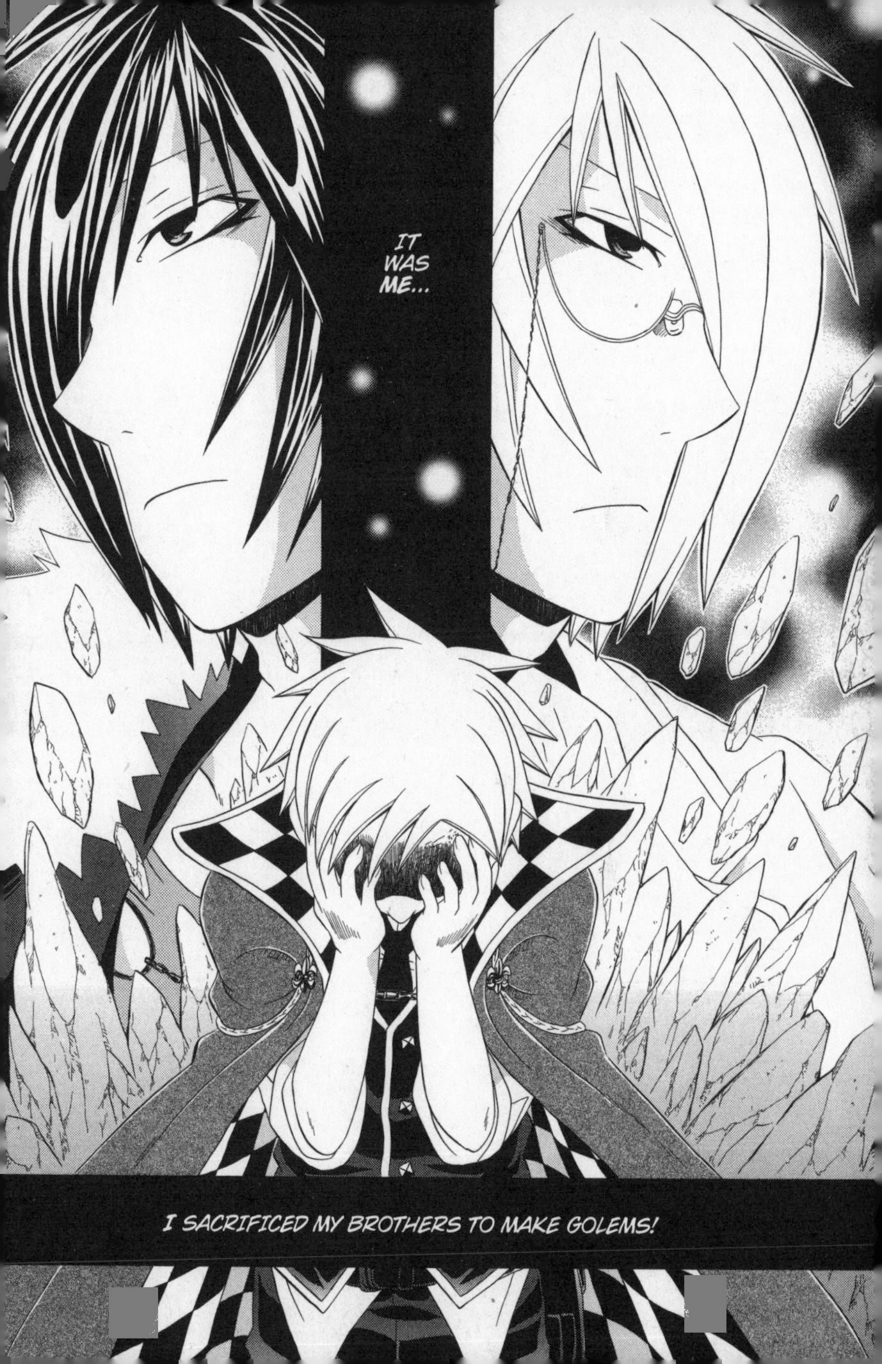
IT WAS ME...
I SACRIFICED MY BROTHERS TO MAKE GOLEMS!

Chapter 11: Things I Want to Protect

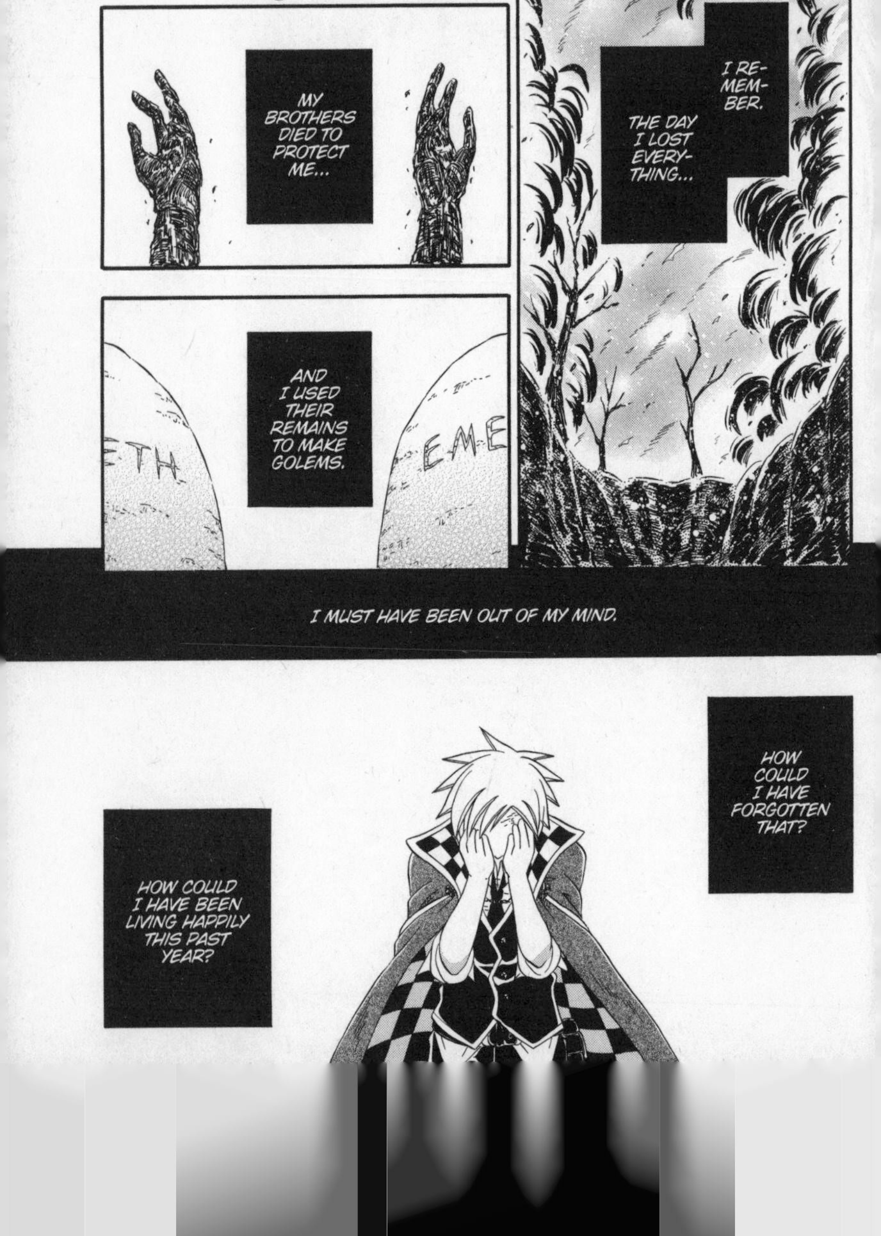
I RE-MEM-BER.
THE DAY I LOST EVERY-THING...
MY BROTHERS DIED TO PROTECT ME...
AND I USED THEIR REMAINS TO MAKE GOLEMS.
I MUST HAVE BEEN OUT OF MY MIND.
HOW COULD I HAVE FORGOTTEN THAT?
HOW COULD I HAVE BEEN LIVING HAPPILY THIS PAST YEAR?

Chapter 11: Things I Want to Protect

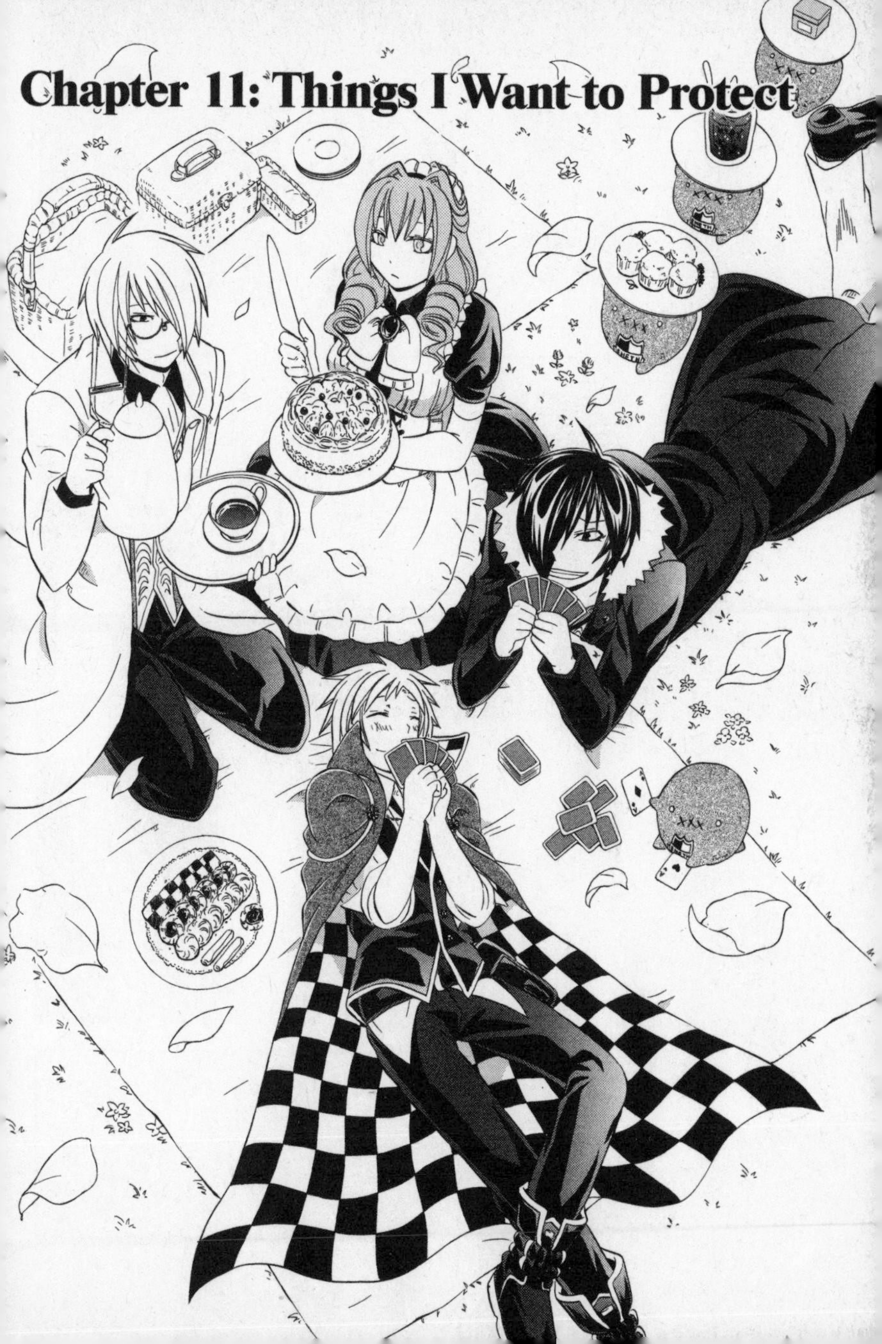

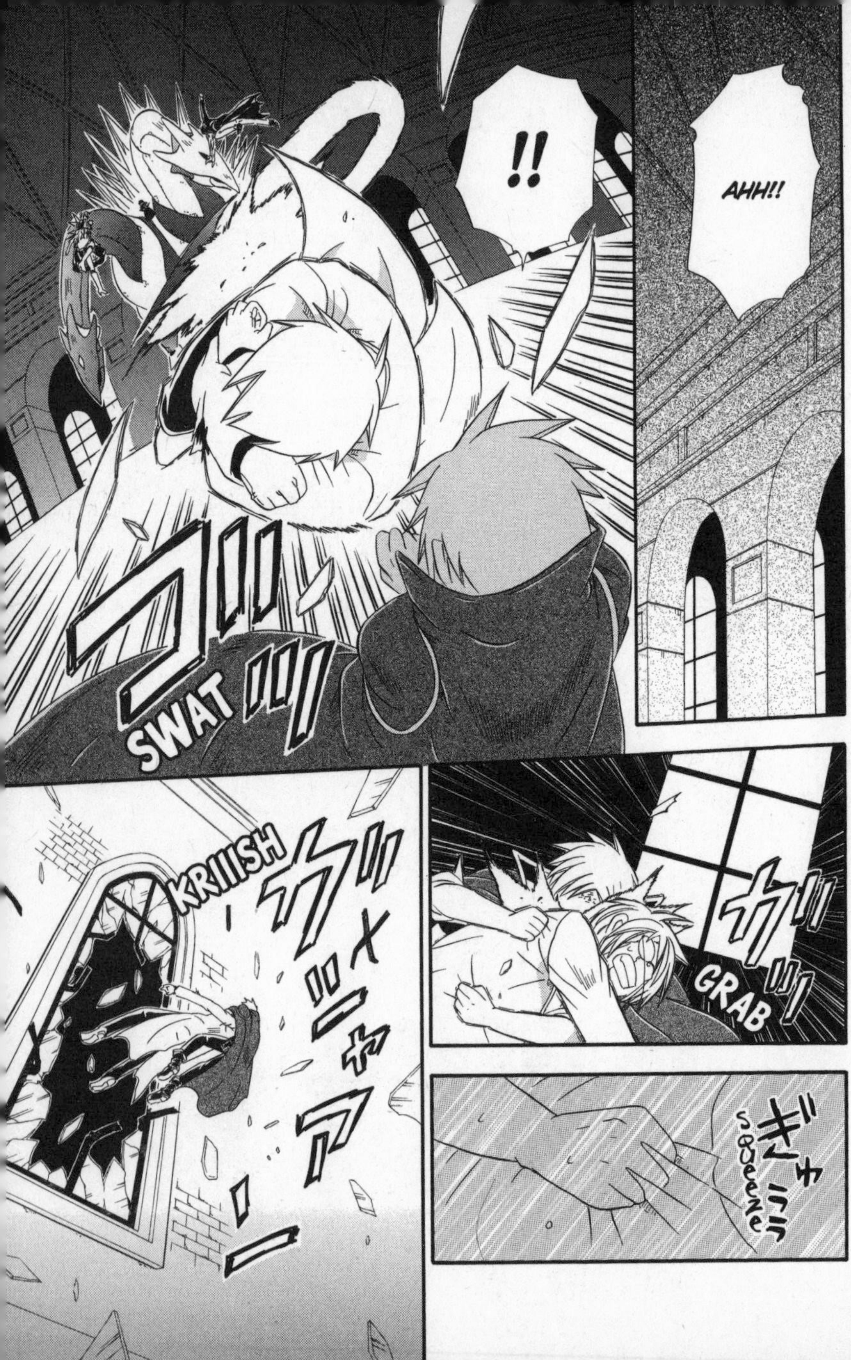

AHH!!
!!
SWAT
GRAB
squeeze
KRIIISH

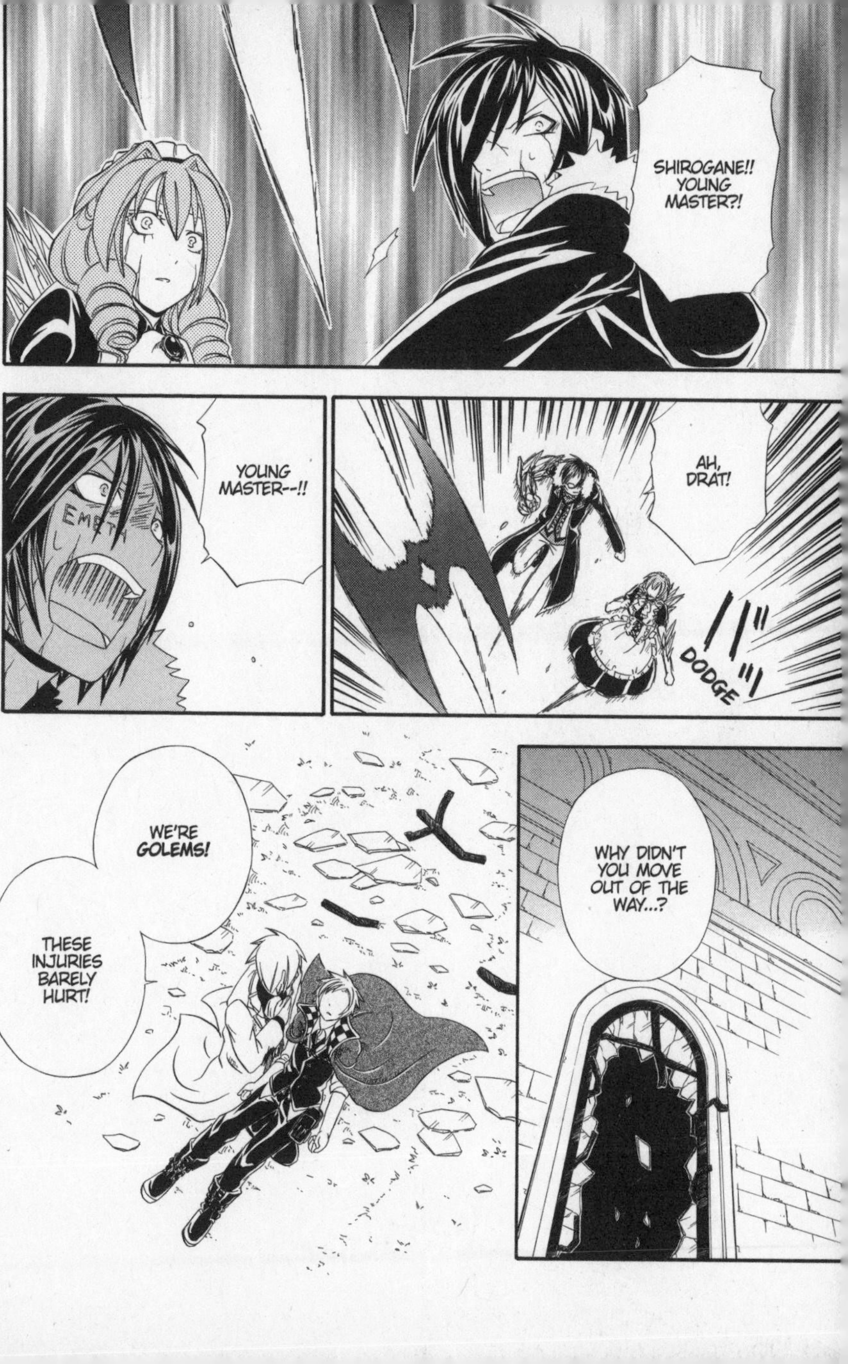
SHIROGANE!! YOUNG MASTER?!
AH, DRAT!
DODGE
YOUNG MASTER--!!
WHY DIDN'T YOU MOVE OUT OF THE WAY...?
WE'RE GOLEMS!
THESE INJURIES BARELY HURT!

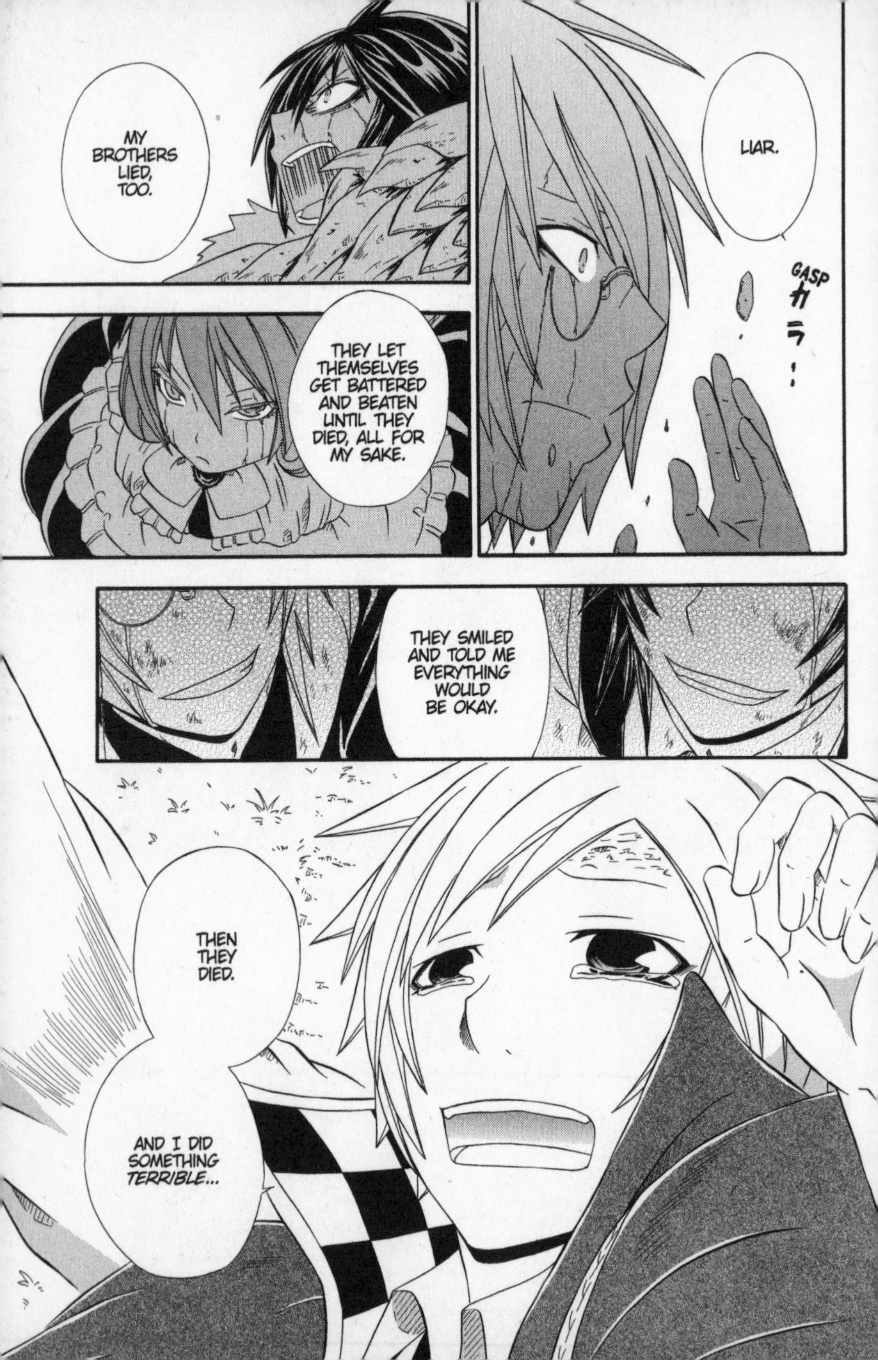
LIAR.
GASP
カラ!
MY BROTHERS LIED, TOO.
THEY LET THEMSELVES GET BATTERED AND BEATEN UNTIL THEY DIED, ALL FOR MY SAKE.
THEY SMILED AND TOLD ME EVERYTHING WOULD BE OKAY.
THEN THEY DIED.
AND I DID SOMETHING *TERRIBLE*...

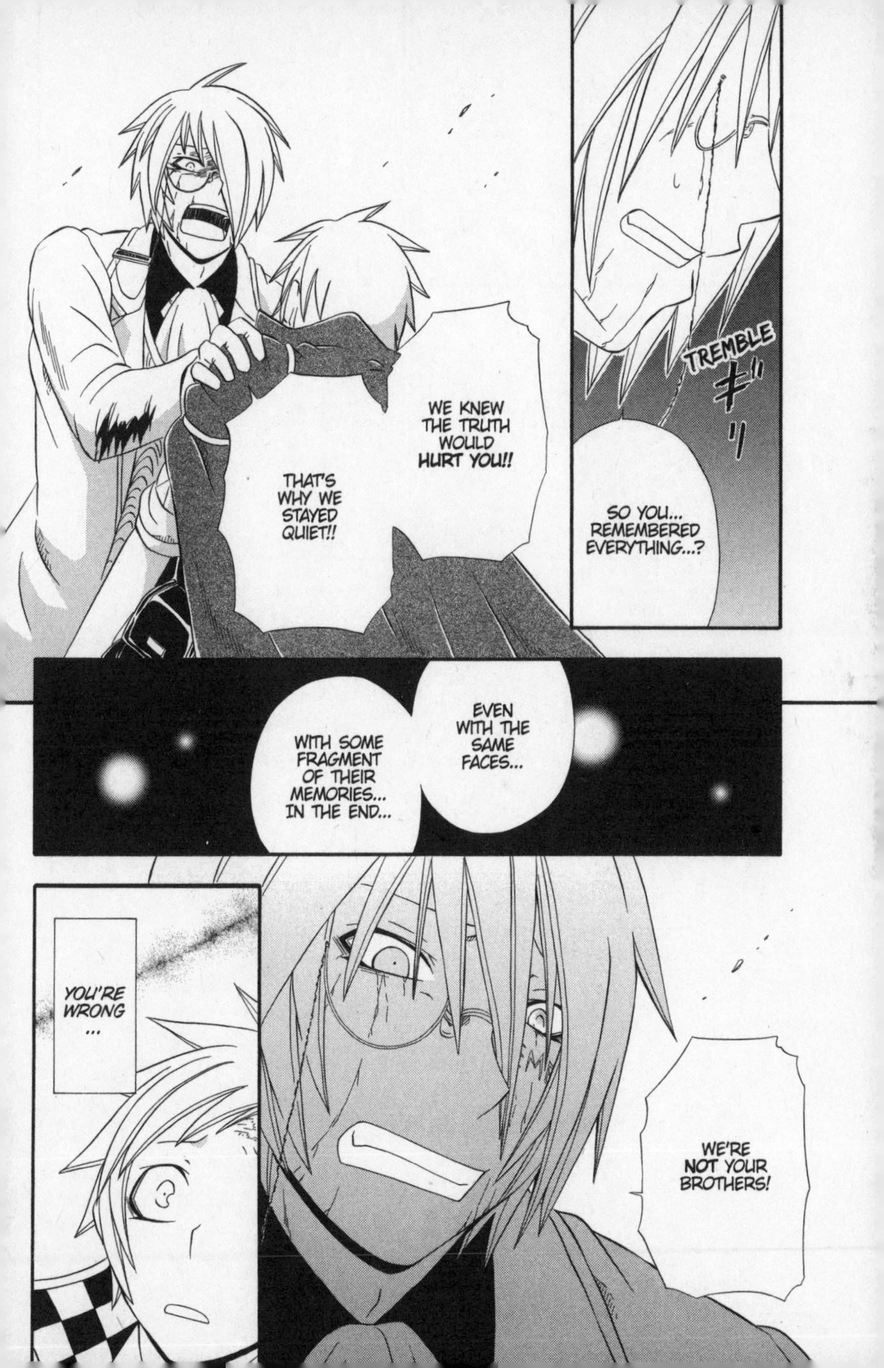
TREMBLE
SO YOU... REMEMBERED EVERYTHING...?
WE KNEW THE TRUTH WOULD HURT YOU!!
THAT'S WHY WE STAYED QUIET!!
EVEN WITH THE SAME FACES...
WITH SOME FRAGMENT OF THEIR MEMORIES... IN THE END...
WE'RE NOT YOUR BROTHERS!
YOU'RE WRONG ...

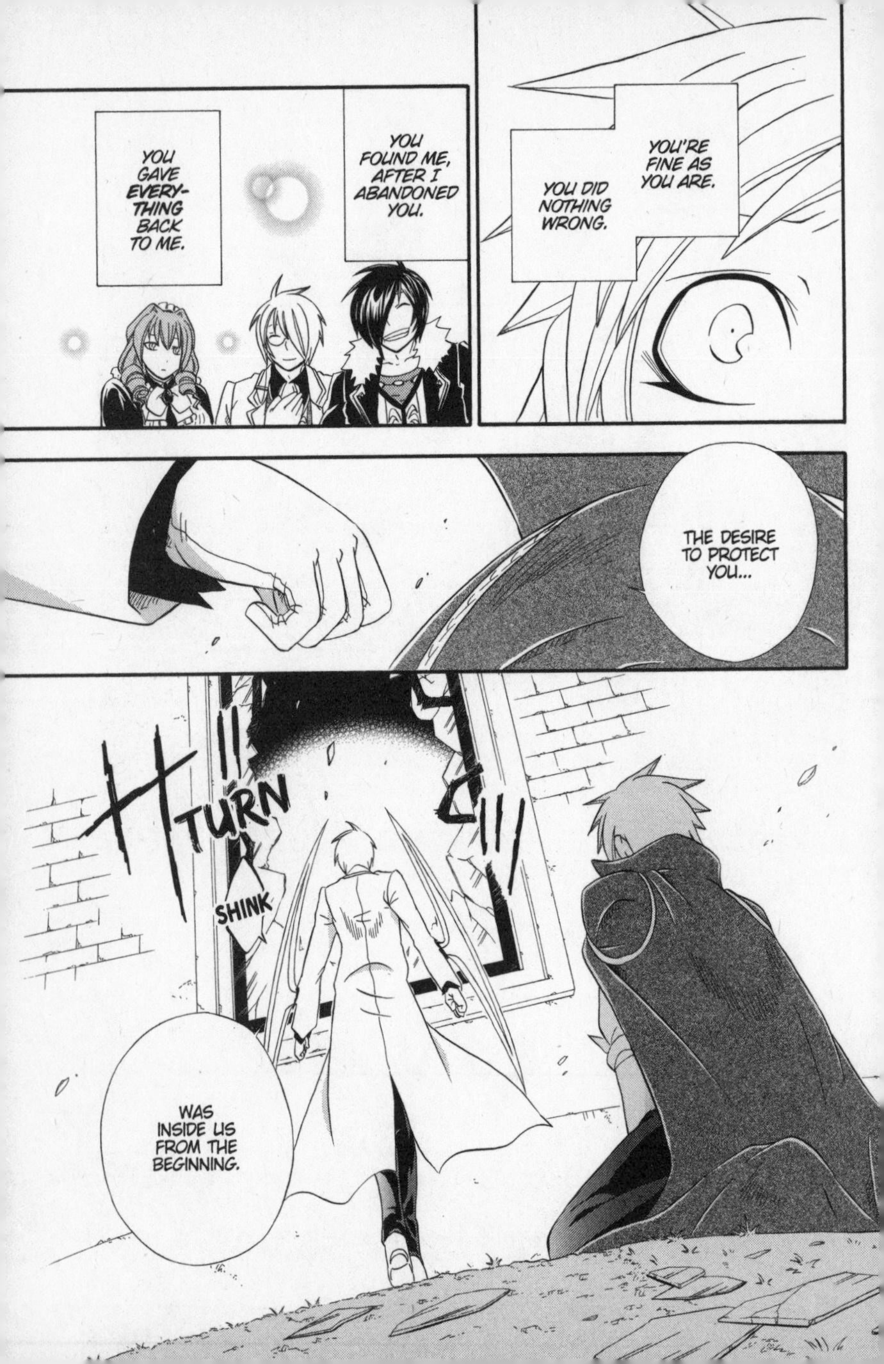
YOU'RE FINE AS YOU ARE.
YOU DID NOTHING WRONG.
YOU FOUND ME, AFTER I ABANDONED YOU.
YOU GAVE EVERY-THING BACK TO ME.
THE DESIRE TO PROTECT YOU...
TURN
SHINK
WAS INSIDE US FROM THE BEGINNING.

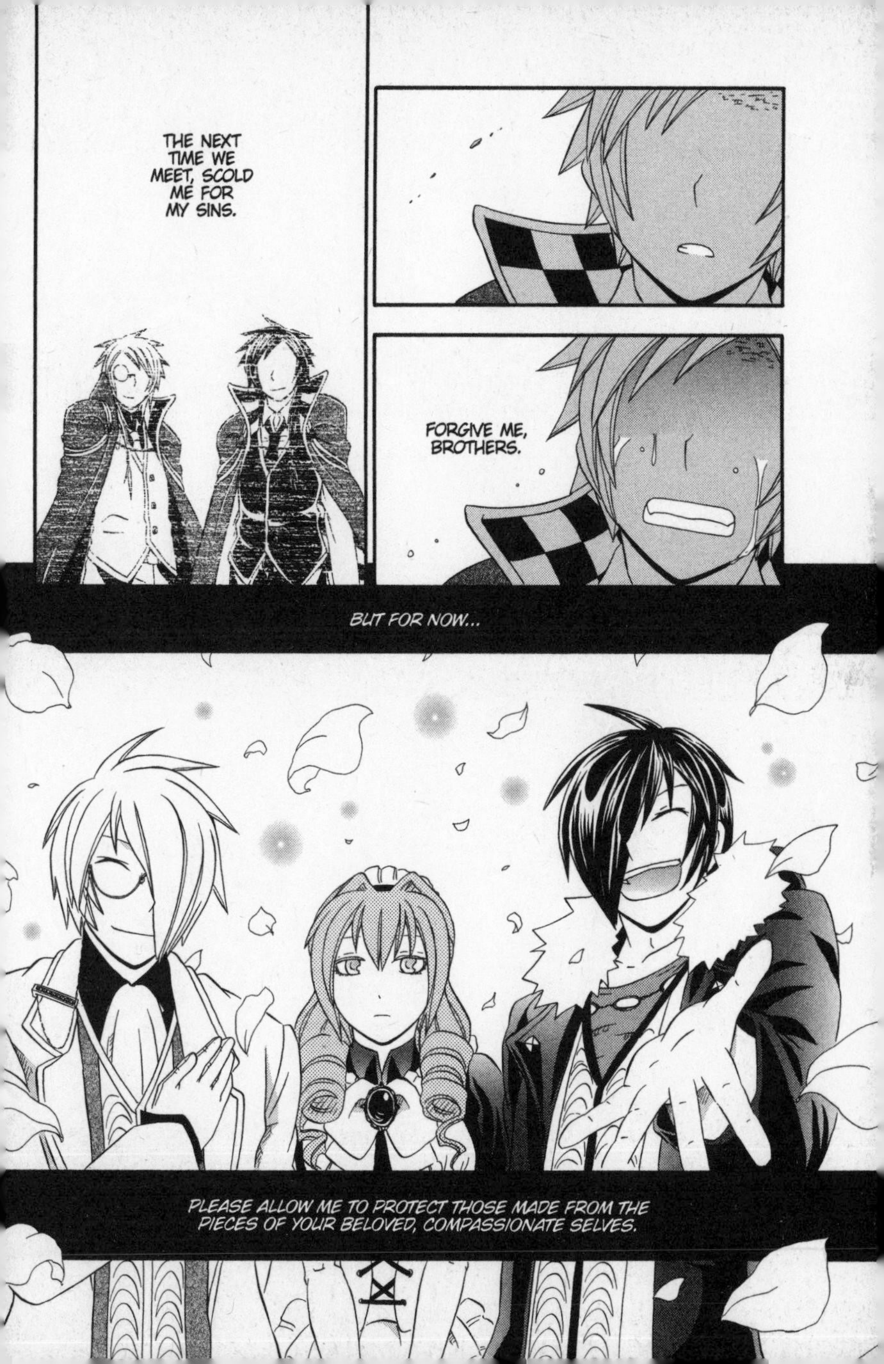
FORGIVE ME, BROTHERS.
THE NEXT TIME WE MEET, SCOLD ME FOR MY SINS.
BUT FOR NOW...
PLEASE ALLOW ME TO PROTECT THOSE MADE FROM THE PIECES OF YOUR BELOVED, COMPASSIONATE SELVES.

WHAT CAN I DO FOR THE ONES I WANT TO PROTECT?

I MUST SHARPEN MY WITS AND...

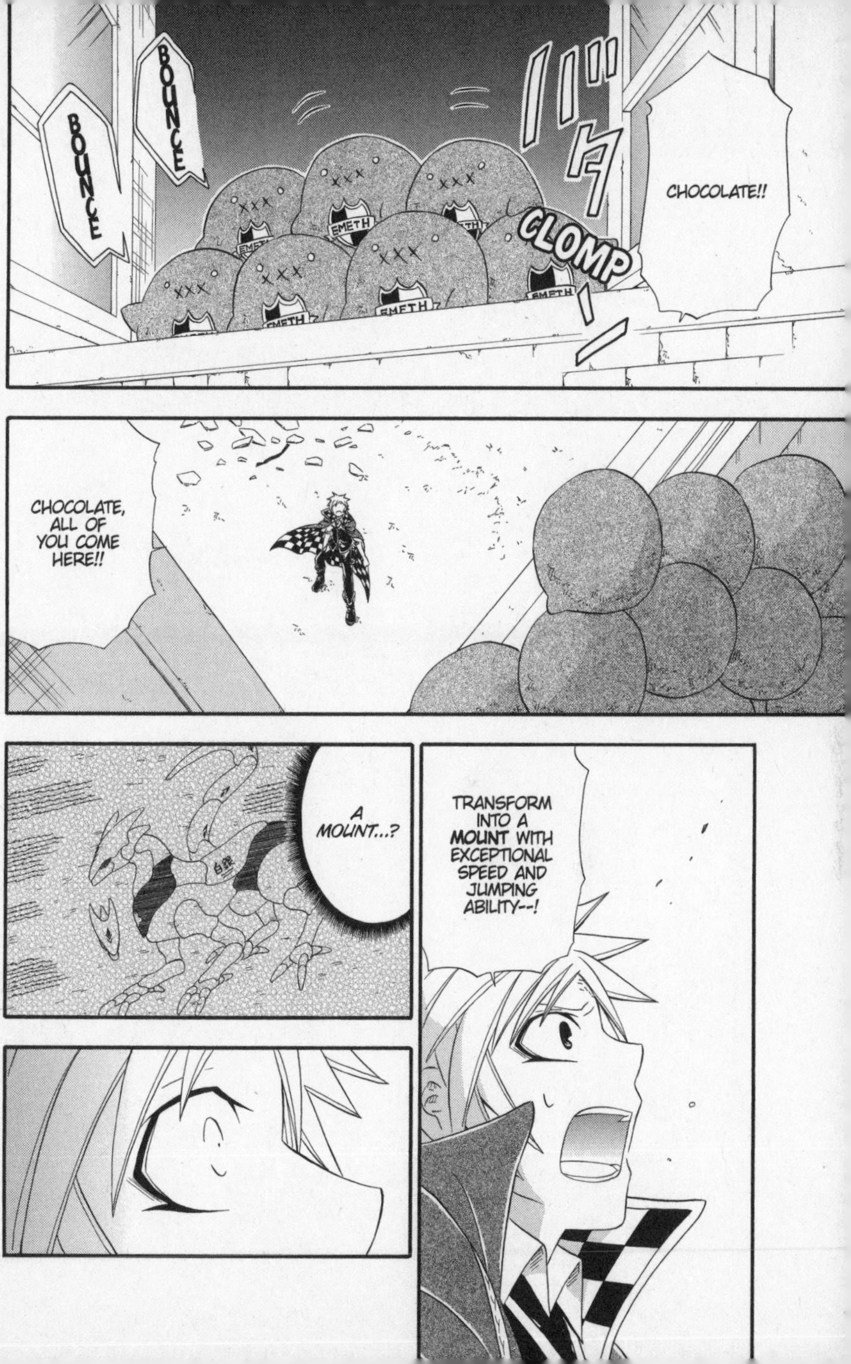
CHOCOLATE!!
CLOMP
BOUNCE
BOUNCE
CHOCOLATE, ALL OF YOU COME HERE!!
TRANSFORM INTO A MOUNT WITH EXCEPTIONAL SPEED AND JUMPING ABILITY--!
A MOUNT...?

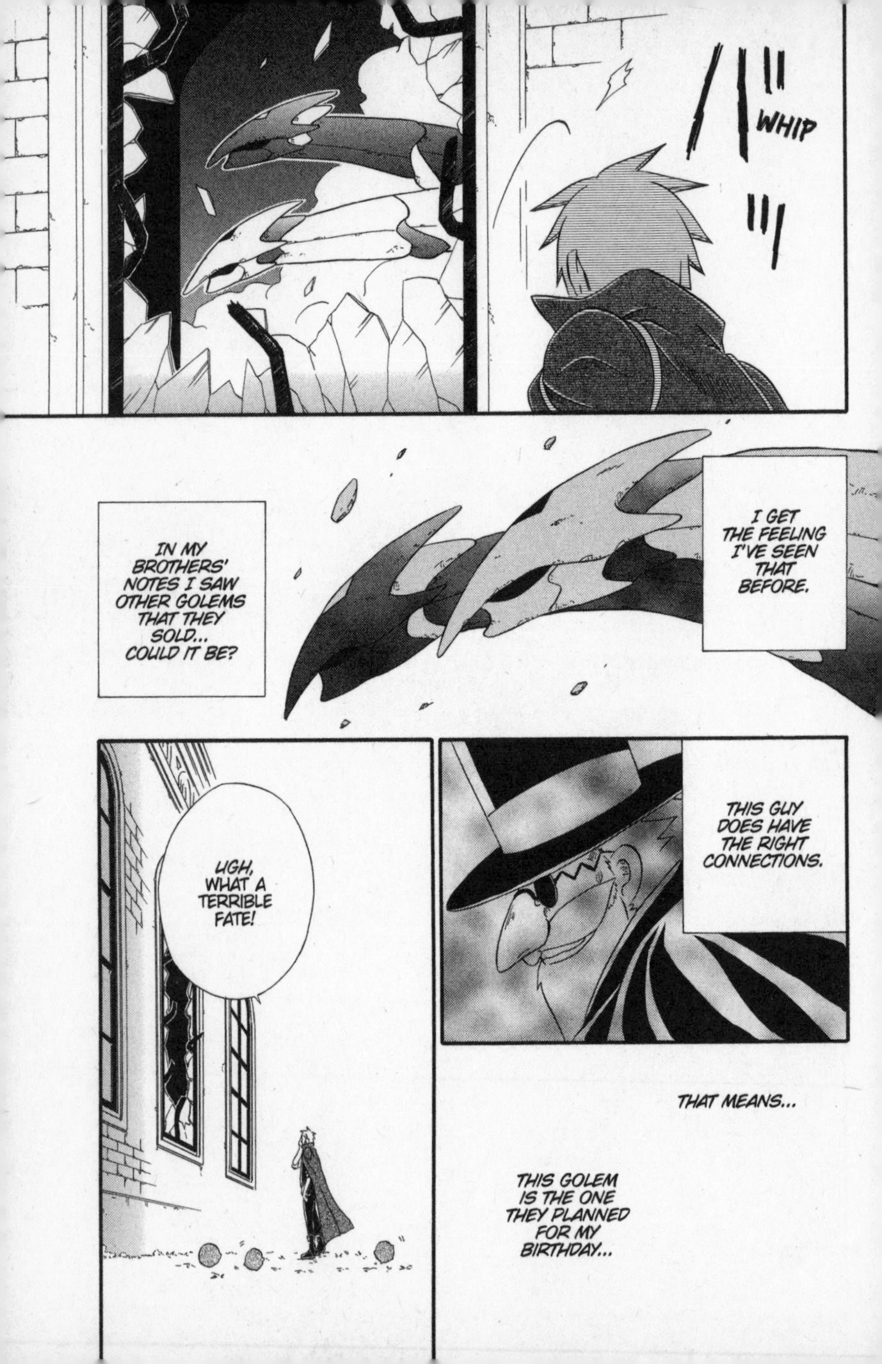
WHIP
I GET THE FEELING I'VE SEEN THAT BEFORE.
IN MY BROTHERS' NOTES I SAW OTHER GOLEMS THAT THEY SOLD... COULD IT BE?
THIS GUY DOES HAVE THE RIGHT CONNECTIONS.
THAT MEANS...
THIS GOLEM IS THE ONE THEY PLANNED FOR MY BIRTHDAY...
UGH, WHAT A TERRIBLE FATE!

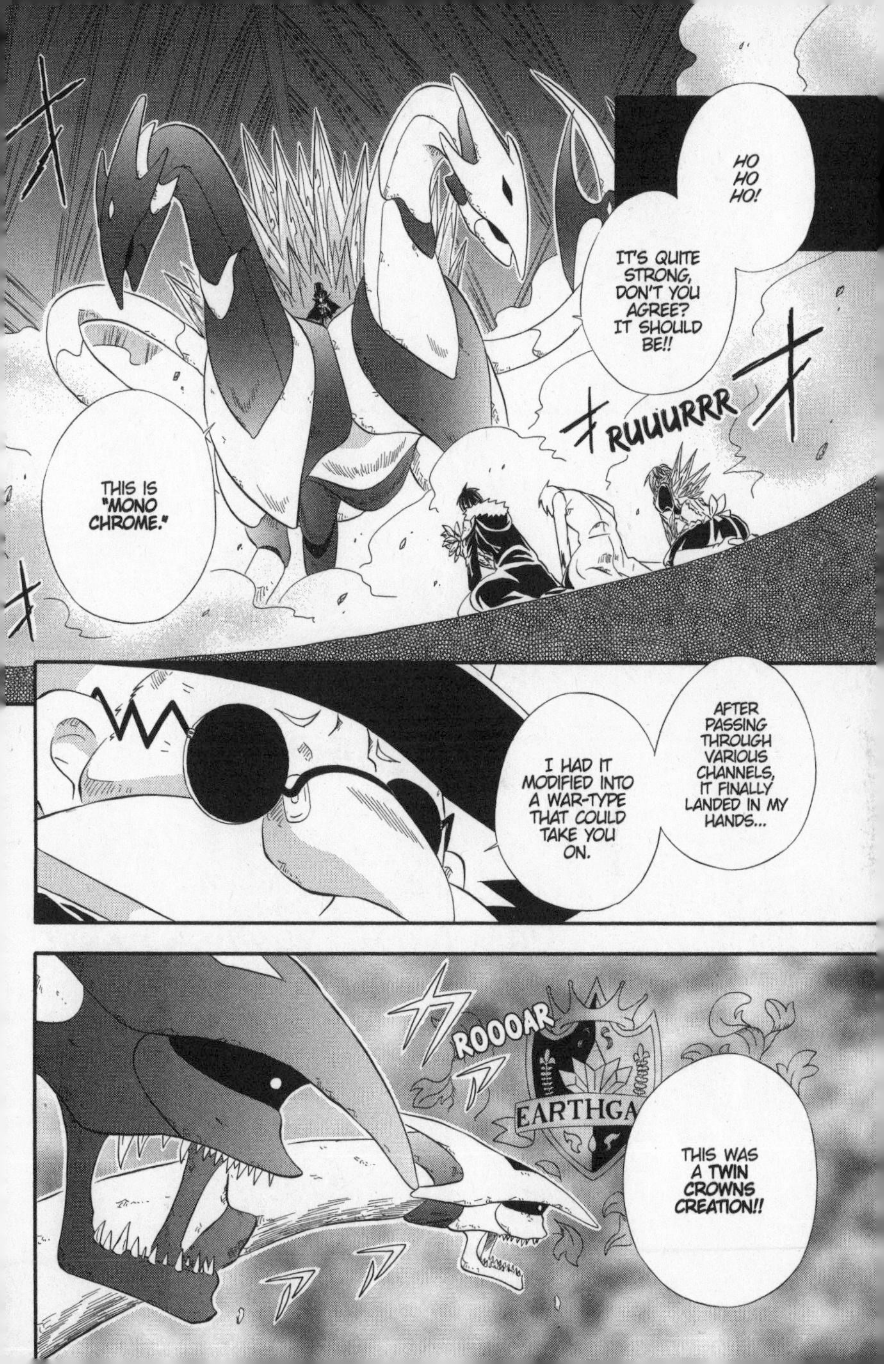
HO HO HO!
IT'S QUITE STRONG, DON'T YOU AGREE? IT SHOULD BE!!
RUUURRR
THIS IS "MONO CHROME."
AFTER PASSING THROUGH VARIOUS CHANNELS, IT FINALLY LANDED IN MY HANDS...
I HAD IT MODIFIED INTO A WAR-TYPE THAT COULD TAKE YOU ON.
THIS WAS A TWIN CROWNS CREATION!!
ROOOAR
EARTHGA

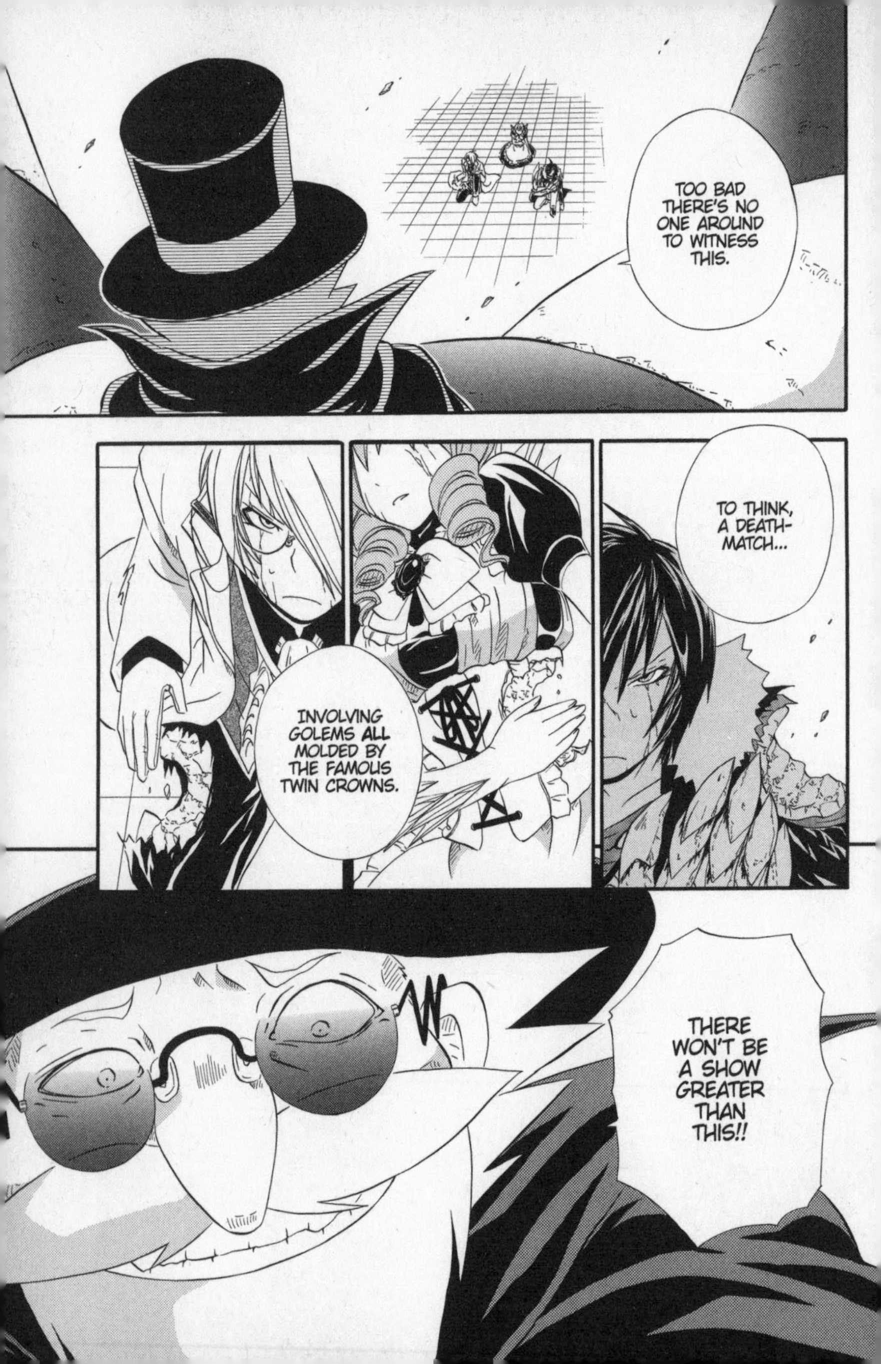
TOO BAD THERE'S NO ONE AROUND TO WITNESS THIS.
TO THINK, A DEATH-MATCH...
INVOLVING GOLEMS ALL MOLDED BY THE FAMOUS TWIN CROWNS.
THERE WON'T BE A SHOW GREATER THAN THIS!!

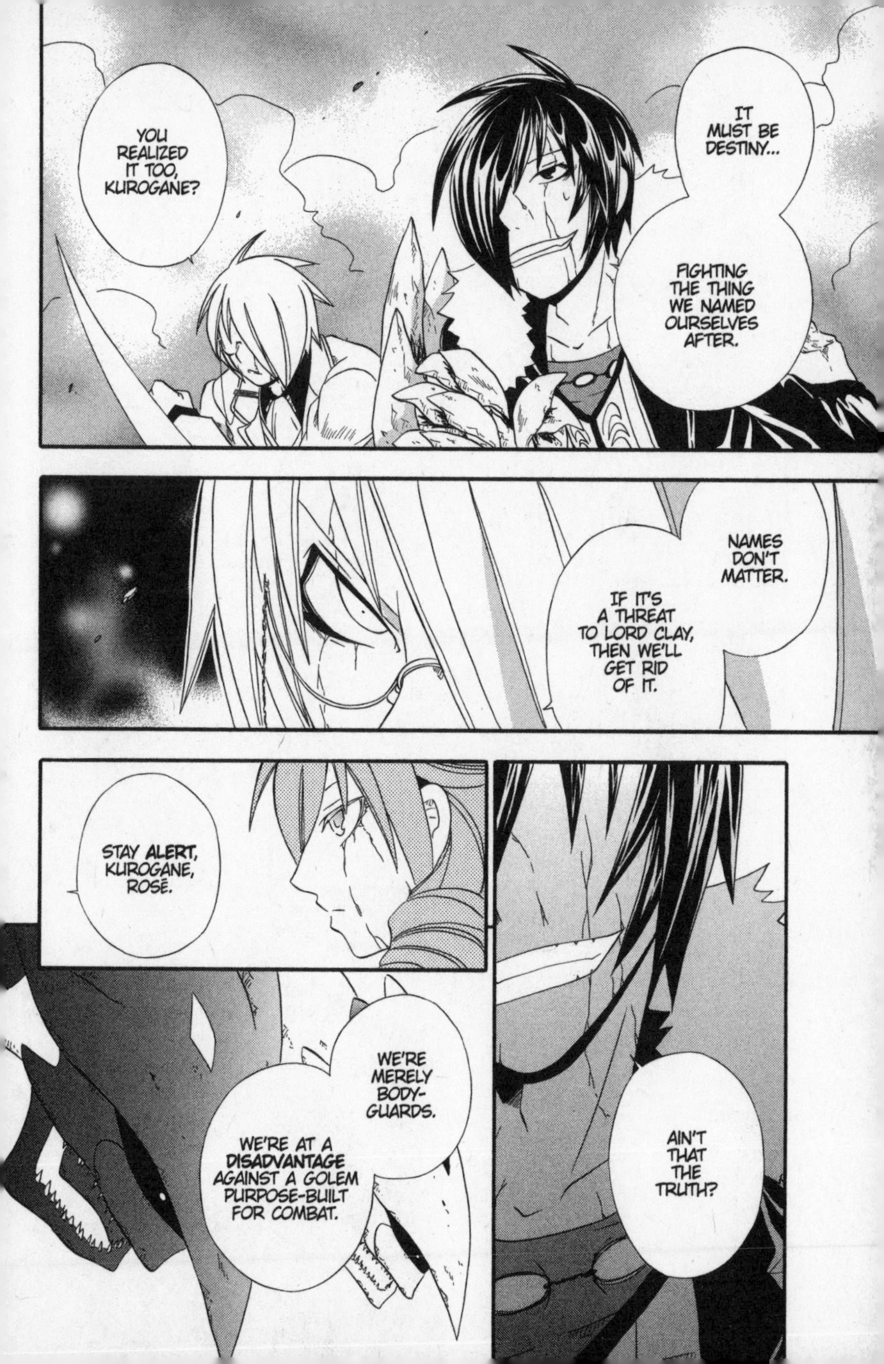
IT MUST BE DESTINY...
FIGHTING THE THING WE NAMED OURSELVES AFTER.
YOU REALIZED IT TOO, KUROGANE?
NAMES DON'T MATTER.
IF IT'S A THREAT TO LORD CLAY, THEN WE'LL GET RID OF IT.
AIN'T THAT THE TRUTH?
STAY ALERT, KUROGANE, ROSË.
WE'RE MERELY BODY-GUARDS.
WE'RE AT A DISADVANTAGE AGAINST A GOLEM PURPOSE-BUILT FOR COMBAT.

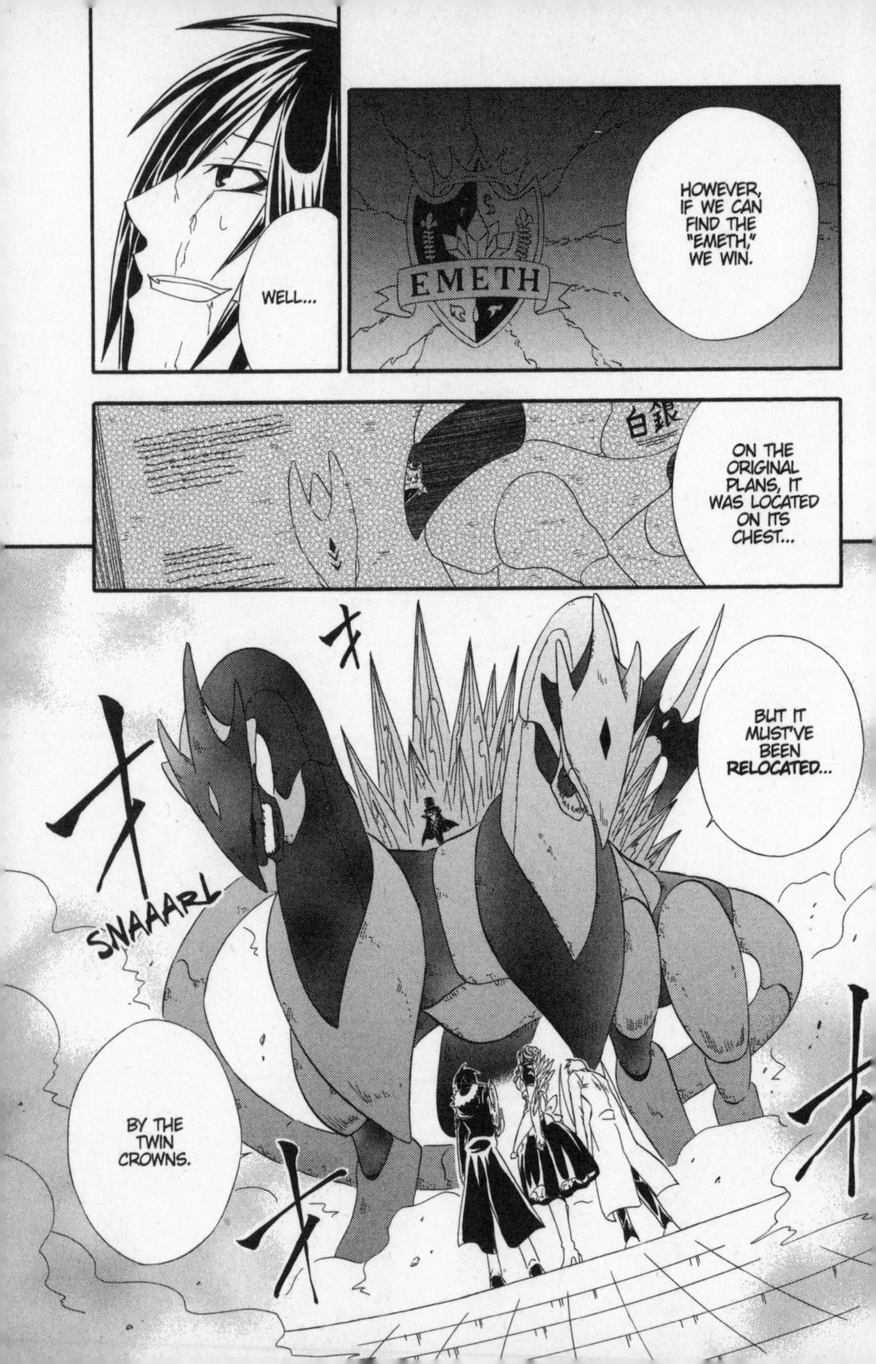
HOWEVER, IF WE CAN FIND THE "EMETH," WE WIN.
EMETH
WELL...
白銀
ON THE ORIGINAL PLANS, IT WAS LOCATED ON ITS CHEST...
BUT IT MUST'VE BEEN RELOCATED...
SNAAARL
BY THE TWIN CROWNS.

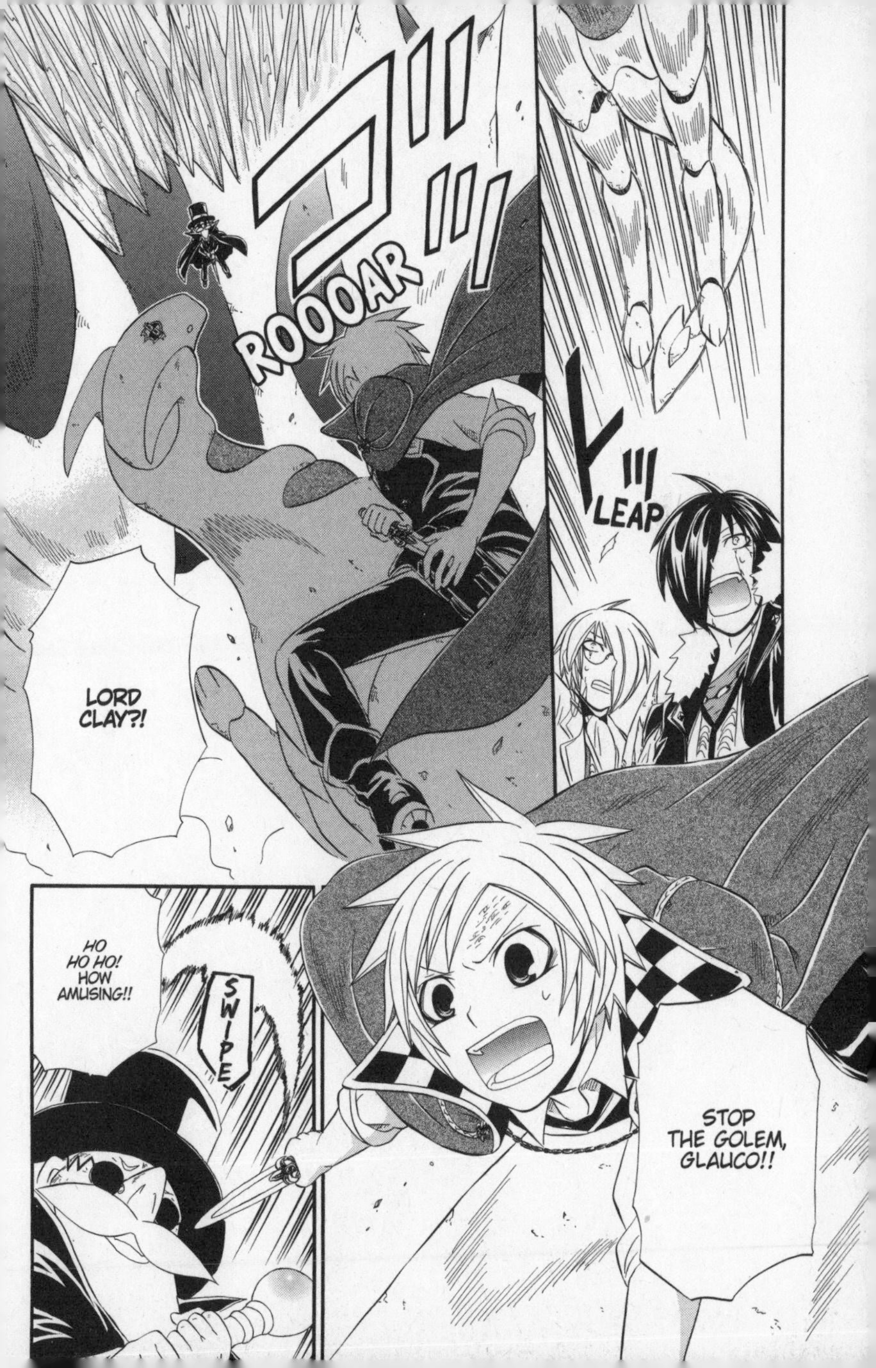
LEAP
ROOOAR
LORD CLAY?!
STOP THE GOLEM, GLAUCO!!
HO HO HO! HOW AMUSING!!
SWIPE

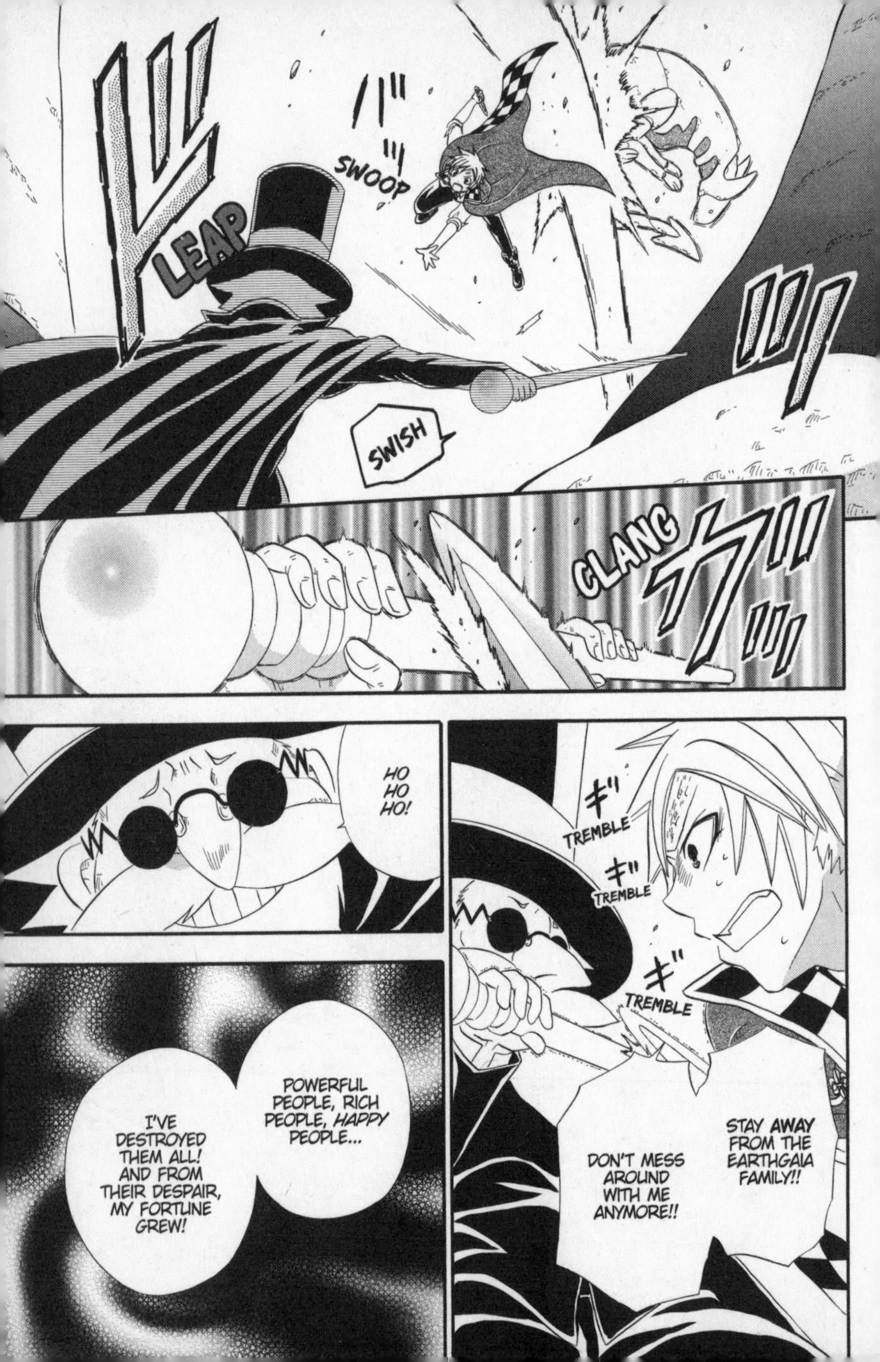
SWOOP
LEAP
SWISH
CLANG
TREMBLE
TREMBLE
TREMBLE
STAY AWAY FROM THE EARTHGAIA FAMILY!!
DON'T MESS AROUND WITH ME ANYMORE!!
HO HO HO!
POWERFUL PEOPLE, RICH PEOPLE, *HAPPY* PEOPLE...
I'VE DESTROYED THEM ALL! AND FROM THEIR DESPAIR, MY FORTUNE GREW!

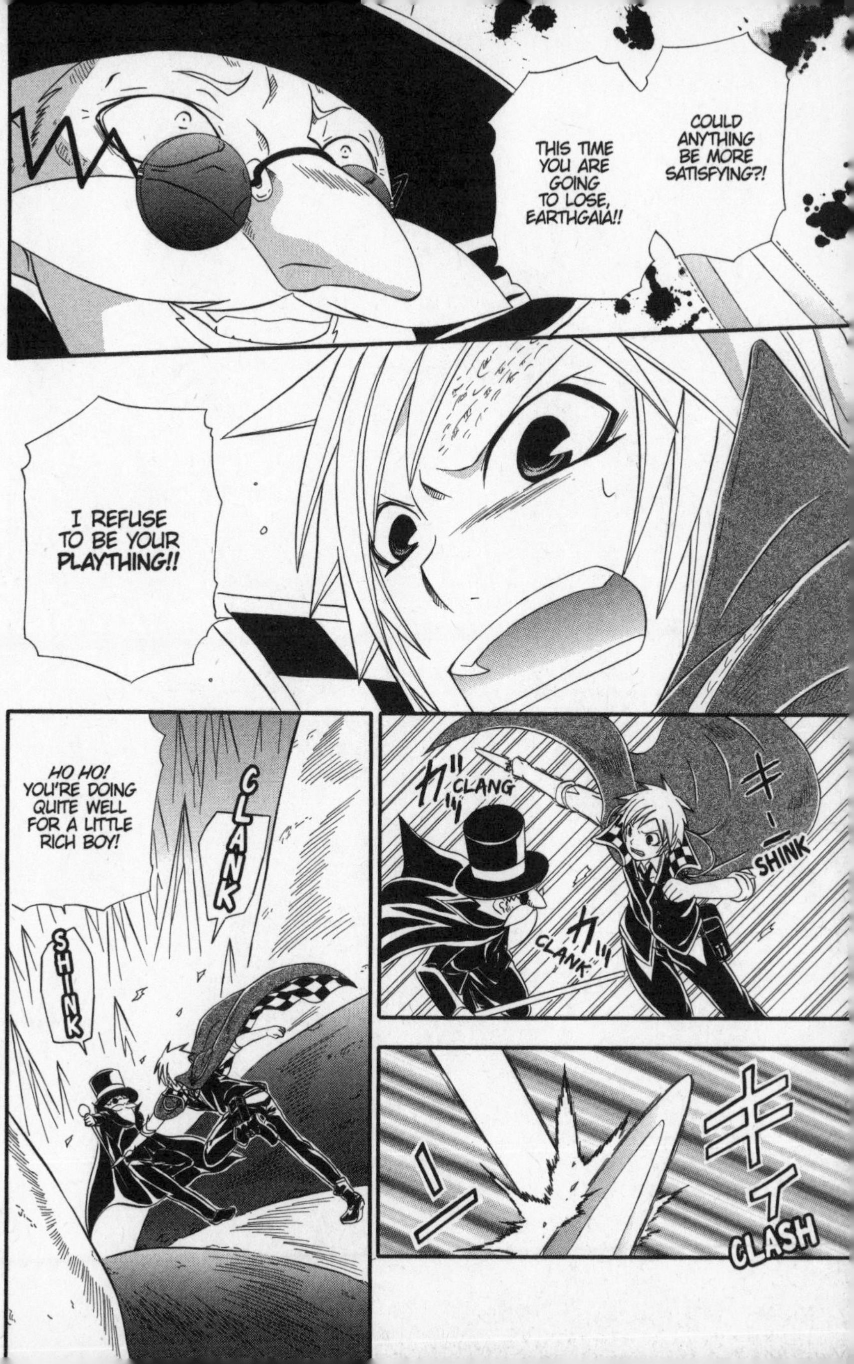
COULD ANYTHING BE MORE SATISFYING?!
THIS TIME YOU ARE GOING TO LOSE, EARTHGAIA!!
I REFUSE TO BE YOUR PLAYTHING!!
CLANG
SHINK
CLANK
CLASH
HO HO! YOU'RE DOING QUITE WELL FOR A LITTLE RICH BOY!
CLANK
SHINK

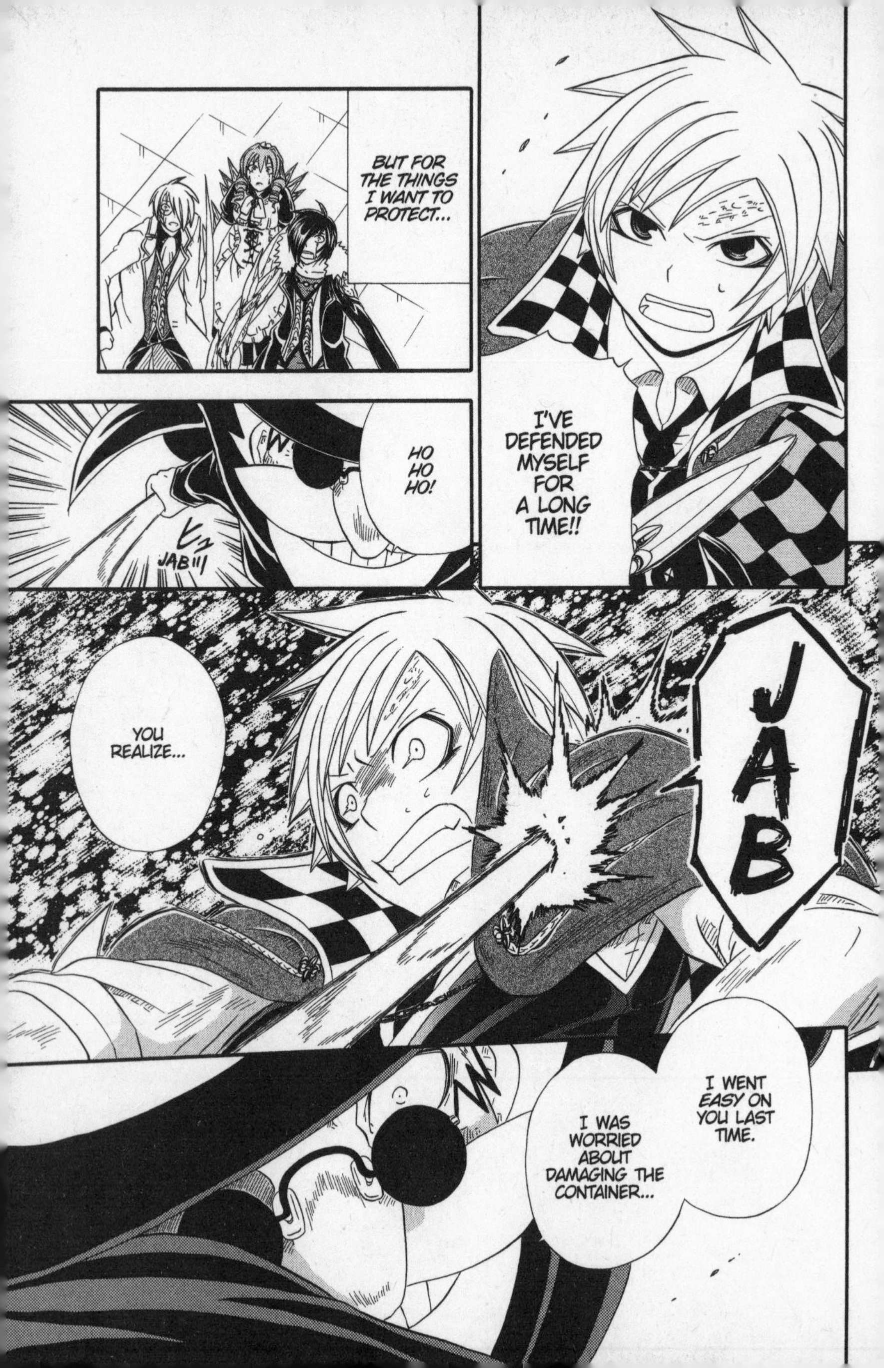
I'VE DEFENDED MYSELF FOR A LONG TIME!!
BUT FOR THE THINGS I WANT TO PROTECT...
HO HO HO!
JAB!!!
JAB
YOU REALIZE...
I WENT EASY ON YOU LAST TIME.
I WAS WORRIED ABOUT DAMAGING THE CONTAINER...

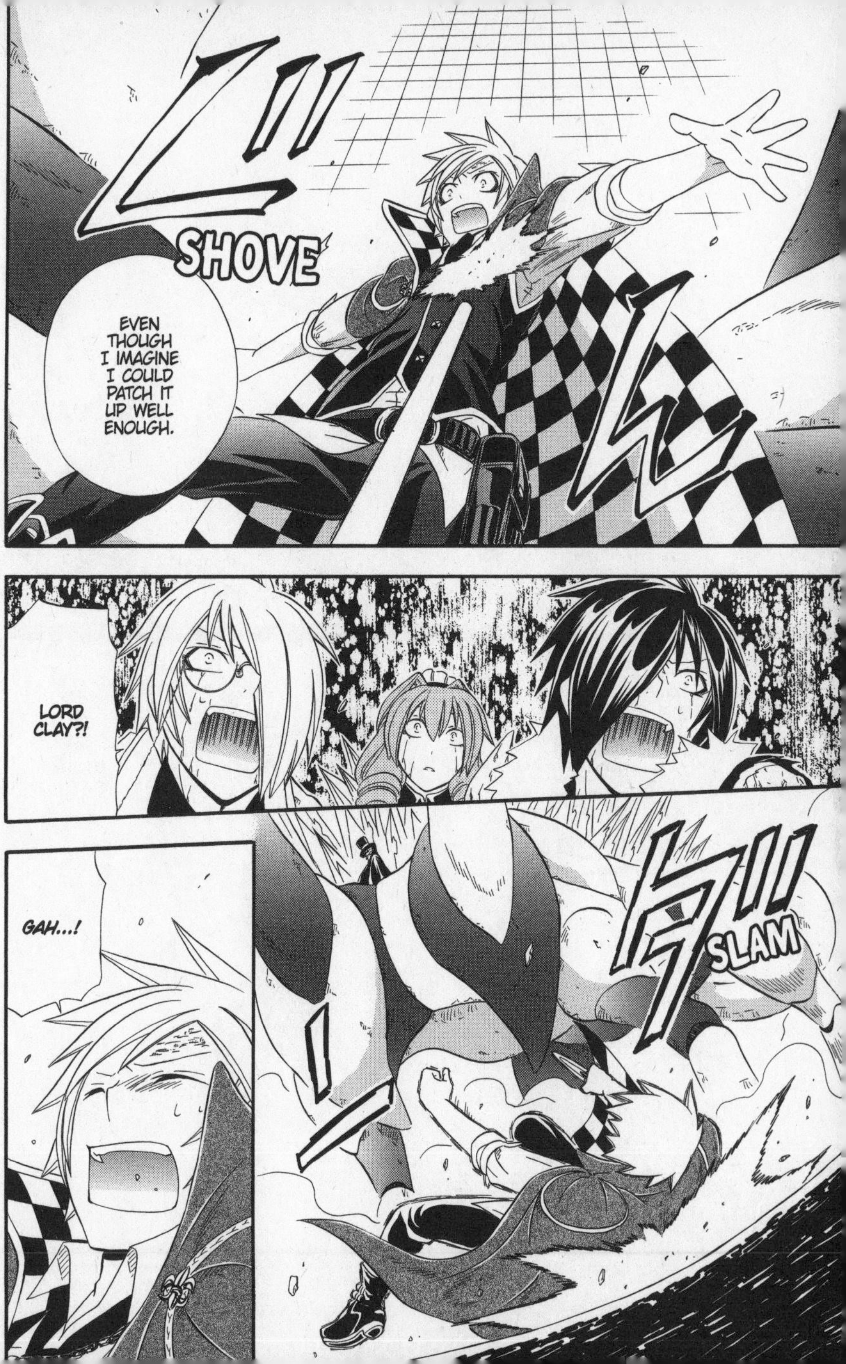

SHOVE
EVEN THOUGH I IMAGINE I COULD PATCH IT UP WELL ENOUGH.
LORD CLAY?!
SLAM
GAH...!

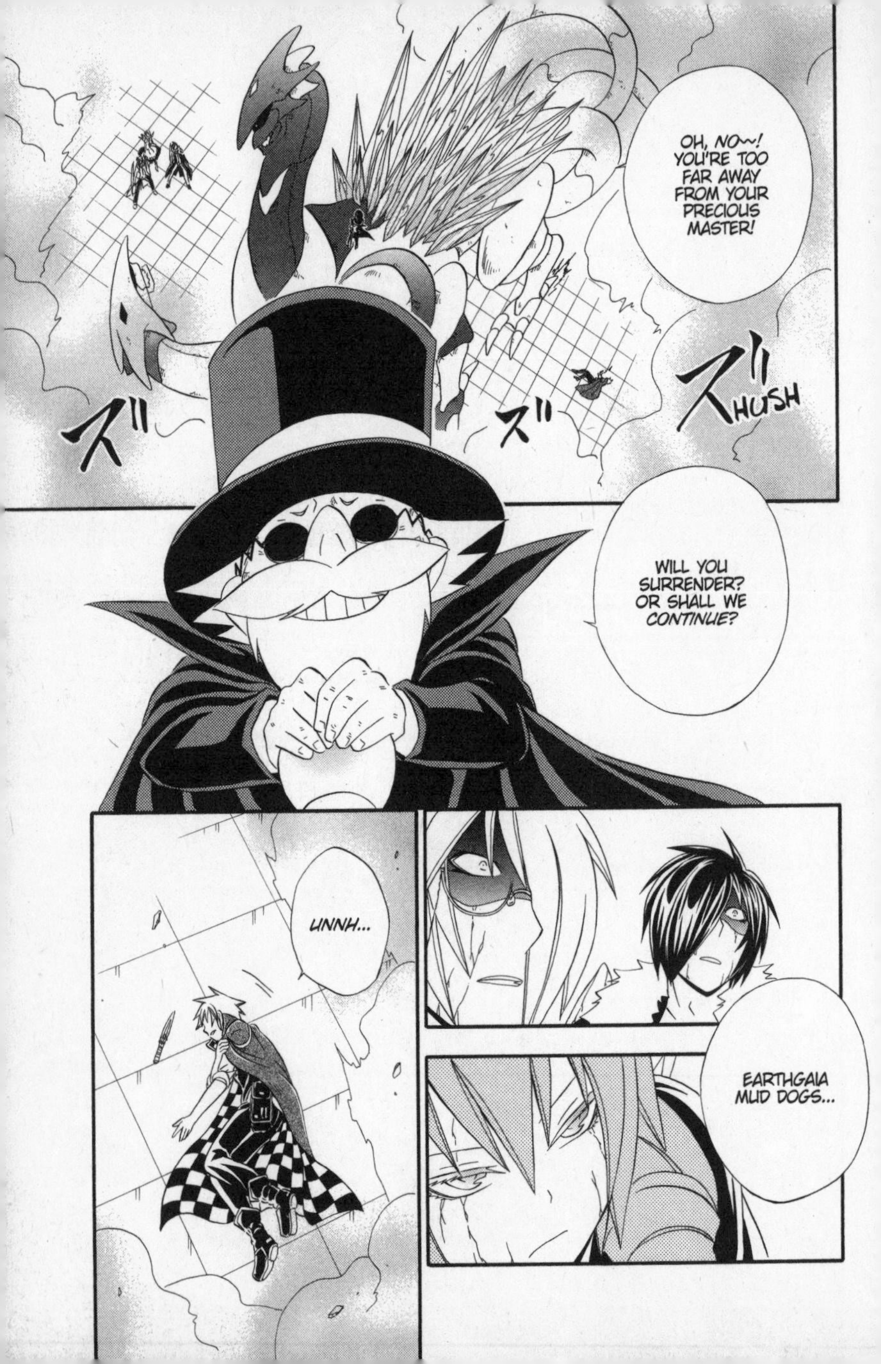
OH, NO~! YOU'RE TOO FAR AWAY FROM YOUR PRECIOUS MASTER!
ズ HUSH
ズ
ズ
WILL YOU SURRENDER? OR SHALL WE CONTINUE?
EARTHGAIA MUD DOGS...
UNNH...

THROB

I SUPPOSE THAT WAS A BIT RECKLESS.

I THOUGHT I COULD AT LEAST TAKE ON GLAUCO, BUT...

MY SHOULDER... IS IT BROKEN? OR JUST DISLOCATED?

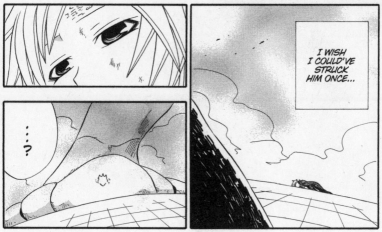

...?

I WISH I COULD'VE STRUCK HIM ONCE...

EMETH

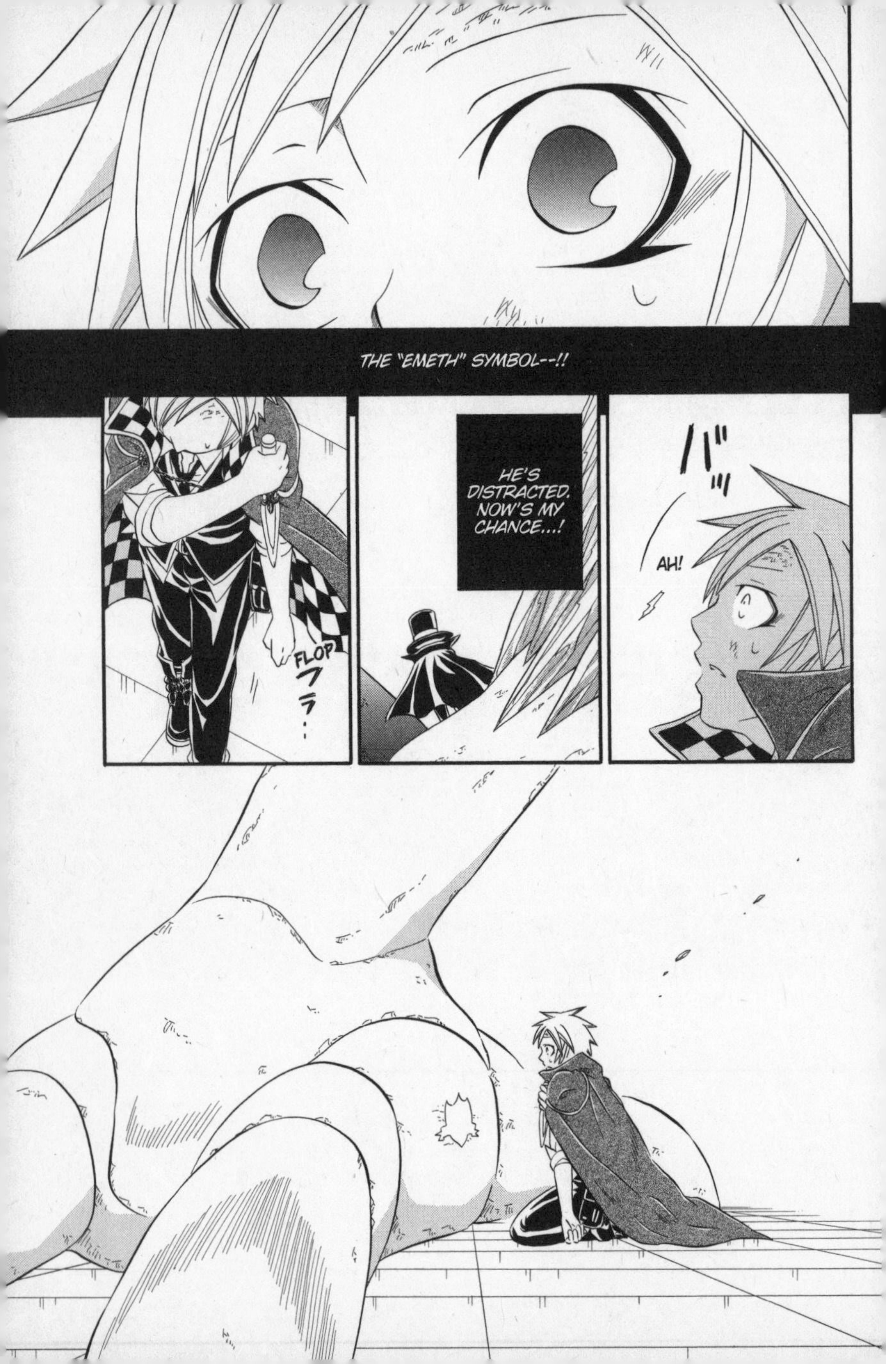
THE "EMETH" SYMBOL--!!
バッ
AH!
HE'S DISTRACTED. NOW'S MY CHANCE...!
FLOP
フラ..

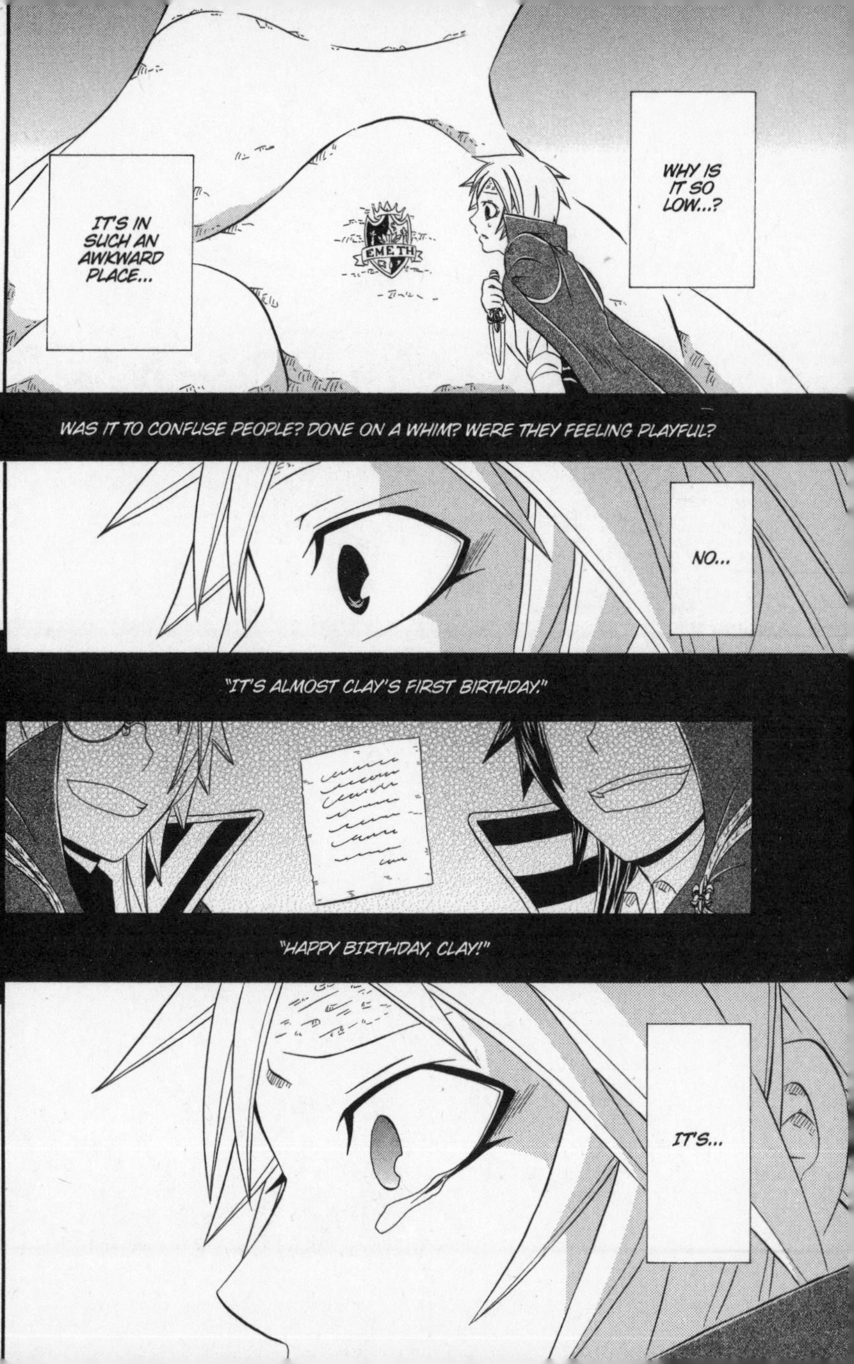
WHY IS IT SO LOW...?
IT'S IN SUCH AN AWKWARD PLACE...
EMETH
WAS IT TO CONFUSE PEOPLE? DONE ON A WHIM? WERE THEY FEELING PLAYFUL?
NO...
"IT'S ALMOST CLAY'S FIRST BIRTHDAY."
"HAPPY BIRTHDAY, CLAY!"
IT'S...

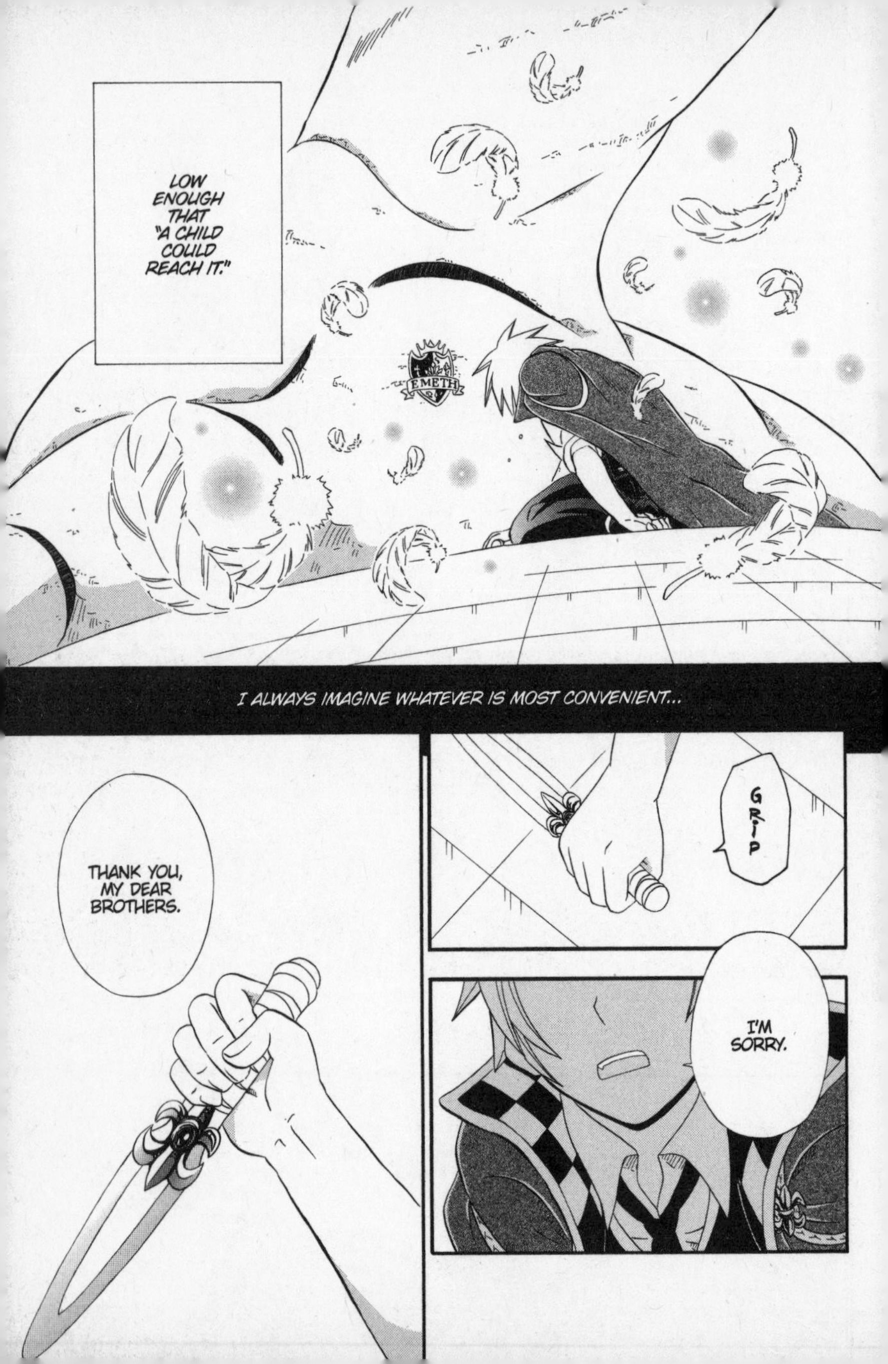
LOW ENOUGH THAT "A CHILD COULD REACH IT."
EMETH
I ALWAYS IMAGINE WHATEVER IS MOST CONVENIENT...
GRIP
I'M SORRY.
THANK YOU, MY DEAR BROTHERS.

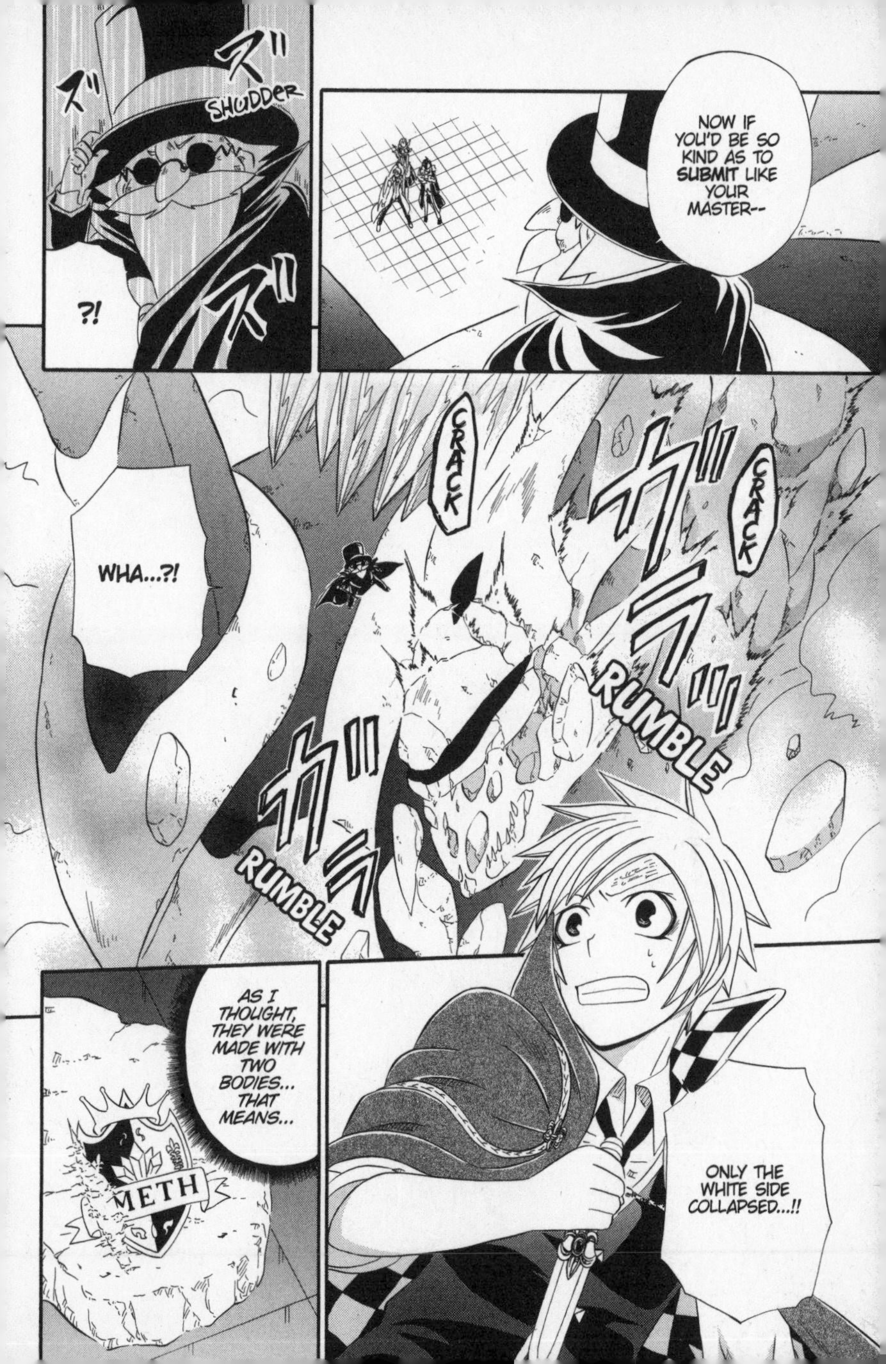

NOW IF YOU'D BE SO KIND AS TO SUBMIT LIKE YOUR MASTER--
ズズ
SHUDDER
ズ
?!
CRACK
ガラ
RUMBLE
CRACK
WHA...?!
ガラ
RUMBLE
ONLY THE WHITE SIDE COLLAPSED...!!
AS I THOUGHT, THEY WERE MADE WITH TWO BODIES... THAT MEANS...
METH

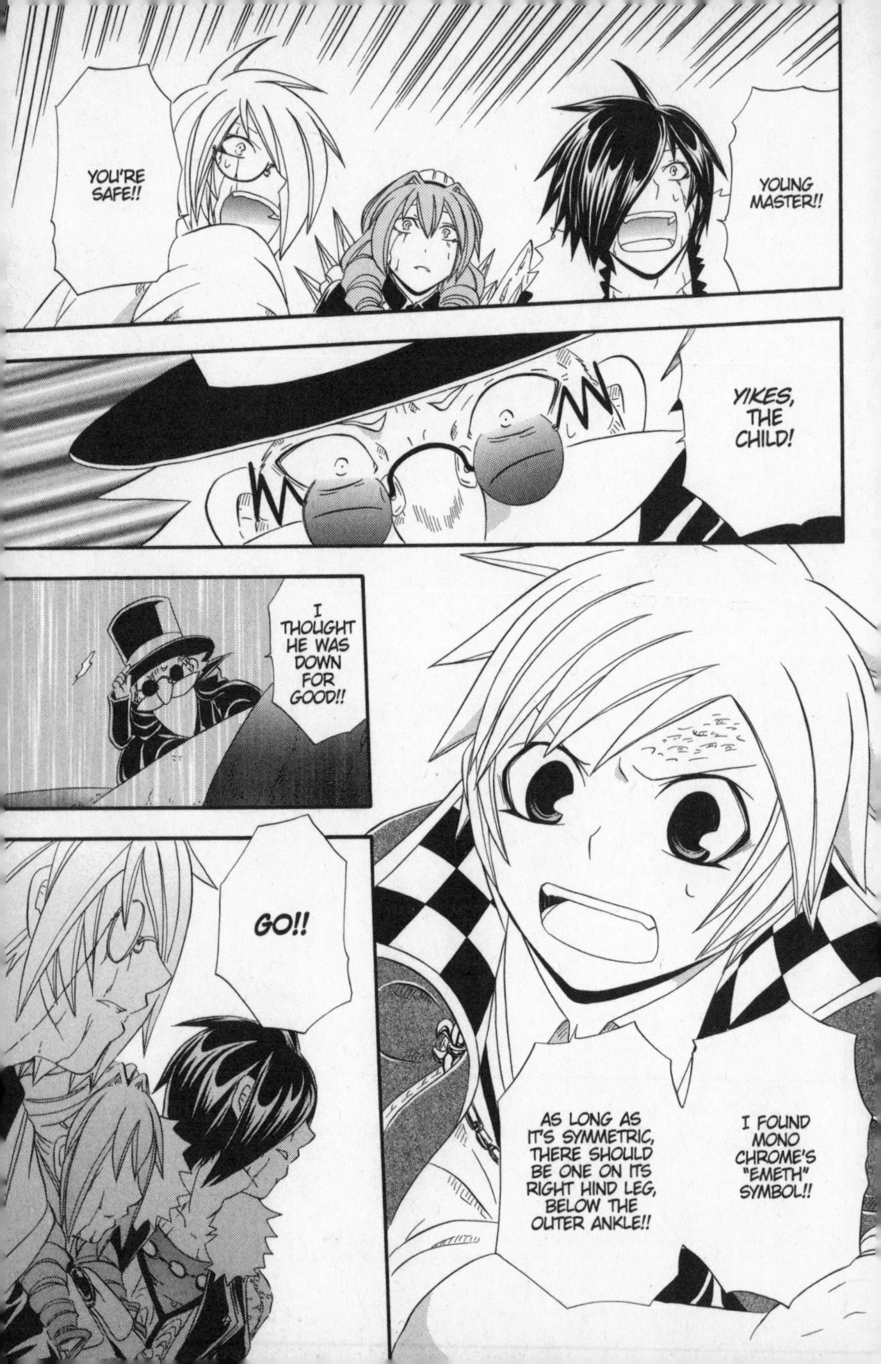
YOUNG MASTER!!
YOU'RE SAFE!!
YIKES, THE CHILD!
I FOUND MONO CHROME'S "EMETH" SYMBOL!!
AS LONG AS IT'S SYMMETRIC, THERE SHOULD BE ONE ON ITS RIGHT HIND LEG, BELOW THE OUTER ANKLE!!
I THOUGHT HE WAS DOWN FOR GOOD!!
GO!!

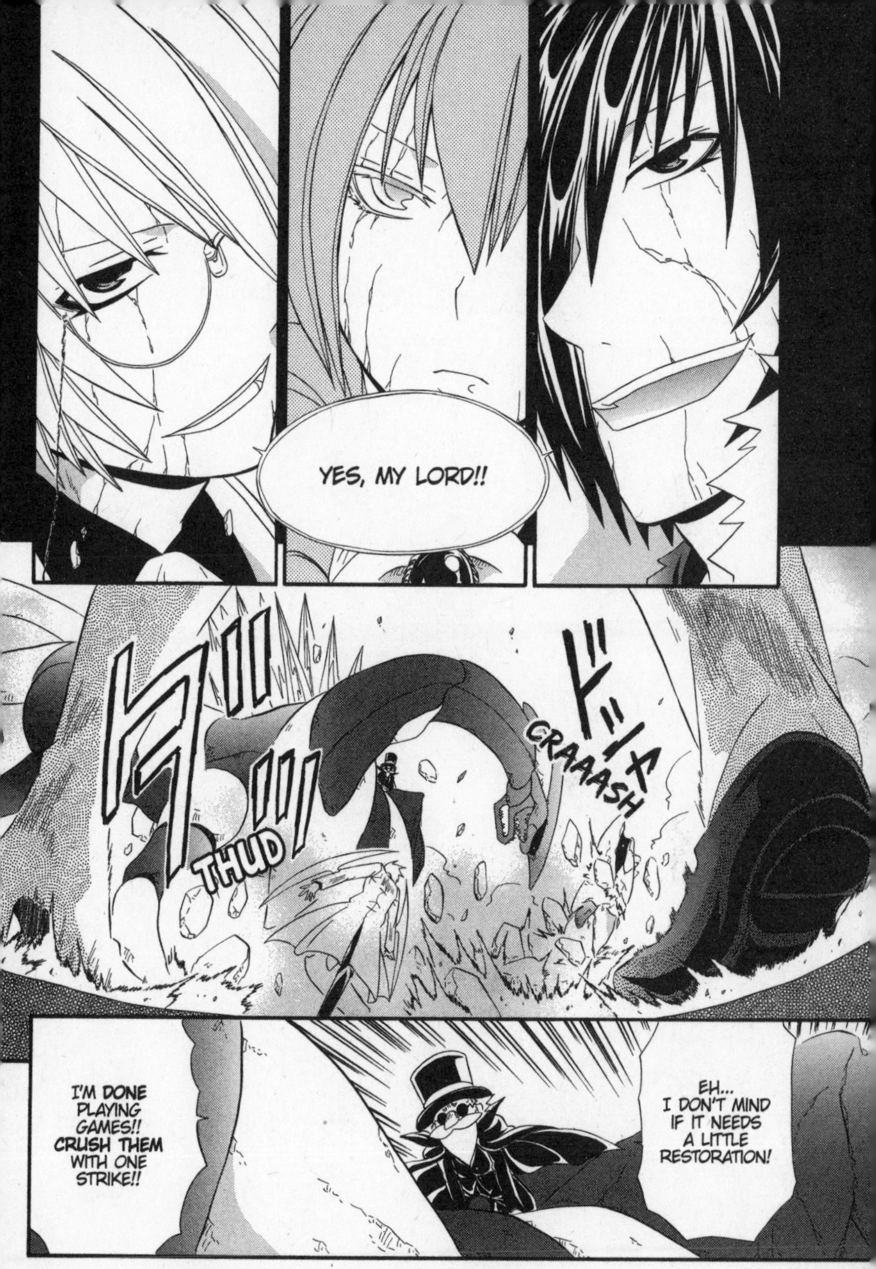
YES, MY LORD!!
CRAAASH
THUD
EH... I DON'T MIND IF IT NEEDS A LITTLE RESTORATION!
I'M DONE PLAYING GAMES!! CRUSH THEM WITH ONE STRIKE!!

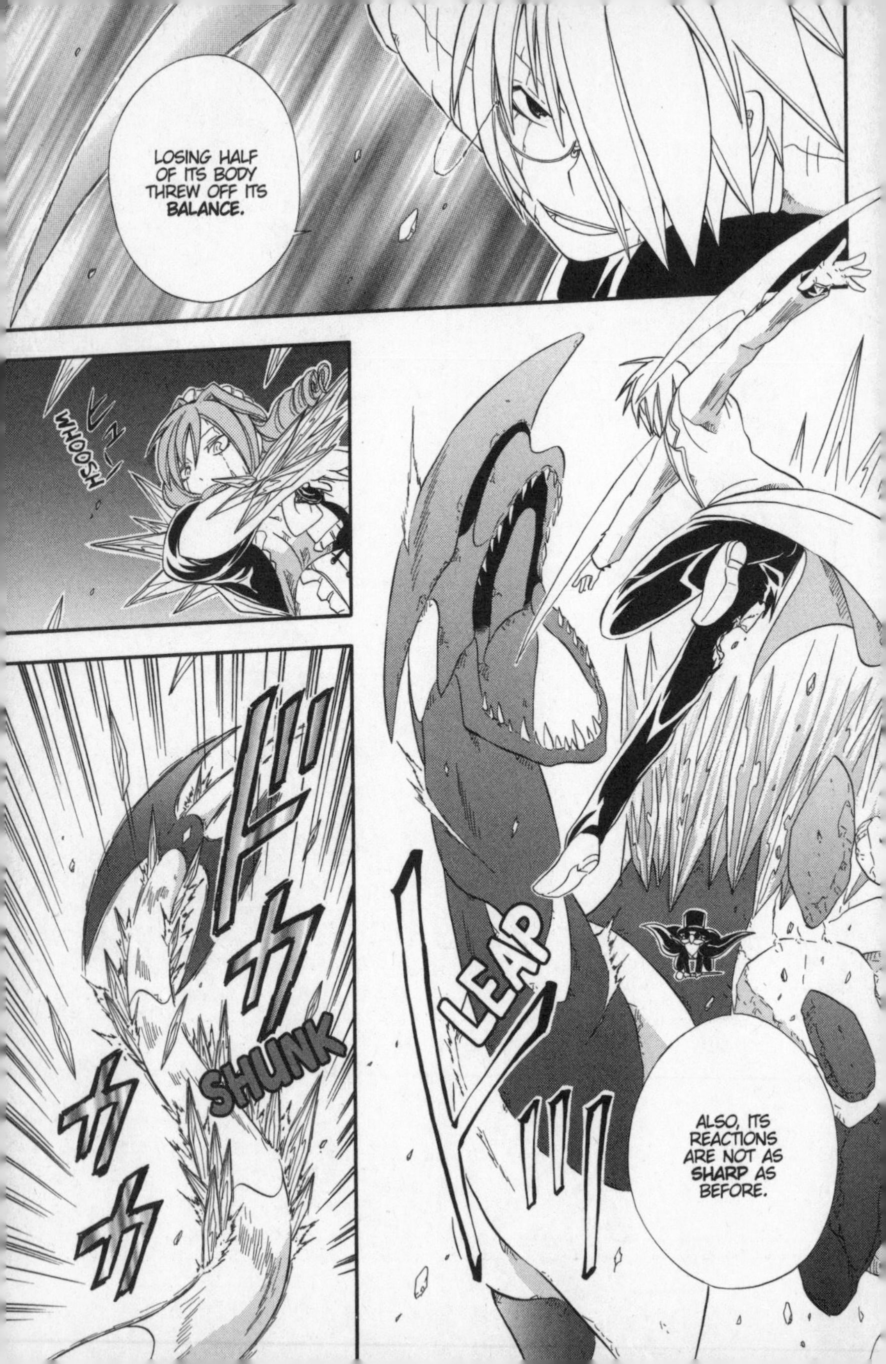
LOSING HALF OF ITS BODY THREW OFF ITS BALANCE.
LEAP
ALSO, ITS REACTIONS ARE NOT AS SHARP AS BEFORE.
WHOOSH
SHUNK

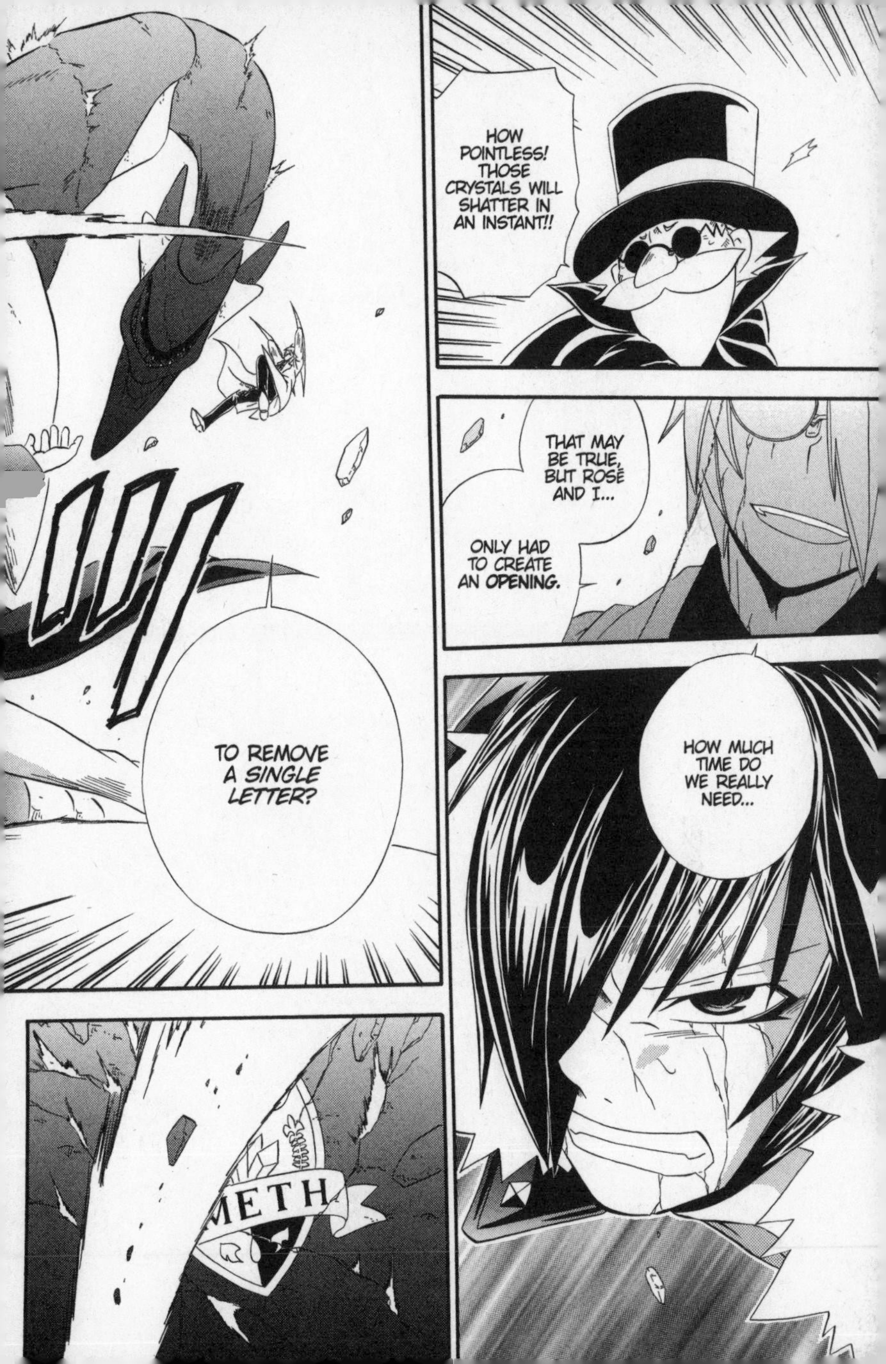
HOW POINTLESS! THOSE CRYSTALS WILL SHATTER IN AN INSTANT!!
THAT MAY BE TRUE, BUT ROSÉ AND I...
ONLY HAD TO CREATE AN **OPENING.**
HOW MUCH TIME DO WE REALLY NEED...
TO REMOVE A *SINGLE* LETTER?
METH

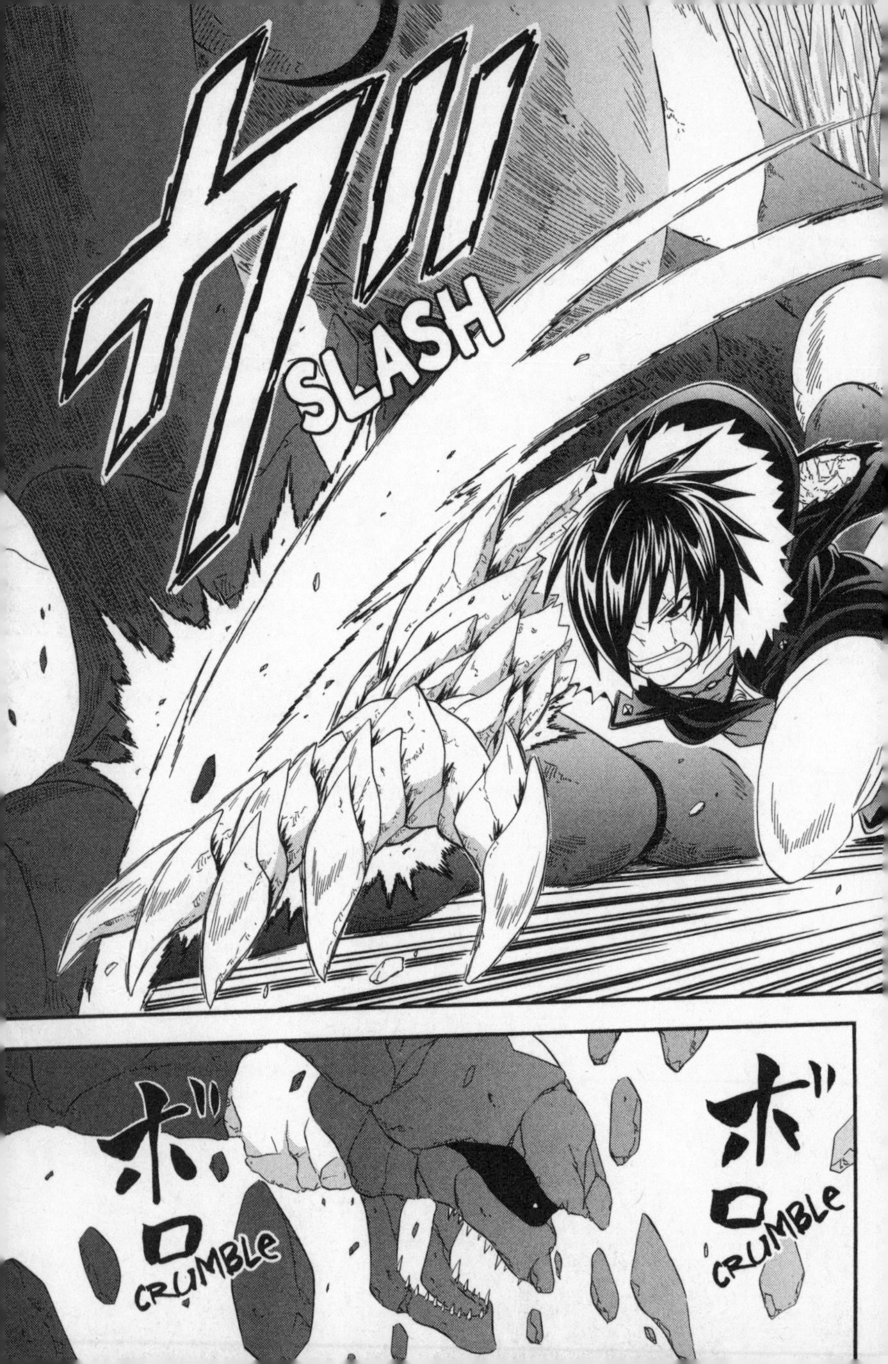
SLASH
ボロ
CRUMBLE
ボロ
CRUMBLE

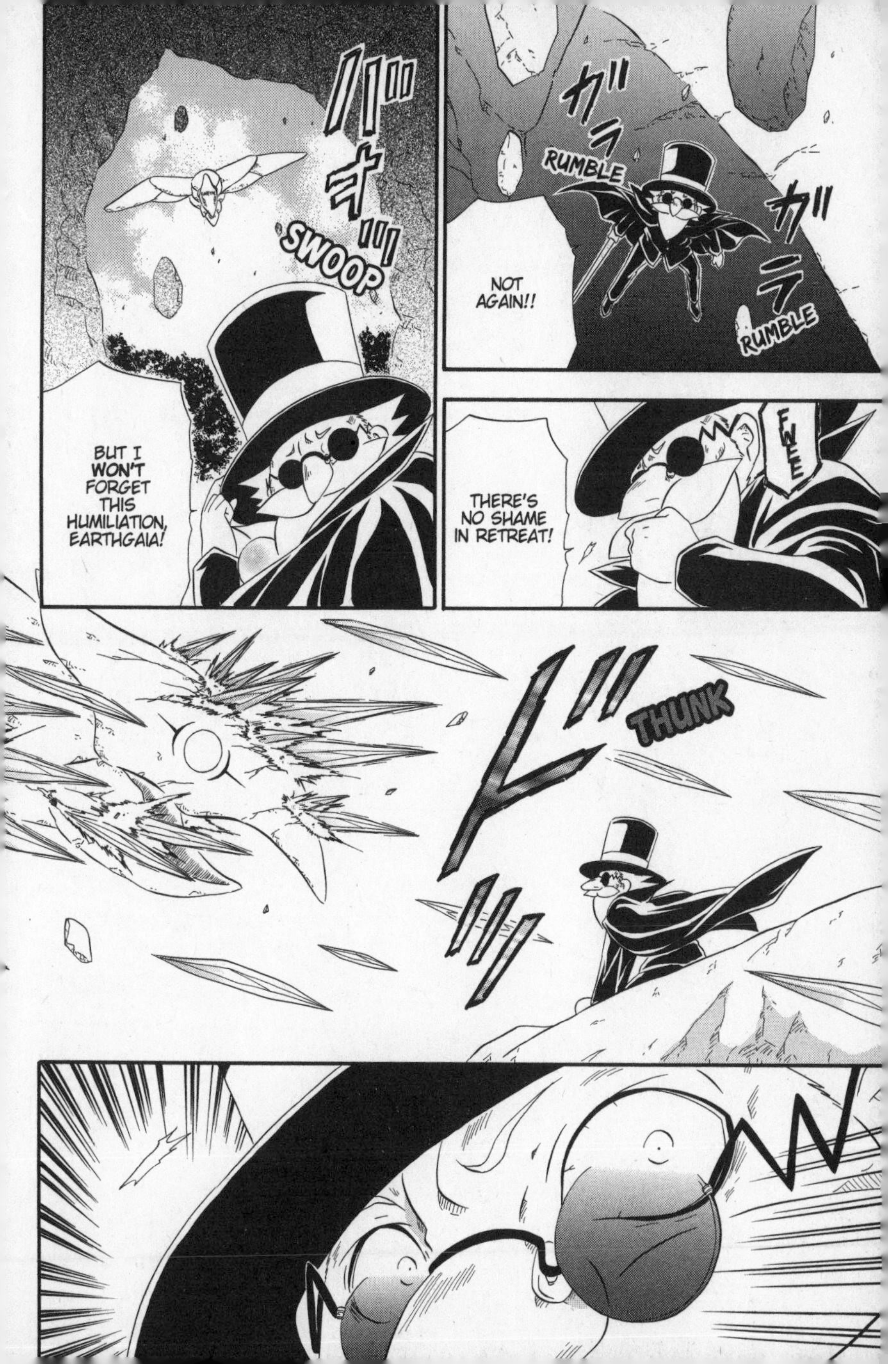
ガラ
RUMBLE
NOT AGAIN!!
ガラ
RUMBLE
FWEE
THERE'S NO SHAME IN RETREAT!
SWOOP
BUT I WON'T FORGET THIS HUMILIATION, EARTHGAIA!
THUNK

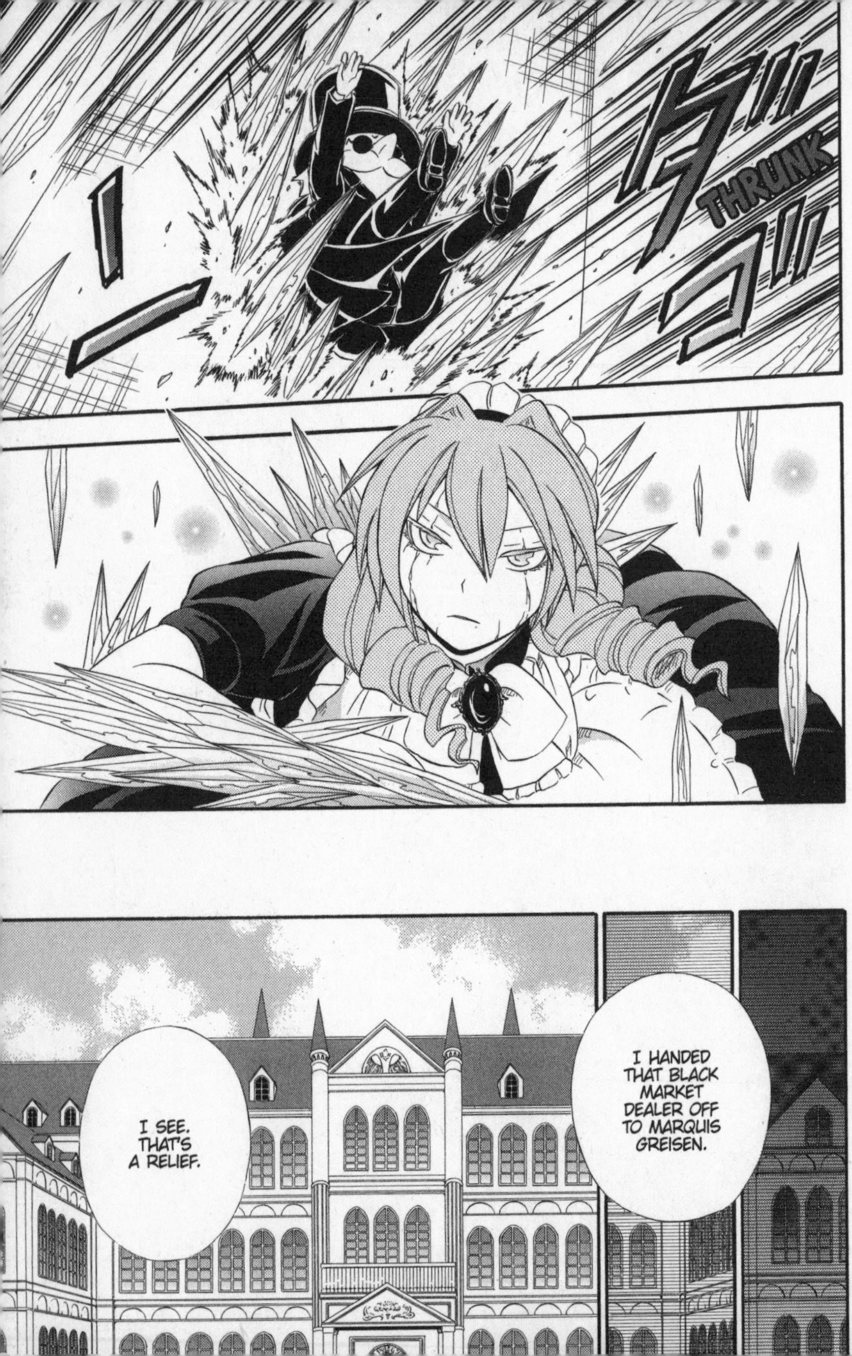
THRUNK
I HANDED THAT BLACK MARKET DEALER OFF TO MARQUIS GREISEN.
I SEE. THAT'S A RELIEF.

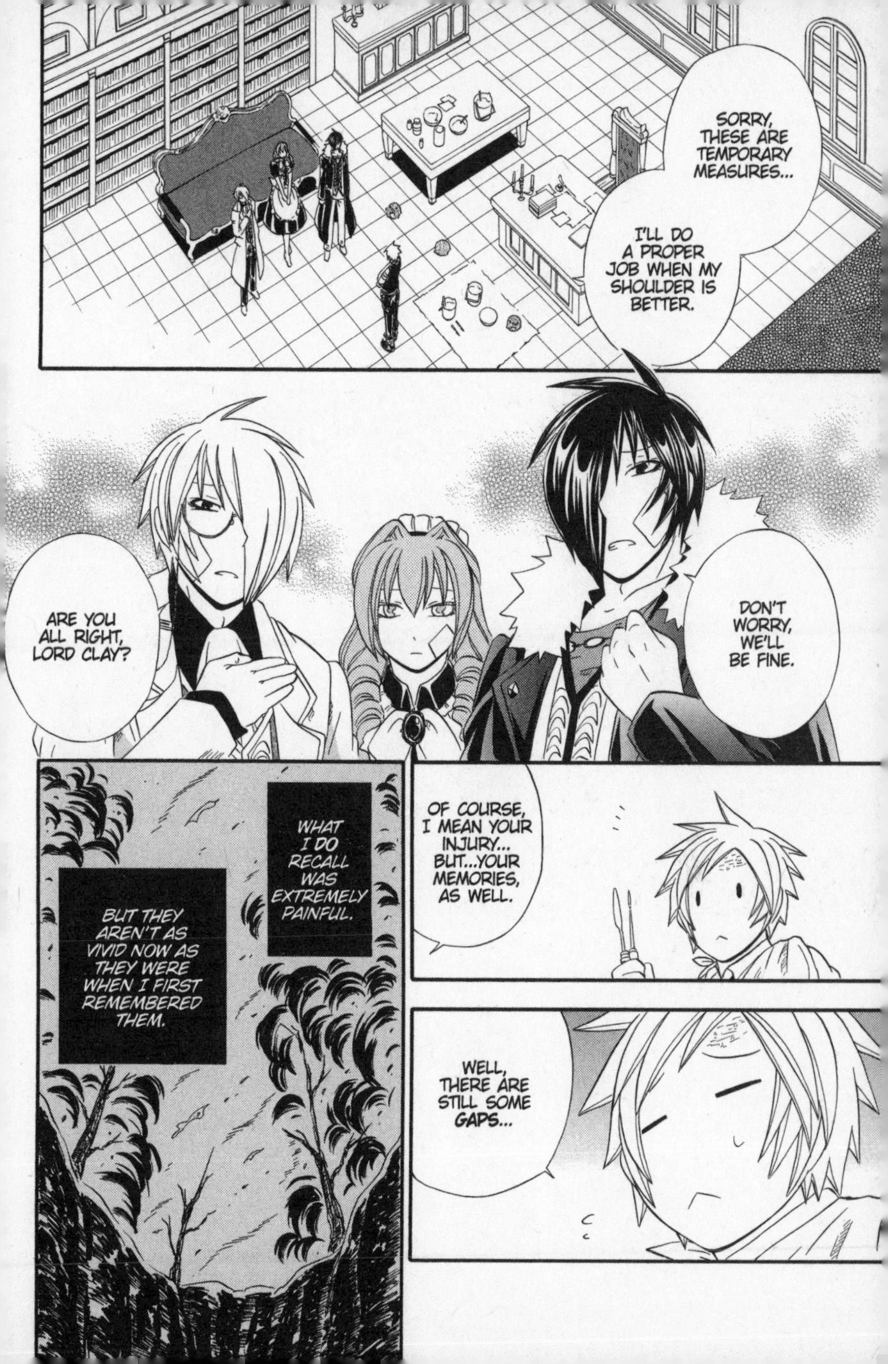
SORRY, THESE ARE TEMPORARY MEASURES...
I'LL DO A PROPER JOB WHEN MY SHOULDER IS BETTER.
ARE YOU ALL RIGHT, LORD CLAY?
DON'T WORRY, WE'LL BE FINE.
OF COURSE, I MEAN YOUR INJURY... BUT...YOUR MEMORIES, AS WELL.
WELL, THERE ARE STILL SOME GAPS...
WHAT I DO RECALL WAS EXTREMELY PAINFUL.
BUT THEY AREN'T AS VIVID NOW AS THEY WERE WHEN I FIRST REMEMBERED THEM.

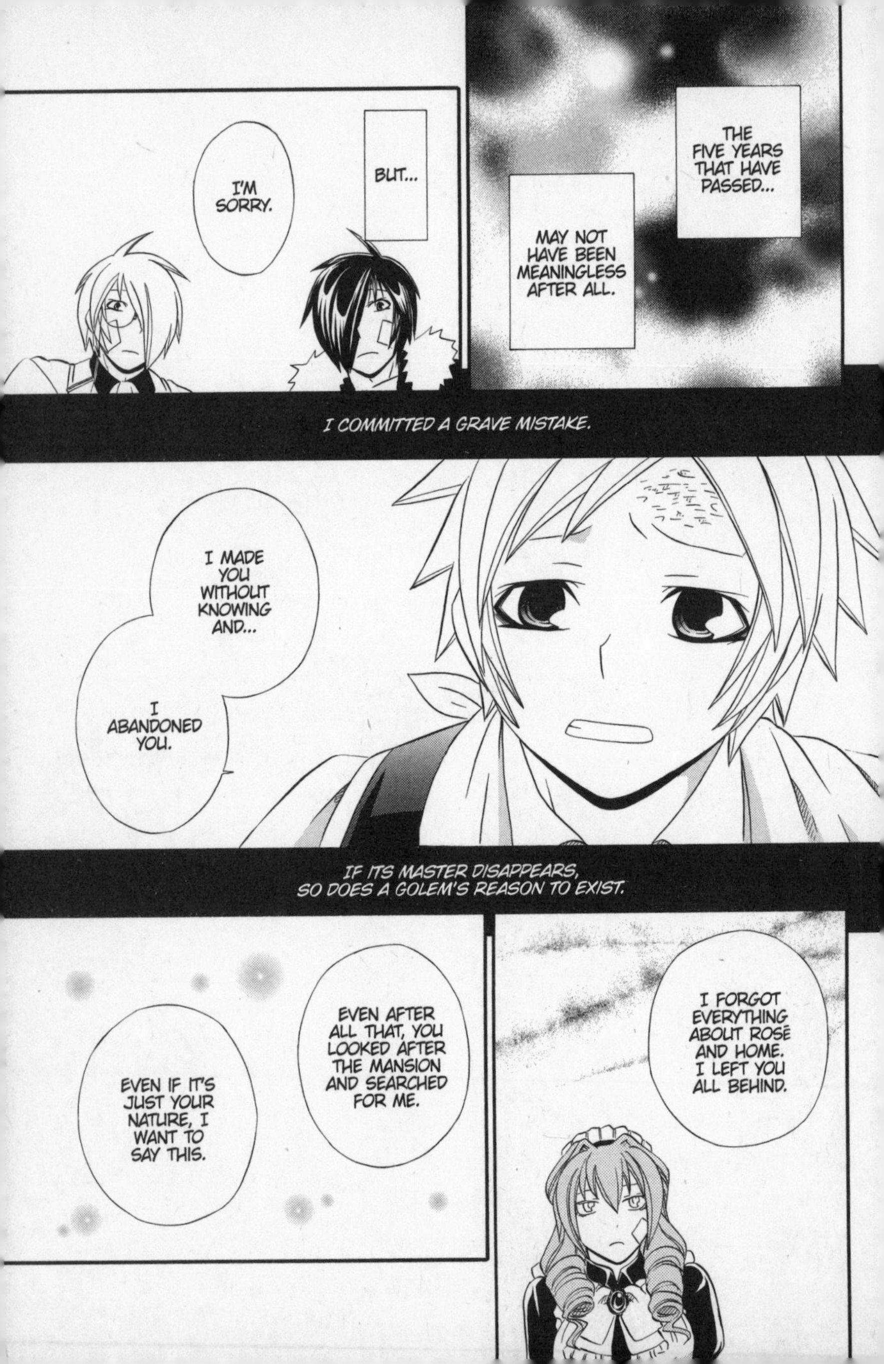
THE FIVE YEARS THAT HAVE PASSED...
MAY NOT HAVE BEEN MEANINGLESS AFTER ALL.
BUT...
I'M SORRY.
I COMMITTED A GRAVE MISTAKE.
I MADE YOU WITHOUT KNOWING AND...
I ABANDONED YOU.
IF ITS MASTER DISAPPEARS, SO DOES A GOLEM'S REASON TO EXIST.
I FORGOT EVERYTHING ABOUT ROSĒ AND HOME. I LEFT YOU ALL BEHIND.
EVEN AFTER ALL THAT, YOU LOOKED AFTER THE MANSION AND SEARCHED FOR ME.
EVEN IF IT'S JUST YOUR NATURE, I WANT TO SAY THIS.

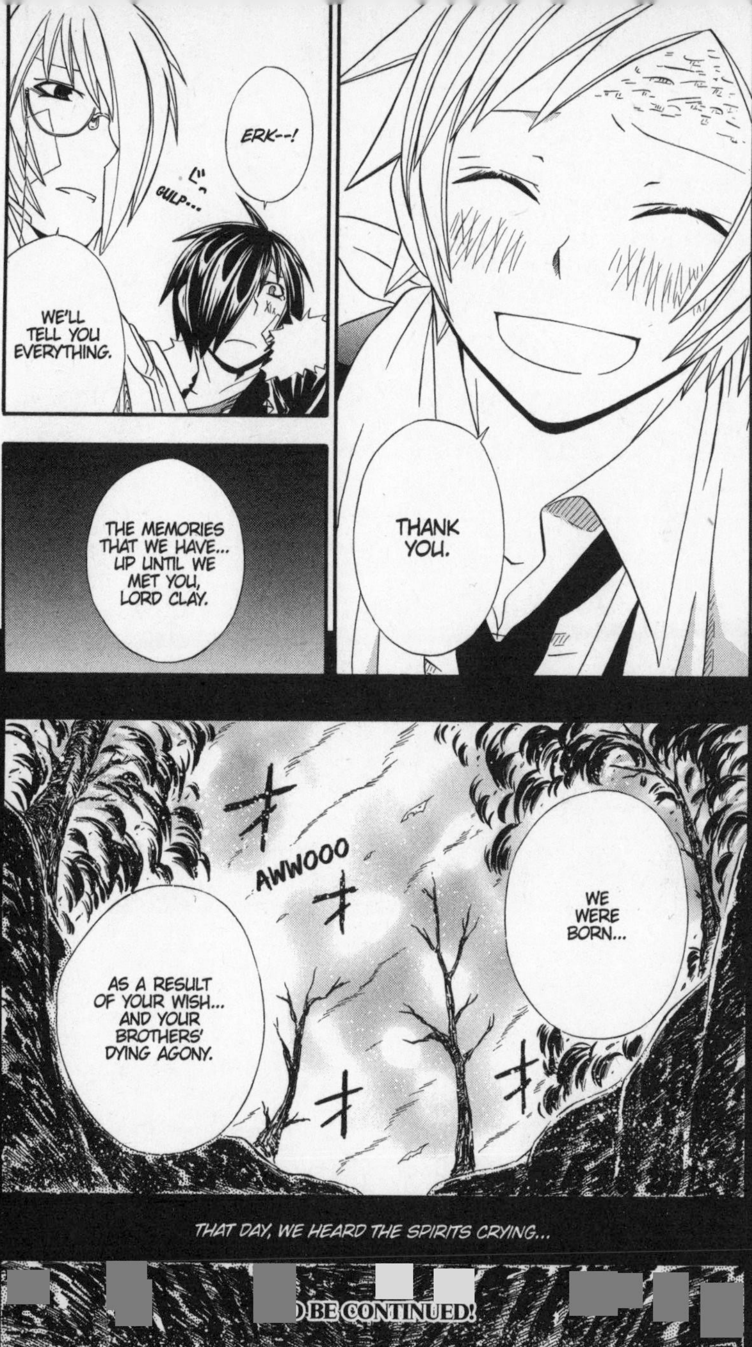
THANK YOU.
ERK--!
GULP...
WE'LL TELL YOU EVERYTHING.
THE MEMORIES THAT WE HAVE... UP UNTIL WE MET YOU, LORD CLAY.
WE WERE BORN...
AWWOOO
AS A RESULT OF YOUR WISH... AND YOUR BROTHERS' DYING AGONY.
THAT DAY, WE HEARD THE SPIRITS CRYING...
D BE CONTINUED!

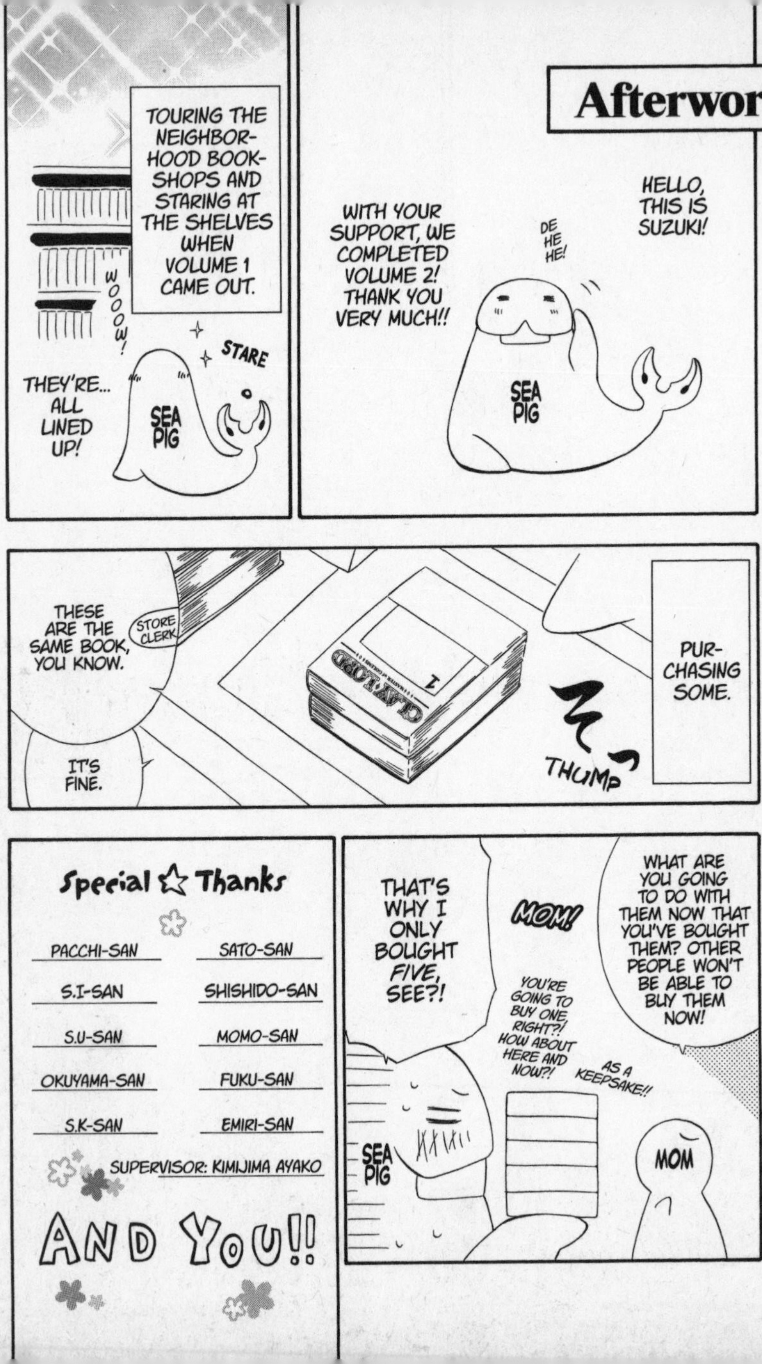
Afterword
HELLO, THIS IS SUZUKI!
DE HE HE!
WITH YOUR SUPPORT, WE COMPLETED VOLUME 2! THANK YOU VERY MUCH!!
SEA PIG
TOURING THE NEIGHBOR-HOOD BOOK-SHOPS AND STARING AT THE SHELVES WHEN VOLUME 1 CAME OUT.
WOOOOW!
STARE
THEY'RE... ALL LINED UP!
SEA PIG
PUR-CHASING SOME.
THUMP
STORE CLERK
THESE ARE THE SAME BOOK, YOU KNOW.
IT'S FINE.
WHAT ARE YOU GOING TO DO WITH THEM NOW THAT YOU'VE BOUGHT THEM? OTHER PEOPLE WON'T BE ABLE TO BUY THEM NOW!
MOM!
THAT'S WHY I ONLY BOUGHT FIVE, SEE?!
YOU'RE GOING TO BUY ONE RIGHT?! HOW ABOUT HERE AND NOW?!
AS A KEEPSAKE!!
SEA PIG
MOM
Special ☆ Thanks
PACCHI-SAN
SATO-SAN
S.I-SAN
SHISHIDO-SAN
S.U-SAN
MOMO-SAN
OKUYAMA-SAN
FUKU-SAN
S.K-SAN
EMIRI-SAN
SUPERVISOR: KIMIJIMA AYAKO
AND YOU!!

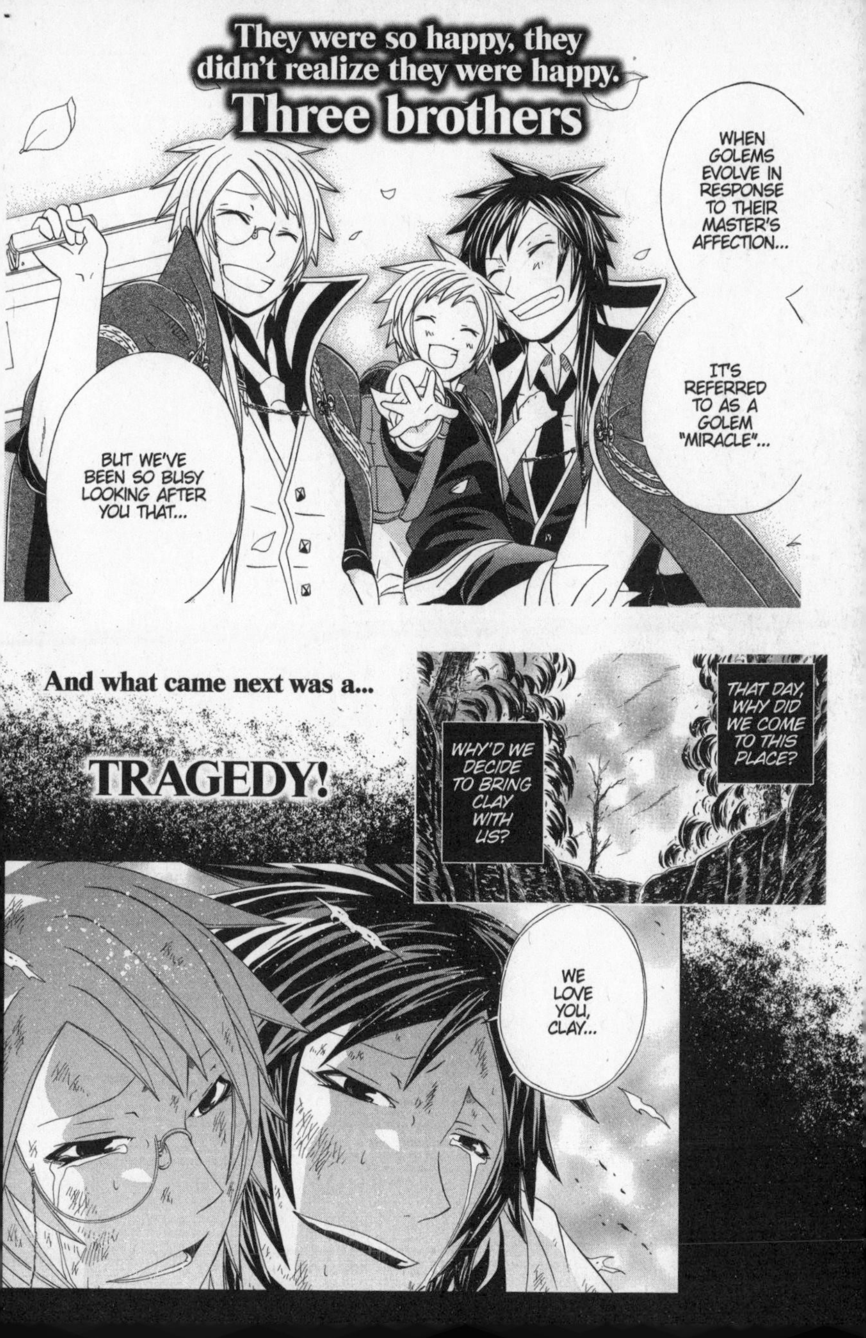
They were so happy, they didn't realize they were happy.
Three brothers
WHEN GOLEMS EVOLVE IN RESPONSE TO THEIR MASTER'S AFFECTION...
IT'S REFERRED TO AS A GOLEM "MIRACLE"...
BUT WE'VE BEEN SO BUSY LOOKING AFTER YOU THAT...
THAT DAY, WHY DID WE COME TO THIS PLACE?
WHY'D WE DECIDE TO BRING CLAY WITH US?
And what came next was a...
TRAGEDY!
WE LOVE YOU, CLAY...

SEVEN SEAS ENTERTAINMENT PRESE

CLAY·LORD
◆ ◆ MASTER of GOLEMS ◆ ◆

story and art by JUN SUZUMOTO

VOLUME 2

TRANSLATION
Jill Morita

ADAPTATION
Patrick King

LETTERING AND LAYOUT
Alexandra Gunawan

COVER DESIGN
Nicky Lim

PROOFREADER
Danielle King

ASSISTANT EDITOR
Lissa Pattillo

MANAGING EDITOR
Adam Arnold

PUBLISHER
Jason DeAngelis

ISBN: 978-1-626921-65-8

Printed in Canada

First Printing: August 2015

10 9 8 7 6 5 4 3 2 1

FOLLOW US ONLINE: www.gomanga.com

READING DIRECTIONS

This book reads from *right to left*, Japanese style.
If this is your first time reading manga, you start
reading from the top right panel on each page and
take it from there. If you get lost, just follow the
numbered diagram here. It may seem backwards at
first, but you'll get the hang of it! Have fun!!

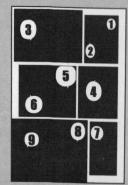

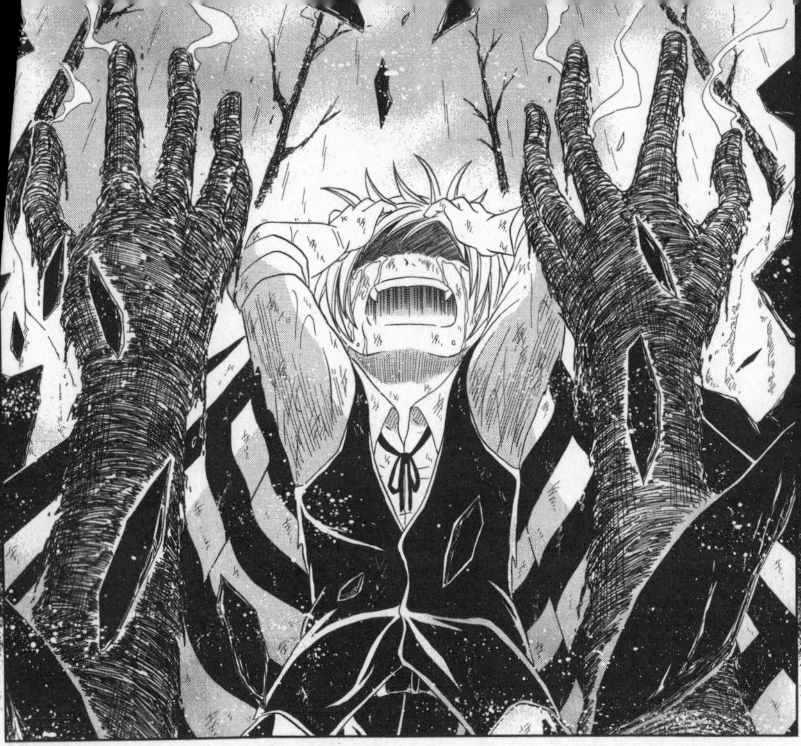

In the throes of his depression, Clay brought something to life...

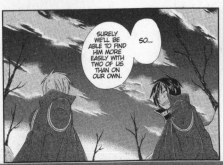

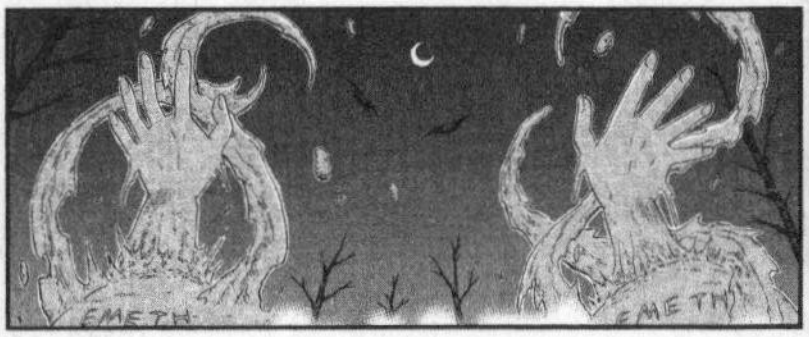
EMETH
EMETH

Two golems...

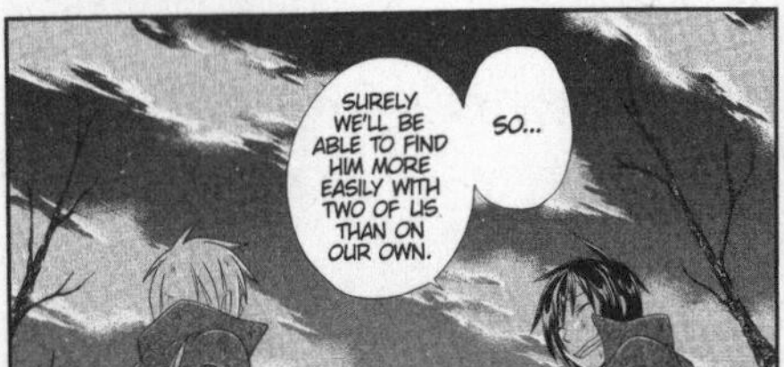
SO...
SURELY WE'LL BE ABLE TO FIND HIM MORE EASILY WITH TWO OF US THAN ON OUR OWN.

Clay Lord: Master of Golems Volume 3 Coming Soon!!

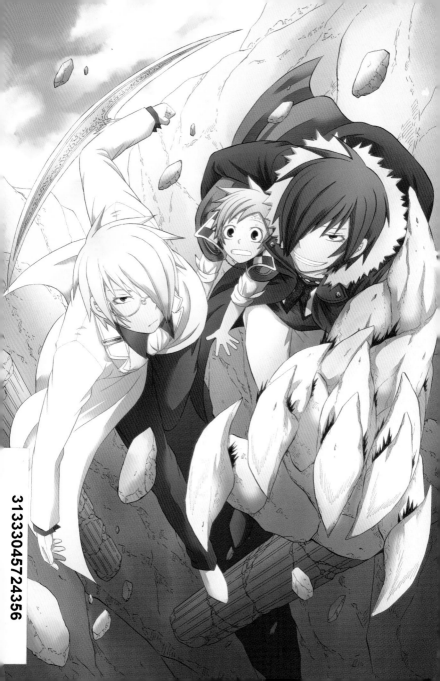

CLAY LORD

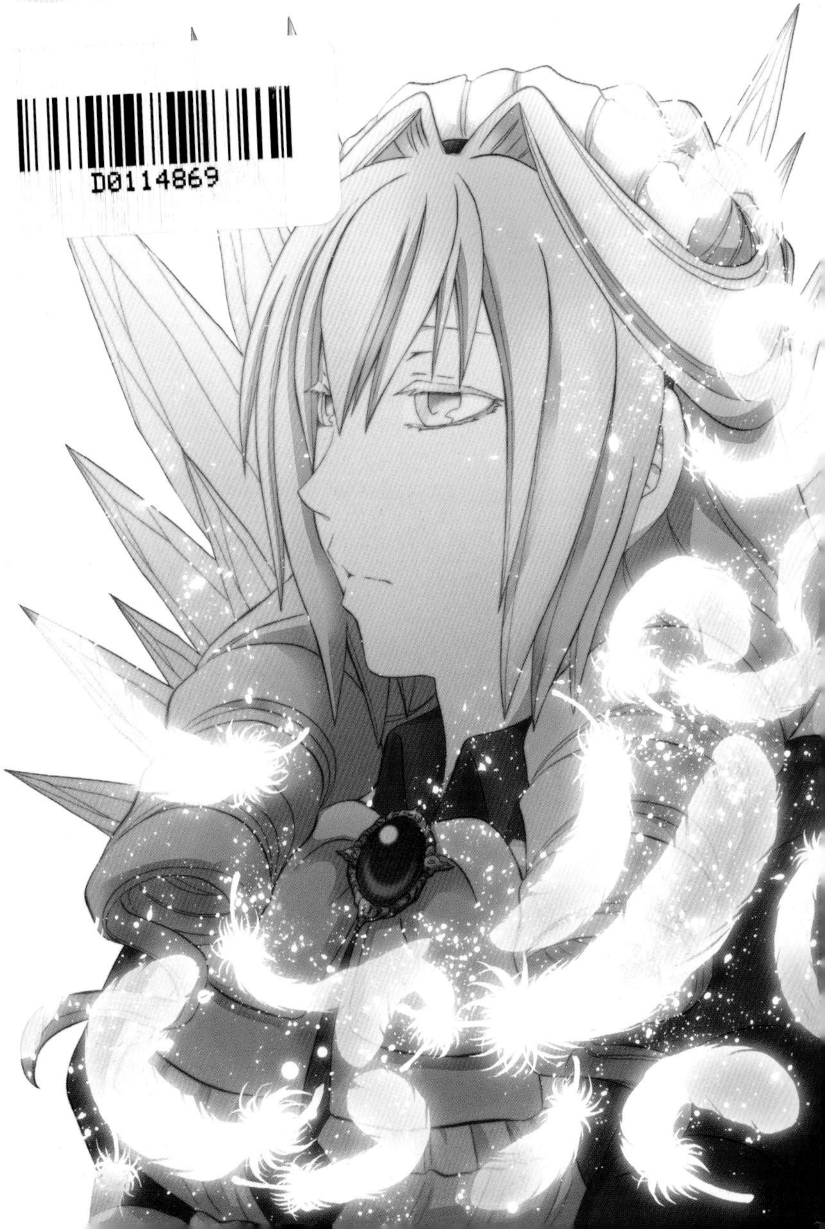